SIGNALS AND SYSTEMS

AUTHOR

Prof. Sanjay L. Nalbalwar

Dean (Academics - FoE&T),

Department of Electronics and Telecommunication Engineering (E&TC),

Dr. Babasaheb Ambedkar Technological University,

Lonere, Raigad, Maharashtra.

REVIEWER

Prof. Satyabrata Jit

Professor (HAG),

Department of Electronics Engineering, IIT(BHU), Varanasi

KHANNA BOOK PUBLISHING CO. (P) Ltd.

4C/4344, Ansari Road, Darya Ganj, New Delhi, India

All India Council for Technical Education

Nelson Mandela Marg, Vasant Kunj, New Delhi, India

Dear Readers,

To prevent the piracy, this book is secured with HIGH SECURITY HOLOGRAM on the front title cover. In case you don't find the hologram on the front cover title, please write us to at contact@khannabooks.com or whatsapp us at +91-99109 09320 and avail special gift voucher for yourself.

Specimen of Hologram on front Cover title:

Moreover, there is a SPECIAL DISCOUNT COUPON for you with EVERY HOLOGRAM.

How to avail this SPECIAL DISCOUNT:

Step 1: Scratch the hologram

Step 2: Under the scratch area, your "coupon code" is available

Step 3: Logon to www.khannabooks.com

Step 4: Use your "coupon code" in the shopping cart and get your copy at a special discount

Step 5: Enjoy your reading!

ISBN: 978-93-5538-545-1

Book Code: UG414EN

Signals and Systems

by Prof. Sanjay L. Nalbalwar

First Edition: 2026

Originally Published by:

All India Council for Technical Education, Ministry of Education, GOI

Exclusively Published & Distributed by:

Khanna Book Publishing Co. (P) Ltd.
4C/4344, Ansari Road, Daryaganj,
New Delhi (INDIA)

Visit us at: **www.khannabooks.com**
Write us at: **contact@khannabooks.com**

To view complete list of books, Please scan the QR Code: KPH

Printed in Bharat.

प्रो. टी. जी. सीताराम
अध्यक्ष
Prof. T. G. Sitharam
Chairman

सत्यमेव जयते

आज़ादी का अमृत महोत्सव

अखिल भारतीय तकनीकी शिक्षा परिषद्
(भारत सरकार का एक सांविधिक निकाय)
(शिक्षा मंत्रालय, भारत सरकार)
नेल्सन मंडेला मार्ग, वसंत कुंज, नई दिल्ली–110070
दूरभाष : 011–26131498
ई–मेल : chairman@aicte-india.org

ALL INDIA COUNCIL FOR TECHNICAL EDUCATION
(A STATUTORY BODY OF THE GOVT. OF INDIA)
(Ministry of Education, Govt. of India)
Nelson Mandela Marg, Vasant Kunj, New Delhi-110070
Phone : 011-26131498
E-mail : chairman@aicte-india.org

FOREWORD

Engineers are the backbone of any modern society. They are the ones responsible for the marvels as well as the improved quality of life across the world. Engineers have driven humanity towards greater heights in a more evolved and unprecedented manner.

The All India Council for Technical Education (AICTE), have spared no efforts towards the strengthening of the technical education in the country. AICTE is always committed towards promoting quality Technical Education to make India a modern developed nation emphasizing on the overall welfare of mankind.

An array of initiatives has been taken by AICTE in last decade which have been accelerated now by the National Education Policy (NEP) 2020. The implementation of NEP under the visionary leadership of Hon'ble Prime Minister of India envisages the provision for education in regional languages to all, thereby ensuring that every graduate becomes competent enough and is in a position to contribute towards the national growth and development through innovation & entrepreneurship.

One of the spheres where AICTE had been relentlessly working since past couple of years is providing high quality original technical contents at Under Graduate & Diploma level prepared and translated by eminent educators in various Indian languages to its aspirants. For students pursuing 2nd year of their Engineering education, AICTE has identified 87 books, which shall be translated into 12 Indian languages - Hindi, Tamil, Gujarati, Odia, Bengali, Kannada, Urdu, Punjabi, Telugu, Marathi, Assamese & Malayalam. In addition to the English medium, books in different Indian Languages are going to support the students to understand the concepts in their respective mother tongue.

On behalf of AICTE, I express sincere gratitude to all distinguished authors, reviewers and translators from the renowned institutions of high repute for their admirable contribution in a record span of time.

AICTE is confident that these outcomes based original contents shall help aspirants to master the subject with comprehension and greater ease.

T. G. Sitharam

(Prof. T. G. Sitharam)

ACKNOWLEDGEMENT

I am deeply grateful to the authorities of AICTE, with special acknowledgment to Prof. T. G. Sitharam, Chairman; Dr. Abhay Jere, Vice-Chairman; Prof. Rajive Kumar, Member-Secretary; and Dr. Ramesh Unnikrishnan, Advisor-II and Dr. Sunil Luthra, Director, Training and Learning Bureau. Their collective vision and planning were instrumental in the publication of the book on ***Signals and Systems***. Sincere appreciation is extended to Prof. Satyabrata Jit, Professor, Department of Electronics Engineering IIT(BHU), Varanasi. As the reviewer of this book, Prof. Satyabrata Jit has made invaluable contributions, ensuring the content is not only student-friendly but also aesthetically pleasing and well-organized.

I extend my heartfelt thanks to Hon'ble Vice Chancellor Prof. Dr. Karbhari Kale for his motivational and continuous encouragement throughout the process. My gratitude also goes to Prof. Dr. A W. Kiwelekar, Dr. B. F. Jogi, Dr. S. M. Pore, Dr. Brijesh Iyer and other senior colleagues in the University for their motivation and unwavering institutional support which was crucial in the successful completion of this book. I extend my deepest appreciation to Dr. Snehal Gaikwad, Dr. Pallavi Ingale and Prof. Prashant Mahajan for their insightful feedback and constructive criticism that has greatly enriched the quality of this work. Their contributions have been indispensable in refining the ideas and arguments presented herein.

Special acknowledgment goes to my wife, daughter and son for their invaluable support for showing patience, excusing my work during weekends and family. I wish to thank my parents, whose nurturing and support have been my pillars through the significant events of my life.

This book is an outcome of various suggestions of AICTE members, experts and authors who shared their opinion and thought to further develop the engineering education in our country. Acknowledgements are due to the contributors and different workers in this field whose published books, review articles, papers, photographs, footnotes, references and other valuable information enriched me at the time of writing the book.

Prof. Sanjay L. Nalbalwar

PREFACE

Welcome to the world of signals and systems – a cornerstone of modern engineering that lies at the heart of countless technological innovations shaping our world today. From telecommunications to medical imaging, from audio processing to control systems, the principles of signals and systems permeate virtually every facet of our lives.

This book serves as a comprehensive guide to understanding the fundamental concepts, theories, and applications of signals and systems. Whether you are a student embarking on your academic journey in engineering or a seasoned professional seeking to deepen your understanding, this text aims to provide you with the knowledge and tools necessary to navigate this fascinating field.

Throughout these pages, you will embark on a journey that explores the mathematics, physics, and engineering principles that underpin signals and systems. From the basic properties of signals to the intricacies of system analysis and design, each chapter is carefully crafted to build upon the previous one, offering a structured approach to learning that facilitates comprehension and retention.

Furthermore, this book emphasizes the practical relevance of signals and systems by incorporating numerous real-world examples and applications. By grounding theoretical concepts in practical scenarios, readers can gain a deeper appreciation for the significance of signals and systems in solving real-world engineering challenges. Moreover, this text is designed to be accessible to readers with a range of backgrounds and expertise levels. Whether you are encountering signals and systems for the first time or seeking to deepen your understanding of advanced topics, this book strives to provide clear explanations, illustrative examples, and helpful insights to aid your learning journey.

As an author, my goal is to provide a valuable resource that inspires curiosity, fosters understanding, and equips readers with the knowledge and skills needed to tackle the complexities of signals and systems. We hope that this book serves as a trusted companion on your exploration of this captivating subject and empowers you to make meaningful contributions to the ever-evolving landscape of engineering.

Thank you for embarking on this journey with us.

Prof. Sanjay L. Nalbalwar

OUTCOME BASED EDUCATION

For the implementation of an outcome based education the first requirement is to develop an outcome based curriculum and incorporate an outcome based assessment in the education system. By going through outcome based assessments evaluators will be able to evaluate whether the students have achieved the outlined standard, specific and measurable outcomes. With the proper incorporation of outcome based education there will be a definite commitment to achieve a minimum standard for all learners without giving up at any level. At the end of the programme running with the aid of outcome based education, a student will be able to arrive at the following outcomes:

PO1. **Engineering knowledge:** Apply the knowledge of mathematics, science, engineering fundamentals, and an engineering specialization to the solution of complex engineering problems.

PO2. **Problem analysis:** Identify, formulate, review research literature, and analyze complex engineering problems reaching substantiated conclusions using first principles of mathematics, natural sciences, and engineering sciences.

PO3. **Design / development of solutions:** Design solutions for complex engineering problems and design system components or processes that meet the specified needs with appropriate consideration for the public health and safety, and the cultural, societal, and environmental considerations.

PO4. **Conduct investigations of complex problems:** Use research-based knowledge and research methods including design of experiments, analysis and interpretation of data, and synthesis of the information to provide valid conclusions.

PO5. **Modern tool usage:** Create, select, and apply appropriate techniques, resources, and modern engineering and IT tools including prediction and modeling to complex engineering activities with an understanding of the limitations.

PO6. **The engineer and society:** Apply reasoning informed by the contextual knowledge to assess societal, health, safety, legal and cultural issues and the consequent responsibilities relevant to the professional engineering practice.

PO7. **Environment and sustainability:** Understand the impact of the professional engineering solutions in societal and environmental contexts, and demonstrate the knowledge of, and need for sustainable development.

PO8. **Ethics:** Apply ethical principles and commit to professional ethics and responsibilities and norms of the engineering practice.

PO9. **Individual and team work:** Function effectively as an individual, and as a member or leader in diverse teams, and in multidisciplinary settings.

PO10. **Communication:** Communicate effectively on complex engineering activities with the engineering community and with society at large, such as, being able to comprehend and write effective reports and design documentation, make effective presentations, and give and receive clear instructions.

PO11. **Project management and finance**: Demonstrate knowledge and understanding of the engineering and management principles and apply these to one's own work, as a member and leader in a team, to manage projects and in multidisciplinary environments.

PO12. **Life-long learning**: Recognize the need for, and have the preparation and ability to engage in independent and life-long learning in the broadest context of technological change.

COURSE OUTCOMES

By the end of the course the students are expected to learn:

CO-1: Analyse the spectral characteristics of continuous-time periodic and Aperiodic Signal.

CO-2: Analyse LTI systems in the time domain.

CO-3: Analyse signals using Fourier series and Fourier transform.

CO-4: Apply DFT to analyse discrete-time systems.

CO-5: Analyse LTI systems using Z-Transform.

CO-6: Understand sampling theorem and its implications.

Mapping of Course Outcomes with Programme Outcomes to be done according to the matrix given below:

Course Outcomes	Expected Mapping with Programme Outcomes (1- Weak Correlation; 2- Medium correlation; 3- Strong Correlation)											
	PO-1	PO-2	PO-3	PO-4	PO-5	PO-6	PO-7	PO-8	PO-9	PO-10	PO-11	PO-12
CO-1	3	3	2	1	1	1	1	2	1	1	1	3
CO-2	3	3	3	1	2	1	1	2	1	1	1	3
CO-3	3	3	3	3	2	3	3	2	1	3	1	3
CO-4	3	3	3	3	2	1	1	2	1	3	1	3
CO-5	3	3	3	3	2	1	1	2	1	3	1	3
CO-6	3	2	2	1	1	1	1	2	1	1	1	3

GUIDELINES FOR TEACHERS

To implement Outcome Based Education (OBE) knowledge level and skill set of the students should be enhanced. Teachers should take a major responsibility for the proper implementation of OBE. Some of the responsibilities (not limited to) for the teachers in OBE system may be as follows:

- Within reasonable constraint, they should manoeuvre time to the best advantage of all students.
- They should assess the students only upon certain defined criterion without considering any other potential ineligibility to discriminate them.
- They should try to grow the learning abilities of the students to a certain level before they leave the institute.
- They should try to ensure that all the students are equipped with the quality knowledge as well as competence after they finish their education.
- They should always encourage the students to develop their ultimate performance capabilities.
- They should facilitate and encourage group work and team work to consolidate newer approach.
- They should follow Blooms taxonomy in every part of the assessment.

Bloom's Taxonomy

Level	Teacher should Check	Student should be able to	Possible Mode of Assessment
Create	Students ability to create	Design or Create	Mini project
Evaluate	Students ability to justify	Argue or Defend	Assignment
Analyse	Students ability to distinguish	Differentiate or Distinguish	Project/Lab Methodology
Apply	Students ability to use information	Operate or Demonstrate	Technical Presentation/ Demonstration
Understand	Students ability to explain the ideas	Explain or Classify	Presentation/Seminar
Remember	Students ability to recall (or remember)	Define or Recall	Quiz

GUIDELINES FOR STUDENTS

Students should take equal responsibility for implementing the OBE. Some of the responsibilities (not limited to) for the students in OBE system are as follows:

- Students should be well aware of each UO before the start of a unit in each and every course.
- Students should be well aware of each CO before the start of the course.
- Students should be well aware of each PO before the start of the programme.
- Students should think critically and reasonably with proper reflection and action.
- Learning of the students should be connected and integrated with practical and real life consequences.
- Students should be well aware of their competency at every level of OBE.

LIST OF FIGURES

1: Introduction to Signals and Systems

Fig. 1.1:	Sinusoidal Signal	5
Fig. 1.2:	ECG Signal	5
Fig. 1.3:	Representation of signal and system	6
Fig. 1.4:	Continuous time signal	7
Fig. 1.5:	Discrete time signal	8
Fig. 1.6:	Pulse signal	8
Fig. 1.7:	CT Unit impulse signal	9
Fig. 1.8:	DT Unit impulse sequence	10
Fig. 1.9:	Unit Step Function	11
Fig. 1.10:	DT unit step sequence	12
Fig. 1.11:	u[n] represented by shifted impulse sequences	13
Fig. 1.12:	CT Signum function	14
Fig. 1.13:	DT Signum sequence	15
Fig. 1.14:	CT ramp function	15
Fig. 1.15:	DT ramp sequence	16
Fig. 1.16:	CT real exponential signal	17
Fig. 1.17:	CT complex exponential signal	17
Fig. 1.18:	DT complex exponential sequence	18
Fig. 1.19:	CT sinusoid signal	19
Fig. 1.20:	CT sinusoid signal (a) Increasing sinusoid signal (b) Decaying sinusoid signal	19
Fig. 1.21:	CT deterministic signal	20
Fig. 1.22:	CT random signal	21
Fig. 1.23:	CT Even signal	21
Fig. 1.24:	CT Odd signal	22
Fig. 1.25:	CT periodic signal	24
Fig. 1.26:	CT aperiodic signal	25
Fig. 1.27:	DT periodic signal	25
Fig. 1.28:	Examples of finite duration signals (a) CT finite-duration signal (b) DT finite duration signal	32

Fig. 1.29:	Examples of infinite duration signals (a) CT infinite-duration signal (b) DT infinite duration signal	32
Fig. 1.30:	Examples of causal signals (a) CT causal signal (b) DT causal signal	33
Fig. 1.31:	Examples of noncausal signals (a) CT noncausal signal (b) DT noncausal signal	33
Fig. 1.32	Example of application of cartesian coordinates	34
Fig. 1.33:	Random (stochastic) Signal	34
Fig. 1.34:	Continuous and Discrete Amplitude Signals	37
Fig. 1.35:	Examples of bounded and unbounded signal	43
	Unit 2: Behavior of Continuous and Discrete-time LTI Systems	
Fig. 2.1:	*Linear scaling*	55
Fig. 2.2:	*Superposition Principle*	56
Fig. 2.3:	*Superposition Principle with Linear Scaling*	56
Fig. 2.4:	*Time-Invariant Systems*	57
Fig. 2.5:	*Linear Time-Invariant Systems*	57
Fig. 2.6:	*Superposition in Linear Time-Invariant Systems*	58
Fig. 2.7:	*CT impulse response*	58
Fig. 2.8:	*DT impulse response*	58
Fig. 2.9:	*Representation of Continuous-Time Signals in Terms of Impulses*	59
Fig. 2.10:	*Convolution operation*	61
Fig. 2.11:	$x(t)$ *input to system*	62
Fig. 2.12:	$\delta(t)$ *input to system*	62
Fig. 2.13:	*Delayed input to system*	62
Fig. 2.14:	$x[n]$ *input to system*	62
Fig. 2.15:	$\delta[n]$ *input to system*	63
Fig. 2.16:	$\delta[n-k]$ *input to system*	63
Fig. 2.17:	$x[k]\,\delta[n-k]$ *input to system*	63
Fig. 2.18:	*Equivalences for the series interconnection of continuous-time LTI systems. The (a) first equivalence (b) second equivalence*	64
Fig. 2.19:	*Equivalence for the parallel interconnection of continuous-time LTI systems*	65
Fig. 2.20:	*System interconnection example*	65
Fig. 2.21:	*State Space representation of CT system*	70

Fig. 2.22 *Periodic input to LTI system* 78

Unit 3: Fourier Series and Transform

Fig. 3.1: *Types of signals and their Fourier representations* 89

Fig. 3.2: *Even, Half wave, Quarter wave symmetry waveform* 98

Fig. 3.3: *Even symmetry waveform* 99

Fig. 3.4: *Odd, Half wave, Quarter wave symmetry waveform* 102

Fig. 3.5: *Odd symmetry waveform* 102

Fig. 3.6: *Half wave symmetry waveform* 103

Fig. 3.7: *Approximation of square waveform using some harmonic frequency components* 106

Unit 4: Laplace Transform

Fig. 4.1: *s-plane* 153

Fig. 4.2: *RoC for right sided signal* 155

Fig. 4.3: *RoC for left sided signal* 156

Fig. 4.4: *RoC for two sided signal* 157

Fig. 4.5: *ROC of* $x(t)=A\,u(t)$ 158

Fig. 4.6: *ROC of* $x(t)=t\,u(t)$ 159

Fig. 4.7: *ROC of* $x(t)=e^{-8t}u(-t)$ 161

Fig. 4.8: *ROC of* $x(t)=e^{-3|t|}$ 162

Unit 5: Z - Transform

Fig. 5.1: *Z-plane* 191

Fig. 5.2: *Poles and zeros in the Z-plane* 192

Fig. 5.3: $x(n) = a^n u(n)$ 196

Fig. 5.4: *Pole-zero plot and ROC* $|z| > |a|$ 196

Fig. 5.5 $x[n]=-a^n u(-n-1)$ 198

Fig. 5.6: *Pole-zero plot and ROC* $|z| < |a|$ 198

Fig. 5.7: *Pole-zero plot and ROC* $|a| < |z| < |b|$ 207

Fig. 5.8:	*Pole-zero plot and ROC : 13 < |z|*	208
Fig. 5.9:	*Pole-zero plot and ROC |z| < 14*	210
	Unit 6: Sampling & Reconstruction	
Fig. 6.1:	*Three continuous time signals*	228
Fig. 6.2:	*Impulse-train sampling*	230
Fig. 6.3:	*Frequency domain representation due to sampling in time domain: (a) Spectrum of original signal; (b) Spectrum of sampling function; (c) Spectrum of sampled signal with* $\omega_s > 2\ \omega_M$ *; (d) Spectrum of sampled signal* $\omega_s < 2\ \omega_M$	231
Fig. 6.4:	*Recovery of original signal by using ideal lowpass filter (a) System for sampling & reconstruction (b) Representative spectrum for x(t) (c) Corresponding spectrum for xp(t) (d) Ideal lowpass filter to recover X(jω) from* X_p *(jω) (e) Spectrum of* x_r *(t)*	232
Fig. 6.5:	*Sampling using Zero-Order Hold*	233
Fig. 6.6:	*Zero order hold as impulse- train sampling followed by an LTI system with rectangular response*	233
Fig. 6.7:	*Interpolation between samples, solid curve represents interpolation*	234
Fig. 6.8:	*Band-limited interpolation using Sinc function: (a) Band-limited signal x(t) (b) Impulse train sampling of x(t) (c) Ideal band-limited interpolation in which impulse train is replaced by superposition of Sinc functions*	235
Fig. 6.9:	*Transfer function for zero-order hold*	236
Fig. 6.10:	*Linear Interpolation (First-order hold) as impulse-train sampling followed with convolution a triangular impulse response: (a) system for sampling & reconstruction; (b) Impulse train of samples; (c) Impulse response representing a first-order hold; (d) First-order hold applied to sampled signal; (e) Comparison of transfer function of ideal interpolating filter & first order hold.*	237
Fig. 6.11:	*Effect of oversampling & under sampling: (a) Spectrum of original sinusoidal signal; (b) (c) Spectrum of sampled signal with* $\omega_s > 2\omega_0$*; (d) (e) Spectrum of sampled signal with* $\omega_s < 2\omega_0$*;*	239
Fig. 6.12:	*Effect of aliasing on sinusoidal signal. For each of the four values of* ω_0*, the original sinusoidal signal (solid curve), its samples, and reconstructed signal (dashed curve) are illustrated: (a)* $\omega_0 = (5\omega_s)/6$*, in (a) and (b) no aliasing occurs, whereas in (c) & (d) there is aliasing*	240
Fig. 6.13:	*Sinusoidal signal for example 6.1*	241
Fig. 6.14:	*Strobe effect*	242
Fig. 6.15:	*Discrete-time processing of Continuous Time signals*	243
Fig. 6.16:	*Notation for A/D conversion and D/A conversion*	244

Fig. 6.17: *Sampling then followed by conversion to Discrete-time sequence: (a) Overall System; (b) x_p (t) for two sampling rates. Dashed envelop represents x_c (t); (c) The output sequence for two different sampling rates.* 245

Fig. 6.18: *The relationship among $X_c(j\omega)$, $X_p(j\omega)$ and X_d ($e^{j\Omega}$) with different sampling rates* 246

Fig. 6.19: *Conversion of discrete time sequence to a continuous time signal* 247

Fig. 6.20: *Frequency Response of ideal band-limited differentiator* 248

Fig. 6.21: *Frequency Response of discrete-time filter used to implement a continuous time band-limited differentiator* 248

Fig. 6.22: *Discrete time sampling* 250

Fig. 6.23: *Impulse-train sampling of discrete-time signal in frequency domain: (a) Original signal spectrum; (b) Spectrum of sampling sequence; (c) Spectrum of sampled signal with $\omega_s > \omega_M$; (d) Spectrum of sampled signal with $\omega_s < \omega_M$. No aliasing occurs.* 251

Fig. 6.24: *Exact recovery of discrete time signal from its samples using an ideal low pass filter: (a) Block diagram for sampling & reconstruction; (b) spectrum of x[n];* 252

Fig. 6.25: *Relationship between x_p [n] corresponding to sampling and x_b [n] corresponding to decimation* 254

Fig 6.26: *Frequency domain illustration of the relationship between sampling & decimation* 255

Fig 6.27: *Continuous time signal that was originally sampled at Nyquist rate. After discrete time filtering, the resulting sequence can be further downsampled. Here $X_c(j\omega)$ is the continuous time Fourier Transform of x_c (t), X_d ($e^{j\omega}$) and Y_d ($e^{j\omega}$) are the discrete time Fourier transforms of $x_d[n]$ & $y_d[n]$ respectively. And H_d ($e^{j\omega}$) is the frequency response of the discrete time low pass filter depicted in the block diagram.* 256

Fig 6.28: *Upsampling: (a) Overall system; (b) associated sequences and spectra for upsampling by a factor of 2* 257

Fig 6.29: *Spectra associated with example 6.4: (a) Spectrum of x[n]; (b) Spectrum after downsampling by 4; (c) Spectrum after upsampling of x(n) by factor of 2; (d) Spectrum after upsampling x[n] by 2 then downsampling by 9* 258

CONTENTS

Foreword — *iii*
Acknowledgement — *iv*
Preface — *v*
Outcome Based Education — *vi*
Course Outcomes — *viii*
Guidelines for Teachers — *ix*
Guidelines for Students — *x*
List of Figures — *xi*

Unit 1: Introduction to Signals and Systems — **1-50**

Unit specifics
Rationale
Pre-requisites
Unit outcomes

1.1 Signals and systems as seen in everyday life, and in various branches of engineering and science — 4
1.1.1 Signal — 4
1.1.2 System — 6
1.2 Classification of signals — 6
1.2.1 Continuous time (CT) signals — 6
1.2.2 Discrete time (DT) signals — 7
1.3 Basic signals — 7
1.3.1 Continuous-Time Unit Impulse $\delta(t)$ — 8
1.3.2 CT Unit Impulse Function Properties — 9
1.3.3 Importance of Impulse Function — 9
1.3.4 Discrete-Time Unit Impulse sequence $\delta[n]$ — 9
1.3.5 DT Unit Impulse Sequence Properties — 10
1.3.6 CT Unit Step Function $u(t)$ — 10
1.3.7 Importance of step function — 11
1.3.8 DT Unit Step Sequence $u[n]$ — 11
1.3.9 CT Signum Function — 13
1.3.10 DT Signum Sequence — 14

1.3.11 CT Ramp Function 14
1.3.12 DT Ramp Sequence 15
1.3.13 CT Exponential signal 15
1.3.14 DT Exponential signal 17
1.3.15 CT Sinusoid Signal 18
1.3.16 DT Sinusoid Sequence 19
1.4 Classification of Continuous Time and Discrete Time signals 19
1.4.1 Deterministic and Random signals 19
1.4.2 Even and Odd signals 21
1.4.3 Periodic and Aperiodic signals 23
1.4.4 Energy and Power signals 27
1.4.5 Finite (Time-limited) and Infinite Duration signals 31
1.4.6 Causal and Noncausal signals 32
1.5 Some signal properties 33
1.5.1 Absolute integrability 33
1.5.2 Determinism 33
1.5.3 Stochastic character 33
1.6 Continuous/Discrete Amplitude Signals 35
1.6.1 Continuous Amplitude Signals 35
1.6.2 Discrete Amplitude Signals 36
1.7 Continuous –Time (CT) and Discrete-Time (DT) systems 37
1.8 System properties: Linearity: additivity and homogeneity, Shift- invariance, Causality, Stability, Realizability 37
1.8.1 Linear and Nonlinear Systems 37
1.8.2 Time-Invariant and Time-Variant Systems 38
1.8.3 Causal and Noncausal Systems 40
1.8.4 Stable and Unstable Systems 41
1.8.5 Realizability 44
Unit summary 44
Exercises 44
Know more 45
References and suggested readings 49

Unit 2: Behavior of Continuous and Discrete-time LTI Systems **51-86**

Unit specifics

Rationale

Pre-requisites

Unit outcomes

2.1 *Introduction* 55

2.1.1 *Linear Time Invariant Systems* 55

2.1.2 *Time Invariant Systems* 57

2.1.3 *Linear Time Invariant Systems* 57

2.2 *Impulse response of LTI System* 58

2.2.1 *Discrete-Time Unit Impulse Response and the Convolution* 58

2.2.2 *Representation of Continuous-Time Signals in Terms of Impulses* 59

2.3 *The Unit Step Response of an LTI System* 60

2.4 *Convolution Integral* 61

2.4.1 *Properties of the Convolution Integral* 61

2.5 *Input-output behaviour with aperiodic convergent inputs* 62

2.5.1 *Response of a continuous time system* 62

2.5.2 *Response of a discrete time system* 62

2.6 *Cascade interconnections* 64

2.7 *Causality for LTI systems* 66

2.8 *Stability for LTI Systems* 66

2.9 *System Representation through Differential Equations and Difference Equations* 67

2.9.1 *Differential Equation Description of CT LTI systems* 67

2.9.2 *Difference Equation Description of DT LTI systems* 68

2.10 *State space representation of systems* 69

2.11 *State Space Analysis* 70

2.11.1 *State equations* 70

2.11.2 *Output equations* 71

2.11.3 *State Model* 72

2.12 *Transfer function of a Continuous Time System* 72

2.13 *State Transition Matrix* 72

2.14 *Multi-Input, Multi-Output Representation* 75

2.15 *Periodic Inputs to LTI system* 78

2.16 The Notion of frequency response and its relation to impulse response 79
Unit summary 81
Exercises 82
Know more 85
References and suggested readings 86

Unit 3: Fourier Series and Transform **87-150**
Unit specifics
Rationale
Pre-requisites
Unit outcomes
3.1 Introduction 89
3.2 Trigonometric Form of Fourier Series 89
3.2.1 Definition 89
3.2.2 Conditions for existence of Fourier series 90
3.2.3 Equations for a_0, a_n and b_n 91
3.3 Exponential form of Fourier Series 94
3.3.1 Definition 94
3.3.2 Derivation for equation for C_n 95
3.3.3 Relationship between the trigonometric and exponential form of Fourier coefficient 95
3.4 Waveform Symmetries 96
3.4.1. Even Symmetry 96
3.4.2. Odd Symmetry 99
3.4.3 Half Wave Symmetry 103
3.4.4 Quarter Wave Symmetry 103
3.5 Properties of Fourier Series in terms of Exponential Form 104
3.5.1. Linearity 104
3.5.2. Time Shifting 104
3.5.3 Frequency Shifting 104
3.5.4 Time Reversal 104
3.5.5. Multiplication 104
3.5.6. Conjugation 105
3.5.7 Time Scaling 105
3.5.8 Differentiation 105
3.5.9. Integration 105

3.5.10. Real and Even 105
3.5.11 Real and Odd 105
3.5.12 Parseval's Relation 105
3.6 Gibb's Phenomenon 106
3.7 Fourier Transform (FT) 111
3.7.1. Definition 111
3.7.2. Definition of Inverse Fourier Transform (IFT) 112
3.7.3 Magnitude and Phase Spectrum using Fourier Transform 112
3.8 Properties of Fourier Transform (FT) 112
3.8.1. Linearity 112
3.8.2. Time Shifting 113
3.8.3 Time Scaling 123
3.8.4 Time Reversal 114
3.8.5. Conjugation 114
3.8.6. Frequency Shifting 115
3.8.7 Time Differentiation 115
3.8.8 Time Integration 116
3.8.9 Differentiation in Frequency 116
3.8.10 Convolution 117
3.8.11 Parseval's Theorem 118
3.8.12 Duality Property 119
3.9 Fourier Transform (FT) Representation of Continuous-Time (CT) LTI System in terms of Convolution and Multiplication 120
3.9.1. Representation of Transfer Function of CT LTI System in Frequency Domain 120
3.9.2. Relation of Impulse Response and Transfer Function of CT LTI System 120
3.9.3 Response of CT LTI System in terms of Fourier Transform 121
3.9.4 Magnitude and Phase Response of CT LTI System 121
3.10 Discrete Time Fourier Series representation 128
3.10.1. Representation of Discrete Time Fourier Series 128
3.10.2. Properties of DTFS in terms of coefficients 128
3.11 Discrete Time Fourier Transform (DTFT) Representation 132
3.11.1. Definition of DTFT 132
3.11.2. Definition of Inverse DTFT 132

3.12 *Properties of DTFT* 132

3.12.1. *Linearity* 132

3.12.2. *Time Shifting* 133

3.12.3 *Periodicity* 134

3.12.4 *Time Reversal* 134

3.12.5 *Conjugation* 134

3.12.6 *Frequency Shifting* 135

3.12.7 *Differentiation in Frequency* 135

3.12.8 *Convolution* 136

3.12.9 *Parseval's Theorem* 137

3.13 *Discrete Fourier Transform (DFT) Representation* 138

3.13.1 *Definition of DFT* 138

3.13.2 *Definition of Inverse DFT* 139

3.14 *Properties of DFT* 139

3.14.1. *Linearity* 139

3.14.2. *Circular Time Shifting* 140

3.14.3 *Periodicity* 140

3.14.4 *Time Reversal* 141

3.14.5 *Conjugation* 142

3.14.6 *Circular Frequency Shifting* 142

3.14.7 *Multiplication* 142

3.14.8 *Convolution* 143

3.14.9 *Parseval's Theorem* 144

Unit summary 144

Exercises 145

Know more 149

References and suggested readings 150

Unit 4 Laplace Transform ***151-187***

Unit specifics

Rationale

Pre-requisites

Unit outcomes

4.1 *Introduction* 153

4.2 *Definition of Complex Frequency* 153

4.2.1 Complex Frequency Plane (s-Plane) 154
4.2.2 Definition of Laplace Transform (LT) 154
4.2.3 Definition of Inverse Laplace Transform (ILT) 155
4.3 Region of Convergence (RoC) 155
4.4 Properties of Laplace Transform 168
4.4.1 Scaling of amplitude 168
4.4.2 Linearity 168
4.4.3 Time differentiation 168
4.4.4 Integration in time domain 169
4.4.5 Shifting in frequency domain 170
4.4.6 Shifting in time domain 170
4.4.7 Differentiation in frequency 170
4.4.8 Time Scaling 171
4.4.9 Initial Value theorem 172
4.4.10 Final Value theorem 172
4.4.11 Convolution Property 172
4.5 Poles and Zeros of System Functions and Signals 173
4.5.1 Poles and Zeros 173
4.6 ROC Properties for Laplace Transform 174
4.7 Inverse Laplace Transform by Partial Fraction Expansion Method 175
4.8 Laplace domain analysis 178
4.8.1 Transfer Function of LTI Continuous Time System 178
4.8.2 Impulse Response and Transfer Function 178
4.9 Solving Differential Equations by Using Laplace Transform 179
Unit summary 179
Exercises 180
Know more 186
References and suggested readings 187

Unit 5 Z Transform **188-266**
Unit specifics
Rationale
Pre-requisites
Unit outcomes

5.1	*Introduction*	*190*
5.2	*Need of Z-transform*	*190*
5.3	*Types of Z-transforms*	*191*
	5.3.1 Unilateral Z-Transform	*191*
	5.3.2 Bilateral Z-Transform	*191*
5.4	*The Z-plane*	*192*
	5.4.1 Poles	*193*
	5.3.2 Zeros	*193*
5.5	*Region of Convergence (ROC) for Z-Transform*	*194*
5.6	*Properties of ROC*	*199*
5.7	*Properties of the Z-transform*	*200*
	5.7.1. Linearity	*200*
	5.7.2. Time Shifting	*201*
	5.7.3 Time Reversal	*202*
	5.7.4 Scaling in z-domain	*202*
	5.7.5 Time scaling property	*203*
	5.7.6 Convolution	*204*
	5.7.7 Differentiation in z-domain	*205*
	5.7.8 Conjugation	*205*
	5.7.9 Initial Value Theorem	*206*
	5.7.10 Final Value Theorem	*206*
	5.7.11 Accumulation	*207*
5.8	*Relationship between DTFT and z-transform*	*211*
5.9	*Inverse Z- transform*	*212*
	5.9.1 Power series expansion method	*213*
	5.9.2 Partial fraction method	*216*
5.10	*Z – Domain Causality and stability analysis*	*219*
	Unit summary	*220*
	Exercises	*221*
	Know more	*225*
	References and suggested readings	*226*

Unit 6 Sampling & Reconstruction **267-283**

Unit specifics

Rationale

Pre-requisites

Unit outcomes

6.1	*Introduction*	230
6.2	*Sampling Theorem*	230
	6.2.1 Impulse train sampling	231
	6.2.2 Sampling with Zero-Order Hold	234
6.3	*Reconstruction of a signal from its samples using interpolation*	236
	6.3.1 The effect of under sampling: Aliasing	238
6.4	*Discrete Time Processing of Continuous Time Signals*	245
	6.4.1 Digital differentiator	249
6.5	*Sampling of discrete time signals*	251
	6.5.1 Impulse train sampling	251
	6.5.2 Discrete time decimation and interpolation	255
	Unit summary	261
	Exercises	275
	Know more	282
	References and suggested readings	283

CO and PO Attainment Table **284**

Index **285**

1 Introduction to Signals and Systems

UNIT SPECIFICS

This unit presents information related to the following topics:

- *Explore fundamentals of signals and systems; understand their significance in engineering and science;*
- *Examine properties of signals: periodicity, integrability, determinism, stochastic character;*
- *Study special signals: unit step, unit impulse, sinusoid, complex exponential, time-limited signals;*
- *Differentiate between continuous-time and discrete-time signals; analyze their characteristics and representations;*
- *Compare continuous and discrete amplitude signals; understand their applications;*
- *Explore system properties: linearity, shift-invariance, causality, stability, realizability;*
- *Discuss practical applications of signals and systems in everyday life and various fields;*
- *Learning outcomes: clear understanding of concepts; ability to analyze signals and comprehend system properties; recognition of signal processing importance;*
- *Unit provides foundational knowledge for further studies and applications in engineering and science.*

This unit provides an introduction to signals and systems, focusing on their fundamental concepts and applications in engineering and science. Students will explore the properties of signals, including periodicity, integrability, determinism, and stochastic character, and understand how these properties relate to real-world scenarios. Special signals such as the unit step, unit impulse, sinusoid, and complex exponential will be studied, along with their characteristics and applications.

The unit will differentiate between continuous-time and discrete-time signals, as well as continuous and discrete amplitude signals, and analyze their representations and characteristics. Students will also explore system properties such as linearity, shift-invariance, causality, stability, and realizability, and understand their impact on signal processing.

The practical applications of signals and systems in various fields will be discussed, highlighting their relevance in everyday life. Students will be encouraged to apply their knowledge to solve practical problems and develop critical thinking and problem-solving skills. Effective communication of concepts using appropriate terminology and notation will be emphasized.

By completing this unit, students will have a strong foundation in signals and systems, enabling them to further their studies and apply their knowledge in engineering and scientific contexts.

RATIONALE

The unit on "Introduction to Signals and Systems" is to provide students with a solid foundation in understanding the fundamental concepts of signals and systems. This knowledge is essential as signals and systems are pervasive in various branches of engineering and science.

By exploring the properties of signals, such as periodicity, integrability, determinism, and stochastic character, students gain insights into the behavior and characteristics of different types of signals encountered in real-world applications. Special signals, including the unit step, unit impulse, sinusoid, and complex exponential, are studied to understand their unique properties and applications. Differentiating between continuous-time and discrete-time signals, as well as continuous and discrete amplitude signals, helps students comprehend the distinctions and representations in both domains. Understanding system properties, such as linearity, shift-invariance, causality, stability, and realizability, provides insights into how signals interact with systems and how system properties impact signal processing. The unit also emphasizes the practical applications of signals and systems, highlighting their relevance in everyday life and across various branches of engineering and science. By applying their knowledge to solve practical problems, students develop critical thinking and problem-solving skills. Effective communication is essential, and students are encouraged to communicate concepts related to signals and systems using appropriate terminology and notation.

Overall, this unit aims to equip students with a strong foundational understanding of signals and systems, enabling them to pursue more advanced topics and apply their knowledge in engineering and scientific contexts.

PRE-REQUISITES

1. *Mathematics: Solid understanding of calculus, algebra, trigonometry, and complex numbers.*

2. *Physics: Basic knowledge of force, motion, energy, and waves.*

3. *Programming: Familiarity with programming languages like MATLAB or Python.*

4. *Algebraic Manipulation: Proficiency in manipulating algebraic expressions and solving equations.*

5. *Analytical Thinking: Ability to think analytically and solve problems systematically.*

6. *These prerequisites are essential for students to effectively engage with the unit on "Introduction to Signals and Systems" and ensure a smooth transition into the study of the subject matter.*

UNIT OUTCOMES

After studying this unit students will be able to:

U1-O1: Understand fundamental concepts of signals and systems.

U1-O2: Identify and analyze different signal types: periodic, deterministic, stochastic.

U1-O3: Recognize the importance of signal properties in real-world applications.

U1-O4: Apply special signals (unit step, unit impulse, sinusoid, complex exponential) in problem-solving and system analysis.

U1-O5: Differentiate and understand representations and characteristics of continuous-time and discrete-time signals; analyze system properties and their impact on signal processing.

Unit-1 Outcomes	***EXPECTED MAPPING WITH COURSE OUTCOMES*** *(1- Weak Correlation; 2- Medium correlation; 3- Strong Correlation)*					
	CO-1	***CO-2***	***CO-3***	***CO-4***	***CO-5***	***CO-6***
U1-O1	3	2	1	2	2	3
U1-O2	3	1	1	1	-	1
U1-O3	3	1	-	-	-	3
U1-O4	3	2	1	1	-	1
U1-O5	3	3	2	1	1	2

1.1 Signals and systems as seen in everyday life, and in various branches of engineering and science

Signals and systems are ubiquitous in everyday life and have significant applications in engineering and science. The term signal is generally applied to something that conveys information. Signals may, for example, convey information about the state or behavior of a physical system. As another class of examples, signals are synthesized for the purpose of communicating information between humans or between humans and machines. Although signals can be represented in many ways, in all cases, the information is contained in some pattern of variations. Signals are represented mathematically as functions of one or more independent variables.

Signals can be any physical quantity that varies with time, space, or other independent variables. They can be represented in either the time domain or frequency domain. Examples of signals include human speech, electric current, and voltage. Signals can be dependent on one or more independent variables, such as time, temperature, position, pressure, or distance. If a signal depends on only one independent variable, it is called a one-dimensional signal, while a signal dependent on two independent variables is called a two-dimensional signal. Examples include audio signals (speech, music), image and video signals, communication signals, biomedical signals (ECG, EEG), control systems, digital signal processing, electrical circuits, mechanical systems, and feedback systems. These concepts find practical use in areas such as audio processing, image recognition, telecommunications, medical diagnostics, robotics, power systems, and scientific research. Signals and systems provide the framework for analyzing, manipulating, and understanding information in various fields.

1.1.1 Signal

A signal can be realized as a physical quantity which conveys the information related to some physical phenomena like any voltage signal, any electromagnetic wave that is transmitted over the air from any base station to the mobile station and this carries the information about the communication between two individuals. A signal can also be predicted in terms of a video or an image carrying information. In this way, a signal is a carrier of data or information.

The examples of the signal can be, when we power on the mobile handset, the electromagnetic field gets associated with the antenna and we receive a signal from a base station. Another example can be, when we listen a whistle of train passing nearby, that is a kind of signal which is identified in our brain. Basically, signals arise in many forms, e.g. acoustic, light, pressure, flow, mechanical, thermal, electrical etc.

For us to study the signal theory, we consider signal as a variation or change of an entity with respect to time or space or any other independent variable. When time signals are considered, they are represented using x(t), y(t) etc., and such 1D signals which varies in time can also be extended for 2D, 3D signals. Signals occurring in many different physical forms are often converted in electrical form by a transducer for ease of processing. For example, a microphone converts sound wave into electrical signal which is convenient for further processing.

To study signals, we must see how the signals look! Below is one signal which is very commonly used i.e., sinusoidal signal.

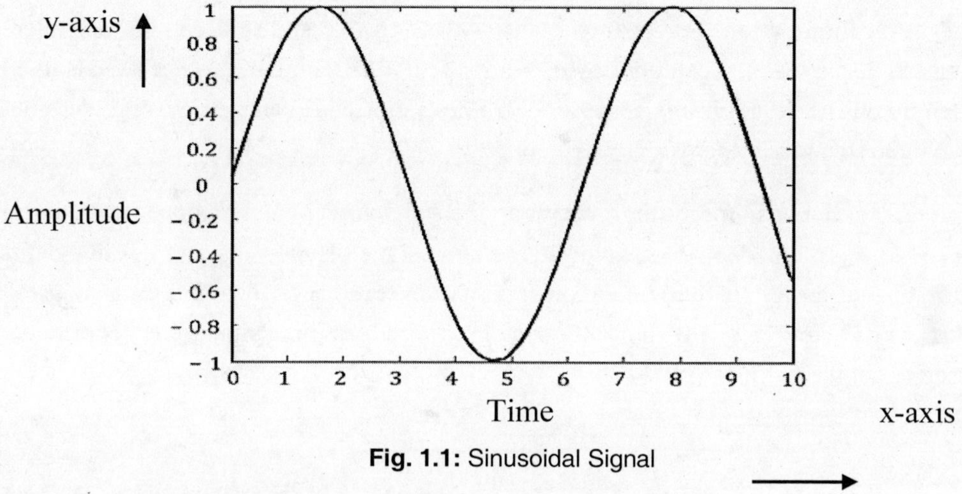

Fig. 1.1: Sinusoidal Signal

Graphically, the independent variable is represented by horizontal axis (x-axis) and the dependent variable is represented by vertical axis (y-axis). In the Fig. 1.1, we must notice that as the time value is changing, the instantaneous value of amplitude (height of the signal waveform) is also changing, so the value plotted on y-axis are dependent on value on x-axis.

The general expression for sinusoidal signal can be written as $\sin(\omega t)$, where ω is constant and t is time which is value on x-axis. Thus, quantity on y-axis is dependent variable and quantity on x-axis is independent variable, as we all know that time depends on nothing and it varies independently. So, from the discussion the definition of Signal is any physical quantity that varies with time, space or any other independent variable, which conveys some information.

Similarly, ECG signal shown in Fig. 1.2 is also a biological signal which depicts the function of heart to find or study any abnormalities in the heart.

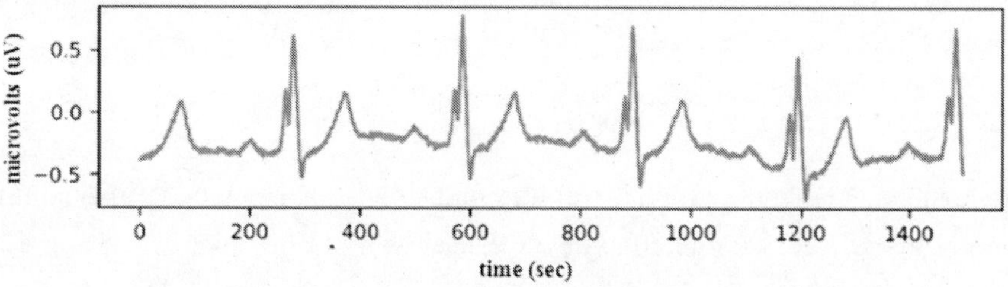

Fig. 1.2: ECG Signal

Other examples of the signals are speech signal, EEG signal, Image/Video signal, Radar signal, AM/FM signal etc.

1.1.2 System

For the examples of the signals given in section 1.1.1, a system is always associated with their generation and extraction of useful information. For example, any waveform like sinusoid can be generated by a function generator and displayed on a cathode-ray oscilloscope (CRO). Similarly, other signals like ECG, EEG are generated by our heart and brain, respectively. These signals are analyzed using the biological equipment with suitable software systems.

From this discussion, a continuous time system accepts an input signal, $x(t)$ and produces an output signal, $y(t)$. A system is often represented as an operator on the input signal. Hence, a system can be defined as any physical device that performs a certain operation or a set of operations on the input signal x(t) to result in a new signal y(t) as its output. Fig. 1.3 shows the system to which an input signal $x(t)$ is provided that is further processed to get the output $y(t)$.

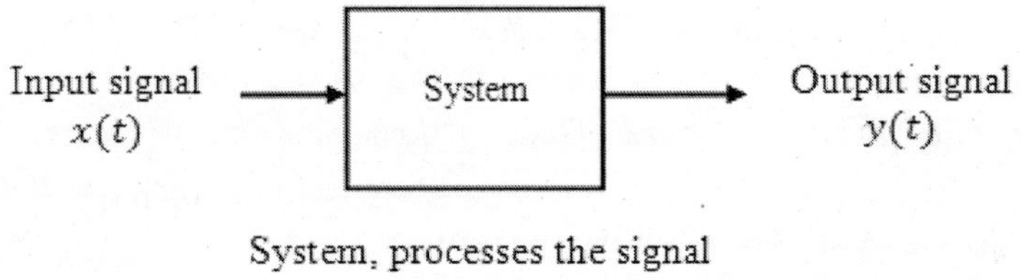

Fig. 1.3: Representation of signal and system

1.2 Classification of signals

According to the nature of independent variable, time, signals can be classified into continuous-time (CT) signals and discrete-time (DT) signals.

1.2.1 Continuous time (CT) signals

If the independent variable is continuous then signal is called as CT signal. Symbol t is used to denote continuous time. Also the independent variable t is enclosed in (.). For example, a signal can be continuous time signal for case,

$$x(t) = \sin(\pi t) \qquad \text{for all } t \qquad (1.1)$$

Above Eq. (1.1) is of sinusoidal signal, which is a continuous time signal as it is defined continuously over time from -∞ to +∞ or over any continuous time interval as shown in Fig. 1.4.

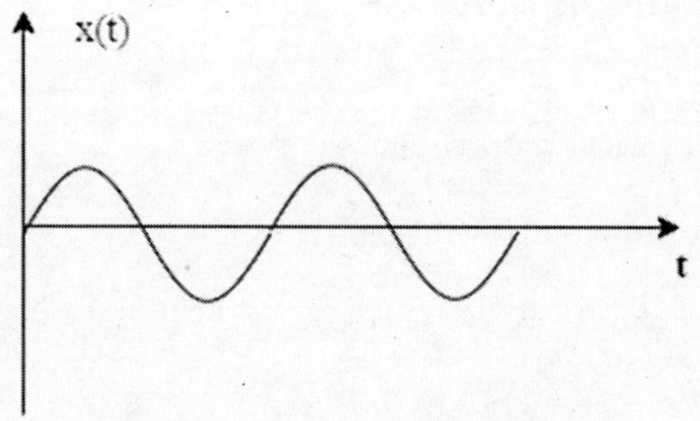

Fig. 1.4: Continuous time signal

1.2.2 Discrete time (DT) signals

If the independent variable has discrete time instances, then signal is called as DT signal. These instances can be either be positive or negative as shown by Fig. 1.5. Symbol n is used to denote discrete time instances. Also, the independent variable n is enclosed in [.]. If a signal is plotted on such discrete time instants the plot is called as a *stem* plot.

So, stem plot contains discrete time instants also called as sequence of numbers. From Fig. 1.5 it can be seen that, at time instant 0, the instance is x (0) that shows the amplitude values at time 0, at time instant 1, the instance is x (1) and so on. Hence, these x (-2), x (-1), x (0), x (1), x (2) are called as time series or sequence of numbers.

For example, a signal can be discrete time signal for case,

$$x[n] = \sin\frac{4\pi n}{20} \quad \text{for all } n \qquad (1.2)$$

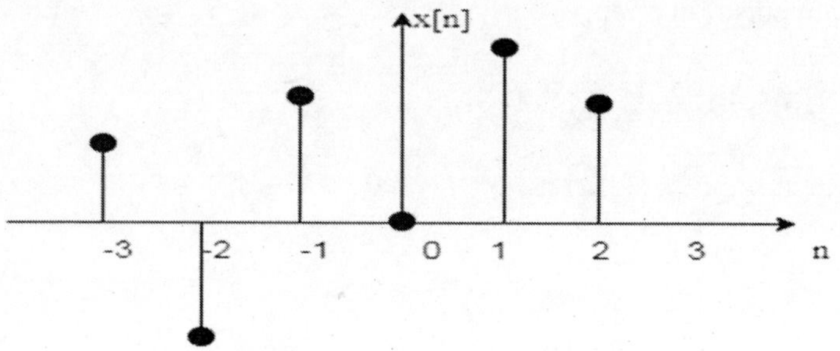

Fig. 1.5: Discrete time signal

1.3 Basic signals

There are many elementary signals which must be studied to better understand the properties of both the signals and systems. These include unit impulse, unit step, signum, ramp, exponential and sinusoid signals.

1.3.1 Continuous-Time Unit Impulse $\delta(t)$

The unit impulse, denoted as $\delta(t)$, is also known as the Dirac delta function. It is one of the most fundamental signals to understand various properties of the system.

The mathematical representation of Impulse function is,

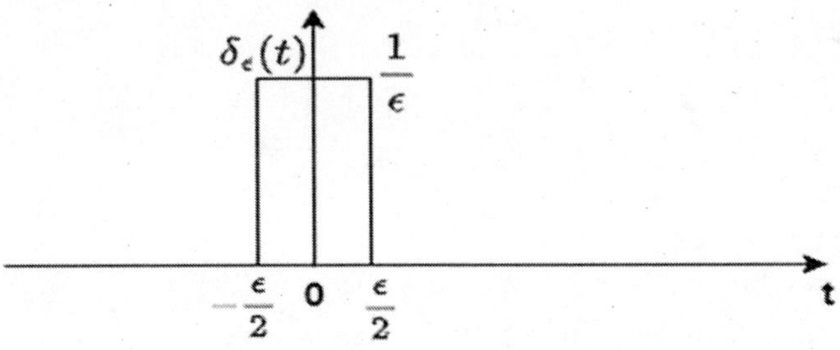

Fig. 1.6: Pulse signal

Consider the given signal which is a pulse from $-\frac{\varepsilon}{2}$ *to* $\frac{\varepsilon}{2}$, hence pulse has a width of ε and height equals $\frac{1}{\varepsilon}$. So, area under the pulse equals $\varepsilon \times \frac{1}{\varepsilon} = 1$. So, for each pulse $\delta_\varepsilon(t)$ for every ε, the area under the pulse equal to 1.

Now, let us consider an impulse function as,

$$\delta(t) = \lim_{\varepsilon \to 0} \delta_\varepsilon(t) \tag{1.3}$$

As, ε tends to 0, the width goes to 0 and height $\frac{1}{\varepsilon}$ to infinity, but area still remains the unity (constant).

Hence, area under the given pulse function,

$$\int_a^b \delta(t)dt = \begin{cases} 1 & a < 0 < b \\ 0 & otherwise \end{cases} \tag{1.4}$$

The representation of CT unit impulse signal is represented by Fig. 1.7.

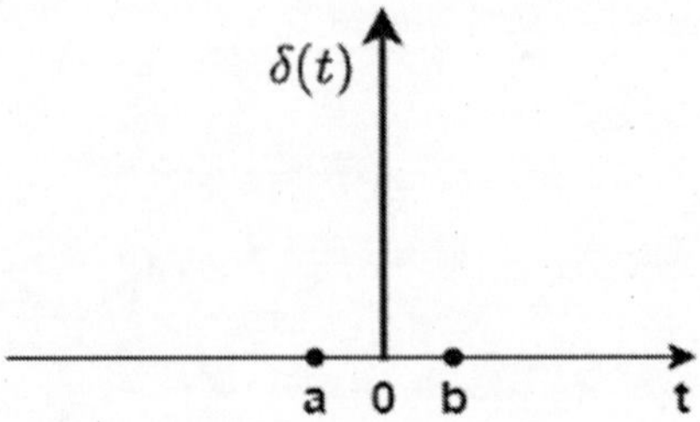

Fig. 1.7: CT Unit impulse signal

In general, a CT impulse function can be described as,

$$\delta(t) = \begin{cases} \infty & t = 0 \\ 0 & otherwise \end{cases} \qquad \text{and} \qquad \int_{-\infty}^{\infty} \delta(t)\, dt = 1$$

The arrow on the top of impulse indicates that it has infinite amplitude as shown in Fig 1.7.

1.3.2. CT Unit Impulse Function Properties

1. $\int_{-\infty}^{\infty} x(t)\delta(t)dt = x(0)$

   i.e., if we multiply the impulse function by any signal x(t) and integrate it, it picks the value of the function x(t) at t = 0

2. $\int_{-\infty}^{\infty} x(t)\delta(t - t_0)dt = x(t_0)$

   Here, $\delta(t - t_0)$ is basically the shifted impulse to $t = t_0$

3. **Scaling property:** $\delta(at) = \frac{1}{|a|}\delta(t), a > 0$

4. **Product property:** $x(t).\delta(t) = x(0).\delta(t)$

   Similarly, $\boldsymbol{x}(t).\delta(t - t_0) = x(t_0).\delta(t - t_0)$

5. **Sifting property:** $\int_{-\infty}^{\infty} x(\tau)\delta(t - \tau)d\tau = x(t)$

6. CT Unit Impulse Function is even: $\delta(-t) = \delta(t)$

1.3.3 Importance of Impulse Function

By applying impulse signal to a system one can get the impulse response of the system. From impulse response, it is possible to get the transfer function of the system. From the impulse response of the system, one can easily get the step response and ramp response by integrating it once and twice respectively. For a linear time invariant system, if the area under the impulse response curve is finite, then the system is said to be stable.

Impulse signal is easy to generate and apply to any system.

1.3.4 Discrete-Time Unit Impulse sequence $\delta[n]$

A DT unit impulse sequence is represented by $\delta[n]$ and is defined by

$$\delta[n] = \begin{cases} 1, & n = 0 \\ 0, & otherwise \end{cases} \qquad (1.5)$$

Graphically $\delta[n]$ is represented by Fig. 1.8,

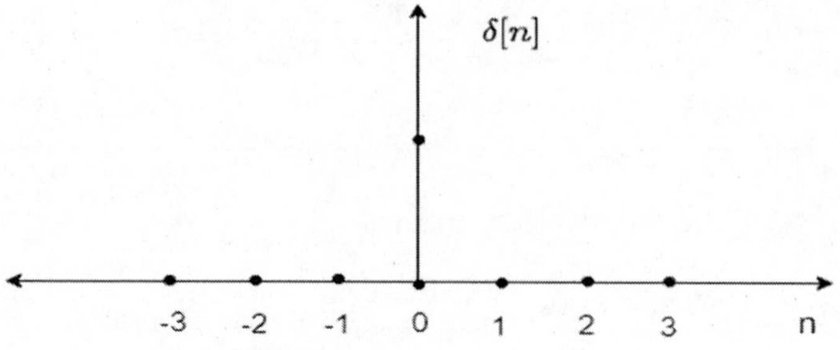

Fig. 1.8: DT Unit impulse sequence

1.3.5 DT Unit Impulse Sequence Properties

1. **Product/multiplication property:**
   Consider $x[n]$ is a DT sequence multiplied with gives output $y[n]$

$$y[n] = x[n].\,\delta[n] = x[0]\,\delta[n] \qquad (1.6)$$

2. **Sifting property:**
   The product property leads to sifting property,

$$\sum_{k=-\infty}^{\infty} x[n]\,\delta[n-k] = x[k] \qquad (1.7)$$

   Eq. (1.7) is true when $\delta[n-k]$ is within the given summation limit otherwise the RHS of the equation becomes zero.

1.3.6 CT Unit Step Function $u(t)$

The unit step signal, denoted as $u(t)$, is a fundamental signal that has a value of 0 for t less than 0 and a value of 1 for t greater than 0.

Mathematically, it can be represented as:

$$u(t) = \begin{cases} 1 & t > 0 \\ \frac{1}{2} & t = 0 \\ 0 & t < 0 \end{cases} \qquad (1.8)$$

At $t = 0$, we sometime define as $\frac{1}{2}$. But, at $t = 0$, there is a discontinuity, that means it jumps from 0 to 1.

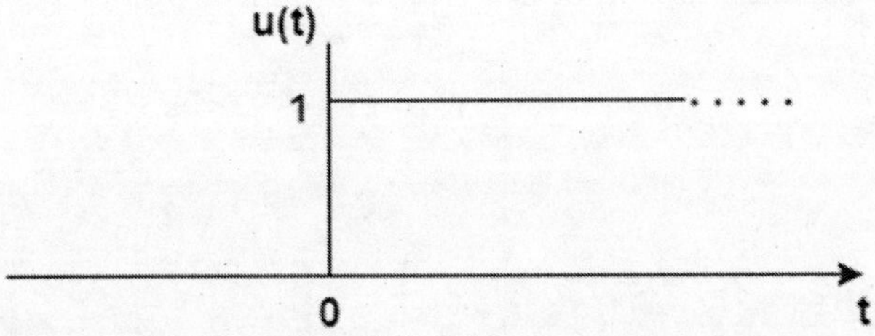

Fig 1.9: Unit Step Function

For example, consider a scenario where a light switch is turned on at time t = 0. The unit step signal can be used to represent this event. Before t = 0, the signal is 0 (light off), and after t = 0, the signal is 1 (light on).

Let us consider the relationship between the unit impulse and unit step function:

$$\delta(t) = \frac{d}{dt}u(t) \qquad (1.9)$$

Derivative of unit step function is unit impulse function. Since, $u(t)$ is discontinuous at $t = 0$, it is not formally differentiable but Eq. (1.9) can be interpreted as approximation to unit step function.

1.3.7 Importance of step function

Step signal is easy to generate and apply to the system, is used in mathematics of control system and signal processing as a signal which switches on at a specified time and stays switched on indefinitely. It is also used in mechanics with impulse function to describe different types of structural loads.

By differentiating the step response impulse response can be obtained.by integrating the step response, ramp response can be obtained.

Application of step signal is equivalent to the application of numerous sinusoidal signals with a wide range of frequencies. Step response is considered as a white noise which is drastic if the system response is satisfactory for a step signal; it is likely to give satisfactory response to other types of signals.

1.3.8 DT Unit Step Sequence $u[n]$

A DT unit step Sequence can be represented by

$$u[n] = \begin{cases} 1, & n \geq 0 \\ 0, & n < 0 \end{cases} \qquad (1.10)$$

Fig. 1.10 shows the graphical representation of unit step sequence.

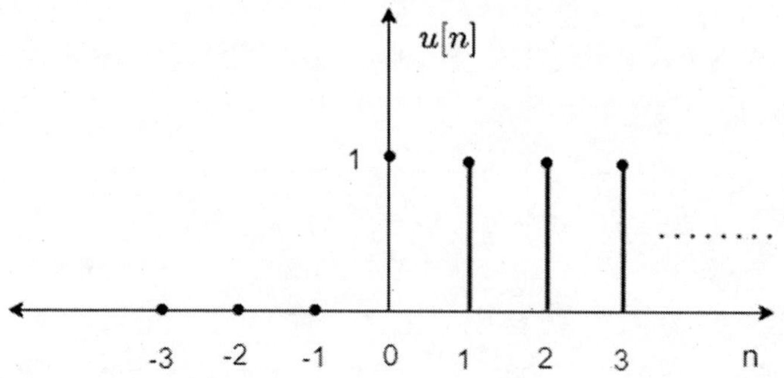

Fig 1.10: DT unit step sequence

The DT unit impulse sequence in forms of DT unit step sequence can be represented by,

$$\delta[n] = u[n] - u[n-1] \qquad (1.11)$$

Conversely, DT unit step sequence can be represented by DT unit impulse sequence as a running sum of impulse. As,

$$u[n] = \sum_{k=0}^{\infty} \delta[n-k] \qquad (1.12)$$

$$u[n] = \delta[n] + \delta[n-1] + \delta[n-2] + \cdots \qquad (1.13)$$

That mean, u[n] can be recognized as a linear combination of shifted impulse sequences as shown by fig. 1.11

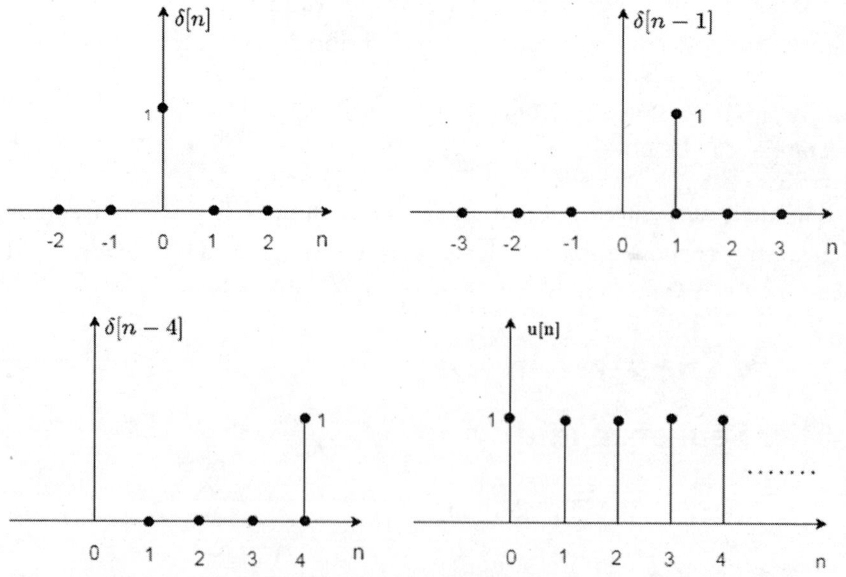

Fig 1.11: u[n] represented by shifted impulse sequences

Example 1.1: $x[n] = \underset{\uparrow}{\{2, -4, 8, 2, 6, 2\}}$. Represent the signal $x[n]$ in terms of weighted shifted impulse functions.

Solution:

$x[n] = \sum_{k=0}^{\infty} x[k]\delta[n-k]$ (1.14)

$x[n]$ has range -2 to 3 i.e. $-2 \leq n \leq 3$

$x[n] = \sum_{k=-2}^{3} x[k]\delta[n-k]$ (1.15)

Expanding the above equation we get

$$x[n] = x[-2]\delta[n+2] + x[-1]\delta[n+1] + x[0]\delta[n] + x[1]\delta[n-1] + x[2]\delta[n-2] + x[3]\delta[n-3] \quad (1.16)$$

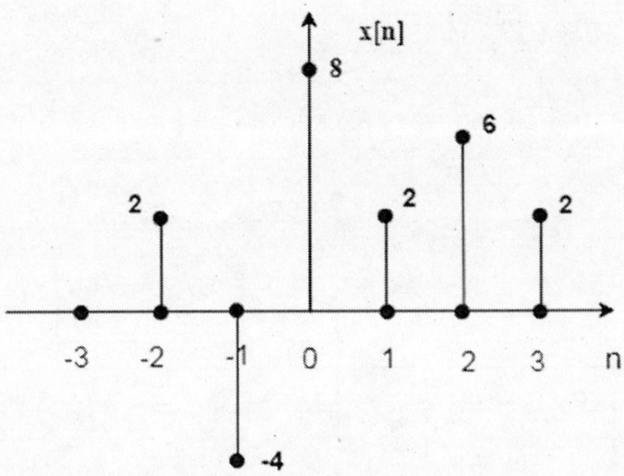

1.3.9 CT Signum Function

A Signum function has amplitude 1 for t> 0 and -1 for t<0. For t=0, the amplitude is discontinuous. The signum function is written as $sgn(t)$ and represented by Eq. (1.13) As,

$$sgn(t) = \begin{cases} 1, & t > 0 \\ -1, & t < 0 \end{cases} \quad (1.17)$$

The Signum Signal is mostly used in the communication theory.

The Signum function can be represented in terms of unit step function as,

$$sgn(t) = 2u(t) - 1 \quad (1.18)$$

Fig. 1.12 show the CT Signum function

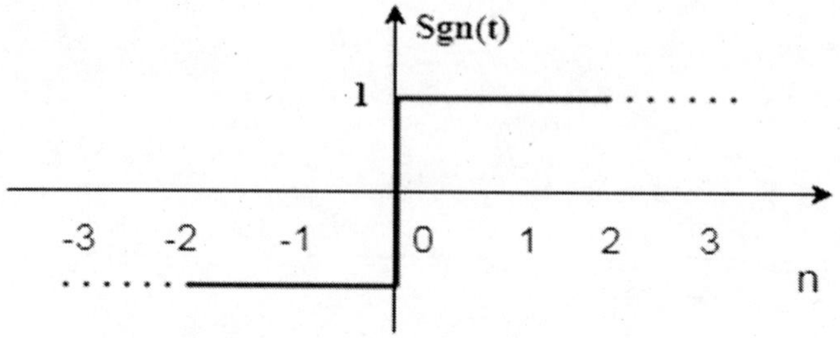

Fig 1.12: CT Signum function

1.3.10 DT Signum Sequence

A DT Signum sequence can be written as

$$sgn[n] = \begin{cases} 1, & n > 0 \\ 0, & n = 0 \\ -1, & n < 0 \end{cases} \quad (1.19)$$

Graphically, DT Signum sequence can be represented by Fig. 1.13

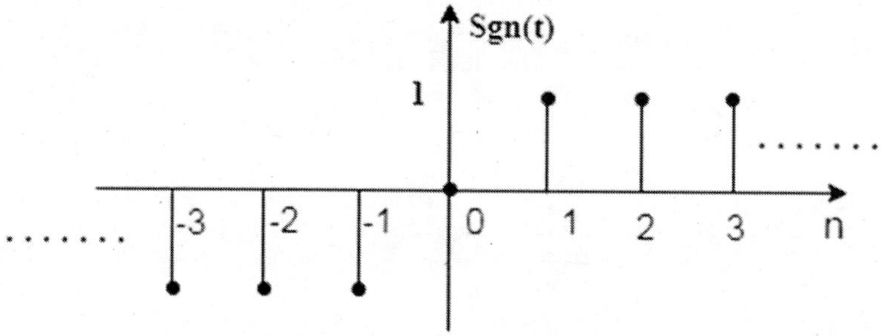

Fig 1.13: DT Signum sequence

A DT Signum sequence can be represented in terms of unit step sequence as,

$$sgn[n] = u[n] - u[-n] \quad (1.20)$$

1.3.11 CT Ramp Function

A CT ramp function is represented by $r(t)$ and given by,

$$r(t) = \begin{cases} t, & t \geq 0 \\ 0, & t < 0 \end{cases} \quad (1.21)$$

The graphical representation of ramp signal is shown by Fig. 1.14.

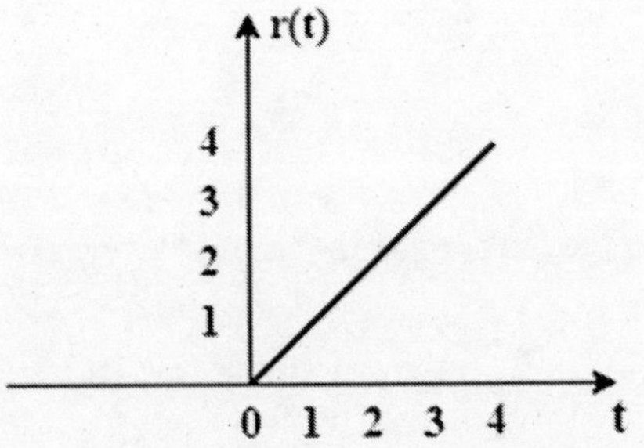

Fig 1.14: CT ramp function

r(t) can be expressed in terms of u(t) as,

$$r(t) = tu(t) \qquad (1.22)$$

Also, when unit step function is integrated it gives ramp function.

$$\int_{-\infty}^{\infty} u(\tau)d\tau = r(t) \qquad (1.23)$$

1.3.12 DT Ramp Sequence

A DT ramp sequence is represented by $r[n]$ and given by

$$r(n) = \begin{cases} n, & n \geq 0 \\ 0, & n < 0 \end{cases} \qquad (1.24)$$

graphical representation of ramp sequence is shown by Fig. 1.15.

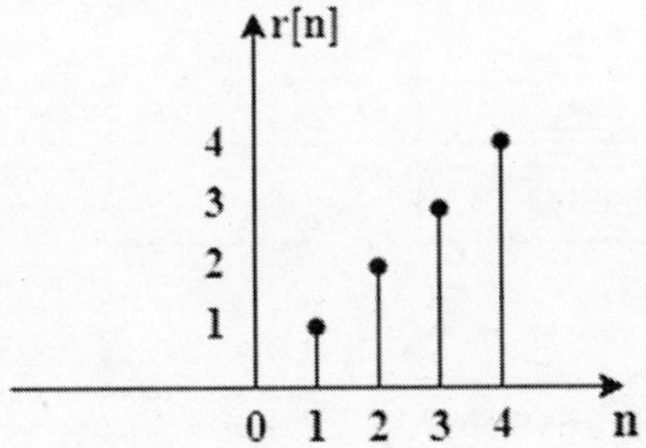

Fig 1.15: DT ramp sequence

1.3.13 CT Exponential signal

It is another important type of signal which is represented by,

$$x(t) = Ae^{\propto t} \qquad (1.25)$$

Depending upon the values of parameters A and α, the exponential signal is categorized into two types.

1. Real Exponential Signal
2. Complex Exponential Signal

1.3.13.1 Real Exponential Signal

For this signal, A and α are real. Depending upon the value of α, the signal increases or decreases exponentially.

If $\alpha > 0$, $x(t)$ increases exponentially with time as shown in Fig. 1.16(a).

If $\alpha < 0$, $x(t)$ decreases exponentially with time as shown in Fig. 1.16(b).

For the value of $\alpha = 0$, $x(t)$ is DC signal as shown in Fig 1.16(c).

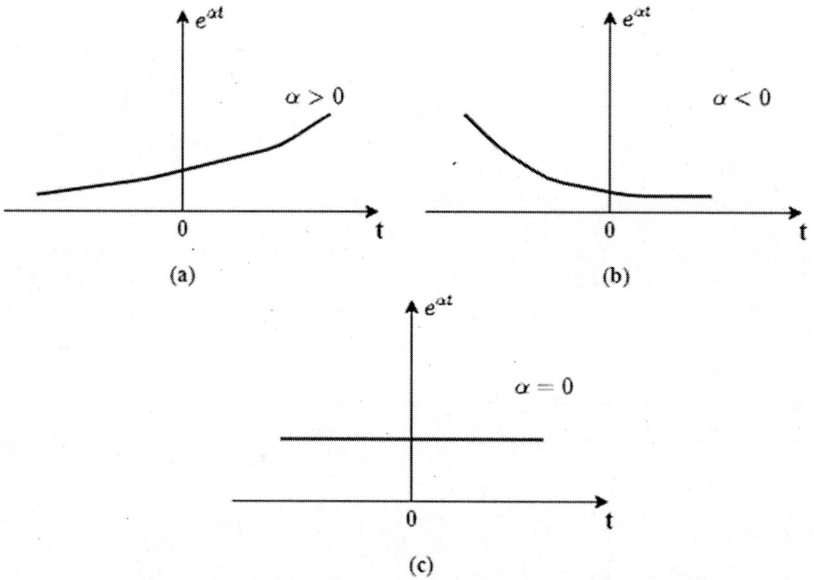

Fig 1.16: CT real exponential signal

1.3.13.2 Complex Exponential Signal

For exponential signal $x(t) = Ae^{\alpha t}$, A and α are complex values.

Here, $x(t)$ can be written as,

$$x(t) = |A|e^{j|\emptyset|}e^{(\sigma+j\Omega_0)t} \qquad (1.26)$$

$$= |A|e^{\sigma t}e^{j(\Omega_0 t+\emptyset)} \qquad (1.27)$$

$$= |A|e^{\sigma t}[\cos(\Omega_0 t + \emptyset) + j\sin(\Omega_0 t + \emptyset)] \qquad (1.28)$$

The complex exponential signal can be represented graphically in terms of sine and cosine waves depending upon value of σ in Eq. (1.28). If value of σ=0, real and imaginary parts of Eq. (1.28) become sinusoidal signals as shown by Fig. 1.17.

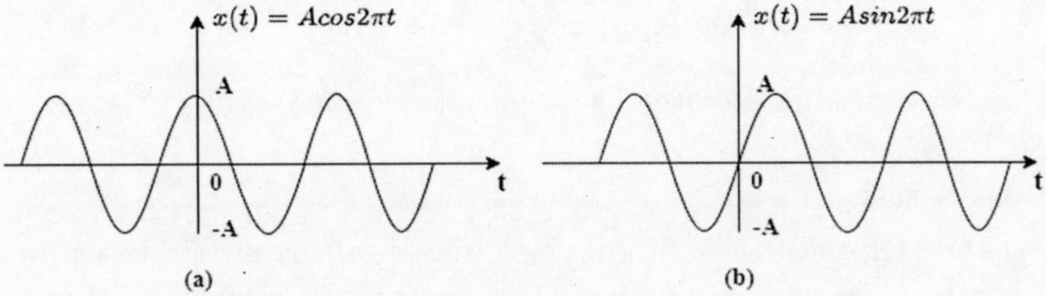

Fig 1.17: CT complex exponential signal

1.3.14 DT Exponential signal

The discrete version of CT exponential signal is defined by DT exponential sequence as

$$x[n] = A\alpha^{n} \qquad (1.29)$$

Depending upon values of the parameters A and α, the DT exponential sequence is categorized into two types.

1) Real Exponential Sequence
2) Complex Exponential Sequence

1.3.14.1 Real Exponential Sequence

For this sequence A and α are real. The exponential signal grows with the value of n for $|\alpha|>1$ and decays with n for $|\alpha|<1$. The nature of DT real exponential sequence is shown in Fig. 1.18.

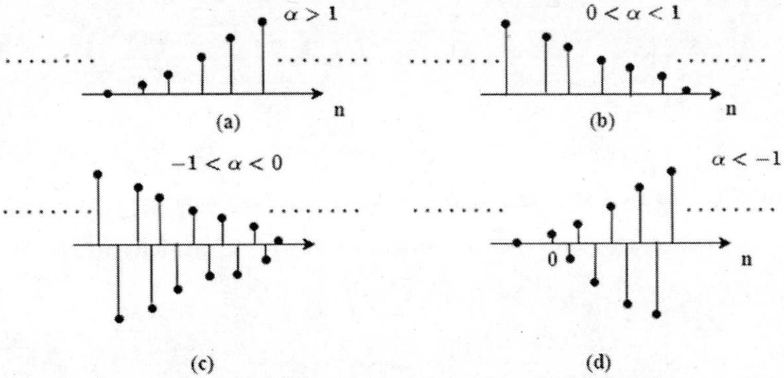

Fig 1.18 DT complex exponential sequence

1.3.14.2 Complex Exponential Sequence

As per the discussion in CT complex exponential signal, $x[n]$ can be written as,

$$x[n] = |A|e^{j\emptyset}|\alpha|^n e^{j(\omega_0 n+\emptyset)} \quad (1.30)$$

$$x[n] = |A||\alpha|^n e^{j(\omega_0 n+\emptyset)} \quad (1.31)$$

$$x[n] = |A||\alpha|^n[cos(\omega_0 n + \emptyset) + jsin(\omega_0 n + \emptyset)] \quad (1.32)$$

1.3.15 CT Sinusoid Signal

From Eq. (1.28) of CT complex exponential signal, when $\sigma = 0$, the real and imaginary parts of a complex exponential become sinusoids as shown by Fig. 1.20.

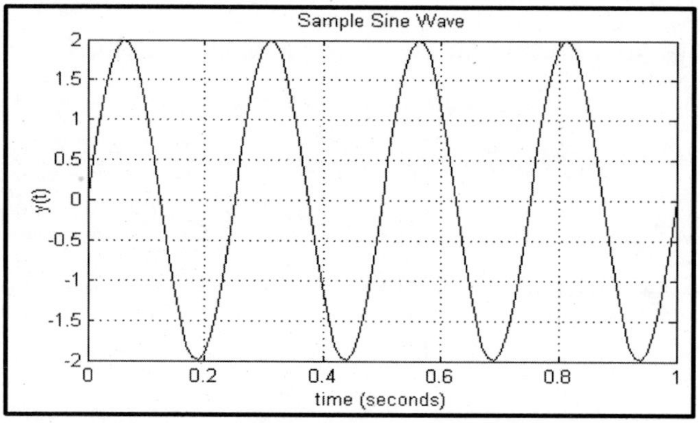

Fig 1.19 CT sinusoid signal

$$x(t) = |A|[cos(\Omega_0 t + \emptyset) + jsin(\Omega_0 t + \emptyset)] \quad (1.33)$$

$$x(t) = |A|\,cos(\Omega_0 t + \emptyset) + j|A|sin(\Omega_0 t + \emptyset)] \quad (1.34)$$

$|A|cos(\Omega_0 t + \emptyset)$ and $|A|sin(\Omega_0 t + \emptyset)$ are continuous time sinusoidal signals. Where, A represents the amplitude value of the signal, $\emptyset$ is the phase angle.

When $\sigma>0$, Eq. (1.28) becomes the increasing sinusoidal signal and for $\sigma<0$, Eq. (1.28) becomes the decaying sinusoidal signal as shown by Fig. 1.21.

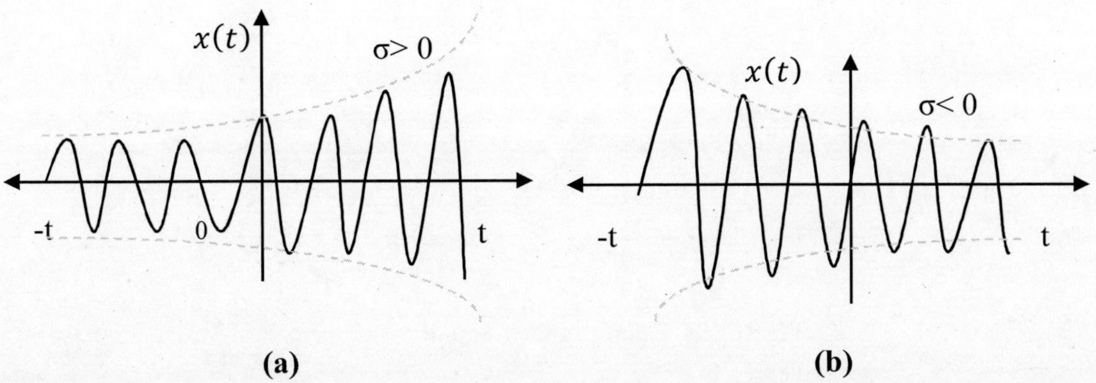

Fig 1.20 CT sinusoid signal (a) Increasing sinusoid signal (b) Decaying sinusoid signal

For example, the sound produced by a tuning fork is a sinusoidal signal. As the prongs of the fork vibrate back and forth, they create a pure tone that can be represented by a sinusoidal waveform.

1.3.16 DT Sinusoid Sequence

From Eq. (5) of DT complex exponential sequence, when $|\alpha|$=1, the real and imaginary parts of a complex exponential sequence becomes sinusoids.

i.e., $x[n] = |A|\, cos(\omega_0 n + \emptyset) + j|A| sin(\omega_0 n + \emptyset)$ (1.35)

$|A| \cos(\omega_0 n + \emptyset)$ and $|A| \sin(\omega_0 n + \emptyset)$ are discrete time sinusoidal sequence where A represents the amplitude, ω_0 is frequency in radians/sample and $\emptyset$ is phase angle in radians.

1.4 Classification of Continuous Time and Discrete Time signals

1.4.1 Deterministic and Random signals

These types of signals class can be either continuous time or discrete time signals. A *deterministic* signal is completely specified that can be deterministically represented at each and every time instant or frequency instant. Deterministic is the fact where all the present, past and future values of the signal amplitude at given time instant are known. For example, $\sin(2\pi f t)$, e^t are the deterministic signals in the sense that at a given time instant t there is no ambiguity, that means given a time instant, one can exactly determine what is the signal. One such example is shown by Fig. 1.22.

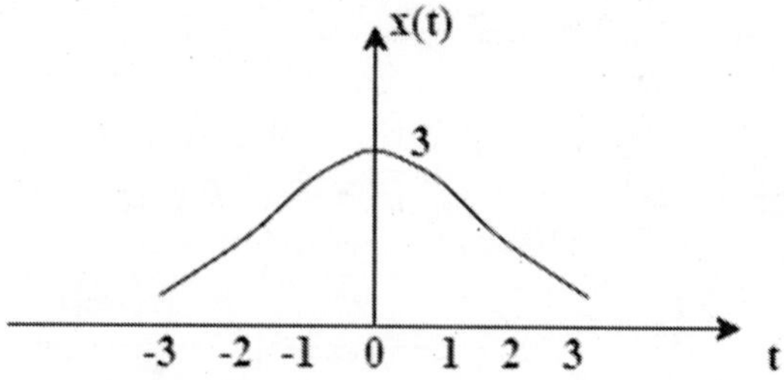

Fig 1.21: CT deterministic signal

In Fig. 1.21, $x(t) = \frac{3}{(1+t^2)}$ for $-\infty<t<\infty$ which determines the values at different time instants. Other examples of deterministic signals include voltage signals, current signals, etc.

Whereas, the *random signals* are random in nature that means it takes random values at various time instants. Mathematically, the behaviour of random signals cannot be predicted. For example, the outcome of a coin toss experiment can lead to a random signal. If its outcome is a head, it is presented by +1 and if the outcome is tail, it is presented by -1. That means, signal $x[n] = +1$, if outcome equals heads or $x[n] = -1$, if outcome equals tails. Since the outcome of the coin toss experiment is random, the signal itself is random in nature and this is a discrete time random signal. On the other hand, a continuous time random signal includes speech signal, record of temperature of the city in a particular month over a time or it can be interpreted as noise with too many variations along the time axis t. This noise tends to limit the performance of a system and hence it is important to understand the behavior of the noise to characterize the performance and behavior of any system. Fig. 1.22 shows the CT random signal.

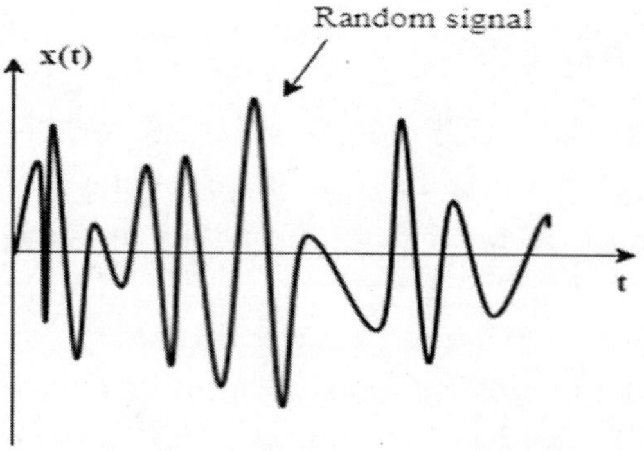

Fig 1.22: CT random signal

1.4.2 Even and Odd signals

Another classification of the signals is even and odd type of the signal. For continuous time signal an even function is represented as,

$$x(t) = x(-t) \qquad (1.36)$$

Or for a discrete time signal an even function is represented as,

$$x[n] = x[-n] \qquad (1.37)$$

For example, $\cos(2\pi ft)$ is a CT even signal as $\cos(2\pi ft) = \cos(-2\pi ft)$ as shown in Fig. 1.23.

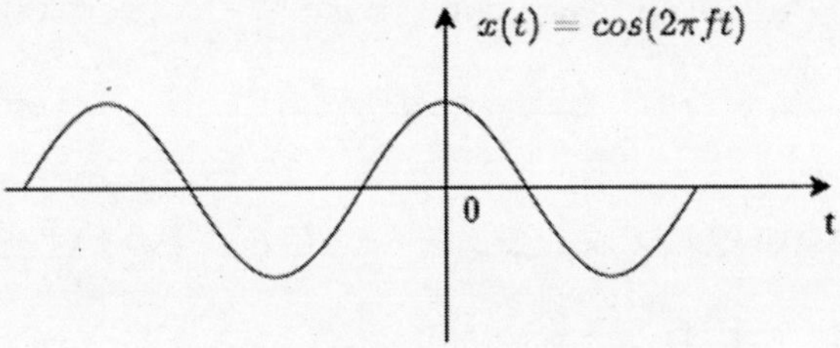

Fig 1.23: CT Even signal

For continuous time signal an odd function is represented as,

$$x(t) = -x(-t) \qquad (1.38)$$

Or for a discrete time signal an even function is represented as,

$$x[n] = -x[-n] \qquad (1.39)$$

For example, $\sin(2\pi ft)$ is an odd signal as $\sin(2\pi ft) = -\sin(2\pi ft)$ as shown in Fig. 1.24.

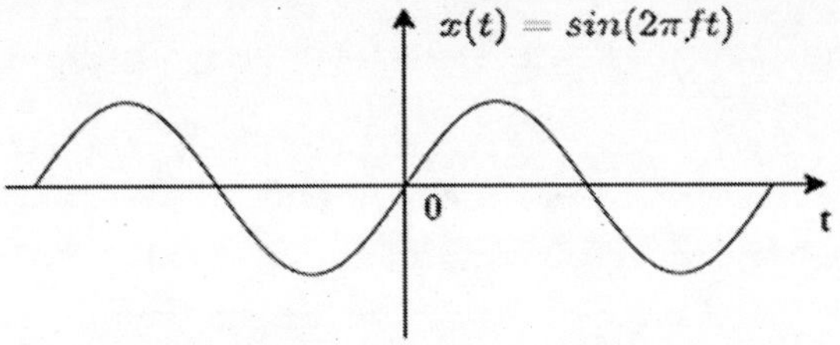

Fig 1.24: CT Odd signal

Hence, it can be seen that the even signals are symmetric about 0 that means they have even symmetry and the odd signals are anti-symmetric about the vertical axis that means they have odd symmetry.

Any real valued CT or DT unsymmetric signal can be represented in terms of its even and odd parts as,

$$x(t) = x_E(t) + x_O(t) \qquad (1.40)$$

and

$$x[n] = x_E[n] + x_O[n] \qquad (1.41)$$

Where, base E represents even part of the signal and base O represents odd part of the signal.

$$x_E(t) = Even\{x(t)\} = \frac{1}{2}\{x(t) + x(-t)\} \qquad (1.42)$$

$$x_O(t) = Odd\{x(t)\} = \frac{1}{2}\{x(t) - x(-t)\} \qquad (1.43)$$

$$x_E[n] = Even\{x[n]\} = \frac{1}{2}\{x[n] + x[-n]\} \qquad (1.44)$$

$$x_O[n] = Odd\{x[n]\} = \frac{1}{2}\{[n] - x[-n]\} \qquad (1.45)$$

1.4.2.1 Important properties of Even and Odd Functions

1. Product of two even or odd signals is an even signal.

Proof: Let $x_1(t)$ and $x_2(t)$ are even signals. If $x(t) = x_1(t)\, x_2(t)$ then,

$$x(-t) = x_1(-t)\, x_2(-t) = x_1(t)\, x_2(t) = x(t)$$

If $x_1(t)$ and $x_2(t)$ are odd signals. If $x(t) = x_1(t)\, x_2(t)$ then,

$$x(-t) = x_1(-t)\, x_2(-t) = (-x_1(t))\,\big(-x_2(t)\big) = x_1(t)\, x_2(t) = x(t)$$

2. Product of one even and one odd signal is an odd signal.

Proof: Let $x_1(t)$ is an even signal and $x_2(t)$ is an odd signal, then

$$-x(-t) = -[x_1(-t)\, x_2] = -[x_1(t)\,(-x_2(t))] = x_1(t)\, x_2(t) = x(t)$$

3. $\int_{-b}^{b} x(t)dt = 2\int_{0}^{b} x(t)dt$ where, $x(t)$ is an even signal.

4. $x(0) = x[0]=0$ and $\int_{-b}^{b} x(t)dt = 0$ where, $x[n]$ is an odd signal.

1.4.3 Periodic and Aperiodic signals

A signal is called as periodic if there exist a time period T such that,

$$x(t+T) = x(t), \ -\infty \le t \le \infty \qquad (1.46)$$

In Fig 1.25, we can see a periodic continuous time triangular wave that is repeating itself after every period T, 2T, 3T towards positive as well as negative direction. For any T which is the smallest positive value for which Eq. (1.46) holds is called the *fundamental period* of the signal. Eq. (1.47) shows the periodic CT signal where same structure is repeating and it follows,

$$x(t) = x(t+T) = x(t+2T) = x(t+3T) = \cdots = x(t+kT) \qquad (1.47)$$

for all t and any integer k. Therefore, a periodic signal is an everlasting signal that exists over the entire interval $-\infty \le t \le \infty$. However, no physical signals are actually periodic as they all begin at some finite time in the past and stop at some finite time in the future.

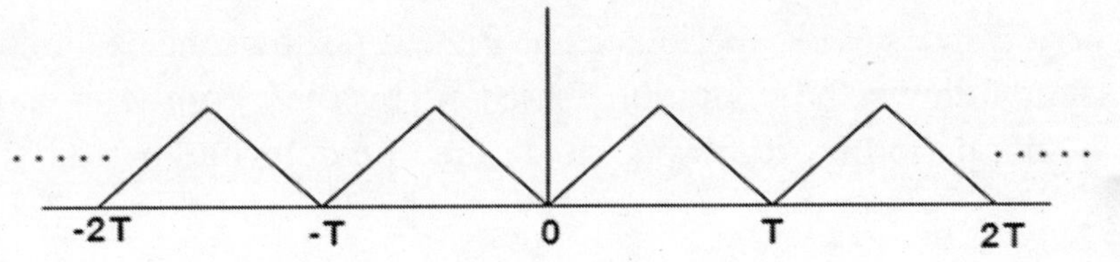

Fig 1.25: CT periodic signal

A regular example of periodic signal is sinusoidal signal which is written as,

$$\mathrm{x(t)} = \mathrm{Asin}(\Omega_0 \mathrm{t} + \emptyset) = Asin(2\pi \mathrm{F}_0 t + \emptyset) \qquad (1.48)$$

where, A represents amplitude, Ω_0 is frequency in radians/second, $\emptyset$ is the phase in radians and F_0 is frequency in Hertz. The fundamental period T for this signal can be written as,

$$T = \frac{2\pi}{\Omega_0} = \frac{1}{\mathrm{F}_0}$$

Now consider two periodic signals, $x_1(t)$ and $x_2(t)$, with fundamental periods T_1 and T_2, respectively. The sum of two periodic signals may or may not be periodic.

$$x_1(t) = x_1(t+pT_1), \ x_2(t) = x_2(t+qT_2) \qquad (1.49)$$

Where, p and q are integers such that

$$x(t) = x_1(t + pT_1) + x_2(t + qT_2) \quad (1.50)$$

In order for $x(t)$ to be periodic with period T,

$$x(t + T) = x_1(t + T) + x_2(t + T) = x_1(t + pT_1) + x_2(t + qT_2) \quad (1.51)$$

Thus,

$$pT_1 = qT_2 = T \quad (1.52)$$

or

$$\frac{T_1}{T_2} = \frac{q}{p} \quad (1.53)$$

The sum of two periodic signals is periodic only if the ratio of their respective periods can be expressed as a rational number. We can say that the fundamental period of $x(t)$ is the smallest positive value of T that is an integer multiple of both T_1 and T_2 and this value is called as least common multiple (LCM) of T_1 and T_2. If $\frac{T_1}{T_2}$ is an irrational number, then $x_1(t)$ and $x_2(t)$ do not have common period and $x(t)$ is aperiodic. The Fig. 1.26 shows the example of aperiodic signal which does not follows the conditions satisfied by the periodic signal that means *aperiodic signals* are not periodic with respect to defined fundamental period.

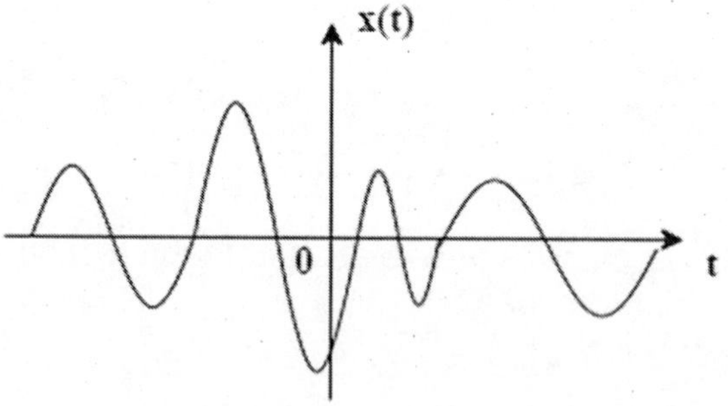

Fig 1.26: CT aperiodic signal

For discrete signal,

$$x[n + N] = x[n] \text{ for all } n \quad (1.54)$$

Where N is positive integer and the period of discrete time signal. It means that signal $x[n]$ repeats itself every N samples as shown in Fig. 1.28. The smallest N for above condition holds is called *fundamental period* N_0.

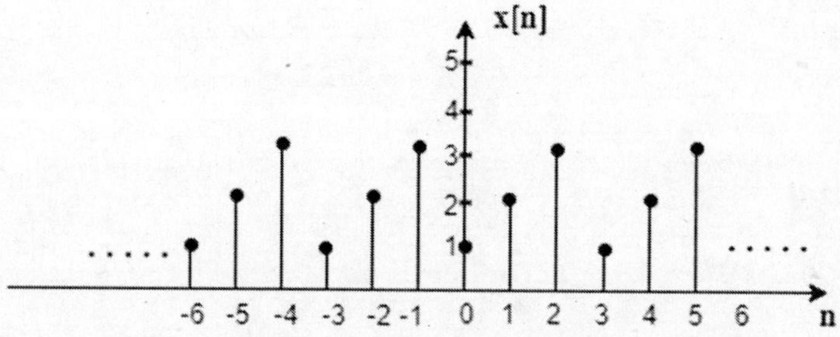

Fig 1.27: DT periodic signal

A discrete time periodic signal follows,

$$x[n] = x[n + N] = x[n + 2N] = x[n + 2N] = \cdots = x[n + N] \qquad (1.55)$$

for all n and any integer k. If $x[n]$ is periodic with period N, then it is also periodic with period $2N, 3N, ...$

A discrete time sinusoid can be written as,

$$x[n] = Asin[\omega_0 n + \emptyset] \qquad (1.56)$$

Where A is amplitude, ω_0 is frequency in radians/sample and $\emptyset$ is phase in radians.

When a DT sequence is not periodic with the fundamental period then it is called as DT *aperiodic sequence.*

Example 1.2:

Determine whether the following continuous time signals are periodic or not. If periodic, find the fundamental period T.

1. $x(t) = Sin\,(50\pi t)$
2. $x(t) = 20\,cos\,(10\,\pi t + \pi/6)$
3. $x\,(t) = 2\cos(10t + 1) - \sin(4t - 1)$
4. $x(t) = cos\,60\pi t + sin\,50\pi t$
5. $x(t) = 3\cos 4t + 2\sin \pi t$

Solution:

1. **Given,** $\boldsymbol{x(t) = Sin\,(50\pi t)}$

$x(t) = sin\,(50\pi t)$, where $\Omega_o = 50\,\pi$.

Time period $T = 2\,\pi\,/\,\Omega_o = 2\,\pi\,/50\,\pi = 1/25$.

2. **Given, $x(t) = 20\ cos\ (10\ \pi t + \pi/6)$**

$\Omega_o = 10\ \pi$

$T = 2\pi/\Omega_o = 2\ \pi/10\ \pi = 1/5$

3. **Given, $x\ (t) = 2cos(10t + 1) - sin(4t - 1)$**

let $x_1(t)$=2cos(10t+1)

$x_2(t)$= sin(4t-1)

T_1 = 2 π / 10 = π /5 and T_2 = 2 π/4 = π /2

Since, ratio T_1 /T_2 = (π /5) / (π /2) = 2/5 is a rational number, signal x (t) is periodic with fundamental period

T=LCM(T_1, T_2)=LCM(π /5, π /2)= π

4. **Given, $x(t) = cos\ 60\pi t + sin\ 50\pi t$**

T1 = 2π / 60π = 1 / 30 sec

T2 = 2π 50π = 1 25 sec

T = $T1$ / $T2$ = (1 / 30) / (1 /25) = 5 / 6

T= 6T1 = 5T2

T = 1 / 5 sec.

5. **Given, $x(t) = 3cos\ 4t + 2sin\ \pi t$**

T1 = 2π /4 = π/ 2 sec

T2 = 2π/ π = 2 sec

T = $T1$ / $T2$ = π / 4

Since it is not a rational number the signal is not periodic.

1.4.4 Energy and Power signals

Energy and power are the two physical characteristics of the signal which are considered in many applications. A familiar example may include, due to current $i(t)$, the power p is delivered to the resistor R and voltage source is $v(t)$ can be written as,

$$p(t) = v(t)i(t) = i^2(t)R = \frac{v^2(t)}{R} \qquad (1.57)$$

Hence the total energy at R equals,

$$E = \int_{-\infty}^{\infty} p(t)\, dt = R\int_{-\infty}^{\infty} i^2(t)\, dt = \frac{1}{R}\int_{-\infty}^{\infty} v^2(t)\, dt$$

Assume, $R = 1\Omega$, then

$$E = \int_{-\infty}^{\infty} i^2(t)\, dt = \int_{-\infty}^{\infty} v^2(t)\, dt$$

Hence for any continuous signal $x(t)$, the energy E can be written as,

$$E = \int_{-\infty}^{\infty} |x(t)|^2 dt \qquad (1.58)$$

Similarly, energy of a discrete time signal $x[n]$ can be written as,

$$E = \sum_{n=-\infty}^{\infty} |x[n]|^2 \qquad (1.59)$$

A signal is called as *energy* signal if the energy is finite, i.e., $0 < E < \infty$. For example, $e^{-t}u(t)$ or $e^{-n}u[n]$ are the energy signals.

The power of a periodic continuous signal $x(t)$ which is periodic with period T can be written as,

$$P = \lim_{T\to\infty} \frac{1}{T}\int_{-\frac{T}{2}}^{\frac{T}{2}} |x(t)|^2 dt \qquad (1.60)$$

The power of a discrete time signal $x(n)$ can be written as,

$$P = \lim_{N\to\infty} \frac{1}{2N+1}\sum_{n=-N}^{N} |x[n]|^2 \qquad (1.61)$$

A signal is called as power signal if the power is finite ($0 < P < \infty$) and non-zero ($P \neq 0$).

A signal with finite energy has zero power and a signal with finite power has infinite energy. A signal neither is an energy signal nor a power signal if it has infinite energy and zero power. For example, CT and DT ramp signal i.e., $r(t)$ and $r[n]$ are neither energy nor power signal.

Example 1.3: Determine the energy E and power P of following signals.

1. $x(t) = 2e^{-\alpha t}u(t) \qquad \alpha > 0$
2. $x(t) = t^{-\frac{1}{4}}\,u(t-2)$
3. $x[n] = 3(0.5)^n\,u[n]$

Solution:

1. **Given, $x(t) = 2e^{-\alpha t}u(t) \qquad \alpha > 0$**

$$E = \int_{-\infty}^{\infty} |x(t)|^2 dt = \int_0^{\infty} 2^2\, e^{-2\alpha t}\, dt$$

$$= 4\int_0^{\infty} e^{-2\alpha t}\, dt$$

$$= 4\left[\frac{e^{-2\alpha t}}{-2\alpha}\right]_0^{\infty}$$

$$= \frac{4}{-2\alpha}\left[e^{-2\alpha t}\right]_0^{\infty}$$

$$= \frac{4}{-2\alpha}\left[e^{-\infty} - e^{-0}\right]$$

$$= \frac{4}{-2\alpha}\left[e^{-\infty} - e^{-0}\right]$$

$$= \frac{4}{-2\alpha}[0-1] = \frac{4}{2\alpha} = \frac{2}{\alpha}$$

As E value is finite, $x(t)$ is an energy signal.

$$P = \lim_{T\to\infty} \frac{1}{T}\int_0^T |x(t)|^2\, dt$$

$$P = \lim_{T\to\infty} \frac{1}{T}\int_0^T 2^2 . e^{-2\alpha t} dt$$

$$P = \lim_{T\to\infty} \frac{4}{T}\int_0^T e^{-2\alpha t} dt$$

$$P = \lim_{T\to\infty} \frac{4}{-2\alpha T} [e^{-2\alpha t}]_0^T$$

$$P = \lim_{T\to\infty} \frac{4}{-2\alpha T} [e^{-2\alpha t} - e^{-0}]$$

$$= 0$$

Since, P=0, $x(t)$ is not a power signal.

2. Given, $x(t) = t^{-\frac{1}{4}} u(t-2)$

$$E = \int_{-\infty}^{\infty} |x(t)|^2 \, dt = \int_2^{\infty} t^{-\frac{2}{4}} dt = \int_2^{\infty} t^{-\frac{1}{2}} dt = \left[\frac{t^{\frac{1}{2}}}{\frac{1}{2}}\right]_2^{\infty}$$

$$= \infty$$

E is infinite, $x(t)$ is not an energy signal

$$P = \lim_{T\to\infty} \frac{1}{T}\int_0^T |x(t)|^2 \, dt$$

$$P = \lim_{T\to\infty} \frac{1}{T}\int_0^T t^{-\frac{1}{2}} \, dt$$

$$= \lim_{T\to\infty} \frac{1}{T}\left[\frac{t^{\frac{1}{2}}}{\frac{1}{2}}\right]_2^T$$

$$= \lim_{T\to\infty} \frac{2}{T}\left[t^{\frac{1}{2}}\right]_2^T$$

$$= \lim_{T\to\infty} \frac{2}{T}\left[T^{\frac{1}{2}} - (2)^{\frac{1}{2}}\right]$$

$$= \lim_{T\to\infty} \frac{2}{T}[\sqrt{T} - \sqrt{2}]$$

$$P = 0$$

Since, $P = 0$, $x(t)$is also not a power signal.

3. Given, $x[n] = 3(0.5)^n\, u[n]$

$$x[n] = 3(0.5)^n \; u[n]$$

$$E = \sum_{n=-\infty}^{\infty} |x(n)|^2$$

$$= \sum_{n=0}^{\infty} |3(0.5)^n|^2$$

$$= \sum_{n=0}^{\infty} 9(0.5)^{2n}$$

$$= 9\sum_{n=0}^{\infty} (0.25)^n$$

Using, $\sum_{n=0}^{\infty} a^n = \frac{1}{1-a}$ for $|a| < 1$

$$\therefore \; E = 9\left[\frac{1}{1-0.25}\right]$$

$$= 9\left(\frac{4}{3}\right)$$

$$= 12$$

E has finite value. Hence, $x(t)$ is an energy signal.

Now,

$$P = \lim_{N\to\infty} \frac{1}{N} \sum_{n=0}^{N-1} |x(n)|^2$$

$$= \lim_{N\to\infty} \frac{1}{N} \sum_{n=0}^{N-1} 9(0.25)^2$$

$$= \lim_{N\to\infty} \frac{9}{N} \sum_{n=0}^{N-1} (0.25)^n$$

Using, $\sum_{n=0}^{N-1} a^n = \frac{1-a^n}{1-a}, \quad a \neq 1$

$$P = \lim_{N\to\infty} \frac{9}{N}\left[\frac{1-(0.25)^n}{1-0.25}\right]$$

$= 0$

Since power P=0, $x[n]$ is not a power signal.

1.4.5 Finite (Time-limited) and Infinite Duration signals

Finite or *Time-limited signals* are signals that exist only over a specific finite duration or time interval. These signals are typically non-zero only within a specific time range. Outside that range, they are considered to be zero. Time-limited signals are often encountered in practical applications, such as audio signals that have a definite start and end time. The examples of CT and DT finite duration signals are shown by Fig 1.28.

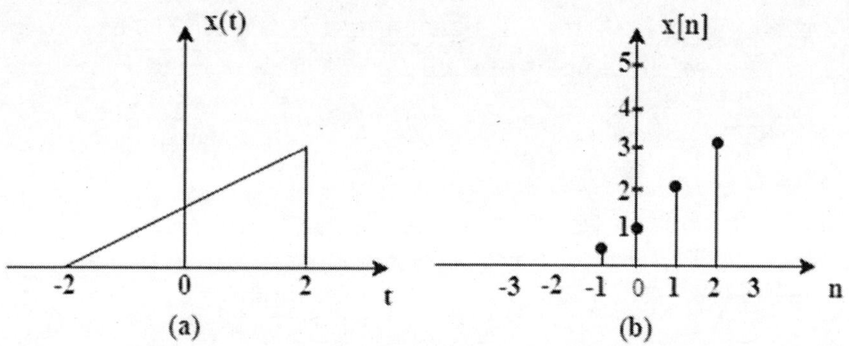

Fig 1.28: Examples of finite duration signals (a) CT finite-duration signal (b) DT finite-duration signal

Infinite duration signals are signals that exists from -∞ to ∞ i.e., for finite interval of time. The examples of CT and DT infinite duration signals are shown by Fig 1.29.

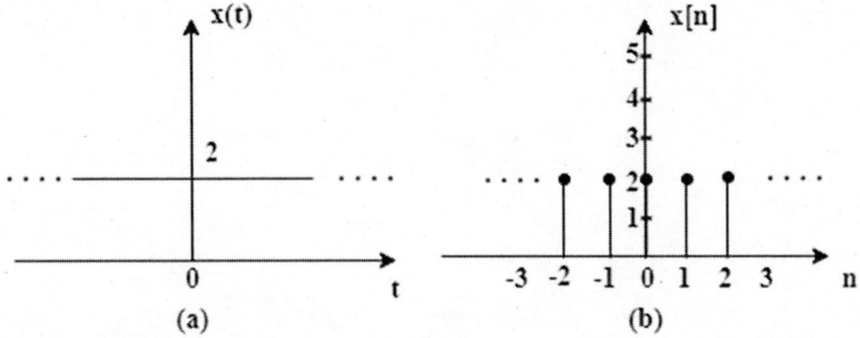

Fig 1.29: Examples of infinite duration signals (a) CT infinite-duration signal (b) DT infinite-duration signal

1.4.6 Causal and Noncausal signals

The signals that are zero for $t < 0$ (for CT signals) or $n < 0$ (for DT signals) are known as *causal* (*right-sided*) *signals*. Examples of such signals are shown by Fig. 1.30.

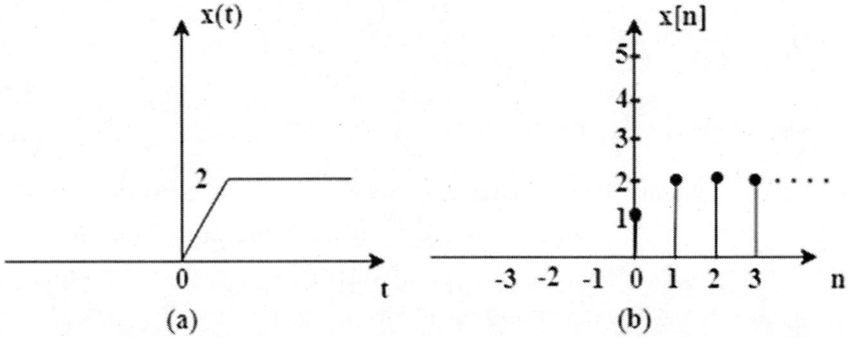

Fig 1.30: Examples of causal signals (a) CT causal signal (b) DT causal signal

The signals that are zero for $t \geq 0$ (for CT signals) or $n \geq 0$ (for DT signals) are known as *Noncausal* (*left-sided*) *signals*. Examples of such signals are shown by Fig. 1.31.

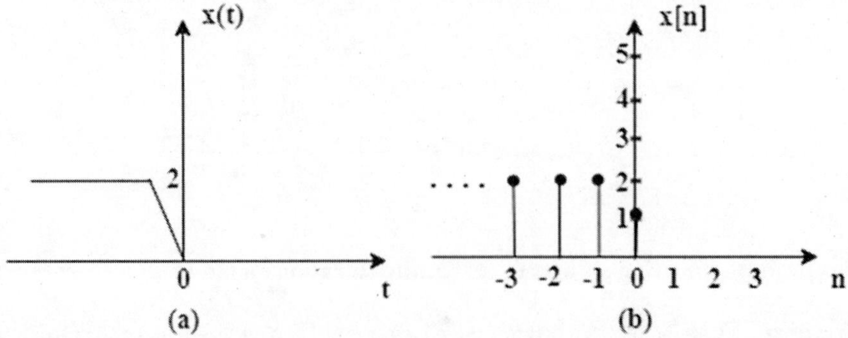

Fig 1.31: Examples of noncausal signals (a) CT noncausal signal (b) DT noncausal signal

1.5 Some signal properties

1.5.1 Absolute integrability:

Absolute integrability is a property that describes the integrability of a signal over its defined domain. A signal is said to be absolutely integrable if the integral of its absolute value exists and is finite. Mathematically, if the integral of $|f\ (t)|$ from $-\infty$ to $+\infty$ is finite, then the signal is absolutely integrable. This property is important in signal processing and analysis as it ensures that the energy or power of the signal is well-defined.

Suppose we have a strictly time limited signal that is a rectangular pulse, so obviously this curve has a finite area under it. Therefore, we can say this signal is absolutely integrable.

1.5.2 Determinism:

Determinism refers to the property of a signal that follows a predictable and deterministic pattern.

A signal is said to be deterministic if there is no uncertainty with respect to its value at any instant of time or the signals which can be defined exactly by a mathematical formula are known as deterministic signals. Examples of deterministic signals include most mathematical functions, such as polynomial functions or exponential functions.

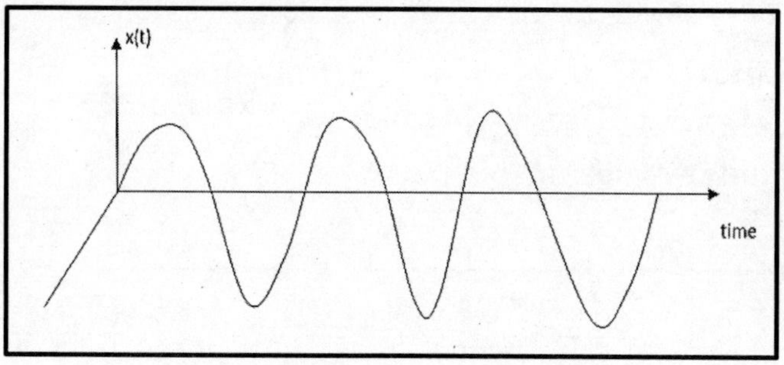

Fig 1.32: Deterministic Signal

1.5.3 Stochastic character:

Stochastic character, also known as randomness or probabilistic behavior, refers to the property of a signal that exhibits randomness or uncertainty. Stochastic signals are characterized by having a random or unpredictable nature, and their future values cannot be precisely determined. Stochastic signals are often modelled using statistical techniques and probability distributions. Examples of stochastic signals include noise signals, stock market fluctuations, or weather patterns.

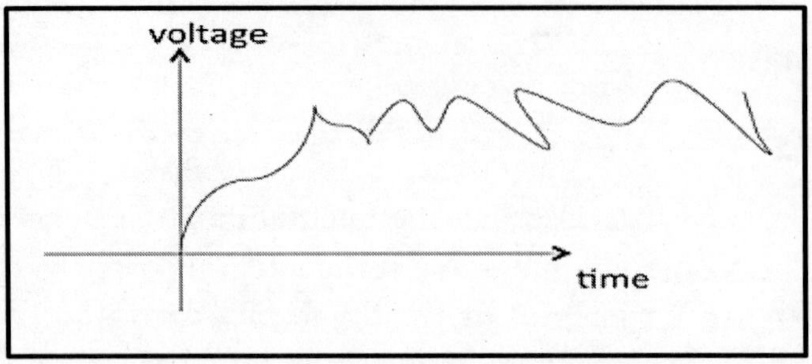

Fig 1.33: Random (stochastic) Signal

<u>Example 1.4:</u> Represent the following discrete time signals graphically. (Arrow indicates position of $n = 0$)

$x[n] = \{1, 2,3,4,5\}$
$\uparrow$ (under 1)

$x[n] = \{-6, -3,2, 5, 1,3,7,8\}$
$\uparrow$ (under 5)

$x[n] = \{ 4,3,1,0,5, 3\}$
$\uparrow$ (under 0)

Solution:

1. **The given sequence is $x[n] = \{1, 2, 3, 4, 5\}$**
$\uparrow$ (under 1)

As the arrow position indicates, $n = 0$

i.e. $x[0] = 1, x[1] = 2, x[2] = 3, x[3] = 4, x[4] = 5$

So, the plot of $x[n]$ (Amplitude) versus time is,

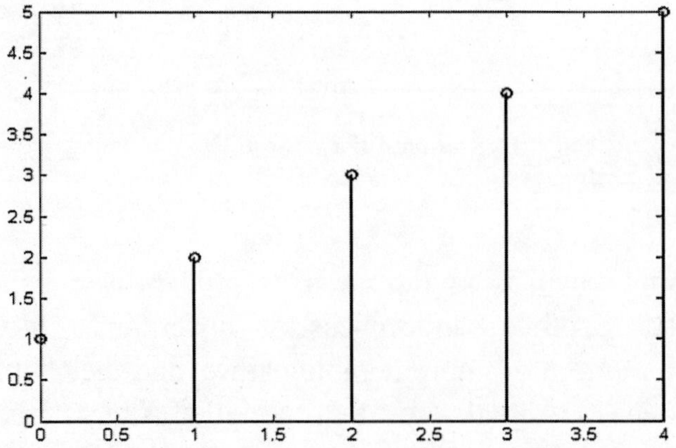

2. The given sequence is, $x[n] = \{-6, -3, 2, 5, 1, 3, 7, 8\}$

$$\uparrow$$

i. e. $x[0] = 5, x[1] = 1\,, x[2] = 3, x[3] = 7, x[4] = 8, x[-1] = 2, x[-2] = -3, x[-3] = -6$

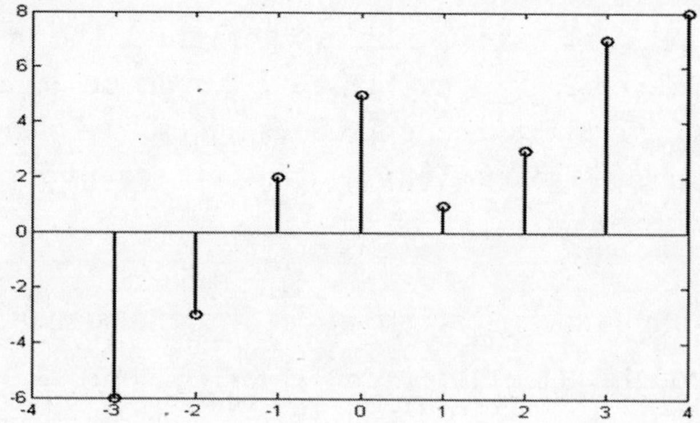

3. The given sequence is $x[n] = \{-4, 3, 1, 0, 5, 3\}$

$$\uparrow$$

i.e. $x[0] = 3, x[1] = 1, x[2] = 0, x[3] = 5, x[4] = 3, x[-1] = -4$

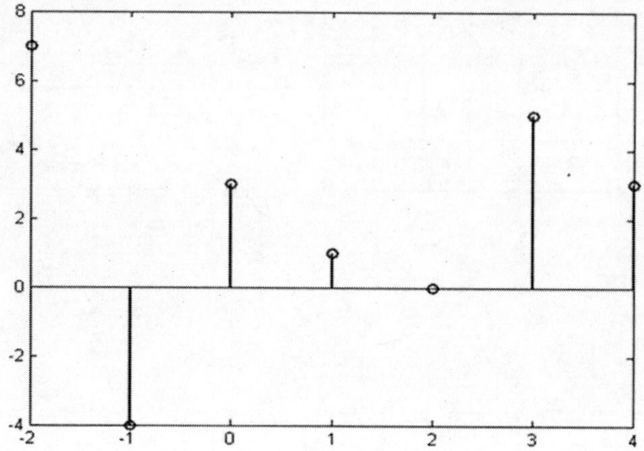

1.6 Continuous/Discrete Amplitude Signals

1.6.1 Continuous Amplitude Signals:

Continuous amplitude signals can take on any value within a continuous range. In other words, the amplitude of the signal can vary continuously over time. These signals are often encountered in analog systems, where the signal can have an infinite number of possible amplitude values. Analog audio signals and continuous waveform signals are examples of continuous amplitude signals.

1.6.2 Discrete Amplitude Signals:

Discrete amplitude signals can only take on a finite set of values. The amplitude of the signal is restricted to specific levels or values. Discrete amplitude signals are commonly encountered in digital systems, where the amplitude is represented using a finite number of bits. Digital audio signals and discrete waveform signals are examples of discrete amplitude signals.

Continuous-time discrete amplitude signals are basically digital signals. Discrete amplitude is one which we get through quantization process and it depends how many levels of quantization one wants. In simple words, quantization means assigning the amplitude values of any analog signal to certain discrete levels, equidistant of each other based on certain criteria. A square wave is a continuous-time discrete amplitude signal. For binary signals, there are only two quantization levels (0, 1). Some examples of continuous-time discrete amplitude signals are shown by Fig. 1.34 (a) and (b).

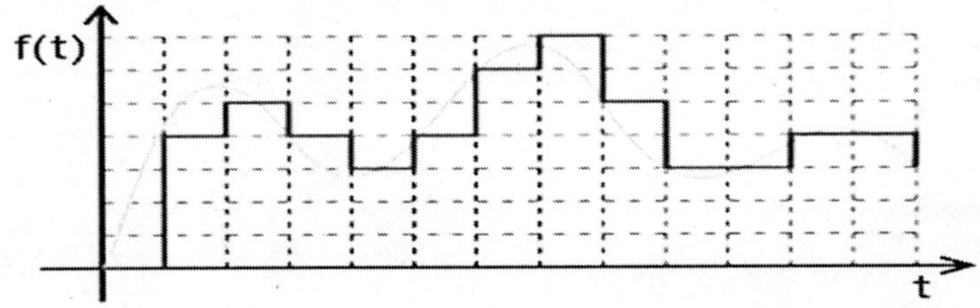

(a)

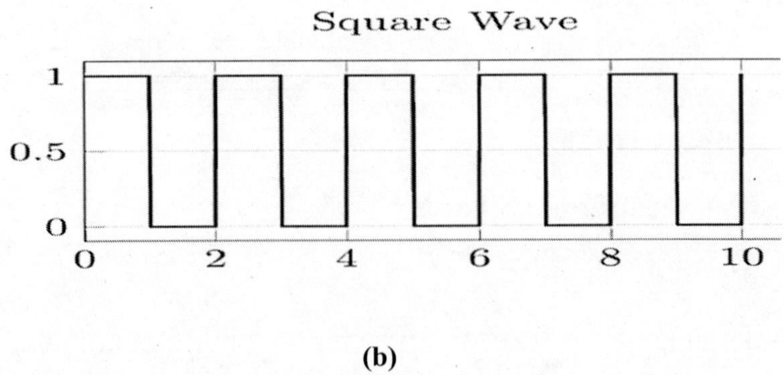

(b)

Fig. 1.34 Continuous and Discrete Amplitude Signals

1.7 Continuous –Time (CT) and Discrete-Time (DT) systems

A *system* can be recognized as an interconnection of the physical components or subsystems or software to perform the activities or tasks. It operates on the provided input signal, processes it accordingly and provides the output. A system that processes continuous–time (CT) signal and generates continuous–time (CT) signal is called *continuous –time (CT) system*. The input to output relation for CT system is given as,

$$x(t) \rightarrow y(t) \qquad (1.62)$$

Similarly, a system that processes discrete–time (DT) signal and generates discrete–time (DT) signal is called *discrete–time (DT) system*. The input to output relation for DT system is given as,

$$x[t] \rightarrow y[t] \qquad (1.63)$$

1.8 System properties: Linearity: additivity and homogeneity, Shift- invariance, Causality, Stability, Realizability.

1.8.1 Linear and Nonlinear Systems

A system is linear if it follows the two principles that are additivity and homogeneity.

1. **Additivity property**: Additivity means that the response of the system to the sum of two inputs is equal to the sum of the individual responses to each input.

Mathematically, if input $x_1(t)$ produces output $y_1(t)$ and input $x_2(t)$ produces output $y_2(t)$, then $x_1(t) + x_2(t)$ must produce $y_1(t) + y_2(t)$.

2. **Homogeneity/scaling property:** Homogeneity means that scaling the input signal by a constant scales the output response by the same constant.

Mathematically, if input $x(t)$ is scaled by a constant a i.e., $ax(t)$, then it must produce the scaled output $ay(t)$. Hence, a system that satisfies both additivity and homogeneity property (combinely called as superposition principle) is called as *linear system*. Mathematically, for CT system, if input $x_1(t)$ produces output $y_1(t)$ and input $x_2(t)$ produces output $y_2(t)$, then a linearly combined input $x(t) = a_1x_1(t) + a_2x_2(t)$ must produce $y(t) = a_1y_1(t) + a_2y_2(t)$.

$$\text{i.e., } a_1x_1(t) + a_2x_2(t) \rightarrow a_1y_1(t) + a_2y_2(t) \qquad (1.64)$$

Mathematically, for DT system, if input $x_1[n]$ produces output $y_1[n]$ and input $x_2[n]$ produces output $y_2[n]$, then a linearly combined input $x[n] = a_1x_1[n] + a_2x_2[n]$ must produce $y[n] = a_1y_1[n] + a_2y_2[n]$.

$$\text{i.e., } a_1x_1[n] + a_2x_2[n] \rightarrow a_1y_1[n] + a_2y_2[n] \qquad (1.65)$$

1.8.2 Time-Invariant and Time-Variant Systems

A system is called as *time invariant* if its behaviour does not change with respect to time. That means, if a system is provided an shifted input in time by t_0, then the system will produce an output shifted by same time t_0. For example in case of CT system, if input $x(t)$ is delayed by t_0 i.e., $x(t - t_0)$, then system produces delayed output $y(t - t_0)$. Similarly, for DT system, if input $x[n]$ is delayed by n_0 i.e., $x[n - n_0]$, then system produces delayed output $y[n - n_0]$.

On the other hand, a system is called as *time variant* if its behaviour changes with respect to time.

Procedure to check for time invariance:

Delay the input signal by t_0 and check the response of the system $y_1(t)$.

Delay the output of the system for unshifted input by t_0. Let this delayed response is $y_2(t)$.

Check whether $y_1(t) = y_2(t)$. If they are equal, system is time invariant otherwise time variant.

Example 1.5

Check whether the following systems are time invariant or not.

1. $y(t) = 5t\,x(t)$
2. $y(t) = x(t)\sin(10\pi t)$
3. $y(t) = 3x(t^2)$
4. $y(t) = 4\,e^{x(t)}$
5. $y(t) = t^2$

Solution:

1. **Given, $y(t) = 5t\,x(t)$**

Delay the input signal by t_0

$$y_1(t) = 5t\,x(t - t_0)$$

Delay the output of the system by t_0

$$y_2(t) = 5(t - t_0)\, x(t - t_0)$$

Here,

$y_1(t) \neq y_2(t)$, hence the system is time variant.

2. Given, $y(t) = x(t)\sin(10\pi t)$

Delay the input signal by t_0

$$y_1(t) = x(t - t_0)\sin(10\pi t)$$

Delay the output of the system by t_0

$$y_2(t) = x(t - t_0)\sin\big(10\pi(t - t_0)\big)$$

Here,

$y_1(t) \neq y_2(t)$, hence the system is time variant.

3. Given, $y(t) = 3x(t^2)$

Delay the input signal by t_0

$$y_1(t) = 3x(t^2 - t_0)$$

Delay the output of the system by t_0

$$y_2(t) = 3x((t - t_0)^2)$$

Here,

$y_1(t) \neq y_2(t)$, hence the system is time variant.

4. Given, $y(t) = 4\, e^{x(t)}$

Delay the input signal by t_0

$$y_1(t) = 4\, e^{x(t - t_0)}$$

Delay the output of the system by t_0

$$y_2(t) = 4\, e^{x(t - t_0)}$$

Here,

$y_1(t) = y_2(t)$, hence the system is time invariant.

5. Given, $y(t) = t^2$

Delay the input signal by t_0

$$y_1(t) = t^2 - t_0$$

Delay the output of the system by t_0

$$y_2(t) = (t - t_0)^2$$

Here,

$y_1(t) \neq y_2(t)$, hence the system is time variant.

1.8.3 Causal and Noncausal Systems

A *causal system* produces an output response that depends only on present and past values of the input signal. In other words, Causality means that the output of the system does not depend on future inputs, but only on past input. On the other hand, the output of a *noncausal system* depends upon present, past as well as future values of the input signal. All the physical systems in the real world are the noncausal systems.

Mathematically, the output response $y(t)$ at time t is determined solely by the input signal $x(\tau)$ for $\tau \leq t$.

Example 1.6: Determine whether the given CT and DT systems are causal or noncausal.

1. $y(t) = x(t + 1)$
2. $y(t) = x(t) + x(t - 1)$
3. $y[n] = n\,x[n] + x[n - 3]$

Solution:

1. Given, $y(t) = x(t + 1)$

When $t = 0$, $y(0) = x(1)$, which implies that, The response at $t = 0$, i.e., $y(0)$ depends on the future value of input $x(0)$.

When $t = 1$, $y(1) = x(2)$, which implies that, The response at $t = 1$, i.e., $y(1)$ depends on the future value of input $x(2)$.

From the above analysis we can say that for any value of t, the system output depends on future inputs. Hence the system is noncausal.

2. Given, $y(t) = x(t) + x(t-1)$

When $t = 0$, $y(0) = x(0) + x(-1)$, which implies that, The response at $t = 0$, i.e., $y(0)$ depends on the present input $x(0)$ and past input $x(-1)$.

When $t = 1$, $y(1) = x(1) + x(0)$, which implies that, The response at $t = 1$, i.e., $y(1)$ depends on the present input $x(1)$ and past input $x(0)$.

From the above analysis we can say that for any value of t, the system output depends on present and past value of inputs. Hence the system is causal.

3. Given, $y[n] = n\,x[n] + x[n-3]$

When $n = 0$, $y[0] = 0\,x[0] + x[-3]$, which implies that, The response at $n = 0$, i.e., $y[0]$ depends on the present input $x[0]$ and past input $x[-3]$.

When $n = 1$, $y[1] = 1\,x[1] + x[-2]$, which implies that, The response at $n = 1$, i.e., $y[0]$ depends on the present input $x[1]$ and past input $x[-2]$.

From the above analysis we can say that for any value of n, the DT system output depends on present and past value of inputs. Hence the system is causal.

1.8.4 Stable and Unstable Systems

Stability refers to the boundedness of the system's response. A system is considered *stable* if, for bounded input signals, the output response remains bounded i.e., small inputs lead to output that do not diverge. For example, if we apply only little pressure to push the object, it will move only a little bit. In other words, if the input signal is finite, the output signal should also be finite.

On the other hand, if a small signal causes the output signal to be arbitrarily large then that system is called as *unstable system*. The examples of bounded and unbounded signals are shown by Fig 1.35.

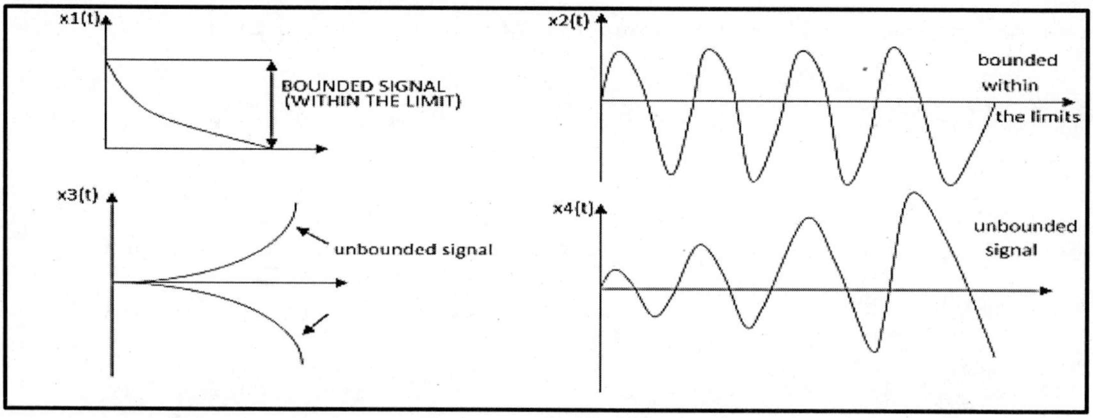

Fig. 1.35 Examples of bounded and unbounded signal

Stability is also defined by the boundedness. The input signal $x(t)$ is said to be *bounded* if there exist a constant M_x $(0 < M_x < \infty)$, such that

$$|x(t)| \leq M_x \quad \text{for all t} \tag{1.66}$$

Similarly, the output signal is bounded if it satisfies the condition $|y(t)| \leq M_y < \infty$

Some of the examples of bounded input signal are step signal, decaying exponential signal and impulse signal. Examples of unbounded input signal are ramp signal and increasing exponential signal.

Note: For a bounded signal, the amplitude is finite.

Example 1.7 Check for the stability of given systems.

1. $y\ (t)\ = \cos(x(t))$
2. $y\ [n]\ = x[n-1]$
3. $y\ (t)\ = tx(t)$
4. $y\ (t)\ = \int x(t)dt$

Solution:

1. Given, $y\ (t)\ = \cos(x(t))$

The value of $cos\theta$ lies between 1 to +1 for any value of θ. Therefore, the output $y(t)$ is bounded for any value of input $x(t)$. Hence the given system is stable.

2. Given, $y\ [n]\ = x[n-1]$

For an arbitrary signal $x[n]$, $|x[n]| \leq M_x$ for all n

Then delayed input $x[n-1]$ is also bounded by M_x,

$$|x[[n-1]| \leq M_x \quad \text{for all } n$$

The output is

$$y[n]= M_x$$

Hence, the DT system is stable.

3. Given, $y\ (t)\ = tx(t)$

The given system is a time variant system, and so the test for stability should be performed for specific inputs. There can be two cases for the existence of $x(t)$.

Case 1: Let $x(t)$ tends to ∞ or constant, as t tends to infinity.

In this case, $y(t)\ = t\,x(t)$ will be infinity as t tends to infinity and so the system is unstable.

Case 2: Let $x(t)$ tends to 0, as t tends to infinity. In this case $y(t)\ = t\,x(t)$ will be zero as t tends to infinity and so the system is stable

4. Given, $y\ (t)\ = \int x(t)dt$

Let the input $x(t)$ be $u(t)$ then

$$y(t) = \int u(t)dt \text{ but } \int u(t)dt = r(t) = \text{ramp signal}$$

It is unbounded because the amplitude of ramp is not finite and tends to become infinite when t →infinite

Hence, the system is unstable.

1.8.5 Realizability:

Realizability is a property that determines whether a given system can be implemented physically. It considers practical considerations like available resources, physical constraints, and feasibility. A realizable system can be physically built and operated.

Consider the first system, $y(t) = x(t-1)$ is a causal system, because its output is a time-delayed version of the original signal.

On the other hand, consider the second system, $y(t) = x(t+1)$, is non-causal, because its output is a time-advanced version of the input signal. This means, that for example at the output time t=0, the system requires access to the value of the input signal at time t=1. Clearly, this is impossible in a realizable system, as nobody can predict the future.

UNIT SUMMARY

This this chapter, we have seen the introduction to signals and systems that covers the fundamental concepts and properties of CT and DT signals. It explores different signal types, including periodicity, determinism, and stochastic character. Special signals such as the unit step, impulse, and ramp are discussed. Signals can exist in continuous or discrete domains with continuous or discrete amplitudes. System properties, including linearity, time-invariance, causality, stability, and realizability are also covered. Understanding signals and systems is crucial for various engineering and scientific applications.

EXERCISES

Multiple Choice Questions and Answers

1. Signals and systems are relevant in which areas?

a) Everyday life

b) Engineering

c) Science

d) All of the above

Answer: d) All of the above

2. Which of the following are signal properties?

a) Periodicity

b) Absolute integrability

c) Determinism

d) Stochastic character

e) All of the above

Answer: e) All of the above

3. Which of the following are special signals?

a) Unit step

b) Unit impulse

c) Sinusoid

d) Complex exponential

e) All of the above

Answer: e) All of the above

4. Continuous-time signals exist in which domain?

a) Continuous

b) Discrete

c) Both

d) None

Answer: a) Continuous

5. Discrete-time signals exist in which domain?

a) Continuous

b) Discrete

c) Both

d) None

Answer: b) Discrete

6. Linearity of a system refers to:

a) Additivity and homogeneity

b) Shift-invariance

c) Causality

d) Stability

Answer: a) Additivity and homogeneity

7. Which property ensures that a system's output remains bounded for bounded input signals?

a) Linearity

b) Shift-invariance

c) Causality

d) Stability

Answer: d) Stability

8. Realizability of a system refers to:

a) Additivity and homogeneity

b) Shift-invariance

c) Causality

d) Feasibility of physical implementation

Answer: d) Feasibility of physical implementation

9. A special time-limited signal is characterized by:

a) Periodicity

b) Absolute integrability

c) Determinism

d) Time limitations

Answer: d) Time limitations

10. Which of the following signal properties relates to randomness?

a) Periodicity

b) Absolute integrability

c) Determinism

d) Stochastic character

Answer: d) Stochastic character

Short and Long Answer Type Questions

1. Give an example of a signal exhibiting periodicity.
2. What does it mean for a signal to have absolute integrability?
3. Define determinism in the context of signals.
4. Provide an example of a special time-limited signal.

5. Explain the concept of shift-invariance in systems.

6. Discuss the applications of signals and systems in engineering and science.

7. Explain the properties and characteristics of the sinusoidal signal.

8. Discuss the importance of linearity in systems and provide examples.

9. Explain the concept of causality in systems and its significance.

10. Discuss the differences between continuous and discrete amplitude signals.

Numerical Problems

1. Consider a periodic signal with a period of $T = 4$ seconds. Find the frequency of the signal.
2. Determine if the following signal is absolutely integrable: x(t) = e^(-2t) for $t \geq 0$.
3. Calculate the average value of the signal $x(t) = 3\sin(2\pi t)$ over the interval $0 \leq t \leq 2$ seconds.
4. Given a system with the impulse response h(t) = 2e^(-t)u(t), where u(t) is the unit step function, find the response of the system to the input signal x(t) = 3u(t).
5. Determine if the system described by the difference equation y[n] = 0.5y[n-1] + x[n] is linear or nonlinear.
6. Consider a discrete-time system with the input signal x[n] = {1, 2, 3, 4} and the impulse response h[n] = {1, -1, 2, -2}. Calculate the output signal y[n] using the convolution sum.
7. Determine if the system described by the following difference equation is time-invariant or time-varying: y[n] = x[n] + x[n-1].
8. Test the stability of the continuous-time system with the transfer function H(s) = 1/(s + 2).
9. Determine if the system with the transfer function H(z) = (1 - z^(-1))/(1 + z^(-1)) is stable in the discrete-time domain.
10. Given a system with the input signal $x(t) = 4\sin(3\pi t)$ and the output signal $y(t) = 2\sin(3\pi t + \pi/4)$, calculate the gain of the system.

KNOW MORE

Signals and systems are fundamental concepts that permeate our daily lives and play a vital role in various fields of engineering and science. Signals exhibit different properties such as periodicity, which describes their repetitive nature, and absolute integrability, which quantifies the energy or power content of a signal. Signals can be deterministic, meaning they have a predictable behavior, or stochastic, displaying random characteristics. Special signals of significance include the unit step, representing abrupt changes, the unit impulse, denoting instantaneous events, sinusoids, fundamental periodic waveforms, and complex exponentials, integral to signal processing. Time-limited signals have finite duration, and they can be continuous or discrete in both the time and amplitude domains. Systems, on the other hand, possess distinct properties that govern their behavior. Linearity signifies that the response of a system to a sum of inputs is the sum of their individual responses, while additivity and homogeneity describe their scaling behavior. Shift-invariance indicates that shifting the input signal leads to a corresponding shift in the output response. Causality denotes that the output depends only on past and present inputs. Stability ensures that the system produces bounded output responses for bounded inputs, and realizability signifies the practical implementability of the system using realizable components or algorithms. Understanding these properties and concepts is vital in comprehending the behavior and characteristics of signals and systems, enabling their analysis, manipulation, and design in numerous applications across engineering and scientific disciplines.

REFERENCES AND SUGGESTED READINGS

1. Signals and Systems by Simon Haykin
2. Signals and Systems by Ganesh Rao
3. Signals and Systems - Course (nptel.ac.in)

Dynamic QR Code for Further Reading

2 Behavior of Continuous and Discrete-time LTI

UNIT SPECIFICS

Through this unit we have discussed the following aspects:

- *Impulse response and step response provide information about a system's characteristics and its response to specific inputs.*
- *Convolution is used to compute the output of a system by integrating the product of the input and the shifted impulse response.*
- *LTI systems can process aperiodic and convergent inputs, and their output can be computed through convolution or other techniques.*
- *Cascade interconnections involve connecting multiple LTI systems in series by convolving their impulse responses.*
- *Causality refers to a system's output depending only on past or present input values, while stability means the output remains bounded for any bounded input.*
- *Differential equations represent continuous-time LTI systems, while difference equations represent discrete-time LTI systems.*
- *State-space representation describes a system using first-order differential or difference equations, including state variables and input-output relationships.*
- *State-space analysis allows for studying the behavior of systems in terms of their state variables and can handle multi-input, multi-output systems.*
- *The state transition matrix relates the initial state to the state at any given time and is essential in solving state-space equations.*
- *Frequency response describes how an LTI system responds to different frequencies in the input, and it is related to the impulse response through Fourier analysis.*
- *Periodic inputs, such as sinusoidal waves, can be analyzed using the notion of frequency response to understand the system's behavior in the frequency domain.*

This unit focuses on the behavior of Continuous and Discrete-time Linear Time-Invariant (LTI) Systems. It covers key topics including impulse response, step response, and convolution. The unit explores how LTI systems respond to aperiodic and convergent inputs, emphasizing techniques such as convolution to determine the output. Cascade interconnections, where multiple systems are connected in series, are examined by convolving their impulse responses. Causality and stability in LTI systems are characterized, where causality refers to the past and present dependency between input and output, and stability ensures bounded output for any bounded input.

The unit addresses system representation through differential equations for continuous-time systems and difference equations for discrete-time systems. It introduces state-space representation, which describes systems using first-order differential or difference equations, facilitating state-space analysis and the study of multi-input and multi-output systems. The role of the state transition matrix is explored, connecting the initial state to the state at any given time. The unit also covers periodic inputs applied to LTI systems, investigating the notion of frequency response and its relationship with the impulse response. This understanding offers insights into how LTI systems respond to different frequencies in the input signal.

Overall, this unit provides comprehensive coverage of impulse response, step response, convolution, input-output behavior, causality, stability, system representation, state-space analysis, state transition matrix, periodic inputs, and the relationship between frequency response and impulse response. It equips learners with a solid foundation in analyzing and understanding the behavior of Continuous and Discrete-time LTI Systems.

RATIONALE

The unit on "Behavior of Continuous and Discrete-time LTI Systems" is to provide students Understanding the behavior of Continuous and Discrete-time Linear Time-Invariant (LTI) Systems is crucial in various engineering and scientific disciplines. This 8-hour unit is designed to provide students with a comprehensive understanding of LTI systems and their characteristics.

Impulse response and step response are fundamental concepts in LTI systems. By studying these responses, students gain insights into how a system reacts to specific inputs and determine its dynamic behavior. Convolution is a key operation used to compute the output of a system, and it plays a vital role in analyzing LTI systems.

The unit focuses on the input-output behavior of LTI systems with a particular emphasis on aperiodic and convergent inputs. Students learn how to analyze and determine the system's response using techniques such as convolution. Cascade interconnections of LTI systems are explored, as they are commonly encountered in real-world applications. By understanding the convolution of impulse responses, students can analyze and predict the behavior of interconnected systems.

Characterizing causality and stability is essential for assessing the reliability and predictability of LTI systems. Students examine the concepts of causality, where the output depends on past and present inputs, and stability, which ensures bounded output for any bounded input. These characterizations provide valuable insights into system behavior and performance.

System representation is an important aspect covered in the unit. Students learn to represent LTI systems using differential equations for continuous-time systems and difference equations for discrete-time systems. State-space representation is introduced as a powerful method to describe and analyze complex systems. It provides a framework for studying multi-input, multi-output systems and understanding their interactions.

The role of the state transition matrix is explored, emphasizing its significance in relating the initial state to the state at any given time. This matrix plays a crucial role in solving state-space equations and analyzing system behavior over time.

Periodic inputs and the notion of frequency response are examined to understand how LTI systems respond to different frequencies in the input. The frequency response is related to the impulse response through Fourier analysis, enabling students to analyze system behavior in the frequency domain.

Overall, this unit equips students with the necessary knowledge and skills to analyze and understand the behavior of Continuous and Discrete-time LTI Systems. The concepts covered, such as impulse response, step response, convolution, input-output behavior, causality, stability, system representation, state-space analysis, state transition matrix, periodic inputs, and frequency response, are essential for successful engineering and scientific applications.

PRE-REQUISITES

1. *Strong understanding of mathematics, including algebra, calculus, and complex numbers.*
2. *Familiarity with basic concepts in signals and systems, such as time-domain and frequency-domain representations, Fourier analysis, and convolution.*
3. *Proficiency in solving ordinary differential equations and understanding linear algebra concepts.*
4. *Basic knowledge of electronics and circuit analysis for understanding continuous-time LTI systems.*
5. *Knowledge of digital signal processing concepts for understanding discrete-time LTI systems.*
6. *These pre-requisites provide the necessary foundations to effectively engage with the content and concepts covered in the unit on the behavior of Continuous and Discrete-time LTI Systems.*

UNIT OUTCOMES

List of outcomes of this unit is as follows:

U2-O1: Understand the concept of impulse response and step response.

U2-O2: Apply convolution to analyze the behavior of LTI systems.

U2-O3: Analyze the input-output behavior of LTI systems with aperiodic convergent inputs.

U2-O4: Understand and apply cascade interconnections of LTI systems.

U2-O5: Characterize the causality and stability of LTI systems.

U2-O6: Represent LTI systems through differential equations and difference equations.

U2-O7: Understand and apply state-space representation of systems.

U2-O8: Perform state-space analysis of LTI systems.

U2-O9: Analyze multi-input, multi-output systems.

U2-O10: Understand the role and application of the State Transition Matrix.

U2-O11: Analyze the behavior of LTI systems with periodic inputs.

U2-O12: Understand the concept of frequency response and its relation to the impulse response.

Unit-2 Outcomes	***EXPECTED MAPPING WITH COURSE OUTCOMES*** *(1- Weak Correlation; 2- Medium correlation; 3- Strong Correlation)*					
	CO-1	***CO-2***	***CO-3***	***CO-4***	***CO-5***	***CO-6***
U2-O1	*3*	*3*	*1*	*2*	*2*	*3*
U2-O2	*3*	*3*	*2*	*1*	-	*1*
U2-O3	*3*	*2*	*2*	-	-	*3*
U2-O4	*3*	*3*	*2*	*1*	-	*2*
U2-O5	*3*	*3*	*2*	*1*	*1*	*2*

"Education is the most powerful weapon which you can use to change the world."

- Nelson Mandela

2.1 Introduction

In chapter 1, we have discussed types of systems and their properties. Two properties namely linearity and time-invariance play very important roles in the analysis of signals and systems since most of the practical systems possess these two properties. We call such systems as *linear time-invariant* (*LTI*) systems. In our study of signals and systems, we will be especially interested in systems that demonstrate both properties, which together allow the use of some of the most powerful tools of signal processing.

2.1.1 Linear Time Invariant Systems

a) Linear Systems

A system is said to be a linear system if the system follows the linear scaling and superposition principle as discussed below.

Linear Scaling: When the input to a given system is scaled by a constant value, if the output of the system is also scaled by the same amount, the system is said to follow the linear scaling property. It is demonstrated in Figure 2.1.

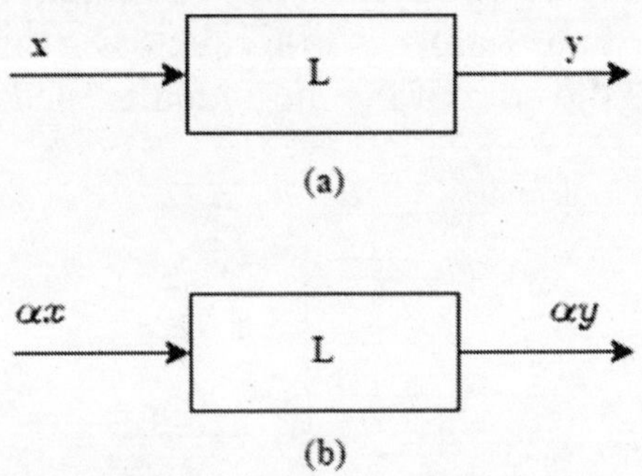

Fig 2.1 Linear scaling

In above Figure 2.1(a), the input x to the linear system L gives the output y. If x is scaled by a value α and passed through this same system, as in Figure 2.1(b), the output will also be scaled by α.

Superposition Principle: The linear system also obeys the principle of superposition. This means that if two inputs are added together and passed through a linear system, the output will be the sum of the outputs corresponding to their individual inputs. It is demonstrated in Figure 2.2.

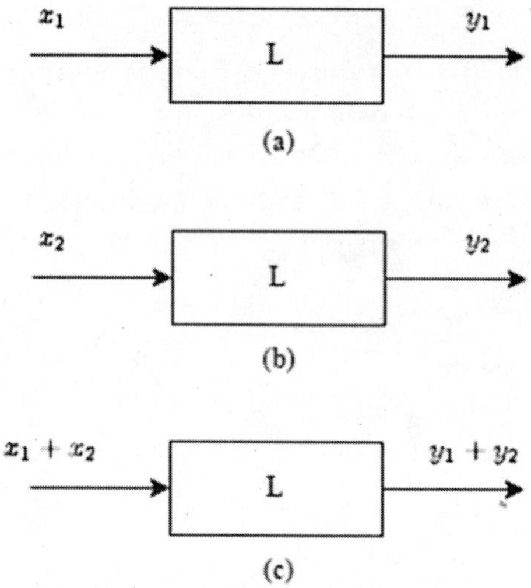

Fig 2.2 Superposition Principle

That is, if cases in Figure 2.2 (a) and (b) are true then Figure 2.2 (c) is also true for a linear system. The scaling property mentioned above still holds in conjunction with the superposition principle. Therefore, if the inputs x and y are scaled by factors α and β, respectively, then the sum of these scaled inputs will give the sum of the individual scaled outputs:

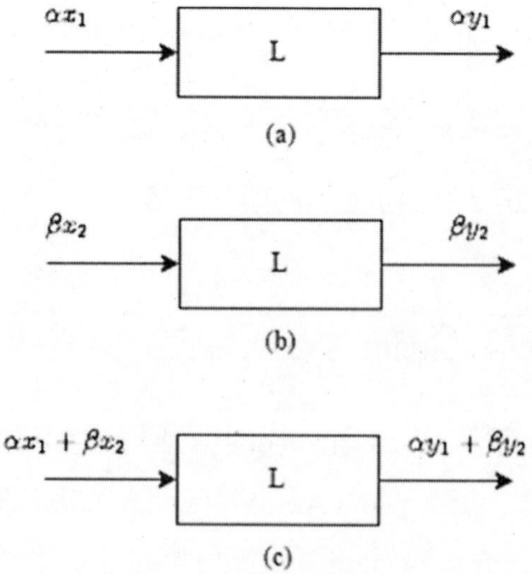

Fig 2.3 Superposition Principle with Linear Scaling

2.1.2 Time Invariant Systems

A time-invariant (TI) system has the property that a certain input will always give the same output (up to timing), without regard to when the input was applied to the system. In other words, if $y(t)$ is the output of the system corresponding to its input $x(t)$, then $y(t-t_0)$ will be the output when a delayed input $x(t-t_0)$ is applied to the system for all values of t_0 as demonstrated in Figure 2.4.

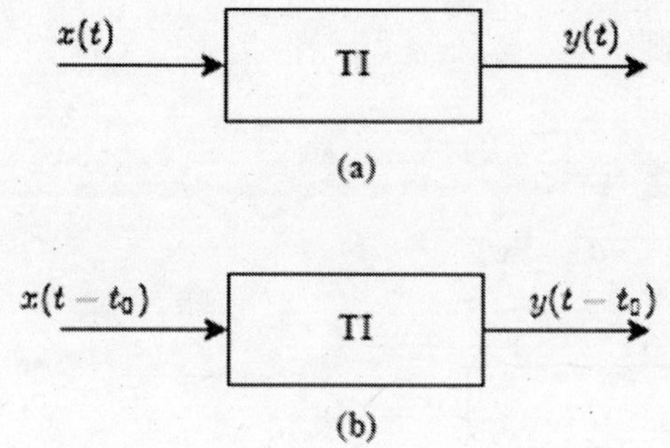

Fig 2.4 Time-Invariant Systems

In this figure, $x(t)$ and $x(t-t_0)$ are passed through the system TI. Because the system TI is time-invariant, the inputs $x(t)$ and $x(t-t_0)$ produce the same output. Whether a system is time-invariant or time-variant can be seen in the differential equation (or difference equation) describing it. Time-invariant systems are modelled with constant coefficient equations. A constant coefficient differential (or difference) equation means that the parameters of the system are not changing over time and an input now will give the same result as the same input later.

2.1.3 Linear Time Invariant Systems

Certain systems are both linear and time-invariant, and are thus referred to as LTI systems.

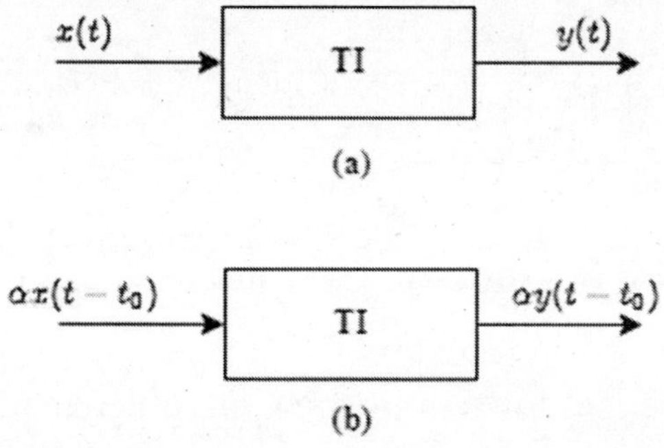

Fig 2.5 Linear Time-Invariant Systems

As LTI systems are a subset of linear systems, they obey the principle of superposition. In the figure below, we see the effect of applying time-invariance to the superposition definition in the linear systems section above.

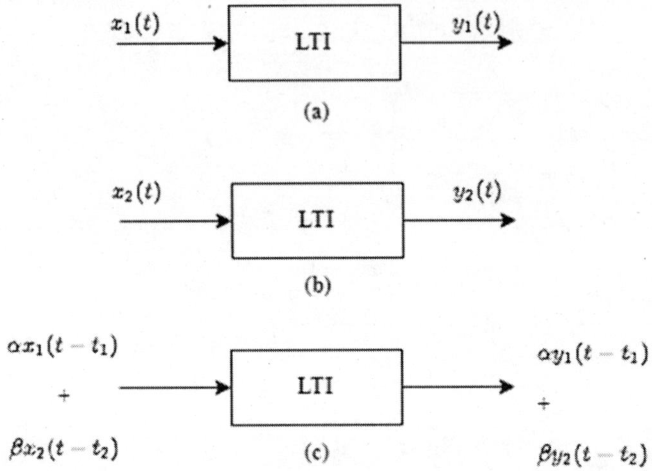

Fig 2.6 Superposition in Linear Time-Invariant Systems

2.2 Impulse response of LTI System

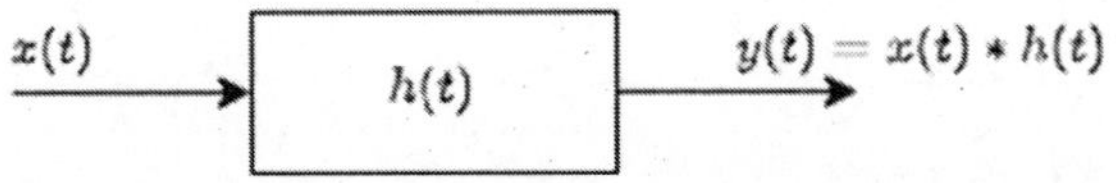

Fig 2.7 CT impulse response

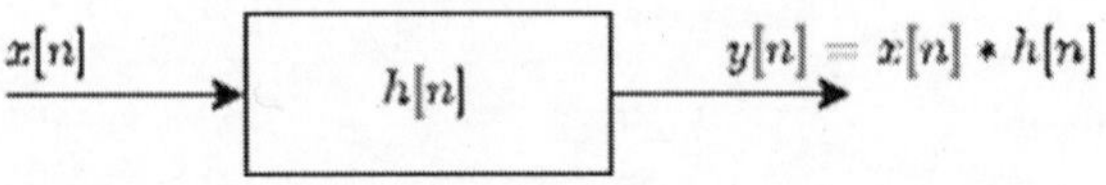

Fig 2.8 DT impulse response

2.2.1 Discrete-Time Unit Impulse Response and the Convolution

Let $h_k[n]$ be the response of the LTI system to the shifted unit impulse $\delta[n-k]$, then from the superposition property for a linear system, the response of the linear system to the input $x[n]$ in Eq. (2.1) is simply the weighted linear combination of these basic responses:

$$y[n] = \sum_{k=-\infty}^{k=+\infty} x[k]\text{h[n]} \quad (2.1)$$

If the linear system is time invariant, then the responses to time-shifted unit impulses are all time-shifted versions of the same impulse responses:

$$h_k[n] = h_0[n-k] \quad (2.2)$$

Therefore, the impulse response $h[n] = h_0[n]$ of an LTI system characterizes the system completely. This is not the case for a linear time-varying system: one has to specify all the impulse responses $h_k[n]$ (an infinite number) to characterize the system. For the LTI system, equation becomes

$$y[n] = \sum_{k=-\infty}^{k=+\infty} x[k]\text{h[n} - \text{k]} \quad (2.3)$$

This result is referred to as the convolution sum or superposition sum and the operation on the right-hand side of the equation is known as the convolution of the sequences of x[n] and h[n]. The convolution operation is usually represented symbolically as

$$y[n] \ = \ x[k] * h[n] \quad (2.4)$$

2.2.2 Representation of Continuous-Time Signals in Terms of Impulses

A continuous-time signal can be viewed as a linear combination of continuous impulses:

$$x(t) = \int_{-\infty}^{\infty} x(\tau)\delta(t-\tau)dx \quad (2.5)$$

The result is obtained by chopping up the signal $x(t)$ in sections of width D, and taking sum

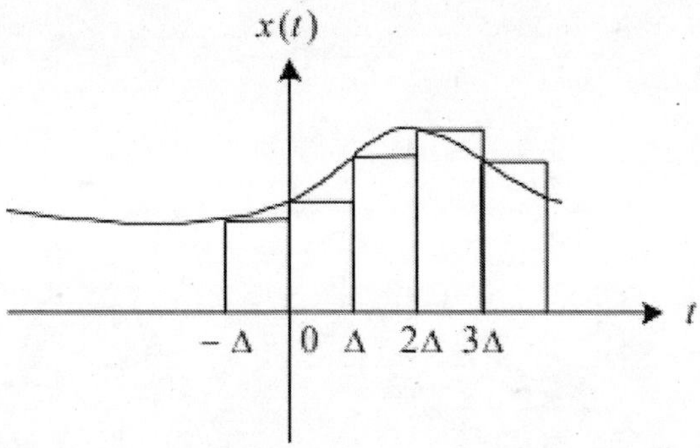

Fig 2.9 Representation of Continuous-Time Signals in Terms of Impulses

Recall the definition of the unit pulse δ_Δ; we can define a signal $x(t)$ as a linear combination of delayed pulses of height $x(k_\Delta)$

$$x(t) = \sum_{k=-\infty}^{k=+\infty}(x(k_\Delta\ \delta(t-k_\Delta))\Delta \qquad (2.6)$$

Taking the limit as $\Delta = 0$, we obtain the integral of Eq. (2.6), in which when $\Delta = 0$

(1) The summation approaches to an integral

(2) $k_\Delta = \tau$ *and* $x(k_\Delta) = x(\tau)$

(3) $\Delta = d\tau$

(4) $\delta(t-k_\Delta) = \delta(t-\tau)$

Eq. (2.7) can also be obtained by using the sampling property of the impulse function. If we consider t is fixed and t is time variable, then we have

$$x(\tau)\delta(t-\tau) = x((\tau)\delta(-(t-\tau)) = x(\tau)\delta(t-\tau). \qquad (2.7)$$

$$\int_{-\infty}^{\infty} x(\tau)\delta(t-\tau)d\tau = \int_{-\infty}^{\infty} x(\tau)\delta(\tau-t)d\tau = x(t)\int_{-\infty}^{\infty}\delta(\tau-t)d\tau = x(t) \qquad (2.8)$$

As in discrete time, this is the sifting property of continuous-time impulse.

2.3 The Unit Step Response of an LTI System

The step response of an LTI system is simply the response of the system to a unit step. It conveys a lot of information about the system. For a discrete-time system with impulse response $h[n]$, the step response is $s[n] = u[n] * h[n]$. However, based on the commutative property of convolution, $s[n] = h[n] * u[n]$, and therefore, s[n] can be viewed as the response to input $h[n]$ of a discrete time LTI system with unit impulse response. We know that $u[n]$ is the unit impulse response of the accumulator. Therefore,

$$s[n] = \sum_{k=-\infty}^{n} h[k] \qquad (2.9)$$

From this equation, $h[n]$ can be recovered from $s[n]$ using the relation

$$h[n] = s[n] - s[n-1] \qquad (2.10)$$

It can be seen that the step response of a discrete-time LTI system is the running sum of its impulse response. Conversely, the impulse response of a discrete-time LTI system is the first difference of its step response.

Similarly, in continuous time, the step response of an LTI system is the running integral of its impulse response,

$$s(t) = \int_{-\infty}^{t} h(\tau)d\tau \qquad (2.11)$$

and the unit impulse response is the first derivative of the unit step response,

$$h(t) = \frac{ds(t)}{dt} = s'(t) \qquad (2.12)$$

Therefore, in both continuous and discrete time, the unit step response can also be used to characterize an LTI system.

2.4 Convolution Integral:

Convolution of two continuous-time signals $x(t)$ and $h(t)$denoted by,

$$y(t) = x(t) * h(t) = \int_{-\infty}^{\infty} x(\tau)h(t-\tau)d\tau \qquad (2.13)$$

Equation (2.13) is commonly called the convolution integral. Thus, we have the fundamental result that the output of any continuous-time LTI system is the convolution of the input $x(t)$ with the impulse response $h(t)$ of the system. Fig. 2.10 illustrates the definition of the impulse response $h(t)$ and the relationship of Eq. (2.13).

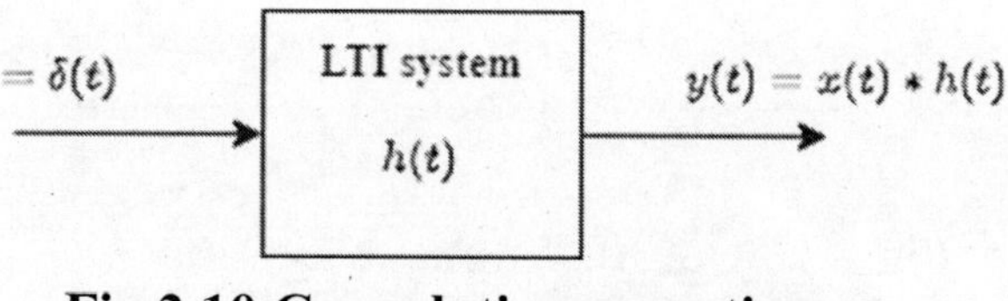

Fig 2.10 Convolution operation

2.4.1 Properties of the Convolution Integral:

The convolution integral has the following properties.

1. Commutative:

$$x(t) * h(t) = h(t) * x(t)$$

2. Associative:

$$\{x(t) * h_1(t)\} * h_2(t) = x(t)\{h_1(t) * h_2(t)\}$$

3. Distributive:

$$x(t) * \{h_1(t) + h_2(t)\} = x(t) * h_1(t) + x(t) * h_2(t)$$

2.5 Input-output behaviour with aperiodic convergent inputs

2.5.1 Response of a continuous time system

If an input $x(t)$ is applied and then output of the system is $y(t)$

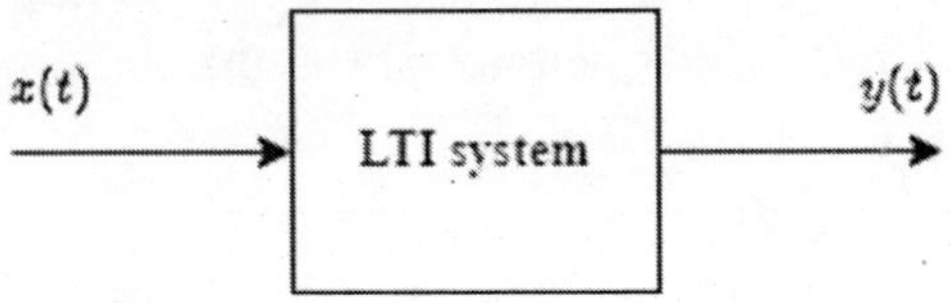

Fig 2.11 $x(t)$ input to system

So, instead of $x(t)$ if we apply a standard elementary signal that is known as impulse signal. If we apply impulse signal then the system's response will be impulse response if delta is replaced by Tau Delta.

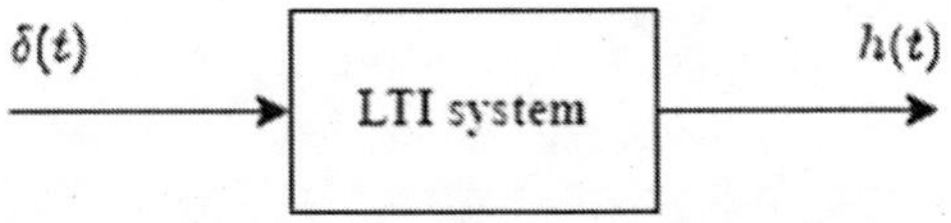

Fig 2.12 $\delta(t)$ input to system

If input is $\delta(t - \Delta\tau)$, so when input is delayed output will be delayed, this is time invariant system.

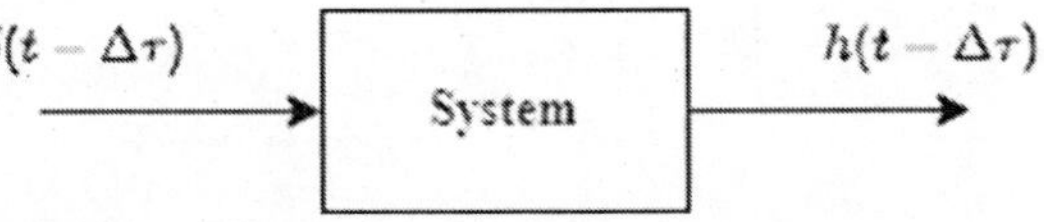

Fig 2.13 Delayed input to system

$$y(t) = \int_{-\infty}^{\infty} x(\tau)h(t - \tau)d\tau \qquad (2.14)$$

So, this equation this convolution in integral equation is very useful for calculating the responses of the systems

2.5.2 Response of a discrete time system

We have input $x[n]$ and discrete time system and this discrete time system is giving output as $y[n]$.

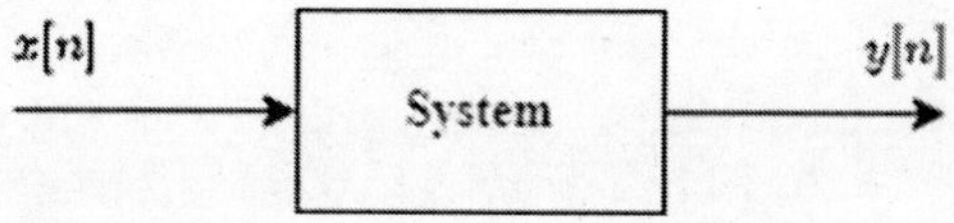

Fig 2.14 $x[n]$ input to system

If this input is an impulse signal $\delta[n]$ then the system will provide the output corresponding to impulse signal the output corresponding to impulse signal is called impulse response $h[n]$.

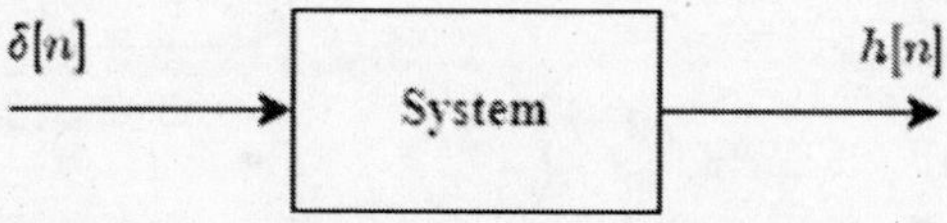

Fig 2.15 $\delta[n]$ input to system

If the input impulse signal is delayed by k, i.e., $\delta[n-k]$ and it is applied to the same discrete time system DTS then the output will also be delayed by k, i.e., $h[n-k]$.

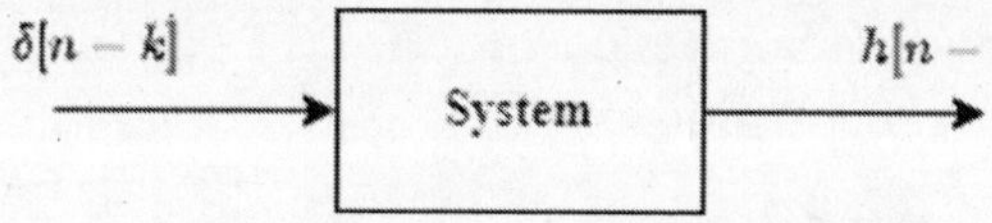

Fig 2.16 δ [n-k] input to system

If another input $x[k]$ is multiplied with $\delta[n-k]$ and provided to the system, because it is a linear time invariant system so multiplying is a scaling of input which will also result in scaling of the output and hence the output will become $x[k]h[n-k]$.

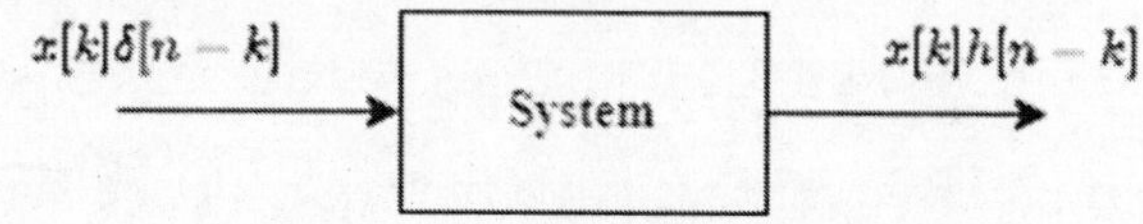

Fig 2.17 x[k] δ [n-k] input to system

Dividing summation of the input from $-\infty$ to $+\infty$ and then passing through the system, the summation will also result in the right side in terms of k which is called convolution sum. Convolution sum is important for calculating output of the discrete time systems.

$$y[n] = \sum_{k=-\infty}^{\infty} x[k]h[n-k] \tag{2.15}$$

$$y[n] = x[n] * h[n] \tag{2.16}$$

2.6 Cascade interconnections

Suppose that we have a LTI system with input x, output y, and impulse response h. We know that x and y are related as $y = x * h$. In other words, the system can be viewed as performing a convolution operation. From the properties of convolution introduced earlier, we can derive several equivalences involving the impulse responses of series and parallel-interconnected systems.

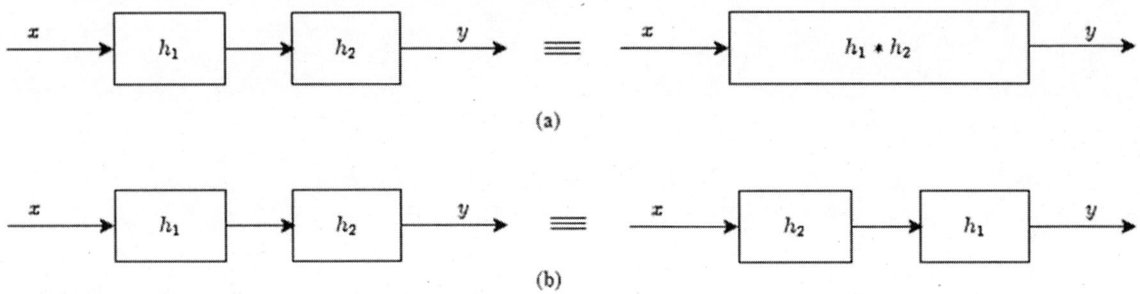

Figure 2.18: Equivalences for the series interconnection of continuous-time LTI systems. The (a) first equivalence (b) second equivalence.

Consider two LTI systems with impulse responses h_1 and h_2 that are connected in a series configuration, as shown on the left-side of Fig 2.18(a). From the block diagram on the left side of Fig. 2.18(a), we have

$$y = (x * h_1) * h_2 \quad (2.17)$$

Due to the associativity of convolution, however, this is equivalent to

$$y = x * (h_1 * h_2) \quad (2.18)$$

Thus, the series interconnection of two LTI systems behaves as a single LTI system with impulse response $h_1 * h_2$. In other words, we have the equivalence shown in Fig. 2.18(a).

Consider two LTI systems with impulse responses h_1 and h_2 that are connected in a series configuration, as shown on the left-side of Figure 2.18(b). From the block diagram on the left side of Figure 2.18(b), we have

$$y = (x * h_1) * h_2 \quad (2.19)$$

Due to the associativity and commutativity of convolution, this is equivalent to

$$y = x * (h_1 * h_2) = x * (h_2 * h_1)$$

$$= (x * h_2) * h_1 \qquad (2.20)$$

Thus, interchanging the two LTI systems does not change the behaviour of the overall system with input x and output y. In other words, we have the equivalence shown in Figure 2.18(b).

Consider two LTI systems with impulse responses h1 and h2 that are connected in a parallel configuration, as shown on the left-side of Figure 2.19. From the block diagram on the left side of Figure 2.19, we have

$$y = x * h_1 + x * h_2 \qquad (2.21)$$

Due to convolution being distributive, however, this equation can be rewritten as

$$y = x * (h_1 + h_2) \qquad (2.22)$$

Thus, the parallel interconnection of two LTI systems behaves as a single LTI system with impulse response $h_1 + h_2$. In other words, we have the equivalence shown in Figure 2.19.

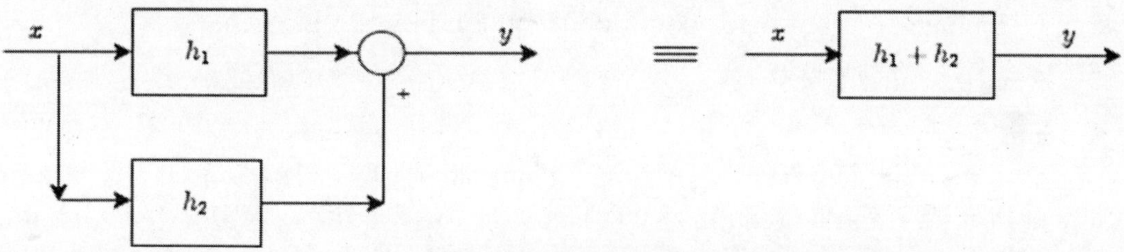

Figure 2.19: Equivalence for the parallel interconnection of continuous-time LTI systems

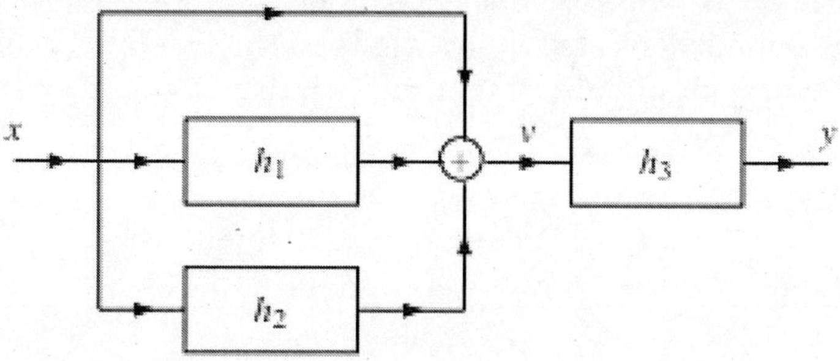

Figure 2.20: System interconnection example

Similarly, from the right half of the block diagram from Figure 2.20, we can write

$$y(t) = v * h_3 \quad (2.23)$$

Substituting the expression for v into the Eq. (2.23) we obtain,

$$= (x * [\delta + h_1 + h_2]) * h_3$$

$$= x * [h_3 + h_1 * h_3 + h_2 * h_3] \quad (2.24)$$

Thus, from Eq. (2.24) the impulse response h of the overall system is

$$h(t) = h_3 + h_1 * h_3 + h_2 * h_3 \quad (2.25)$$

2.7 Causality for LTI systems

A system is causal if its output depends only on the past and present values of the input signal. Specifically, for a discrete-time LTI system, this requirement is $y[n]$ should not depend on $x[k]$for $k > n$. Based on the convolution sum equation, all the coefficients $h[n - k]$ that multiply values of $x[k]$ for $k > n$ must be zero, which means that the impulse response of a causal discrete-time LTI system should satisfy the condition

$$h[n] = 0, \; for\, n < 0 \quad (2.26)$$

A causal system is causal if its impulse response is zero for negative time; this makes sense as the system should not have a response before impulse is applied.

A similar conclusion can be arrived for continuous-time LTI systems, namely

$$h(t) = 0, \; for\, t < 0 \quad (2.27)$$

Examples: The accumulator $h[n] = u[n]$, and its inverse $h[n] = \delta[n] - \delta\,[n-1]$ are causal. The pure time shift with impulse response $y\,(t) = x\,(t - t_0)\; for\; t_0 > 0$ is causal, but is not causal for $t_0 < 0$.

2.8 Stability for LTI Systems

Recall that a system is stable if every bounded input produces a bounded output. For LTI system, the input $x[n]$ is bounded in magnitude $x[n] \le B$, for all n. If this input signal is applied to an LTI system with unit impulse response $h[n]$, the magnitude of the output,

$$|y[n]| = \left|\sum_{k=-\infty}^{+\infty} h[k]x[n-k]\right| \le \sum_{k=-\infty}^{+\infty} |h[k]||x[n-k]| \le B\sum_{k=-\infty}^{+\infty} |h[k]| \quad (2.28)$$

$y[n]$ is bounded in magnitude, and hence is stable if

$$\sum_{k=-\infty}^{\infty} h[k] < \infty \quad (2.29)$$

So discrete-time LTI system is stable is Eq. (2.29) is satisfied. The similar analysis applies to continuous-time LTI systems, for which the stability is equivalent to

$$\int_{-\infty}^{\infty} h(\tau)d\tau < \infty \tag{2.30}$$

Example: consider a system that is pure time shift in either continuous time or discrete time. In discrete time,

$$\sum_{k=-\infty}^{+\infty} |h[k]| = \sum_{k=-\infty}^{+\infty} |\delta[n-n_0| = 1,$$

While, in continuous time,

$$\int_{-\infty}^{+\infty} |h(\tau)|d\tau = \int_{-\infty}^{+\infty} |\delta(t-t_0)|d\tau = 1,$$

Hence, we can conclude that both systems are stable.

Example: The accumulator h[n] = u[n] is unstable because

$$\sum_{k=-\infty}^{+\infty} |h[k]| = \sum_{k=0}^{+\infty} |u[n]| = \infty.$$

2.9 System Representation through Differential Equations and Difference Equations.

Linear, time-invariant (LTI) systems are represented by linear constant-coefficient differential equations in continuous-time (CT) and linear constant-coefficient difference equations in discrete-time (DT).

CT LTI system through differential equations can be of form electrical circuits, mechanical systems etc. DT LTI system through difference equations can be described by a wide variety of data filtering, time series analysis, and digital filtering systems.

2.9.1 Differential Equation Description of CT LTI systems

Differential equations are used to represent CT systems, where the system variables are functions of continuous time, typically denoted as t. These equations describe the relationship between the system's input, output, and their derivatives with respect to time. The general structure of such a representation is given by Eq. (2.31),

$$\sum_{m=0}^{M} a_m \frac{d^m y(t)}{dt^m} = \sum_{n=0}^{N} a_n \frac{d^n x(t)}{dt^n} \tag{2.31}$$

Where, $x(t)$ is the input to the system and $y(t)$ is the response.

Any general output $y(t)$ can also be represented in terms of two signals and that are particular solution and homogeneous solution.

The homogeneous solution can be given as,

$$\sum_{m=0}^{M} a_m \frac{d^m y_{homogeneous}(t)}{dt^m} = 0 \tag{2.32}$$

To solve the above equation, we required the M auxiliary (initial) conditions.

The system is said to be linear when described by the above differential equation if all the initial conditions are equal to 0. Similarly, the system is said to be time invariant if it is at initial rest, i.e., if $x(t) = 0 \text{ for } t \leq t_0$ then assume, $y(t) = 0 \text{ for } t \leq t_0$. Hence, the initial condition becomes,

$$y(t_0) = \frac{dy(t)}{dt}\bigg|\bigg|_{t=t_0} = \ldots.. = \frac{d^{M-1}y(t)}{dt^{M-1}} = 0 \tag{2.33}$$

That means the value of the output at t_0 and its derivatives up to degree $(M - 1)$ is 0. So, if the system satisfies both the conditions of linearity and time invariance then it is linear time-invariant (LTI) system.

2.9.2 Difference Equation Description of DT LTI systems

Similar to CT LTI systems we can be represented by differential equations, a DT LTI system is represented by Difference equations. A general structure of difference equation is,

$$\sum_{m=0}^{M} a_m y(n-m) = \sum_{m=0}^{N} b_m x(n-m) \qquad (2.34)$$

Where, $x(m)$ is an input and $y(m)$ is an output.

2.10 State space representation of systems

Earlier we have seen LTI systems based on input-output relationships known as external description of a system. Now we will examine the state space representation of systems known as internal description of systems.

State space representation of systems consists of two parts, state equations and output equations. State equations represent set of equations relating state variables to inputs. Whereas, Output equations represents set of equations relating outputs to state variables and inputs. Advantage of state space representation is it provides new insight into the system behaviour with the use of matrix linear algebra. It can also handle multiple-input multiple-output (MIMO) systems.

The state of a CT system at time t_0 is defined as the minimal information that is sufficient to determine the state and output of a system for all times.

State variables are the variables that contain all state information related to the memory. For LTI system with output signal $y(t)$ with input signal $u(t)$ and impulse response $h(t)$. Therefore,

$$y(t) = h(t) * u(t) -> Y(s) = H(s)\,U(s) \qquad (2.35)$$

This representation of the system expresses the input output relation. It does not provide us the internal specification of the system. State space representation not only provides information on I/O but also gives good view on the internal specification of the system. The states of the system at time to include min required information to express the system situation at time t_0. These are the first-degree equations. CT LTI state space representation of LTI system is given by,

$$\frac{dx}{dt} = \dot{x}(t) = Ax(t) + B\,u(t) \qquad (2.36)$$

$$y(t) = Cx(t) + Du(t) \qquad (2.37)$$

Eq. (2.36) and Eq. (2.37) represents the state equations and output equations respectively.

Where, $\frac{dx}{dt} = \dot{x}(t)$ is the vector whose entries are the derivative $\frac{dx}{dt}$.

2.11 State Space Analysis

The state of a CT system is the condition of a system at any time instant. The state variables are the variables that completely describe the state of a system at any given time. These variables at t = 0 with inputs for t > 0 completely describes the behavior of system for $t \geq 0$.

2.11.1 State equations

Let us consider a CT system has P inputs, Q state variables and Y outputs.
Hence, let $q_1(t), q_2(t), \dots \dots q_Q(t)$ be the Q state variables,
$p_1(t), p_2(t), \dots \dots p_P(t)$ be the P input.
$y_1(t), y_2(t), \dots \dots y_Y(t)$ be the Y outputs

Now, the CT system can be represented by Fig. 2.21 as shown below,

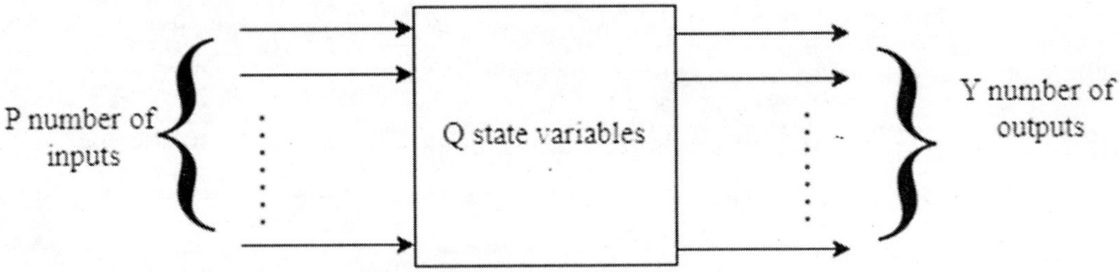

Fig. 2.21 State Space representation of CT system

Take first derivative of state variables as a function of state variables and input to form the state equations.

$$q_1(t) = F\{q_1(t), q_2(t), \dots \dots q_Q(t) \qquad p_1(t), p_2(t), \dots \dots p_P(t)\}$$

$$\vdots$$

$$q_Q(t) = F\{q_1(t), q_2(t), \dots \dots q_Q(t) \qquad p_1(t), p_2(t), \dots \dots p_P(t)\}$$

Above state equation can be represented in q matrix form given by Eq. (2.38),

$$\begin{bmatrix} q_1(t) \\ q_2(t) \\ q_3(t) \\ \vdots \\ \vdots \end{bmatrix} = \begin{bmatrix} a_{11}\, a_{12} a_{13} \cdots \\ a_{21}\, a_{22} a_{23} \cdots \\ a_{31}\, a_{32} a_{33} \cdots \\ \vdots \\ \vdots \end{bmatrix} \begin{bmatrix} q_1(t) \\ q_2(t) \\ q_3(t) \\ \vdots \\ \vdots \end{bmatrix} + \begin{bmatrix} b_{11}\, b_{12} b_{13} \cdots \\ b_{21}\, b_{22} b_{23} \cdots \\ b_{31}\, b_{32} b_{33} \cdots \\ \vdots \\ \vdots \end{bmatrix} \begin{bmatrix} p_1(t) \\ p_2(t) \\ p_3(t) \\ \vdots \\ \vdots \end{bmatrix} \quad (2.38)$$

$$Q(t) \qquad A \qquad Q(t) \qquad B \qquad P(t)$$

Where

A= System matrix

B = Input matrix

$Q(t)$ = State vector

$X(t)$ = Input vector

Hence, State equation can be written as,

$$Q(t) = AQ(t) + BX(t) \quad (2.39)$$

2.11.2 Output equations

The output equation in terms of y can be written as,

$$y_1(t) = F\{q_1(t), q_2(t), \dots \dots q_Q(t) \qquad p_1(t), p_2(t), \dots \dots p_P(t)\}$$

$$\vdots$$

$$\vdots$$

$$\vdots$$

$$y_Y(t) = F\{q_1(t), q_2(t), \dots \dots q_Q(t) \qquad p_1(t), p_2(t), \dots \dots p_P(t)\}$$

The output equations can be written in terms of matrix form as in Eq. (2.40)

$$\begin{bmatrix} y_1(t) \\ y_2(t) \\ y_3(t) \\ \vdots \\ \vdots \end{bmatrix} = \begin{bmatrix} c_{11}\, c_{12} c_{13} \cdots \\ c_{21}\, c_{22} c_{23} \cdots \\ c_{31}\, c_{32} c_{33} \cdots \\ \vdots \\ \vdots \end{bmatrix} \begin{bmatrix} q_1(t) \\ q_2(t) \\ q_3(t) \\ \vdots \\ \vdots \end{bmatrix} + \begin{bmatrix} d_{11}\, d_{12} d_{13} \cdots \\ d_{21}\, d_{22} d_{23} \cdots \\ d_{31}\, d_{32} d_{33} \cdots \\ \vdots \\ \vdots \end{bmatrix} \begin{bmatrix} p_1(t) \\ p_2(t) \\ p_3(t) \\ \vdots \\ \vdots \end{bmatrix} \quad (2.40)$$

$$Y(t) \qquad C \qquad Q(t) \qquad D \qquad P(t)$$

Where

C = Output matrix

D = Transition matrix

Q(t) = State vector

P(t) = Input vector

Hence,

$$Y(t) = CQ(t) + DP(t) \qquad (2.41)$$

2.11.3 State Model

The state model of a CT system can be represented in terms of state equations and output equations.

$Q(t) = AQ(t) + BX(t)$ (2.42)

$Y(t) = CQ(t) + DP(t)$ (2.43)

2.12 Transfer function of a Continuous Time System

Consider the equation

$Q(t) = AQ(t) + BX(t)$

Take Laplace transform on both sides assuming zero initial condition.

$sQ(s) = AQ\ (s) + BP(s)$

$sQ(s) - AQ(s) = BP(s)$

$Q(s)(I_s - A) = B.P(s)$ .....I is unit matrix

$Q(s) = B.P(s)(sI - A)^{-1}$ (2.44)

Now consider output equation

$Y(t) = CQ(t) + D\ P\ (t)$

Take Laplace transform on both Sides

$Y(s) = CQ\ (s) + D\ P\ (s)$ (2.45)

Put Eq. (2.7) in Eq. (2.8)

$Y\ (s) = C\ [B.P(s)\ (sI\text{-}A)\ \ \text{-}1\ ] + D\ P\ (s)$

$Y\ (s) +[C.B\ (Is\text{-}A)^{-1}\ PC(s)$

$\frac{Y(s)}{P(s)} = C.B.\ (Is\text{-}A)^{-1} + D$ (2.46)

Hence, Eq (2.46) is called transfer function of CT system.

2.13 State Transition Matrix

The State Equation can be written as

$$\dot{Q}(t) - A\ Q\ (t) = B\ P\ (t)$$

Multiplying above equation by e^{-At} we get,

$$e^{-At}[\dot{Q}(t) - AQ(t)] = e^{-At}BP(t)$$

$$e^{-At}\dot{Q}(t) - Ae^{-At}Q(t) = e^{-At}BP(t) \qquad (2.47)$$

Using derivative formula of, $d(uv) = udv + vdu$ in the above equation we get,

$$\frac{d}{dt}\left(e^{-At}Q(t)\right) = e^{-At}\dot{Q}(t) + (-A)e^{-At}Q(t) \qquad (2.48)$$

Using Eq. (2.48) in Eq. (2.47) we get,

$$\frac{d}{dt}\left(e^{-At}Q(t)\right) = e^{-At}BP(t) \qquad (2.49)$$

On integrating Eq. (2.49) we get,

$$e^{-At}Q(t) = \int_0^t e^{-A\tau}\, B.P(\tau)d\tau + Q(0) \qquad (2.50)$$

We have, $Q(0)$ is the intitial condition vector, τ is the dummy variable used instead of t.

On multiplying Eq. (2.50) by e^{At} we get,

$$e^{At}e^{-At}Q(t) = e^{At}\int_0^t e^{-A\tau}\, B.P(\tau)d\tau + e^{At}Q(0)$$

$$Q(t) = e^{At}\int_0^t e^{A(t-\tau)}\, B.P(\tau)d\tau + e^{At}Q(0) \qquad (2.51)$$

Eq. (2.51) is the time domain solution of state equations of the CT system.

Matrix e^{At} is called state transition matrix of CT System.

Example 2.1: Compute the continuous convolution of the following functions:

x (t) = e^(-t) * u(t)

h (t) = 2 * e^(2t) * u(t)

Solution:

To compute the continuous convolution, we can use the integral formula:

y(t) = ∫(x(τ) * h(t-τ)) dτ

Let's calculate it step by step:

For t > 0:

y(t) = ∫(e^(-τ) * 2 * e^(2(t-τ))) dτ

= 2 * ∫(e^(-τ) * e^(2(t-τ))) dτ

= 2 * ∫(e^(2t - 3τ)) dτ

= 2 * e^(2t) * ∫(e^(-3τ)) dτ

= 2 * e^(2t) * (-1/3) * e^(-3τ) | from 0 to t

= -2/3 * e^(2t) * (e^(-3t) - 1)

For t <= 0:

y(t) = 0

Therefore, the continuous convolution of x(t) and h(t) is:

y(t) = -2/3 * e^(2t) * (e^(-3t) - 1) for t > 0

0 for t <= 0

Example 2.2: Compute the discrete convolution of the following sequences:

x[n] = [1, 2, 3]

h[n] = [2, -1, 3, 0]

Solution:

To compute the discrete convolution, we can use the formula:

y[n] = ∑(x[k] * h[n-k])

Let's calculate it step by step:

For n = 0:

y[0] = (1 * 2) = 2

For n = 1:

y[1] = (1 * -1) + (2 * 2) = 3

For n = 2:

y[2] = (1 * 3) + (2 * -1) + (3 * 2) = 5

For n = 3:

y[3] = (2 * 3) + (3 * -1) = 3

For n = 4:

y[4] = (3 * 3) = 9

Therefore, the discrete convolution of x[n] and h[n] is:

y[n] = [2, 3, 5, 3, 9]

2.14 Multi-Input, Multi-Output Representation

MIMO refers to systems that have multiple inputs and multiple outputs. These systems are characterized by their ability to handle multiple control inputs and generate multiple outputs simultaneously. The state-space representation for a MIMO system is an extension of the single-input, single-output (SISO) case. In the MIMO representation, the state equations and output equations are modified to accommodate multiple inputs and outputs.

Let's consider an example of a multi-input, multi-output (MIMO) system with a numerical representation. Suppose we have a MIMO system with two inputs (u1, u2) and two outputs (y1, y2). The state-space representation of the system is given by the following equations:

State equations:

$$\frac{dx}{dt} = \begin{bmatrix} -2 & 0 \\ 1 & -3 \end{bmatrix} . x + \begin{bmatrix} 1 & 0 \\ 0 & 2 \end{bmatrix} \cdot \begin{bmatrix} u1 \\ u2 \end{bmatrix} \qquad (2.52)$$

Output equations:

$$\begin{bmatrix} y1 \\ y2 \end{bmatrix} = \begin{bmatrix} 1 & 2 \\ -1 & 0 \end{bmatrix} . x + \begin{bmatrix} 1 & 0 \\ 0 & -1 \end{bmatrix} \cdot \begin{bmatrix} u1 \\ u2 \end{bmatrix} \tag{2.53}$$

In this representation:

- x $=\begin{bmatrix} x1 \\ x2 \end{bmatrix}$ is a 2-dimensional state vector representing the internal state of the system.
- u $=\begin{bmatrix} u1 \\ u2 \end{bmatrix}$ is a 2-dimensional input vector representing the inputs to the system.
- y $=\begin{bmatrix} y1 \\ y2 \end{bmatrix}$ is a 2-dimensional output vector representing the outputs from the system.
- The state matrix A is $\begin{bmatrix} -2 & 0 \\ 1 & -3 \end{bmatrix}$.
- The input matrix B is $\begin{bmatrix} 1 & 0 \\ 0 & 2 \end{bmatrix}$
- The output matrix C is $\begin{bmatrix} 1 & 2 \\ -1 & 0 \end{bmatrix}$
- The feed forward matrix D is $\begin{bmatrix} 1 & 0 \\ 0 & -1 \end{bmatrix}$.

To analyze this system, we can perform various analyses such as stability analysis, controllability analysis, observability analysis and system response analysis.

For stability analysis, we can determine the eigenvalues of the state matrix A. In this case, the eigenvalues are -2 and -3, indicating that the system is stable. For controllability analysis, we can check if the controllability matrix Co has full rank. The controllability matrix Co is formed by concatenating the input matrix B with powers of the state matrix A. For observability analysis, we can examine if the observability matrix Ob has full rank. The observability matrix Ob is formed by concatenating the output matrix C with powers of the state matrix A. To analyze the system's response, we can simulate the state equations and output equations with appropriate inputs. For example, if we apply a step input $u_1(t) = 1$ and $u_1(t) = 0$, we can numerically solve the state equations and output equations to obtain the time-domain response of the system.

By analyzing the state variables $x_1(t)$, $x_2(t)$, and the outputs $y_1(t)$, $y_1(t)$, we can observe the behavior of the system, including transient response, steady-state behavior, and the interaction between inputs and outputs.

Example 2.4: Find Laplace domain and time domain state transition matrix if

$$A = \begin{pmatrix} 0 & 1 \\ -2 & -3 \end{pmatrix}$$

Solution:

$$\phi(s) = (sI - A)^{-1} = \left(s\begin{pmatrix} 1 & 0 \\ 0 & 1 \end{pmatrix} - \begin{pmatrix} 0 & 1 \\ -2 & -3 \end{pmatrix}\right)^{-1} = \left(\begin{pmatrix} s & 0 \\ 0 & s \end{pmatrix} - \begin{pmatrix} 0 & 1 \\ -2 & -3 \end{pmatrix}\right)^{-1}$$

$$= \begin{pmatrix} s & -1 \\ -2 & s+3 \end{pmatrix}^{-1}$$

The inverse of a 2×2 matrix is

$$\phi(s) = \begin{pmatrix} s & -1 \\ 2 & s+3 \end{pmatrix}^{-1} = \frac{\begin{pmatrix} s+3 & 1 \\ -2 & s \end{pmatrix}}{s(s+3)+2} = \frac{\begin{pmatrix} s+3 & 1 \\ -2 & s \end{pmatrix}}{s^2+3s+2}$$

To find φ(t) we must take the inverse Laplace Transform of every term in the matrix

$$\varphi(t) = \mathcal{L}^{-1}(\phi(s)) = \mathcal{L}^{-1}\left(\frac{\begin{pmatrix} s+3 & 1 \\ -2 & s \end{pmatrix}}{s^2+3s+2}\right) = \mathcal{L}^{-1}\left(\frac{\begin{pmatrix} s+3 & 1 \\ -2 & s \end{pmatrix}}{(s+1)(s+2)}\right)$$

$$= \mathcal{L}^{-1}\begin{pmatrix} \frac{s+3}{(s+1)(s+2)} & \frac{1}{(s+1)(s\_2} \\ -\frac{2}{(s+1)(s+2)} & \frac{s}{(s+1)(s+2)} \end{pmatrix}$$

Using partial fraction expansion of each term we get

$$\varphi(t) = e^{-1}\begin{pmatrix} \frac{2}{s+1} + \frac{-1}{s+2} & \frac{1}{s+1} + \frac{-1}{s+2} \\ -\frac{2}{s+1} + \frac{2}{s+2} & -\frac{1}{s+1} + \frac{2}{s+2} \end{pmatrix} = \begin{pmatrix} 2e^{-t} - e^{-2t} & e^{-t} - e^{-2t} \\ -2e^{-t} + 2e^{-2t} & 2 \mp 2e^{-2t} \end{pmatrix}$$

2.15 Periodic Inputs to LTI system

When a periodic input signal is applied to a linear time-invariant (LTI) system, the response of the system also becomes periodic. In this scenario, the output of the LTI system exhibits the same periodicity as the input signal, but with potentially different amplitudes and phases.

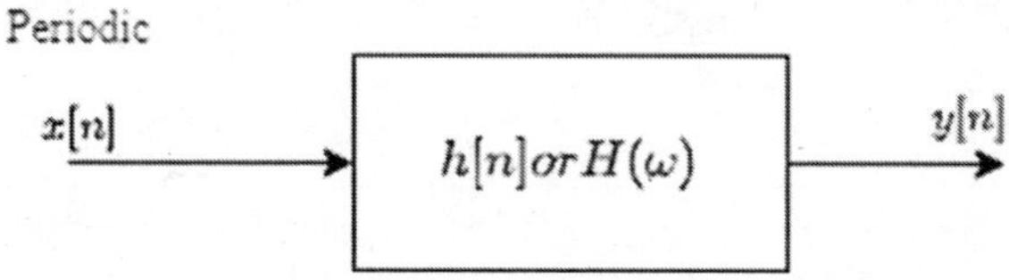

Figure 2.22: Periodic input to LTI system

When a periodic signal with period N_0 is passed through a linear, time-invariant system, the output is also periodic and can be expressed as a sum of complex exponential signals.

Let's consider the input signal $x[n] \;=\; e^{(j2\pi k\,/N_0\, *\, n)}$

Where n is the discrete time index and k range from 0 to N_0-1. This signal represents a complex exponential with a frequency of $2\pi k/N_0$.

According to the properties of linear, time-invariant systems, the output signal can be obtained by multiplying the frequency response of the system, denoted by $h[2\pi k/N_0]$, with the input signal's complex exponential component $x[k]$.

Hence, the output for each component signal can be written as:

$$y[n] = x[k] * h\left[\frac{2\pi k}{N_0}\right] * e^{(j2\pi k/N_0 * n)} \tag{2.54}$$

Now, let's simplify the expression further.

Since $h[2\pi k/N_0]$ is a constant value for each component signal, we can combine it with the exponential term:

$$y[n] = h\left[\frac{2\pi k}{N_0}\right] * e^{(j(2\pi k/N_0 * n+\theta))} \tag{2.55}$$

Here, θ represents the phase shift introduced by the frequency response of the system.

When a periodic input signal is passed through a linear, time-invariant system, the output signal remains periodic and can be represented as a sum of complex exponential signals. Each component signal's frequency response, $h[2\pi k/N_0]$, is multiplied by the input signal's complex exponential component, resulting in a modified exponential term in the output.

The linearity property of the filter allows us to express the output signal as

$$y[n] = h\left[\frac{2\pi k}{N_0}\right] * e^{(j(2\pi k/N_0 * n+\theta))} \tag{2.56}$$

Where, $h\left[\frac{2\pi k}{N_0}\right]$ represents the frequency response of the system.

2.16 The Notion of frequency response and its relation to impulse response

The notion of frequency response is an important concept in the field of signal processing. It provides information about how a system or a filter responds to different frequencies present in the input signal. It is obtained by taking the Fourier transform of the impulse response. The frequency response reveals how the system responds to different frequencies, while the impulse response shows its response to an impulse signal.

Let's start with the convolution sum equation:

$$y\,(n) \;=\; \Sigma[x(n-m)h(m)] \qquad (2.57)$$

Where x (n) is the input signal, h (n) is the impulse response of the system, and y (n) is the output signal. The convolution sum represents the mathematical operation of convolving the input signal with the impulse response to obtain the output signal.

Now, let's consider a specific input signal in the form of a complex exponential function:

$$x\,(n) \;=\; e^{\,j\omega n}$$

Where j represents the imaginary unit, ω is the angular frequency, and n belongs to the set of integers.

By substituting this input signal into the convolution sum equation, we get:

$$y[n] \;=\; \Sigma\, e^{\,j\omega[n-m]}h[m \qquad (2.58)$$

Next, we can simplify this expression by factoring out the term $e^{\,j\omega n}$:

$$y[n] \;=\; e^{\,j\omega n}\Sigma\, e^{\,j\omega[n-m]}h[m] \qquad (2.59)$$

Notice that the term inside the summation, $e^{\,-j\omega n}$, is the complex conjugate of $e^{\,j\omega n}$. Therefore, we can rewrite it as:

$$y[n] \;=\; e^{\,j\omega n}\Sigma\, h[m]e^{\,-j\omega m}$$

Now, if we compare this expression to the form of the output signal when the input is a complex exponential with frequency ω, given as $y\ (n)\ =\ H\ (\omega)e^{\ j\omega n}$, we can conclude that:

$$H\ (\omega)\ =\ \sum\ [h\ [m]\ e^{\ -j\omega n}] \qquad (2.60)$$

The term $H(\omega)$ in this equation is referred to as the frequency response. It represents the relationship between the input signal's frequency ω and the output signal's amplitude and phase shift. The frequency response provides information about how the system or filter amplifies or attenuates specific frequencies.

Therefore, the frequency response H (ω) is obtained by taking the discrete-time Fourier transform (DTFT) of the impulse response h (n). The frequency response describes how the system or filter responds to different frequencies present in the input signal, and it is a fundamental concept in signal processing.

UNIT SUMMARY

In this unit on the behavior of continuous and discrete-time LTI systems, we covered various important topics. These include understanding impulse and step responses, analysing input-output behavior with aperiodic convergent inputs, cascade interconnections, causality and stability characterization, system representation through differential equations and difference equations, state-space representation, state-space analysis, multi-input multi-output systems, the role of the state transition matrix, periodic inputs and the notion of frequency response. Overall, this unit provided a comprehensive overview of the behavior and analysis of LTI systems in both continuous and discrete-time domains.

EXERCISES

Multiple Choice Questions and Answers

1. The impulse response of an LTI system provides information about:

a) The system's stability

b) The system's causality

c) The system's input-output behavior

d) The system's frequency response

Answer: c) The system's input-output behavior

2. Convolution is a mathematical operation used to:

a) Compute the impulse response of an LTI system

b) Determine the step response of an LTI system

c) Analyze the behavior of LTI systems

d) Calculate the transfer function of an LTI system

Answer: c) Analyze the behavior of LTI systems

3. Causality in LTI systems implies that the output of the system depends on:

a) Future inputs

b) Past inputs

c) Present inputs only

d) Both past and future inputs

Answer: b) Past inputs

4. Stability of an LTI system ensures that:

a) The output is bounded for any bounded input

b) The output is zero for any input

c) The system has a linear transfer function

d) The system has a constant impulse response

Answer: a) The output is bounded for any bounded input

5. System representation through differential equations is commonly used for:
a) Analyzing the frequency response of LTI systems
b) Describing the input-output behavior of LTI systems
c) Evaluating the stability of LTI systems
d) Modeling continuous-time LTI systems
Answer: d) Modeling continuous-time LTI systems

6. State-space representation of systems involves describing the system behavior using:
a) Impulse response
b) Transfer function
c) Differential equations
d) Convolution
Answer: c) Differential equations

7. The State Transition Matrix in state-space analysis represents the:
a) Impulse response of the system
b) Transfer function of the system
c) Evolution of state variables over time
d) Frequency response of the system
Answer: c) Evolution of state variables over time

8. Multi-input, multi-output (MIMO) representation of LTI systems deals with:
a) Systems with multiple state variables
b) Systems with multiple inputs and multiple outputs
c) Systems with nonlinear behavior
d) Systems with periodic inputs
Answer: b) Systems with multiple inputs and multiple outputs

9. The frequency response of an LTI system is obtained through:
a) Fourier transform
b) Laplace transform

c) Z-transform

d) Convolution.

Answer: b) Laplace transform

10. The relationship between the frequency response and impulse response of an LTI system given by:

a) Convolution theorem

b) Parseval's theorem

c) Nyquist criterion

d) Plancherel's theorem

Answer: a) Convolution theorem

Short and Long Answer Type Questions

1. What is the impulse response of an LTI system?
2. How is the step response of an LTI system defined?
3. What role does convolution play in analyzing LTI systems?
4. How would you characterize causality in LTI systems?
5. What does stability refer to in the context of LTI systems?
6. How are LTI systems represented using differential equations?
7. What are difference equations, and how are they used to represent LTI systems?
8. What is the state-space representation of a system?
9. What is the significance of the State Transition Matrix in state-space analysis?
10. How do periodic inputs affect LTI systems, and what is the relationship between the frequency response and the impulse response?

Numerical Problems

1. Given the impulse response h(t) = 3e^(-2t), calculate the step response of the system.
2. Find the convolution of the two sequences x[n] = {1, 2, 3} and h[n] = {2, -1, 0}.

3. Consider an LTI system with the input x(t) = 2cos(3t). If the impulse response is h(t) = e^(-t), determine the output y(t).
4. Analyze the stability of the difference equation y[n] = 0.5y[n-1] + x[n].
5. Represent an LTI system through a differential equation: y''(t) + 3y'(t) + 2y(t) = x(t), where y(0) = 0 and y'(0) = 1.
6. Calculate the state-space representation of a multi-input, multi-output LTI system with two state variables and two inputs.
7. Find the State Transition Matrix for a second-order LTI system described by the state-space equations: $\dot{x}(t) = Ax(t) + Bu(t)$ and $y(t) = Cx(t) + Du(t)$.
8. Determine the response of a continuous-time LTI system with the impulse response h(t) = sin(2πt) to a periodic input signal with a frequency of 10 Hz and an amplitude of 3.
9. Analyze the frequency response of an LTI system with the impulse response h(t) = e^(-t)cos(2πt).
10. Investigate the relationship between the impulse response and the frequency response of an LTI system using a specific example.

KNOW MORE

The study of continuous and discrete-time LTI systems involves analyzing their behavior using concepts like impulse response, step response, convolution, and input-output behavior with periodic inputs. Understanding causality and stability is crucial for characterizing these systems. System representation can be done through differential equations or difference equations, with state-space analysis providing a comprehensive approach. Multi-input, multi-output systems and the role of the state transition matrix are also studied. Additionally, the notion of frequency response and its relation to the impulse response is explored. These concepts form the foundation for analyzing and designing LTI systems in various applications. In summary, the study of continuous and discrete-time LTI systems includes analyzing impulse and step responses, convolution, input-output behavior with periodic inputs, causality, stability, system representation through differential or difference equations, state-space analysis, multi-input multi-output systems, state transition matrix, and the relation between frequency response and impulse response. These concepts are essential for understanding and designing LTI systems in diverse applications.

REFERENCES AND SUGGESTED READINGS

1. Signals and Systems by Simon Haykin
2. Signals and Systems by Ganesh Rao
3. Signals and Systems - Course (nptel.ac.in)

Dynamic QR Code for Further Reading

3 Fourier Series and Transform

UNIT SPECIFICS

Through this unit we have discussed the following aspects:

- *What is Fourier series, why it was developed?*
- *Fourier series representation of periodic signals, Waveform Symmetries, Calculation of Fourier Coefficients.*
- *Fourier Transform, convolution/ multiplication and their effect in the frequency domain,*
- *Magnitude and phase response, Fourier domain duality.*
- *The Discrete-Time Fourier Transform (DTFT) and the Discrete Fourier Transform (DFT).*

RATIONALE

The unit on "Fourier Series and Transform" provide students to understand the behavior of Continuous and Discrete-time signals. This 6-hour unit is designed to provide students with a comprehensive understanding of periodic and non-periodic signals along with their frequency domain representation.

The unit focuses on Fourier series representation of periodic signals along with the properties. The students can analyze the behavior of signal by extracting the frequency components from the signal. The behavior will be found for both CT and DT signals.

The concepts covered, such as Fourier series representation of periodic signals, waveform symmetries, calculation of Fourier coefficients, Fourier transform, convolution/ multiplication and their effect in the frequency domain, magnitude and phase response, Fourier domain duality, the Discrete-Time Fourier Transform (DTFT) and the Discrete Fourier Transform (DFT).

PRE-REQUISITES

1. *Strong understanding of mathematics, including algebra, calculus, and complex numbers.*
2. *Familiarity with basic concepts in signals and systems, such as time-domain and periodic, non-periodic signals*
3. *Proficiency in solving ordinary differential equations and understanding linear algebra concepts.*

UNIT OUTCOMES

List of outcomes of this unit is as follows:

U3-O1: Be able to compute the frequency components of the signal.

U3-O2: Be able to predict how the signal will interact with linear systems and circuits using frequency response methods.

U3-O3: Be able to extract the Fourier coefficients from the signal.

U3-O4: Be able to analyze the signal directly from its properties.

U3-O5: Be able to analyze the magnitude and phase response of the given signal.

Unit-3 Outcomes	***EXPECTED MAPPING WITH COURSE OUTCOMES*** *(1- Weak Correlation; 2- Medium correlation; 3- Strong Correlation)*					
	CO-1	***CO-2***	***CO-3***	***CO-4***	***CO-5***	***CO-6***
U3-O1	3	-	3	3	-	-
U3-O2	3	-	3	-	-	-
U3-O3	3	-	3	3	-	-
U3-O4	3	-	3	3	-	-
U3-O5	3	-	3	2	-	-

3.1 Introduction

Earlier we have discussed the time domain representation of signals and systems. We have also seen the types of signals that are periodic and non-periodic. The French mathematician Jean Baptiste Joseph Fourier showed that any periodic non-sinusoidal signal could be represented in terms of linear weighted sum of harmonic sinusoidal signals. This representation is called as *Fourier series* representation.

On the other hand, the Fourier representation of the aperiodic or non-periodic signals is performed by treating them as periodic signals with an infinite fundamental period. In this case, the non-periodic signals are represented as a function of frequency called *Fourier Transform.* Fourier domain representation of the signal is another name for Fourier Transform.

The Fourier representations of the signals are used for the frequency domain analysis of signals. It enables us to extract the amplitude and phase of various frequency components present in the signal.

Figure 3.1 shows the types of signals and their corresponding Fourier representations.

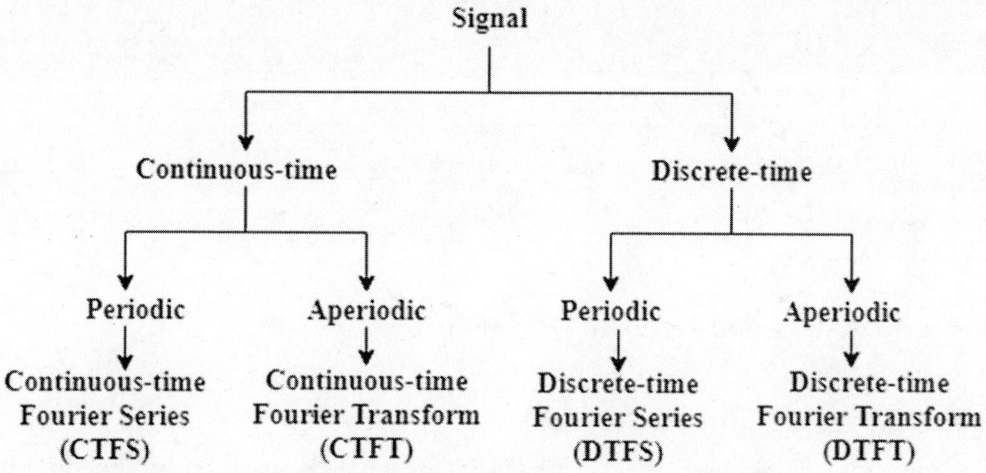

Fig. 3.1 Types of signals and their Fourier representations

3.2 Trigonometric Form of Fourier Series

3.2.1 Definition

In this form of Fourier representation, any periodic signal $x(t)$ with a fundamental period T is represented in terms of trigonometric functions as,

$$x(t) = \frac{a_0}{2} + \sum_{m=1}^{\infty} a_m \cos m\,\Omega_0 t + \sum_{n=1}^{\infty} b_n \sin n\,\Omega_0 t \qquad (3.1)$$

Where $\Omega_0 = \frac{2\pi}{T}$ and, a_m and b_n are constants.

It may be noted that $\cos m\,\Omega_0 t$ and $\sin n\,\Omega_0 t$ are orthogonal functions over one period for all integer values of m and n. This implies that $\int_{\alpha}^{\alpha+T} \cos m\,\Omega_0 t \sin n\,\Omega_0 t\, dt = 0$ for any arbitrary value of α.

Equation (3.1) can be extended as,

$$x(t) = \frac{1}{2}a_0 + a_1 \operatorname{Cos} \Omega_0 t + a_2 \operatorname{Cos} 2\,\Omega_0 t + \cdots + b_1 \operatorname{Sin} \Omega_0 t + b_2 \operatorname{Sin} 2\,\Omega_0 t + \cdots \quad (3.2)$$

Where, $\Omega_0 = 2\pi F_0 \; = \frac{2\pi}{T} \; = \text{Fundamental frequency in rad/sec}$

$F_0 \; = \text{Fundamental frequency in } H_z$

$n\,\Omega_0 \; = \text{Harmonic frequencies}$

$a_0, a_n, b_n \; = \text{Fourier coefficients of trigonometric form}$

Here, $\frac{a_0}{2}$ is a constant representing the average value or dc component of $x(t)$.

The Fourier Coefficients in Eq. (3.1) can be expressed as,

$$a_0 = \frac{2}{T}\int_{-\frac{T}{2}}^{\frac{T}{2}} x(t) \quad \text{or}$$

$$\text{or} \qquad a_0 = \frac{2}{T}\int_0^T x(t)dt \qquad (3.3)$$

$$a_n = \frac{2}{T}\int_{-\frac{T}{2}}^{\frac{T}{2}} x(t) \operatorname{Cos} n\,\Omega_0\, t\, dt \qquad \text{or} \qquad a_n = \frac{2}{T}\int_0^T x(t) \operatorname{Cos} n\,\Omega_0\, t\, dt \qquad (3.4)$$

$$b_n = \frac{2}{T}\int_{-\frac{T}{2}}^{\frac{T}{2}} x(t) \operatorname{Sin} n\,\Omega_0\, t\, dt \qquad \text{or} \qquad b_n = \frac{2}{T}\int_0^T x(t) \operatorname{Sin} n\,\Omega_0\, t\, dt \qquad (3.5)$$

The integration is over one period i.e. $\frac{-T}{2}$ to $\frac{T}{2}$ or 0 to T.

3.2.2 Conditions for existence of Fourier series

The following conditions called as *Dirichlet's conditions* must be satisfied by the signals for the existence or convergence of Fourier series:

1. The signal x(t) should be absolutely integrable over one period.

i.e. $\int_0^T |x(t)|\, dt < \infty$

2. The signal x(t) must have finite number of maxima and minima in one period.
3. The signal x(t) must have finite number of discontinuities in one period.

If any signal x(t) satisfies the above Dirichlet's conditions, the Fourier series represented by equation (3.1) converges i.e., the sum becomes equal to x(t) except at the point of discontinuities.

3.2.3 Equations for a_0, a_n and b_n.

1) Derivation equation for a_0

$$a_0 = \frac{2}{T}\int_{-T/2}^{T/2} x(t)dt$$

or

$$a_0 = \frac{2}{T}\int_0^T x(t)dt$$

Proof: Consider Trigonometric FS in Eq. (3.1)

$$x(t) = \frac{a_0}{2} + \sum_{n=1}^{\infty} a_n \cos n\Omega_0 t + \sum_{n=1}^{\infty} b_n \sin n\Omega_0 t$$

Integrate the above equation for 0 to *T*

$$\int_0^T x(t)dt = \int_0^T \frac{a_0}{2} dt + \int_0^T \sum_{n=1}^{\infty} a_n \cos n\Omega_0 t\, dt + \int_0^T \sum_{n=1}^{\infty} b_n \sin n\Omega_0 t\, dt$$

$$= \frac{a_0}{2}\int_0^T dt + \sum_{n=1}^{\infty} a_n \int_0^T \cos n\Omega_0 t\, dt + \sum_{n=1}^{\infty} b_n \int_0^T \sin n\Omega_0 t\, dt$$

$$= \frac{a_0}{2}[t]_0^T + \sum_{n=1}^{\infty} a_n \left[\frac{\sin n\,\Omega_0 t}{n\,\Omega_0}\right]_0^T + \sum_{n=1}^{\infty} b_n \left[\frac{-\cos n\,\Omega_0 t}{n\,\Omega_0}\right]_0^T$$

$$= \frac{a_0}{2}[T-0] + \sum_{n=1}^{\infty} a_n \left[\frac{\sin n\,\Omega_0 t}{n\,\Omega_0} - \frac{\sin n\,\Omega_0\, 0}{n\,\Omega_0}\right] + \sum_{n=1}^{\infty} b_n \left[\frac{-\cos n\,\Omega_0 t}{n\,\Omega_0} + \frac{\cos n\,\Omega_0\, 0}{n\,\Omega_0}\right]$$

$$= \frac{T}{2}a_0 + \sum_{n=1}^{\infty} a_n \left[\frac{\sin n\frac{2\pi}{T}.T}{n\frac{2\pi}{T}}\right] + \sum_{n=1}^{\infty} b_n \left[\frac{-\cos n\frac{2\pi}{T}.T}{n\frac{2\pi}{T}} + \frac{1}{n\frac{2\pi}{T}}\right]$$

As, $\Omega_0 = \frac{2\pi}{T}$, $\cos 0 = 1, \sin 0 = 0.$

$$\therefore \int_0^T x(t)dt = \frac{T}{2}a_0 + \sum_{n=1}^{\infty} a_n T\left[\frac{\sin n2\pi}{n2\pi}\right] + \sum_{n=1}^{\infty} b_n T\left[\frac{-\cos n2\pi}{n2\pi} + \frac{1}{n2\pi}\right]$$

$$= \frac{T}{2}a_0 + \sum_{n=1}^{\infty} a_n T.0 + \sum_{n=1}^{\infty} b_n T\left[-\frac{1}{n2\pi} + \frac{1}{n2\pi}\right]$$

$$\int_0^T x(t)dt = \frac{T}{2}a_0$$

$$\therefore a_0 = \frac{2}{T}\int_0^T x(t)dt$$

2) Derivation equation for a_n

$a_n = \frac{2}{T}\int_{-T/2}^{T/2} x(t)\cos n\,\Omega_0 tdt$ or $a_n = \frac{2}{T}\int_0^T x(t)\cos n\Omega_0\, t\, dt$

Proof: Consider trigonometric FS in Eq. (3.1)

$x(t) = \frac{a_0}{2} + \sum_{n=1}^{\infty} a_n \cos n\Omega_0 t + \sum_{n=1}^{\infty} b_n \sin n\Omega_0\, t$

Let us multiply above equation by $\cos m\Omega_0 t$

$$\therefore x(t)\cos m\Omega_0 t = \frac{a_0}{2}\cos m\,\Omega_0 t + \cos m\,\Omega_0 t\left[\sum_{n=1}^{\infty} a_n \cos n\,\Omega_0 t\right] + \cos m\,\Omega_0 t\left[\sum_{n=1}^{\infty} b_n \sin n\,\Omega_0 t\right]$$

Integrate the above equation over 0 to *T* and expand,

$$\therefore \int_0^T x(t)\cos m\Omega_0 t\, dt = \int_0^T \frac{a_0}{2}\cos m\Omega_0\, t + \int_0^T a_1 \cos\Omega_0 t.\cos m\Omega_0 t\, dt + \cdots + \int_0^T a_m \cos^2 m\Omega_0 t\, dt + \cdots + \int_0^T b_1 \sin\Omega_0 t.\cos m\Omega_0 t dt + \cdots + \int_0^T b_m \sin m\,\Omega_0\, t.\cos m\Omega_0 t\, dt + \cdots$$

In above equation all the definite integrations becomes zero except $\int_0^T a_m \cos^2 m\Omega_0 t\, dt$

$\therefore \int_0^T x(t)\cos m\Omega_0 t\, dt = \int_0^T a_m \cos^2 m\Omega_0 t\, dt$

$= \int_0^T a_m \frac{1+\cos 2m\Omega_0 t}{2} dt$

$= \frac{a_m}{2}\int_0^T (1 + \cos 2m\,\Omega_0 t)dt$

$= \frac{a_m}{2}\left[t + \frac{\sin 2m\,\Omega_0 t}{2m\Omega_0}\right]_0^T$

$= \frac{a_m}{2}\left[T + \frac{\sin 2\,m\,\Omega_0 t}{2m\,\Omega_0} - 0 - \frac{\sin 0}{2m\,\Omega_0}\right]$

$$= \frac{a_m}{2}\left[T + \frac{\text{Sin } 2m\frac{2\pi}{T}T}{2m\frac{2\pi}{T}}\right]$$

$= \frac{T}{2}\ a_m$ ……as $sin\ 2m2\pi = 0$ for integer m. Hence,

$$a_m = \frac{2}{T}\int_0^T x(t)\cos m\Omega_0 t\, dt \tag{3.6}$$

As m is the mth coefficient, the nth coefficient will be,

$$\boxed{a_n = \frac{2}{T}\int_0^T x(t)\cos n\,\Omega_0\, t\, dt}$$

3) Derivation Equation for b_n

$b_n = \frac{2}{T}\int_{-T/2}^{T/2} x(t)\sin n\Omega_0\, t$ or $b_n = \frac{2}{T}\int_0^T x(t)\sin\ n\Omega_0\, t\, dt$

Proof: Consider trigonometric FS in Eq. (3.1)

$$x(t) = \frac{a_0}{2} + \sum_{n=1}^{\infty} a_n\cos n\ \Omega_0 t + \sum_{n=1}^{\infty} b_n\ \sin n\,\Omega_0 t$$

Let us multiply above equation by $\sin m\,\Omega_0 t$

$$x(t)\sin m\,\Omega_0\, t = \frac{a_0}{2}\text{Sin } m\Omega_0 t + \sin m\,\Omega_0 t\left[\sum_{n=1}^{\infty} a_n\cos n\,\Omega_0\, t\right] + \sin m\,\Omega_0 t\left[\sum_{n=1}^{\infty} b_n\sin n\,\Omega_0\, t\right]$$

Integrate above equation over 0 to T and expand.

$$\int_0^T x(t)\sin m\,\Omega_0 t\, dt$$

$$= \int_0^T \frac{a_0}{2}\sin m\,\Omega_0\, t + \int_0^T a_1\cos\Omega_0 t\sin m\Omega_0\, t + \cdots$$

$$+ \int_0^T a_m\cos m\Omega_0 t\sin m\Omega_0\, t\, dt + \cdots + \int_0^T b_1\sin\Omega_0\, t\sin m\,\Omega_0 t\, dt$$

$$+ \cdots .. + \int_0^T b_m\sin^2 m\,\Omega_0 t\, dt + \cdots$$

In above equation all the definite integrations becomes zero except $\int_0^T b_m \, Sin^2 m\Omega_0 t \, dt$

$$\int_0^T x(t) \sin m \, \Omega_0 \, t \, dt = \int_0^T b_m \sin^2 m\Omega_0 t \, dt$$

$= b_m \int_0^T \frac{1-\cos 2m\Omega_0 t}{2} \, dt$

$= \frac{b_m}{2} \int_0^T [1 - \cos 2m\Omega_0 t] \, dt$

$= \frac{b_m}{2} \left[t - \frac{Sin \, 2 \, m \, \Omega_0 t}{2m \, \Omega_0}\right]_0^T$

$= \frac{b_m}{2} \left[T - \frac{Sin \, 2 \, m\Omega_0 \, T}{2m\Omega_0} - 0 + \frac{Sin \, 0}{2m \, \Omega_0}\right]$

$= \frac{b_m}{2} \left[T - \frac{Sin \, 2 \, m \frac{2\pi}{T} T}{2m\frac{2\pi}{T}}\right]$

$= \frac{T}{2} \, b_m$........ as $\sin 2m \, 2\pi = 0$ for integer m.

$$b_m = \frac{2}{T} \int_0^T x(t) \sin m \, \Omega_0 t \, dt \qquad (3.7)$$

as m is the mth coefficient, the nth coefficient will be,

$$\boxed{b_n = \frac{2}{T} \int_0^T x(t) \sin n \, \Omega_0 \, t \, dt}$$

3.3 Exponential form of Fourier Series

3.3.1 Definition

A periodic signal can also be represented in terms of *exponential form of Fourier Series*. Let us consider $x(t)$ be a periodic signal with period T. Then we can write

$$x(t) = \sum_{n=-\infty}^{+\infty} c_n e^{jn \, \Omega_0 t} \qquad (3.8)$$

where, $\Omega_0 = 2\pi F_0 = \frac{2\pi}{T}$ =Fundamental frequency in rad/sec

F_0 =Fundamental frequency in H_z

$\pm n \, \Omega_0$ =Harmonic frequencies

c_n =Fourier coefficients of exponential form

The value of c_n can be evaluated as

$$c_n = \frac{1}{T} \int_{-\frac{T}{2}}^{\frac{T}{2}} x(t) e^{-jn \, \Omega_0 t} \quad \text{or} \quad c_n = \frac{1}{T} \int_0^T x(t) e^{-jn \, \Omega_0 t} \qquad (3.9)$$

The integration is over one period i.e. $\frac{-T}{2}$ to $\frac{T}{2}$ or 0 to T.

This form consists of both positive and negative frequencies of exponential harmonic components. When these exponential components are added, we get real sine and cosine signals.

3.3.2 Derivation for equation for c_n

As we know the Fourier coefficient of exponential form is written as,

$c_n = \frac{1}{T}\int_{-\frac{T}{2}}^{\frac{T}{2}} x(t)e^{-jn\,\Omega_0 t}\,dt$ or $c_n = \frac{1}{T}\int_0^T x(t)e^{-jn\,\Omega_0 t}\,dt$

Proof: Consider the exponential form of Fourier series of $x(t)$ given by Eq. (3.8),

$x(t) = \sum_{n=-\infty}^{+\infty} c_n e^{jn\,\Omega_0 t} = \cdots + c_{-k}e^{-jk\,\Omega_0 t} + \ldots + c_{-1}e^{-j\,\Omega_0 t} + c_0 + c_1 e^{j\,\Omega_0 t} + \cdots + c_k e^{jk\,\Omega_0 t} + \cdots$

Multiply the above equation by $e^{-jk\,\Omega_0 t}$

$x(t)e^{-jk\,\Omega_0 t} = \cdots + c_{-k}e^{-j2k\,\Omega_0 t} + \ldots + c_{-1}e^{-j\,\Omega_0 t}e^{-jk\,\Omega_0 t} + c_0 e^{-jk\,\Omega_0 t} + c_1 e^{j\,\Omega_0 t}e^{-jk\,\Omega_0 t} + \cdots + c_k + \cdots$

Now integrate the above equation over a period 0 *to* T.

$\int_0^T x(t)e^{-jk\,\Omega_0 t}dt = \cdots + \int_0^T c_{-k}e^{-j2k\,\Omega_0 t}dt + \ldots + \int_0^T c_{-1}e^{-j\,\Omega_0 t}e^{-jk\,\Omega_0 t}\,dt + \int_0^T c_0 e^{-jk\,\Omega_0 t}\,dt + \int_0^T c_1 e^{j\,\Omega_0 t}e^{-jk\,\Omega_0 t}dt + \cdots + \int_0^T c_k dt + \cdots$

In the above equation all the definite integrations beocmes zero except $\int_0^T c_k dt$. Hence,

$\int_0^T x(t)e^{-jk\,\Omega_0 t}dt = \int_0^T c_k dt = c_k[t]_0^T = c_k[T-0] = Tc_k$

$$c_k = \frac{1}{T}\int_0^T x(t)e^{-jk\,\Omega_0 t}dt$$

Above equation is for k^{th} coefficient. Hnece we can write for n^{th} coefficient c_n,

$$c_n = \frac{1}{T}\int_0^T x(t)e^{-jn\,\Omega_0 t}\,dt$$

3.3.3 Relationship between the triginimetric and exponential form of Fourier coefficient

The relationship between the triginimetric and exponential form of Fourier coefficient can be written as,

$$c_0 = \frac{a_0}{2} \qquad (3.10)$$

$$c_{\pm n} = \frac{1}{2}(a_n \mp jb_n) \text{ for } n = \pm 1, \pm 2, \pm 3, \ldots \qquad (3.11)$$

$$|c_n| = \frac{1}{2}\sqrt{a_n{}^2 + b_n{}^2} \qquad \text{for all values of } n, \text{ except when } n = 0 \qquad (3.12)$$

3.4 Waveform Symmetires

3.4.1 Even Symmetry

If $x(t)$ is an even signal, then it should satisfy the condition $x(-t) = x(t)$. The waveform of an even symmetry signal is symmetric about the vertical axis or it is symmetric at $t = 0$.

A waveform can be represented in terms of even symmetry by folding the waveform with respect to vertical axis. After folding, if the shape remains same then waveform adopts even symmetry.

The value of Fourier coefficient a_0 is zero if the average value of one period is equal to zero. For an even signal a_0, a_n exists but b_n does not exist. Hnece the Fourier coefficients are given by,

$$a_0 = \frac{4}{T}\int_0^{\frac{T}{2}} x(t)dt \qquad (3.13)$$

$$a_n = \frac{4}{T}\int_0^{\frac{T}{2}} x(t)\cos n\,\Omega_0 t\ dt \qquad (3.14)$$

$$b_n = 0 \qquad (3.15)$$

Proof 1: Consider Eq. (3.3),

$$a_0 = \frac{2}{T}\int_{-\frac{T}{2}}^{\frac{T}{2}} x(t)dt = \frac{2}{T}\int_{-\frac{T}{2}}^{0} x(t)dt = \frac{2}{T}\int_{0}^{\frac{T}{2}} x(t)dt$$

Let $t = -\tau$; $\therefore\ dt = -d\tau$

$$a_0 = \frac{2}{T}\int_{\frac{T}{2}}^{0} x(-\tau)(-d\tau) + \frac{2}{T}\int_{0}^{\frac{T}{2}} x(t)dt$$

$$= \frac{2}{T}\int_{0}^{\frac{T}{2}} x(-\tau)d\tau + \frac{2}{T}\int_{0}^{\frac{T}{2}} x(t)dt$$

$$= \frac{2}{T}\int_0^{\frac{T}{2}} x(-t)dt + \frac{2}{T}\int_0^{\frac{T}{2}} x(t)dt$$

Since, $x(t)$ is even, $x(-t) = x(t)$,

$$= \frac{2}{T}\int_0^{\frac{T}{2}} x(t)dt + \frac{2}{T}\int_0^{\frac{T}{2}} x(t)dt$$

$$\boxed{a_0 = \frac{4}{T}\int_0^{\frac{T}{2}} x(t)dt}$$

Proof 2: Consider Eq. (3.4),

$$a_n = \frac{2}{T}\int_{-\frac{T}{2}}^{\frac{T}{2}} x(t)\cos n\,\Omega_0\,t\,dt = \frac{2}{T}\int_{-\frac{T}{2}}^{0} x(t)\cos n\,\Omega_0\,t\,dt + \frac{2}{T}\int_0^{\frac{T}{2}} x(t)\cos n\,\Omega_0\,t\,dt$$

Let $t = -\tau$; $\therefore\ dt = -d\tau$

$$a_n = \frac{2}{T}\int_{\frac{T}{2}}^{0} x(-\tau)\cos n\,\Omega_0(-\tau)\,(-d\tau) + \frac{2}{T}\int_0^{\frac{T}{2}} x(t)\cos n\,\Omega_0\,t\,dt$$

$$= \frac{2}{T}\int_0^{\frac{T}{2}} x(-\tau)\cos n\,\Omega_0\tau\,d\tau + \frac{2}{T}\int_0^{\frac{T}{2}} x(t)\cos n\,\Omega_0 t\,dt$$

$$= \frac{2}{T}\int_0^{\frac{T}{2}} x(-t)\cos n\,\Omega_0 t\,dt + \frac{2}{T}\int_0^{\frac{T}{2}} x(t)\cos n\,\Omega_0 t\,dt$$

Since, $x(t)$ is even, $x(-t) = x(t)$,

$$= \frac{2}{T}\int_0^{\frac{T}{2}} x(t)\cos n\,\Omega_0 t\,dt + \frac{2}{T}\int_0^{\frac{T}{2}} x(t)\cos n\,\Omega_0 t\,dt$$

$$\boxed{a_n = \frac{4}{T}\int_0^{\frac{T}{2}} x(t)\cos n\,\Omega_0 t\,dt}$$

Proof 3: Consider Eq. (3.5),

$$b_n = \frac{2}{T}\int_{-\frac{T}{2}}^{\frac{T}{2}} x(t)\sin n\,\Omega_0\,t\,dt = \frac{2}{T}\int_{-\frac{T}{2}}^{0} x(t)\sin n\,\Omega_0\,t\,dt + \frac{2}{T}\int_{0}^{\frac{T}{2}} x(t)\sin n\,\Omega_0\,t\,dt$$

Let $t = -\tau$; $\therefore\ dt = -d\tau$

$$a_n = \frac{2}{T}\int_{\frac{T}{2}}^{0} x(-\tau)\sin n\,\Omega_0(-\tau)\,(-d\tau) + \frac{2}{T}\int_{0}^{\frac{T}{2}} x(t)\sin n\,\Omega_0\,t\,dt$$

Since, $\sin(-\theta) = -\sin(\theta)$,

$$= -\frac{2}{T}\int_{0}^{\frac{T}{2}} x(-\tau)\sin n\,\Omega_0\tau\,d\tau + \frac{2}{T}\int_{0}^{\frac{T}{2}} x(t)\sin n\,\Omega_0 t\,dt$$

$$= -\frac{2}{T}\int_{0}^{\frac{T}{2}} x(-t)\sin n\,\Omega_0 t\,dt + \frac{2}{T}\int_{0}^{\frac{T}{2}} x(t)\sin n\,\Omega_0 t\,dt$$

Since, $x(t)$ is even $x(-t) = x(t)$,

$$= -\frac{2}{T}\int_{0}^{\frac{T}{2}} x(t)\sin n\,\Omega_0 t\,dt + \frac{2}{T}\int_{0}^{\frac{T}{2}} x(t)\sin n\,\Omega_0 t\,dt$$

$$\boxed{b_n = 0}$$

3.4.1.1 Some even symmetry signals with their Fourier series expansion

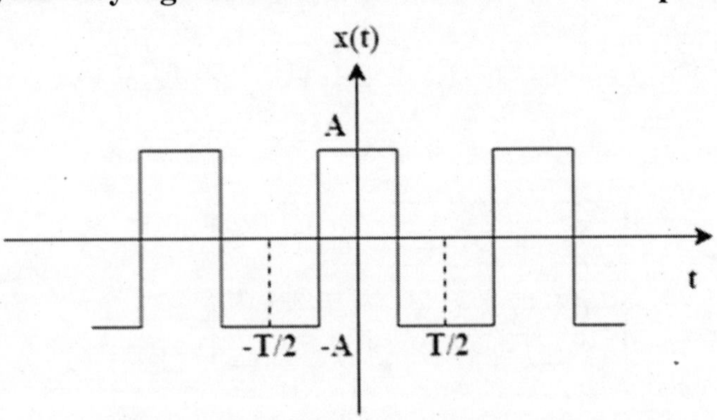

Fig. 3.2 Even, Half wave, Quarter wave symmetry waveform

Figure 3.2 shows the waveform with even symmetry as well as half wave and quarter wave symmetry. Hence for this waveform,

$$\boxed{a_0 = 0}$$

$$\boxed{b_n = 0}$$

$$\boxed{a_n \text{ exists for odd values of } n \text{ and equation of Fourier series consists of odd harmonics of all cosine terms}}$$

$$x(t) = \frac{4A}{\pi}\left[\frac{\cos \Omega_0 t}{1} - \frac{\cos 3\Omega_0 t}{3} + \frac{\cos 5\Omega_0 t}{5} - \frac{\cos 7\Omega_0 t}{7} + \cdots\right] \quad (3.16)$$

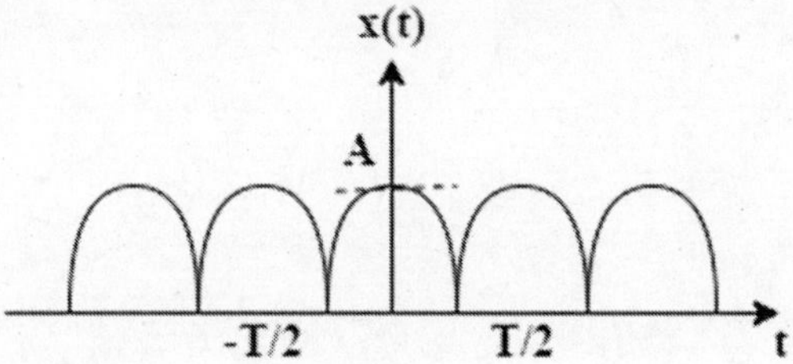

Fig. 3.3 Even symmetry waveform

Figure 3.3 shows the waveform with even symmetry. Hence for this waveform,

$$\boxed{a_0 \text{ exists}}$$

$$\boxed{a_n \text{ exists}}$$

$$\boxed{b_n = 0}$$

$$x(t) = \frac{2A}{\pi} + \frac{4A}{\pi}\left[\frac{\cos 2\,\Omega_0 t}{2^2-1} - \frac{\cos 4\,\Omega_0 t}{4^2-1} + \frac{\cos 6\,\Omega_0 t}{6^2-1} - \frac{\cos 8\,\Omega_0 t}{8^2-1} + \cdots\right] \quad (3.17)$$

3.4.2 Odd Symmetry

If $x(t)$ is an odd signal, then it should satisfy the condition $x(-t) = -x(t)$. The waveform of an odd symmetry signal is anti-symmetric about the vertical axis or it is anti-symmetric at $t = 0$.

a waveform can be represented in terms of odd symmetry by folding the waveform with respect to vertical axis. After folding, if the shape is exaclty opposite of the the another side of vertical axis then waveform adopts odd symmetry.

The value of Fourier coefficient a_0 is zero, a_n is zero but b_n exists. Hnece the Fourier coefficients are given by,

$$a_0 = 0 \quad (3.18)$$

$$a_n = 0 \quad (3.19)$$

$$b_n = \frac{4}{T}\int_0^{\frac{T}{2}} x(t)\sin n\,\Omega_0 t\ dt \qquad (3.20)$$

Proof 1: Consider Eq. (3.3),

$$a_0 = \frac{2}{T}\int_{-\frac{T}{2}}^{\frac{T}{2}} x(t)dt = \frac{2}{T}\int_{-\frac{T}{2}}^{0} x(t)dt = \frac{2}{T}\int_{0}^{\frac{T}{2}} x(t)dt$$

Let $t = -\tau;\ \therefore\ dt = -d\tau$

$$a_0 = \frac{2}{T}\int_{\frac{T}{2}}^{0} x(-\tau)(-d\tau) + \frac{2}{T}\int_{0}^{\frac{T}{2}} x(t)dt$$

$$= \frac{2}{T}\int_{0}^{\frac{T}{2}} x(-\tau)d\tau + \frac{2}{T}\int_{0}^{\frac{T}{2}} x(t)dt$$

$$= \frac{2}{T}\int_0^{\frac{T}{2}} x(-t)dt + \frac{2}{T}\int_0^{\frac{T}{2}} x(t)dt$$

Since, $x(t)$ is odd, $x(-t) = -x(t)$,

$$= -\frac{2}{T}\int_0^{\frac{T}{2}} x(t)dt + \frac{2}{T}\int_0^{\frac{T}{2}} x(t)dt$$

$$\boxed{a_0 = 0}$$

Proof 2: Consider Eq. (3.4),

$$a_n = \frac{2}{T}\int_{-\frac{T}{2}}^{\frac{T}{2}} x(t)\cos n\,\Omega_0\,t\ dt = \frac{2}{T}\int_{-\frac{T}{2}}^{0} x(t)\cos n\,\Omega_0\,t\ dt + \frac{2}{T}\int_{0}^{\frac{T}{2}} x(t)\cos n\,\Omega_0\,t\ dt$$

Let $t = -\tau;\ \therefore\ dt = -d\tau$

$$a_n = \frac{2}{T}\int_{\frac{T}{2}}^{0} x(-\tau)\cos n\,\Omega_0(-\tau)\,(-d\tau) + \frac{2}{T}\int_{0}^{\frac{T}{2}} x(t)\cos n\,\Omega_0\,t\ dt$$

$$= \frac{2}{T}\int_{0}^{\frac{T}{2}} x(-\tau)\cos n\,\Omega_0\tau\,d\tau + \frac{2}{T}\int_{0}^{\frac{T}{2}} x(t)\cos n\,\Omega_0 t\,dt$$

$$= \frac{2}{T}\int_{0}^{\frac{T}{2}} x(-t)\cos n\,\Omega_0 t\,dt + \frac{2}{T}\int_{0}^{\frac{T}{2}} x(t)\cos n\,\Omega_0 t\,dt$$

Since, $x(t)$ is odd, $x(-t) = -x(t)$,

$$= -\frac{2}{T}\int_{0}^{\frac{T}{2}} x(t)\cos n\,\Omega_0 t\,dt + \frac{2}{T}\int_{0}^{\frac{T}{2}} x(t)\cos n\,\Omega_0 t\,dt$$

$$\boxed{a_n = 0}$$

Proof 3: Consider Eq. (3.5),

$$b_n = \frac{2}{T}\int_{-\frac{T}{2}}^{\frac{T}{2}} x(t)\sin n\,\Omega_0\,t\,dt = \frac{2}{T}\int_{-\frac{T}{2}}^{0} x(t)\sin n\,\Omega_0\,t\,dt + \frac{2}{T}\int_{0}^{\frac{T}{2}} x(t)\sin n\,\Omega_0\,t\,dt$$

Let $t = -\tau$; $\therefore\ dt = -d\tau$

$$a_n = \frac{2}{T}\int_{\frac{T}{2}}^{0} x(-\tau)\sin n\,\Omega_0(-\tau)\,(-d\tau) + \frac{2}{T}\int_{0}^{\frac{T}{2}} x(t)\sin n\,\Omega_0\,t\,dt$$

Since, $\sin(-\theta) = -\sin(\theta)$,

$$= -\frac{2}{T}\int_{0}^{\frac{T}{2}} x(-\tau)\sin n\,\Omega_0\tau\,d\tau + \frac{2}{T}\int_{0}^{\frac{T}{2}} x(t)\sin n\,\Omega_0 t\,dt$$

$$= -\frac{2}{T}\int_{0}^{\frac{T}{2}} x(-t)\sin n\,\Omega_0 t\,dt + \frac{2}{T}\int_{0}^{\frac{T}{2}} x(t)\sin n\,\Omega_0 t\,dt$$

Since, $x(t)$ is odd $x(-t) = -x(t)$,

$$= \frac{2}{T}\int_{0}^{\frac{T}{2}} x(t)\sin n\,\Omega_0 t\,dt + \frac{2}{T}\int_{0}^{\frac{T}{2}} x(t)\sin n\,\Omega_0 t\,dt$$

$$\boxed{b_n = \frac{4}{T}\int_{0}^{\frac{T}{2}} x(t)\sin n\,\Omega_0 t\ dt}$$

3.4.2.1 Some odd symmetry signals with their Fourier series expansion

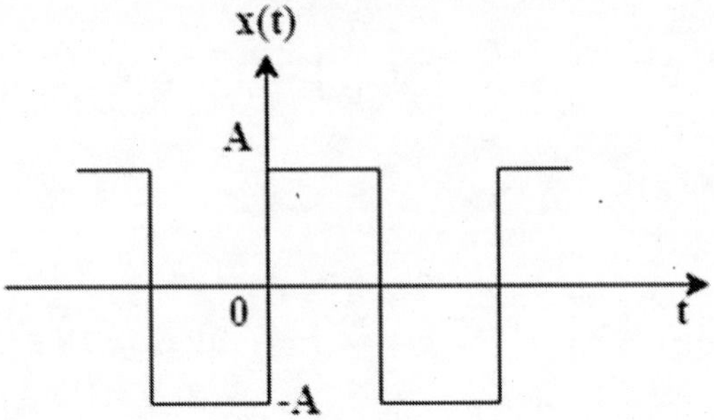

Fig. 3.4 Odd, Half wave, Quarter wave symmetry waveform

Figure 3.4 shows the waveform with odd symmetry as well as half wave and quarter wave symmetry. Hence for this waveform,

$$\boxed{a_0 = 0}$$

$$\boxed{a_n = 0}$$

b_n exists for odd values of n and equation of Fourier series consists of odd harmonics of all cosine terms

$$x(t) = \frac{4A}{\pi}\left[\frac{\sin \Omega_0 t}{1} + \frac{\sin 3\Omega_0 t}{3} + \frac{\sin 5\Omega_0 t}{5} + \frac{\sin 7\Omega_0 t}{7} + \cdots\right] \tag{3.21}$$

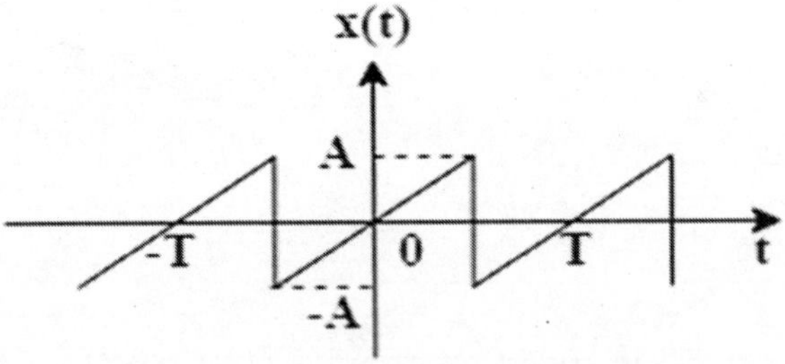

Fig. 3.5 Odd symmetry waveform

Figure 3.5 shows the waveform with odd symmetry. Hence for this waveform,

$$\boxed{a_0 = 0}$$

$$\boxed{a_n = 0}$$

b_n exists for all values of n and Fourier series consists both even and odd harmonics of sine terms

$$x(t) = \frac{2A}{\pi}\left[\frac{\sin \Omega_0 t}{1} - \frac{\sin 2\Omega_0 t}{2} + \frac{\sin 3\Omega_0 t}{3} - \frac{\sin 4\Omega_0 t}{4} + \cdots\right] \qquad (3.22)$$

3.4.3 Half Wave Symmetry

A periodic waveform satisfying the condition of having two equal and opposite half period/cycle in one period/cycle are said to have half wave symmetry.

The conditin of half wave symmetry should satisfy the below equation,

$$x\left(t \pm \frac{T}{2}\right) = -x(t) \qquad (3.23)$$

If any waveform satisfies the half wave symmetry condition then, the Fourier series will consist of odd harmonic terms alone.

The waveform shown in Fig. 3.6 shows the example of half wave symmetry.

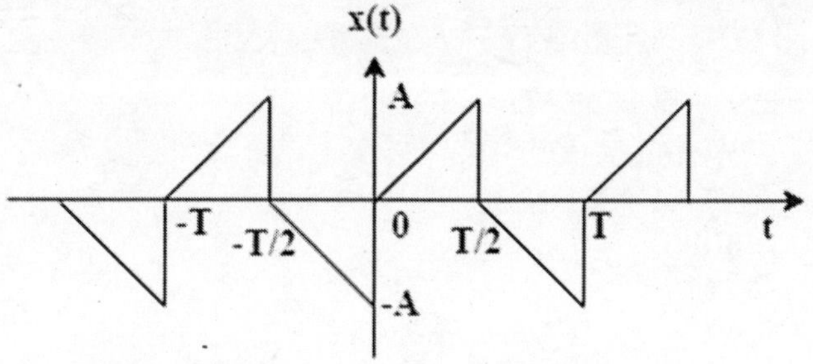

Fig. 3.6 Half wave symmetry waveform

$$x(t) = -\frac{4A}{\pi^2}\left[\cos\Omega_0 t + \frac{\cos 3\Omega_0 t}{3^2} + \frac{\cos 5\Omega_0 t}{5^2} + \cdots\right] + \frac{2A}{\pi}\left[\sin\Omega_0 t + \frac{\sin 3\Omega_0 t}{3} + \frac{\sin 5\Omega_0 t}{5} + \cdots\right] \qquad (3.24)$$

3.4.4 Quarter Wave Symmetry

A waveform that satisfies half wave symmetry condition along with even or odd symmetry then that waveform is said to have quarter wave symmetry. In this type of symmetry, each quarter period will be of same identical shape and may or may not have opposite sign. The conditin of quarter wave symmetry should satisfy the below equation,

$$x\left(t \pm \frac{T}{2}\right) = -x(t) \qquad (3.23)$$

Where $x(t)$ has half wave symmetry and its Fourier series coefficients consists of all odd hrmonic terms.

If $x(t)$ has *even and half wave symmetry*, then $x(-t) = x(t)$ and Fourier series will have odd harmonics of only cosine terms.

If $x(t)$ has *odd and half wave symmetry*, then $x(-t) = -x(t)$ and Fourier series will have odd harmonics of only sine terms.

The waveforms shown in Fig. 3.2, 3.4 are the examples of quarter wave symmetry.

3.5 Properties of Fourier Series in terms of Exponential Form

Suppose $x(t)$ and $y(t)$ have the Fourier series coefficients c_n and d_n in exponential form, respectively.

3.5.1 Linearity:

For continuous time periodic signal,

$$Ax(t)+By(t)$$

In terms of Fourier coefficients,

$$Ac_n+Bd_n$$

3.5.2 Time Shifting:

For continuous time periodic signal,

$$x(t - t_0)$$

In terms of Fourier coefficients,

$$c_n e^{-jn\,\Omega_0 t_0}$$

3.5.3 Frequency Shifting

For continuous time periodic signal,

$$x(t)e^{-jk\,\Omega_0 t}$$

In terms of Fourier coefficients,

$$c_{n-k}$$

3.5.4 Time Reversal

For continuous time periodic signal,

$$x(-t)$$

In terms of Fourier coefficients,

$$c_{-n}$$

3.5.5 Multiplication

For continuous time periodic signal,

$$x(t)\,y(t)$$

In terms of Fourier coefficients,

$$\sum_{k=-\infty}^{+\infty} c_k d_{n-k}$$

3.5.6 Conjugation

For continuous time periodic signal,

$$x^*(t)$$

In terms of Fourier coefficients,

$$c^*_{-n}$$

3.5.7 Time Scaling

For continuous time periodic signal,

$$x(\beta t)\,;\ \text{where } \beta > 0$$

In terms of Fourier coefficients,

$$c_n$$

3.5.8 Differentiation

For continuous time periodic signal,

$$\frac{d}{dt}x(t)$$

In terms of Fourier coefficients,

$$jn\,\Omega_0 c_n$$

3.5.9 Integration

For continuous time periodic signal,

$$\int_{-\infty}^{t} x(t)dt$$

In terms of Fourier coefficients,

$$\frac{1}{jn\,\Omega_0}c_n$$

3.5.10 Real and Even

For continuous time periodic signal,

$x(t)$ is real and even

In terms of Fourier coefficients,

c_n are real and even

3.5.11 Real and Odd

For continuous time periodic signal,

$x(t)$ is real and odd

In terms of Fourier coefficients,

c_n are imaginary and odd

3.5.12 Parseval's Relation

For continuous time periodic signal,

Average power of signal $x(t)$ is,

$$P = \frac{1}{T}\int_{T} |x(t)|^2 dt$$

In terms of Fourier coefficients, the average power is

$$P = \sum_{n=-\infty}^{+\infty} |c_n|^2$$

3.6 Gibb's Phenomenon

Consider a periodic signal $x(t)$ and it's exponential form of Fourier Series expansion

$$x(t) = \sum_{n=-\infty}^{+\infty} c_n e^{jn\,\Omega_0 t}$$

Above expansion consists the terms as a sum of infinite series of harmonic frequency components. When the signal $x(t)$ is to be reconstructed with some N terms from infinite series of harmonic frequency components, the signal displays some oscillations also called as ripples that have discontinuities with it.

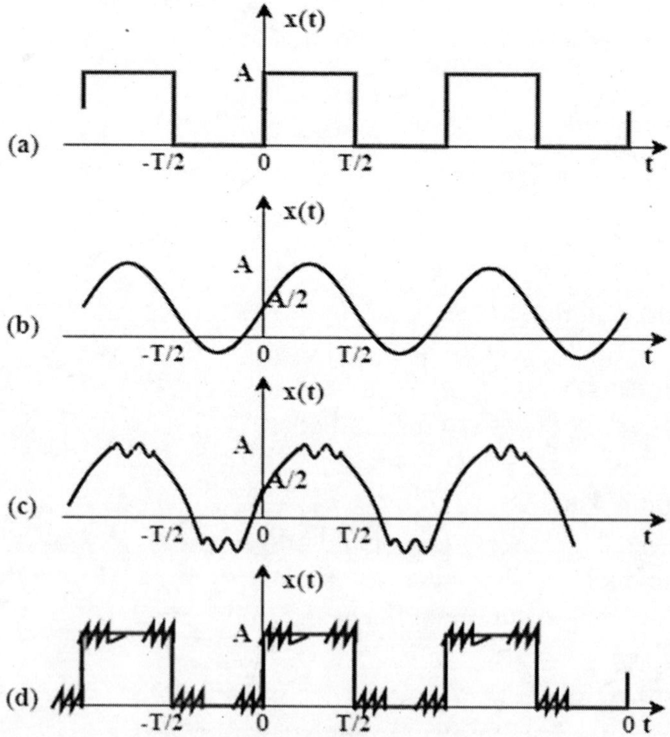

Fig. 3.7 Approximation of square waveform using some harmonic frequency components

Consider the Fig. 3.7(a) of periodic square waveform. Figure 3.7(b), (c), (d) shows the reconstruction using some N harmonic frequency components. It can be easily seen that the reconstructed signals have some ripples with it at the edge points. Also it can be observed that, at the points of discontinuity, the Fourier series converges to average value of the signal on either side of discontinuity. This phenomenon is called as Gibbs phenomenon after the name of great scientist, Josiah Gibbs. He had shown that as the value of N increases, the peak overshoot shifts towards the point of discontinuity.

Solved examples on Fourier series

Example 3.1 Determine the trigonometric form of Fourier series of the waveform shown in fig 3.1.1.

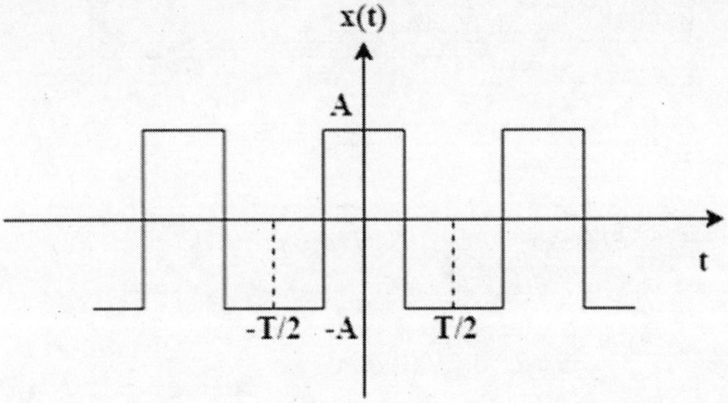

Fig. 3.1.1.

Solution: The waveform has even symmetry, half wave symmetry and quarter wave symmetry.

$a_0 = 0,\, b_n = 0,\, a_n = \frac{4}{T}\int_0^{\frac{T}{2}} x(t)cosn\Omega_0 tdt$

Equation for square wave is written as,

$x(t) = A;$ for $t = 0\ to\ \frac{T}{4}$

$= -A;$ for $t = \frac{T}{4}\ to\ \frac{T}{2}$

Now,

$$a_n = \frac{4}{T}\int_0^{\frac{T}{2}} x(t)cosn\Omega_0 tdt$$

$$a_n = \frac{4}{T}\int_0^{\frac{T}{4}} A cosn\Omega_0 t dt + \frac{4}{T}\int_{\frac{T}{4}}^{\frac{T}{2}} (-A) cosn\Omega_0 t dt$$

$$= \frac{4A}{T}\left[\frac{sinn\Omega_0 t}{n\Omega_0}\right]_0^{\frac{T}{4}} - \frac{4A}{T}\left[\frac{sinn\Omega_0 t}{n\Omega_0}\right]_{\frac{T}{4}}^{\frac{T}{2}}$$

$$= \frac{4A}{T}\left[\frac{sinn\frac{2\pi}{T}t}{n\frac{2\pi}{T}}\right]_0^{\frac{T}{4}} - \frac{4A}{T}\left[\frac{sinn\frac{2\pi}{T}t}{n\frac{2\pi}{T}}\right]_{\frac{T}{4}}^{\frac{T}{2}}$$

$$= \frac{4A}{T}\left[\frac{sin\left(n\frac{2\pi T}{T\,4}\right)}{n\frac{2\pi}{T}} - \frac{sin0}{n\frac{2\pi}{T}}\right] - \frac{4A}{T}\left[\frac{sin\left(n\frac{2\pi}{T}\frac{T}{2}\right)}{n\frac{2\pi}{T}} - \frac{in\left(n\frac{2\pi}{T}\frac{T}{4}\right)}{n\frac{2\pi}{T}}\right]$$

$$= \frac{4A}{T}\left[\frac{T}{2n\pi}sin\frac{n\pi}{2} - 0\right] - \frac{4A}{T}\left[\frac{T}{2n\pi}sinn\pi - \frac{T}{2n\pi}sin\frac{n\pi}{2}\right]$$

$$= \frac{2A}{n\pi}sin\frac{n\pi}{2} + \frac{2A}{n\pi}sin\frac{n\pi}{2} = \frac{4A}{n\pi}sin\frac{n\pi}{2}$$

$sin\frac{n\pi}{2} = 0;$

for even values of n

$sin\frac{n\pi}{2} = \pm 1;$

for odd values of n

$\therefore a_n = 0;$

for even values of n

$a_n = \frac{4A}{n\pi}sin\frac{n\pi}{2};$

for odd values of n

$$x(t) = \sum_{odd\ n} a_n cosn\Omega_0 t$$

$$x(t) = \frac{4A}{\pi}\left[\frac{cos\,\Omega_0 t}{1} - \frac{cos3\Omega_0 t}{3} + \frac{cos5\Omega_0 t}{5} - \frac{cos7\Omega_0 t}{7} + \cdots\right]$$

Example 3.2 Determine the trigonometric form of Fourier series of the waveform shown in fig 3.1.2.

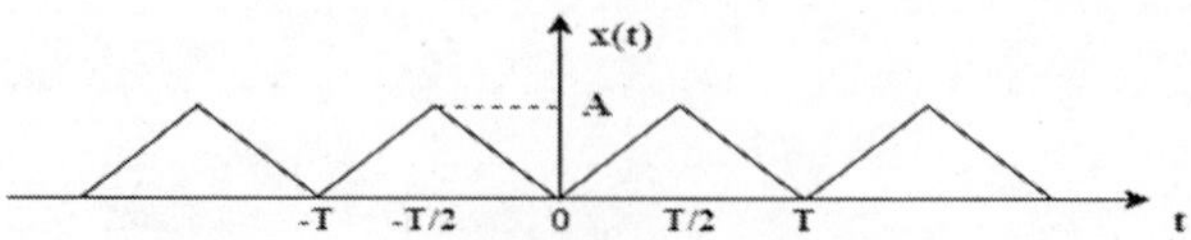

Fig. 3.1.2.

Solution: The waveform has even symmetry.

$a_0 = \frac{4}{T}\int_0^{\frac{T}{2}} x(t)dt;\ a_n = \frac{4}{T}\int_0^{\frac{T}{2}} x(t)cosn\Omega_0 tdt;\ b_n = 0$

$straight\ line\ equation = \frac{y-y_1}{y_1-y_2} = \frac{x-x_1}{x_1-x_2} = \frac{x(t)-x(t_1)}{x(t_1)-x(t_2)} = \frac{t-t_1}{t_1-t_2}$

$coordinates\ of\ (t_1, x(t_1)) = [0,0]$ and $coordinates\ of\ (t_2, x(t_2)) = [\frac{T}{2}, A]$

$\therefore \frac{x(t)-0}{0-A} = \frac{t-0}{0-\frac{T}{2}} => \frac{x(t)}{-A} = \frac{-2t}{T} => x(t) =$

$\frac{2At}{T}$ for $t = 0\ to\ \frac{T}{2}$

Now,

$a_0 = \frac{4}{T}\int_0^{\frac{T}{2}} x(t)dt = \frac{4}{T}\int_0^{\frac{T}{2}} \frac{2A}{T} t\ dt = \frac{8A}{T^2}\int_0^{\frac{T}{2}} t\ dt = \frac{8A}{T^2}\left[\frac{t^2}{2}\right]_0^{\frac{T}{2}} = \frac{8A}{T^2}\left[\frac{T^2}{8} - 0\right] = A$

$$a_n = \frac{4}{T}\int_0^{\frac{T}{2}} x(t)cosn\Omega_0 tdt = \frac{4}{T}\int_0^{\frac{T}{2}} \frac{2A}{T} t\ cosn\Omega_0 tdt$$

$$= \frac{8A}{T^2}\left[\frac{tsinn\frac{2\pi}{T}t}{n\frac{2\pi}{T}} + \frac{cos\ n\frac{2\pi}{T}t}{n^2\frac{4\pi^2}{T^2}}\right]_0^{\frac{T}{2}}$$

$$= \frac{8A}{T^2}\left[\frac{T^2}{n4\pi}\sin n\pi + \frac{T^2}{n^2 4\pi^2}\cos n\pi - \frac{T^2}{n^2 4\pi^2}\right]$$

$cos\ n\pi = +1;$ for even values of n

$cos\ n\pi = -1;$ for odd values of n

$\therefore a_n = 0;$ for even values of n

$a_n = \frac{2A}{n^2\pi^2}\cos[n\pi - 1] = -\frac{4A}{n^2\pi^2}$; for odd values of n

$$x(t) = \frac{a_0}{2} + \sum_{odd\ n} a_n cosn\Omega_0 t$$

$$x(t) = \frac{A}{2} - \frac{4A}{\pi^2}\left[\frac{cos\ \Omega_0 t}{1^2} + \frac{cos3\Omega_0 t}{3^2} + \frac{cos5\Omega_0 t}{5^2} + \frac{cos7\Omega_0 t}{7^2} + \cdots\right]$$

Example 3.3 Given the Fourier series coefficients as a_k determine the signalx(t):

$$a_k = j\delta[k-1] + \frac{j}{2}\delta[k+1] + \frac{1}{3}\delta[k+3] + \frac{1}{6}\delta[k-3] + \delta[k+4] + \delta[k-4]$$

Solution:

$$a_k = j\delta[k-1] + \frac{j}{2}\delta[k+1] + \frac{1}{3}\delta[k+3] + \frac{1}{6}\delta[k-3] + \delta[k+4] + \delta[k-4]$$

The Fourier series coefficients are identified as

$$a_0 = 0, \quad a_1 = j, \quad a_2 = 0, \quad a_3 = \frac{1}{6}, a_4 = 1$$

$$a_{-1} = \frac{j}{2}, \quad a_{-2} = 0, \quad a_{-3} = \frac{1}{3}, \quad a_{-4} = 1$$

$$x(t) = \sum_{k=-\infty}^{\infty} a_k e^{jk\Omega_0 t}$$

Substituting the values of a_k, we get

$$x(t) = je^{\Omega_0 t} + \frac{j}{2}e^{-j\Omega_0 t} + \frac{1}{6}e^{j3\Omega_0 t} + \frac{1}{3}e^{-j3\Omega_0 t} + e^{j4\Omega_0 t} + e^{-j4\Omega_0 t}$$

Expanding by using Euler's relation, we get

$$x(t) = j(cos\Omega_0 t + j\, sin\Omega_0 t) + \frac{j}{2}(\cos\Omega_0 t - jsin\Omega_0 t) + \frac{1}{6}(\cos 3\Omega_0 t + jsin3\Omega_0 t)$$
$$+ \frac{1}{3}(\cos 3\Omega_0 t - jsin3\Omega_0 t) + 2cos4\Omega_0 t$$

Simplifying, we get

$$x(t) = \frac{3j}{2}cos\Omega_0 t - \frac{1}{2}\sin\Omega_0 t + 2cos4\Omega_0 t - \frac{j}{6}\sin 3\Omega_0 t + \frac{1}{2}cos3\Omega_0 t$$

Example 3.4 Given the Fourier series coefficients as a_k determine the signal$x(t)$:

$x(t) = \frac{1}{2} + cost + \frac{1}{4}cos2t$

Solution:

Given

$$x(t) = \frac{1}{2} + cost + \frac{1}{4}cos2t$$

Now cost is periodic with period $T_1 = \frac{2\pi}{1} = 2\pi$ and cos2t s periodic with period $T_2 = \frac{2\pi}{2} = \pi$.

Hence,

It is periodic with period $T = LCM(T_1, T_2) = LCM(2\pi, \pi) = 2\pi$

The fundamental frequency Ω_0

Using Euler'srelation, the signal $x(t)$ can be written as

$$x(t) = \frac{1}{2} + \frac{e^{jt} + e^{-jt}}{2} + \frac{1}{4}\frac{e^{2jt} + e^{-2jt}}{2}$$

$$= \frac{1}{2} + \frac{e^{jt} + e^{-jt}}{2} + \frac{e^{j2t} + e^{-j2t}}{8}$$

$$= \frac{1}{2} + \frac{1}{2}e^{jt} + \frac{1}{2}e^{-jt} + \frac{1}{8}e^{j2t} + \frac{1}{8}e^{-j2t}$$

Since $\Omega_0 = 1, we\ can\ write$

$$x(t) = \frac{1}{8}e^{-j2\Omega_0 t} + \frac{1}{2}e^{-j\Omega_0 t} + \frac{1}{2} + \frac{1}{2}e^{j\Omega_0 t} + \frac{1}{8}e^{-j2\Omega_0 t}$$

We can identify the Fourier series coefficients as,

$a_{-2} = \frac{1}{8}, a_{-1} = \frac{1}{2}; a_0 = \frac{1}{2}, a_1 = \frac{1}{2}\ a_2 = \frac{1}{8}, a_k = 0,\ |k| > 2$

3.7 Fourier Transform (FT)

3.7.1 Definition

Let $x(t)$ is a continuous time signal, $X(j\Omega)$ is the Fourier transform of signal $x(t)$. The Fourier signal of signal $x(t)$ is defined as,

$X(j\Omega) = \int_{-\infty}^{+\infty} x(t)e^{-j\Omega t}dt = \int_{-\infty}^{+\infty} x(t)e^{-j2\pi f t}dt =$
$\mathcal{F}\{x(t)\}$
(3.24)

Where, f =Cyclic frequency

Condition for Fourier Transform Existence:

The Fourier transform exists for the signal $x(t)$ if it follows Dirichlet condition.

1. Signal $x(t)$ is absolutely integrable.

$$\int_{-\infty}^{+\infty} x(t)\,dt < \infty$$

2. The signal $x(t)$ should have a finite number of maxima and minima within a finite duration of interval.
3. The signal $x(t)$ can have a finite number of discontinuities within a interval.

3.7.2 Definition of Inverse Fourier Transform (IFT)

Inverse Fourier transform of $X(j\Omega)$ is given by,

$$x(t) = \frac{1}{2\pi}\int_{-\infty}^{+\infty} X(j\Omega)e^{j\Omega t}\, d\Omega = \int_{-\infty}^{+\infty} X(jf)e^{j2\pi ft}\, d\Omega = F^{-1}\{X(j\Omega)\} \qquad (3.25)$$

Signal $x(t)$ and its Fourier transform $X(j\Omega)$ makes the Fourier trasnform pair and the relation is given by,

$$x(t) \overleftrightarrow{\boldsymbol{FT, IFT}} X(j\Omega)$$

3.7.3 Magnitude and Phase Spectrum using Fourier Transform

Let Fourier transform of $X(j\Omega)$ is a complex function of frequency Ω and it can be defined in terms of real and imaginary parts as shown below,

$$X(j\Omega) = X_{real}(j\Omega) + X_{imag}(j\Omega)$$

Where, $X_{real}(j\Omega)$ = Real part of $X(j\Omega)$

$X_{imag}(j\Omega)$ =Imaginary part of $X(j\Omega)$

The ***Magnitude spectrum*** of $X(j\Omega)$ can be written as,

$$|X(j\Omega)| = \sqrt{X_{real}{}^2(j\Omega) + X_{imag}{}^2(j\Omega)} \qquad (3.26)$$

Magnitude spectrum has always even symmetry.

The ***Phase spectrum*** of $X(j\Omega)$ can be written as,

$$\angle X(j\Omega) = \tan^{-1}\frac{X_{imag}(j\Omega)}{X_{real}(j\Omega)} \qquad (3.27)$$

Phase spectrum has always odd symmetry.

Both magnitude spectrum and phase spectrum are called as ***frequency spectrum***.

3.8 Properties of Fourier Transform (FT)

3.8.1 Linearity

If $x_1(t) \overrightarrow{FT} X_1(j\Omega)$,

$x_2(t) \overrightarrow{FT} X_2(j\Omega)$

Then,

$$F\{a_1x_1(t) + a_2x_2(t)\} = a_1X_1(j\Omega) + a_2X_2(j\Omega) \qquad (3.28)$$

Proof: By definition of FT,

$X(j\Omega) = \int_{-\infty}^{\infty} x(t)\, e^{-j\Omega t} dt$

$\therefore\ X_1(j\Omega) = \int_{-\infty}^{\infty} x_1(t)\, e^{-j\Omega t} dt$

$\therefore\ X_2(j\Omega) = \int_{-\infty}^{\infty} x_2(t)\, e^{-j\Omega t} dt$

Consider linear combination, $a_1x_1(t) + a_2x_2(t)$

$\therefore\ F\{a_1x_1(t) + a_2x_2(t)\} = \int_{-\infty}^{\infty} [a_1x_1(t) + a_2x_2(t)]\, e^{-j\Omega t} dt$

$= \int_{-\infty}^{\infty} a_1x_1(t)\, e^{-j\Omega t} dt + \int_{-\infty}^{\infty} a_2x_2(t)\, e^{-j\Omega t} dt$

$= a_1X_1(j\Omega) + a_2X_2(j\Omega)$

3.8.2 Time Shifting:

If $x(t) \underset{FT}{\rightarrow} X(j\Omega)$

Then,

$F\{x(t - t_0)\} = X(j\Omega)e^{-j\Omega t}$ (3.29)

Proof: By definition of FT,

$X(j\Omega) = \int_{-\infty}^{\infty} x(t)\, e^{-j\Omega t} dt$

$\therefore F\{x(t - t_0)\} = \int_{-\infty}^{\infty} x(t - t_0)e^{-j\Omega t}\, dt$

Let $t - t_0 = \tau$, $\therefore t = \tau + t_0$, $dt = d\tau$

$\therefore F\{x(t - t_0)\} = \int_{-\infty}^{\infty} x(\tau)e^{-j\Omega(\tau+t_0)}\, d\tau$

$= \int_{-\infty}^{\infty} x(\tau)e^{-j\Omega\tau} . e^{-j\Omega t_0} d\tau$

$= e^{-j\Omega t_0} \int_{-\infty}^{\infty} x(\tau)e^{-j\Omega\tau}\, d\tau$

$= e^{-j\Omega t_0}\, X(j\Omega)$

3.8.3 Time Scaling:

If $x(t)\overrightarrow{FT}x(j\Omega)$

then,

$F\{x(at)\} = \frac{1}{|a|} * \left(\frac{j\Omega}{a}\right)$ (3.30)

Proof: By definition of FT,

$$x(j\Omega) = \int_{-\infty}^{\infty} x(t)\, e^{-j\Omega t}\, dt$$

$$F\{x(at)\} = \int_{-\infty}^{\infty} x(at)e^{-j\Omega t}\, dt$$

Let $= \tau,\ t = \frac{\tau}{a},\ dt = \frac{d\tau}{a}$

$$\therefore F\{x(at)\} = \frac{1}{a}\int_{-\infty}^{\infty} x(\tau)e^{-j\Omega\left(\frac{\tau}{a}\right)}\, d\tau$$

$$= \frac{1}{a}\int_{-\infty}^{\infty} x(\tau)e^{-j\left(\frac{\Omega}{a}\right)\tau} d\tau$$

'a' can be negative or positive. Hence, in general $F\{x(at)\} = \frac{1}{|a|} * \left(\frac{j\Omega}{a}\right)$

3.8.4 Time Reversal:

If $x(t) \overrightarrow{\ FT\ } X(j\Omega)$
then,
$F\{x(at)\} = x\,(j\Omega)$ (3.31)

Proof: By using the Time Scaling Property in Eq. (3.30)

$$F\{x(at)\} = \frac{1}{|a|}X\left(\frac{j\Omega}{a}\right)$$

For $a = -1$,

$$F\{x(-t)\} = \frac{1}{|-1|}X\left(\frac{j\Omega}{-1}\right) = X(-j\,\Omega)$$

3.8.5 Conjugation:

If $x(t) \overrightarrow{\ FT\ } X(j\Omega)$
then,
$F\{x^*(t)\} = X^*(-j\Omega)$ (3.32)

Proof: By definition of FT,

$$X(j\Omega) = \int_{-\infty}^{\infty} x(t)\, e^{-j\Omega t} dt$$

$$\therefore F\{x^*(t)\} = \int_{-\infty}^{\infty} x^*(t)e^{-j\Omega t} dt$$

$$= \left[\int_{-\infty}^{\infty} x(t)\, e^{j\Omega t} dt\right]^*$$

$$=\left[\int_{-\infty}^{\infty} x(t)\, e^{-j(-\Omega)t} dt\right]^*$$

$$= X^*(-j\Omega)$$

3.8.6 Frequency Shifting:

$If\ x(t)\ \overrightarrow{FT}\ X(j\Omega)$

then,

$F\{e^{j\Omega_0 t}x(t)\} = X(j(\Omega - \Omega_0))$ (3.33)

Proof: By definition of FT,

$$X(j\Omega) = \int_{-\infty}^{\infty} x(t)\, e^{-j\Omega t} dt$$

$$\therefore F\{e^{j\Omega_0 t}x(t)\} = \int_{-\infty}^{\infty} x(t)e^{j\Omega_0 t}e^{-j\Omega t} dt$$

$$= \int_{-\infty}^{\infty} x(t)e^{-j(\Omega-\Omega_0)t}\, dt$$

$$= X(j(\Omega - \Omega_0))$$

3.8.7 Time differentiation

If $x(t)\ \overrightarrow{FT}\ X(j\Omega)$

then,

$F\left\{\frac{d}{dt}\, x(t)\right\} = j\Omega X(j\Omega)$ (3.34)

Proof: By definition of FT,

$$X(j\Omega) = \int_{-\infty}^{\infty} x(t)\, e^{-j\Omega t} dt$$

$$\therefore F\left\{\frac{d}{dt} x(t)\right\} = \int_{-\infty}^{\infty} \left(\frac{d}{dt} x(t)\right) e^{-j\Omega t}\ dt$$

$$= \int_{-\infty}^{\infty} e^{-j\Omega t} \left(\frac{d}{dt}\, x(t)\right) dt$$

$$Using, \int uv = u\int v - \int\left[du \int v\right]$$

$$\therefore F\left\{\frac{d}{dt}x(t)\right\} = e^{-j\Omega t}x(t)|_{-\infty}^{\infty} - \int (-j\Omega)\, e^{-j\Omega t}x(t)dt$$

$$= 0 + j\Omega \int_{-\infty}^{\infty} x(t)\, e^{-j\Omega t} dt$$

$$= j\Omega\, X(j\Omega)$$

3.8.8 *Time Integration*

$$x(t) \overrightarrow{FT} X(j\Omega)$$

then,

$F\left\{\int_{-\infty}^{t} x(t)dt\right\} = \frac{1}{j\Omega}X(j\Omega)$ (3.35)

Proof: Let,

$$x(t) = \frac{d}{dt}\left[\int_{-\infty}^{t} x(t)dt\right]$$

Take FT on both sides,

$$F\{x(t)\} = F\left\{\frac{d}{dt}\left[\int_{-\infty}^{t} x(t)dt\right]\right\}$$

$$X(j\Omega) = F\left\{\int_{-\infty}^{t} \left[\frac{d}{dt}x(t)\right] dt\right\}$$

$$X(j\Omega) = (j\Omega)F\left\{\int_{-\infty}^{t} x(t)dt\right\}$$

$$\therefore F\left\{\int_{-\infty}^{t} x(t)dt\right\} = \frac{1}{j\Omega}X(j\Omega)$$

3.8.9 *Differentiation in Frequency*

If $x(t) \overrightarrow{FT} X(j\,\Omega)$

then,

$F\{tx(t)\} = j\frac{d}{d\Omega}X(j\,\Omega)$ (3.36)

Proof: By definition of FT

$$X(j\Omega) = \int_{-\infty}^{\infty} x(t)e^{-j\Omega t}dt$$

Take differentiation on both sides, w. r. t. Ω

$$\frac{d}{d\Omega}X(j\Omega) = \frac{d}{d\Omega}\left[\int_{-\infty}^{\infty} x(t)e^{-j\Omega t}\,dt\right]$$

$$= \int_{-\infty}^{\infty} x(t)\left[\frac{d}{d\Omega}\,e^{-j\Omega t}\right]dt$$

$$\int_{-\infty}^{\infty} x(t)\left[(-jt)e^{-j\Omega t}\right]dt$$

As, $-j = \frac{1}{j}$

$$\frac{d}{d\Omega}X(j\Omega) = \frac{1}{j}\int_{-\infty}^{\infty}[tx(t)]e^{-j\Omega t}dt$$

$$= \frac{1}{j}\,F\{tx(t)\}$$

$$\therefore F\{tx(t)\} = j\frac{d}{d\Omega}X(j\Omega)$$

3.8.10 Convolution

If $x_1(t)\overrightarrow{\,FT\,}X_1(j\Omega)$

$x_2(t)\overrightarrow{\,FT\,}X_2(j\Omega)$

then,

$F\{x_1(t) * x_2(t)\} = X_1(j\Omega)X_2(j\Omega)$ (3.37)

Proof: By definition of FT,

$$X_1\,(j\Omega) = \int_{-\infty}^{\infty} x_1(t)e^{-j\Omega t}\,dt$$

$$X_2\,(j\Omega) = \int_{-\infty}^{\infty} x_2(t)e^{-j\Omega t}\,dt$$

$$\therefore F\{x_1(t) * x_2(t)\} = \int_{-\infty}^{\infty} [x_1(t) * x_2(t)]e^{-j\Omega t}\, dt$$

$$\int_{-\infty}^{\infty}\left[\int_{-\infty}^{\infty} x_1(\tau) * x_2(t-\tau)d\tau\right]e^{-j\Omega t}\, dt$$

$let\ m = t - \tau,$

$dm = dt,$

$t = m + \tau,$

$e^{j\Omega t} = e^{-j\Omega\tau}e^{-j\Omega m}$

$$\therefore F\{x_1(t) * x_2(t)\} = \int_{-\infty}^{\infty}\int_{-\infty}^{\infty} x_1(\tau)e^{-j\Omega\tau}x_2(m)\, e^{-j\Omega\tau}e^{-j\Omega m}\, d\tau\, dm$$

$$\therefore F\{x_1(t) * x_2(t)\} = \int_{-\infty}^{\infty} x_1(\tau)e^{-j\Omega\tau}d\tau \int_{-\infty}^{\infty} x_2(m)e^{-j\Omega m}\, dm$$

Replace τ *and* m *to* t,

$$\therefore\ F\{x_1(t) * x_2(t)\} = X_1(j\Omega)X_2(j\Omega)$$

3.8.11 Parseval's Theorem:

If $x(t) \overrightarrow{\ FT\ } X(j\,\Omega)$

then,

$\int_{-\infty}^{\infty}|x(t)|^2 dt = \frac{1}{2\pi}\int_{-\infty}^{\infty}|X(j\Omega|^2\, d\Omega$ (3.38)

Proof:

Let $|x(t)|^2 = x(t)x^*(t)dt$ (3.39)

$\therefore\ \int_{-\infty}^{\infty}|x(t)|^2 = \int_{-\infty}^{\infty}x\,(t)x^*(t)dt$ (3.40)

Recall the inverse FT definition,

$x(t) = \frac{1}{2\pi}\int_{-\infty}^{\infty}X(j\,\Omega)e^{j\Omega t}d\Omega$

$\therefore x^*(t) = \frac{1}{2\pi}\int_{-\infty}^{\infty}X^*(j\Omega)e^{-j\Omega t}\, d\Omega$ (3.41)

R.H.S. of Eq. (3.40) becomes,

$$\therefore \int_{-\infty}^{\infty} x(t)\left[\frac{1}{2\pi}\int_{-\infty}^{\infty} X^*(j\Omega)e^{-j\Omega t}d\Omega\right]dt$$

$$\therefore \int_{-\infty}^{\infty} |x(t)|^2\, dt = \frac{1}{2\pi}\int_{-\infty}^{\infty} X^*(j\Omega)\left[\int_{-\infty}^{\infty} x(t)e^{-j\Omega t}dt\right]d\Omega$$

$$= \frac{1}{2\pi}\int_{-\infty}^{\infty} X^*(j\Omega)X(j\Omega)d\Omega$$

$$\int_{-\infty}^{\infty} |x(t)|^2\, dt = \frac{1}{2\pi}\int_{-\infty}^{\infty} |X(j\Omega|^2\, d\Omega$$

3.8.12 Duality Property:

If $x(t) \overrightarrow{\ FT\ } X(j\Omega)$

then,

$X(t) \leftrightarrow 2\pi x(-j\Omega)$ (3.42)

Proof: By definition of IFT,

$$x(t) = \frac{1}{2\pi}\int_{-\infty}^{\infty} X(j\Omega)e^{j\Omega t}d\Omega$$

$x(-t) = \frac{1}{2\pi}\int_{-\infty}^{\infty} X(j\Omega)e^{-j\Omega t}d\Omega$ (3.43)

Put t= jΩ in Eq. (3.43)

$x(-j\Omega) = \frac{1}{2\pi}\int_{-\infty}^{\infty} X(t)e^{-j\Omega t}\ d\Omega$

$$\therefore 2\pi\, x(-j\Omega) = \int_{-\infty}^{\infty} X(t)e^{-j\Omega t}dt$$

Where R.H.S. is FT of $X(t)$.

3.9 Fourier Transform (FT) Representation of Continuous-Time (CT) LTI System in terms of Convolution and Multiplication

3.9.1 Representation of Transfer Function of CT LTI System in Frequency Domain

Transfer function if CT LTI system is defined as the ratio of output of Fourier transform to the input of Fourier transform.

Let $x(t)$=Input of CT system

$y(t)$=Output of CT system

$X(j\Omega)$=FT of $x(t)$

$Y(j\Omega)$=FT of $y(t)$

Then, the transfer funtion (TF) can be written as,

$$TF = \frac{Y(j\Omega)}{X(j\Omega)} \tag{3.44}$$

Frequency domain representation of CT LTI system can be written in terms of differential equation as,

$$\frac{d^n}{dt^n}y(t) + p_1\frac{d^{n-1}}{dt^{n-1}}y(t)+p_2\frac{d^{n-2}}{dt^{n-2}}y(t) + \cdots + p_n y(t) = q_0\frac{d^m}{dt^m}x(t) + q_1\frac{d^{m-1}}{dt^{m-1}}x(t) + q_2\frac{d^{m-2}}{dt^{m-2}}x(t) + \cdots + q_m x(t) \tag{3.45}$$

Transfer function of CT LTI system can be obtained by taking the FT of above equation and arranging as a ration of $Y(j\Omega)$ to $X(j\Omega)$.

3.9.2 Relation of Impulse Response and Transfer Function of CT LTI System

Let $x(t)$ and $y(t)$ are the input and output of CT LTI system respectively. When input $x(t)$ is replaced by impulse signal $\delta(t)$, the system output is called as *impulse response* which is denoted by $h(t)$.

The impulse response is represented as the convolution of input and impulse response itself for any input to LTI system. Let the convolution opertaion,

$$y(t) = x(t) * h(t) = \int_{-\infty}^{\infty} x(\tau)h(t-\tau)d\tau$$

Let,

$H(j\Omega)$=FT of $h(t)$

$X(j\Omega)$=FT of $x(t)$

$Y(j\Omega)$=FT of $y(t)$

Using the convolution property,

$$F\{x(t) * h(t)\} = F\{y(t)\} = X(j\Omega)H(j\Omega)$$

$$\therefore Y(j\Omega) = X(j\Omega)H(j\Omega)$$

$$H(j\Omega) = \frac{Y(j\Omega)}{X(j\Omega)} \qquad (3.46)$$

Equation (3.46) shows that the transfer function in frequency domain is given by Fourier transform of impulse response which is the ratio of Fourier transform of output to input.

3.9.3 Response of CT LTI System in terms of Fourier Trasnform

Consider Eq. (3.46) of transfer function,

$$H(j\Omega) = \frac{Y(j\Omega)}{X(j\Omega)}$$

$$\therefore Y(j\Omega) = X(j\Omega)H(j\Omega)$$

$$\therefore Y(j\Omega) = \frac{(z_1+j\Omega)(z_2+j\Omega)+\cdots}{(p_1+j\Omega)(p_2+j\Omega)+\cdots} \qquad (3.47)$$

Using partial fraction expansion,

$$Y(j\Omega) = \frac{A_1}{(p_1+j\Omega)} + \frac{A_2}{(p_2+j\Omega)} + \frac{A_3}{(p_3+j\Omega)} + \cdots \qquad (3.48)$$

Where $A_1,\ A_2,\ A_3, ..$ are residues.

$$\text{The Fourier transform of } e^{-at} = \frac{1}{a+j\Omega} \qquad (3.49)$$

Using Eq. (3.49), the inverse Fourier transform of Eq. (3.48) can be written as,

$$y(t) = A_1 e^{-p_1 t}u(t) + A_2 e^{-p_2 t}u(t) + A_3 e^{-p_3 t}u(t) + \cdots \qquad (3.50)$$

The response obtained by using Eq. (3.50) is the time domain steady state response of the LTI continuous time system as the transfer function is defined with zero initial conditions.

3.9.4 Magnitude and Phase Response of CT LTI System

The output of LTI system in terms of the convolution opertaion is written as,

$$y(t) = x(t) * h(t) = h(t) * x(t) = \int_{-\infty}^{\infty} h(\tau)x(t-\tau)d\tau$$

Let,

$$x(t) = Ae^{j\Omega t} \qquad (3.51)$$

$$\therefore\ x(t-\tau) = Ae^{j\Omega(t-\tau)} \qquad (3.52)$$

$$y(t) = \int_{-\infty}^{\infty} h(\tau)Ae^{j\Omega(t-\tau)}d\tau \qquad (3.53)$$

$$y(t) = \int_{-\infty}^{\infty} h(\tau) A e^{j\Omega t} e^{-j\Omega\tau} d\tau \qquad (3.54)$$

$$y(t) = A e^{j\Omega t} \int_{-\infty}^{\infty} h(\tau) e^{-j\Omega\tau} d\tau \qquad (3.55)$$

Recall the definition of FT,

$$H(j\Omega) = \int_{-\infty}^{\infty} h(t) e^{-j\Omega t} dt = \int_{-\infty}^{\infty} h(\tau) e^{-j\Omega\tau} d\tau \qquad (3.56)$$

Using Eq. (3.51), (3.56), the Eq. (3.55) can be written as,

$$y(t) = x(t) H(j\Omega) \qquad (3.57)$$

Equation (3.57) says that if a complex signal is given as input signal to CT LTI system, then the output has the same frequency as that of input signal multiplied by $H(j\Omega)$. Hence, $H(j\Omega)$ is called the frequency response of the CT LTI system. The

The $H(j\Omega)$ can be represented in terms of magnitude and phase as,

$$H(j\Omega) = |H(j\Omega)| \angle H(j\Omega)$$

Where,

$$|H(j\Omega)| = Magnitude\ function$$

$$\angle H(j\Omega) = Phase\ function$$

$$H(j\Omega) = H_{real}(j\Omega) + H_{imaginary}(j\Omega)$$

The ***magnitude function*** is written as,

$$|H(j\Omega)| = \sqrt{H^2{}_{real}(j\Omega) + H^2{}_{imaginary}(j\Omega)} \qquad (3.58)$$

The ***phase function*** is written as,

$$\angle H(j\Omega) = tan^{-1}\left[\frac{H_{imaginary}(j\Omega)}{H_{real}(j\Omega)}\right] \qquad (3.59)$$

Solved examples on Fourier transform

Example 3.5 Determine the Fourier transform of given continuous time signals.

1. $x(t) = \begin{cases} 1 - t^2; & \text{for } |t| < 1 \\ 0; & \text{for } |t| > 1 \end{cases}$
2. $x(t) = e^{-at} cos\Omega_0 t\, u(t)$

Solution:

1. Given, $\boldsymbol{x(t) = \begin{cases} 1 - t^2; & \text{for } |t| < 1 \\ 0; & \text{for } |t| > 1 \end{cases}}$

That means

$x(t) = 1 - t^2;$ for t= -1 to +1

Using the definition of FT,

$$X(j\Omega) = \int_{-\infty}^{\infty} x(t)e^{-j\Omega t}\,dt$$

$$X(j\Omega) = \int_{-1}^{+1} (1 - t^2)e^{-j\Omega t}\,dt$$

$$X(j\Omega) = \int_{-1}^{+1} e^{-j\Omega t}\,dt - \int_{-1}^{+1} t^2 e^{-j\Omega t}\,dt$$

$$Using\ integration\ rule, \int uv = u\int v - \int\left[du\int v\right]$$

$$= \left[\frac{e^{-j\Omega t}}{-j\Omega}\right]_{-1}^{+1} - \left[t^2\frac{e^{-j\Omega t}}{-j\Omega} - \int 2t\frac{e^{-j\Omega t}}{-j\Omega}dt\right]_{-1}^{+1}$$

$$= \left[\frac{e^{-j\Omega t}}{-j\Omega}\right]_{-1}^{+1} - \left[\frac{-t^2e^{-j\Omega t}}{j\Omega} + \frac{2}{j\Omega}\int te^{-j\Omega t}dt\right]_{-1}^{+1}$$

$$Again\ using\ integration\ rule, \int uv = u\int v - \int\left[du\int v\right]$$

$$= \left[\frac{e^{-j\Omega t}}{-j\Omega}\right]_{-1}^{+1} - \left[\frac{-t^2e^{-j\Omega t}}{j\Omega} + \frac{2}{j\Omega}\left[\frac{te^{-j\Omega t}}{-j\Omega} - \int 1\frac{e^{-j\Omega t}}{-j\Omega}dt\right]\right]_{-1}^{+1}$$

$$= \left[\frac{e^{-j\Omega t}}{-j\Omega}\right]_{-1}^{+1} - \left[-\frac{t^2e^{-j\Omega t}}{j\Omega} + \frac{2}{(j\Omega)^2}\left[-te^{-j\Omega t} - \int e^{-j\Omega t}dt\right]\right]_{-1}^{+1}$$

$$= \left[-\frac{e^{-j\Omega t}}{j\Omega}\right]_{-1}^{+1} - \left[-\frac{t^2e^{-j\Omega t}}{j\Omega} - \frac{2}{(\Omega)^2}\left[-te^{-j\Omega t} + \frac{e^{-j\Omega t}}{-j\Omega}\right]\right]_{-1}^{+1}$$

$$= \left[-\frac{e^{-j\Omega t}}{j\Omega}\right]_{-1}^{+1} - \left[-\frac{t^2e^{-j\Omega t}}{j\Omega} + \left[\frac{2te^{-j\Omega t}}{\Omega^2} + \frac{2e^{-j\Omega t}}{j\Omega^3}\right]\right]_{-1}^{+1}$$

$$= -\frac{e^{-j\Omega}}{j\Omega} + \frac{e^{j\Omega}}{j\Omega} - \left[-\frac{e^{-j\Omega}}{j\Omega} + \frac{2e^{-j\Omega}}{\Omega^2} + \frac{2e^{-j\Omega}}{j\Omega^3} + \frac{e^{j\Omega}}{j\Omega} + \frac{2e^{j\Omega}}{\Omega^2} - \frac{2e^{j\Omega}}{j\Omega^3}\right]$$

Using, $sin\Omega = \frac{e^{j\Omega} - e^{-j\Omega}}{2j}$ and $cos\Omega = \frac{e^{j\Omega} + e^{-j\Omega}}{2}$

$$= -\frac{2}{\Omega^2}\left(e^{j\Omega} + e^{-j\Omega}\right) + \frac{2}{j\Omega^3}\left(e^{j\Omega} + e^{-j\Omega}\right)$$

$$= -\frac{2}{\Omega^2}2cos\Omega + \frac{2}{j\Omega^3}2jsin\Omega$$

$$= \frac{4}{\Omega^2}\left(\frac{sin\Omega}{\Omega} - cos\Omega\right)$$

2. Given, $x(t) = e^{-at}cos\Omega_0 t\, u(t)$

Given signal can be written as,

$x(t) = e^{-at}cos\Omega_0 t$ for $t \geq 0$

Using the definition of FT,

$$X(j\Omega) = \int_{-\infty}^{\infty} x(t)e^{-j\Omega t}dt$$

$$= \int_0^{\infty} e^{-at}cos\Omega_0 t e^{-j\Omega t}dt = \int_0^{\infty} e^{-at}\left(\frac{e^{j\Omega_0 t}+e^{-j\Omega_0 t}}{2}\right)e^{-j\Omega t}dt$$

$$= \frac{1}{2}\int_0^{\infty} e^{-at}\, e^{j\Omega_0 t}e^{-j\Omega t}dt + \frac{1}{2}\int_0^{\infty} e^{-at}\, e^{-j\Omega_0 t}e^{-j\Omega t}dt$$

$$= \frac{1}{2}\int_0^{\infty} e^{-(a-j\Omega_0+j\Omega)t}\, dt + \frac{1}{2}\int_0^{\infty} e^{-(a+j\Omega_0+j\Omega)t}dt$$

$$= \frac{1}{2}\left[\frac{e^{-(a-j\Omega_0+j\Omega)t}}{-(a-j\Omega_0+j\Omega)}\right]_0^{\infty} + \frac{1}{2}\left[\frac{e^{-(a+j\Omega_0+j\Omega)t}}{-(a+j\Omega_0+j\Omega)}\right]_0^{\infty}$$

$$= \frac{1}{2}\left[\frac{e^{-\infty}}{-(a-j\Omega_0+j\Omega)} - \frac{e^0}{-(a-j\Omega_0+j\Omega)}\right] + \frac{1}{2}\left[\frac{e^{-\infty}}{-(a+j\Omega_0+j\Omega)} - \frac{e^0}{-(a+j\Omega_0+j\Omega)}\right]$$

$$= \frac{1}{2}\left[0 + \frac{1}{(a-j\Omega_0+j\Omega)}\right] + \frac{1}{2}\left[0 + \frac{1}{(a+j\Omega_0+j\Omega)}\right]$$

$$= \frac{1}{2}\left[\frac{1}{(a+j\Omega)-j\Omega_0} + \frac{1}{(a+j\Omega)+j\Omega_0}\right]$$

$$= \frac{1}{2}\left[\frac{(a+j\Omega)+j\Omega_0+(a+j\Omega)-j\Omega_0}{(a+j\Omega)^2+{\Omega_0}^2}\right]$$

$$= \frac{1}{2}\left[\frac{2\,(a+j\Omega)}{(a+j\Omega)^2+{\Omega_0}^2}\right] = \frac{(a+j\Omega)}{(a+j\Omega)^2+{\Omega_0}^2}$$

Example 3.6 Determine the Fourier transform of the rectangular pulse shown in fig 3.10.1.

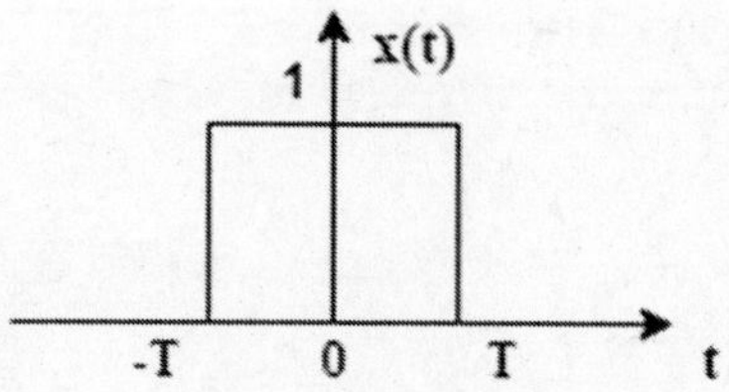

Fig. 3.10.1

Solution:

From fig. 3.10.1, the equation can be written as,

x(t) = 1; for $t = -T \ to + T$

Using the definition of FT,

$$X(j\Omega) = \int_{-\infty}^{\infty} x(t)e^{-j\Omega t}dt$$

$$= \int_{-T}^{+T} 1\, e^{-j\Omega t}dt$$

$$= \left[\frac{e^{-j\Omega t}}{-j\Omega}\right]_{-T}^{+T} = \frac{e^{-j\Omega T}}{-j\Omega} - \frac{e^{j\Omega T}}{-j\Omega} = \frac{1}{j\Omega}(e^{j\Omega T} - e^{-j\Omega T}) = \frac{1}{j\Omega}2jsin\Omega T$$

$$= 2\frac{sin\Omega T}{\Omega} = 2T\frac{sin\Omega T}{\Omega T} = 2Tsinc\Omega T \text{..........as } \frac{sin\theta}{\theta} = sinc\theta$$

Example 3.7 Determine the inverse Fourier transform of the following functions.

1. $X(j\Omega) = \frac{3(j\Omega)+14}{j\Omega^2+7j\Omega+12}$

2. $X(j\Omega) = \frac{j\Omega+7}{(j\Omega+3)^2}$

Solution:

1.Given, $\boldsymbol{X(j\Omega) = \frac{3(j\Omega)+14}{j\Omega^2+7j\Omega+12}}$

$$X(j\Omega) = \frac{3(j\Omega) + 14}{(j\Omega + 3)(j\Omega + 4)}$$

Using partial fraction,

$$X(j\Omega) = \frac{A_1}{(j\Omega + 3)} + \frac{A_2}{(j\Omega + 4)}$$

$$A_1 = \frac{3(j\Omega) + 14}{(j\Omega + 3)(j\Omega + 4)} (j\Omega + 3)\bigg|_{j\Omega=-3} = 5$$

$$A_2 = \frac{3(j\Omega) + 14}{(j\Omega + 3)(j\Omega + 4)} (j\Omega + 4)\bigg|_{j\Omega=-4} = -2$$

$$X(j\Omega) = \frac{5}{(j\Omega+3)} - \frac{2}{(j\Omega+4)} \tag{3.60}$$

Using Fourier transform of $F\{e^{-at}u(t)\} = \frac{1}{j\Omega+a}$

The inverse Fourier transform of Eq. (3.60) can be written as,

$$x(t) = 5e^{-3t}u(t) - 2e^{-4t}u(t)$$

2. **Given,** $\boldsymbol{X(j\Omega)} = \frac{j\Omega+7}{(j\Omega+3)^2}$

Using partial fraction, above function can be written as,

$$X(j\Omega) = \frac{A_1}{(j\Omega + 3)^2} + \frac{A_2}{j\Omega + 3}$$

$$A_1 = \frac{j\Omega + 7}{(j\Omega + 3)^2} (j\Omega + 3)^2\bigg|_{j\Omega=-3} = -3 + 7 = 4$$

Using rule of repeating poles,

$$A_2 = \frac{d}{d(j\Omega)} \left[\frac{j\Omega + 7}{(j\Omega + 3)^2} (j\Omega + 3)^2\right] \bigg|_{j\Omega=-3} = \frac{d}{d(j\Omega)} (j\Omega + 7)\bigg|_{j\Omega=-3} = 1$$

$$X(j\Omega) = \frac{4}{(j\Omega+3)^2} + \frac{1}{j\Omega+3} \tag{3.61}$$

Using Fourier transform of $F\{te^{-at}u(t)\} = \frac{1}{(j\Omega+a)^2}$

The inverse Fourier transform of Eq. (3.61) cann be written as,

$$x(t) = 4te^{-3t}u(t) + e^{-3t}u(t)$$

Example 3.8 Given $X(j\Omega) = 2\pi\delta(\Omega - \Omega_0)$

Determine the time-domain signal $x(t)$.

Solution: The inverse Fourier transform can be found as,

$$x(t) = \frac{1}{2\pi}\int_{-\infty}^{\infty} X(j\Omega)e^{j\Omega t}\,d\Omega$$

Substituting for $X(j\Omega)$, we get

$$x(t) = \frac{1}{2\pi}\int_{-\infty}^{\infty} 2\pi\delta(\Omega - \Omega_0)\,e^{j\Omega t}d\Omega$$

$$x(t) = \int_{-\infty}^{\infty} e^{j\Omega t}\delta(\Omega - \Omega_0)d\Omega$$

Using the Sifting property of impulse,

$$\int_{-\infty}^{\infty} x(t)\delta(t - t_0)\,dt = x(t_0)$$

$$\therefore x(t) = e^{j\Omega t}$$

For this time–domain signal, the Fourier transform given as,

$$e^{j\Omega_0 t} \overset{FT}{\leftrightarrow} 2\pi\delta(\Omega - \Omega_0)$$

Example 3.9 Find the Fourier transform of the periodic signal

$$x(t) = \sin\Omega_0 t$$

Solution: Using Euler's identity, $x(t)$ can be written as

$$x(t) = \frac{e^{j\Omega_0 t} - e^{-j\Omega_0 t}}{2j} = \frac{1}{2j}e^{j\Omega_0 t} - \frac{1}{2j}\,e^{-j\Omega_0 t}$$

The Fourier series coefficients can be identified as,

$$a_1 = \frac{1}{2j},\ a_{-1} = \frac{-1}{2j},$$

Substituting the values, we get the Fourier transform ofsin$\Omega_0 t$ as

$$X(j\Omega) = \frac{\pi}{j}\delta(\Omega - \Omega_0) - \frac{\pi}{j}\delta(\Omega + \Omega_{0)}$$

3.10 Discrete Time Fourier Series representation

A discrete time signal which is periodic with fundamental period N can be decomposed into N harmonics of frequency components (frequency spectrum). When we combine these related frequency components it must give the Fourier series representation of that particular periodic discrete time signal which is a function of angular frequency denoted as ω, . This representation of Fourier series of discrete time signal is called ***Discrete Time Fourier Series (DTFS)***.

3.10.1 Representation of Discrete Time Fourier Series

The Discrete Time Fourier Series, (DTFS) of discrete time periodic signal $x[n]$ with period N is defined as,

$$x[n] = \sum_{k=0}^{N-1} a_k e^{\frac{j2\pi kn}{N}}$$

$$let, \omega_0 \; = \text{Fundamental frequency of } x[n]$$

$$x[n] = \sum_{k=0}^{N-1} a_k e^{j\omega_0 kn}$$

$let, k = k^{th}$ harmonic frequency component of $x[n]$

$$x[n] = \textstyle\sum_{k=0}^{N-1} a_k e^{j\omega_k n} \qquad (3.62)$$

Where, a_k= Fourier coefficients

This coefficient represents the amplitude and phase of the kth frequency component that provides the presentation of $x[n]$ in the Fourier/frequency domain.

These Fourier coefficients a_k can be evaluated using following formula,

$$a_k = \frac{1}{N}\textstyle\sum_{n=0}^{N-1} x[n]e^{\frac{-j2\pi kn}{N}}; \text{ for } k = 0, 1, 2, .. N-1 \qquad (3.63)$$

3.10.2 Properties of DTFS in terms of coefficients

The properties of DTFS coefficients are given in table 3.1 in terms of Fourier coefficients. Let $x[n]$ has Fourier series coefficients a_k and $y[n]$ has Fourier series coefficients b_k.

Table 3.1 : Properties of DTFS in terms of coefficients

Sr. No.	Property name	Discrete periodic signal	FS coefficients
1	Linearity	$Ax[n] + By[n]$	$Aa_k + Bb_k$
2	Time shifting	$x[n - n_0]$	$a_k e^{\frac{j2\pi k n_0}{N}}$
3	Frequency shifting	$x[n]e^{\frac{j2\pi n n_0}{N}}$	a_{k-n_0}
4	Conjugation	$x^*[n]$	a^*_{-k}
5	Time reversal	$x[-n]$	a_{-k}
6	Time scaling	$x\left[\frac{n}{m}\right]$ where n is multiple of m	$\frac{1}{m} a_k$
7	Multiplication	$x[n]y[n]$	$\sum_{m=0}^{N-1} a_m b_{k-m}$
8	Convolution	$\sum_{m=0}^{N-1} x[m]y[n - m]_N$	$Na_k b_k$
9	Symmetry	If $x[n]$ is real	$a_k = a^*_{-k}$ $\lvert a_k\rvert = \lvert a_{-k}\rvert$ $\angle a_k = -\angle a_{-k}$
		If $x[n]$ is real and even	a_k are real and even
		If $x[n]$ is real and odd	a_k are imaginary and odd
10	Parseval's theorem	$P = \frac{1}{N}\sum_{n=0}^{N-1} \lvert x[n]\rvert^2$	$P = \sum_{k=0}^{N-1} \lvert a_k\rvert^2$

Solved examples on DTFS

Example 3.6 Determine the DTFS representation of the following signals.

1. $x[n] = 4cos\sqrt{5}\pi n$
2. $x[n] = 8cos\frac{\pi n}{4}$

Solution:

1. **Given, $x[n] = 4cos\sqrt{5}\pi n$**

Let us check for the periodicity,

$$x[n+N] = 4cos\sqrt{5}\pi[n+N] = 4\cos[\sqrt{5}\pi n + \sqrt{5}\pi N]$$

For periodicity $\sqrt{5}\pi n$ should be equal to integral multiple of 2π.

Let $\sqrt{5}\pi N = M \times 2\pi$; where M and N are integers $\xrightarrow{yields} N = \frac{2}{\sqrt{5}}M$

Here N cannot be an integer for any integer value of M and so $x[n]$ will not be periodic and for nonperiodic signal FS does not exists.

2. **Given, $x[n] = 8cos\frac{\pi n}{4}$**

Let us check for the periodicity,

$$x[n+N] = 8cos\frac{\pi[n+N]}{4} = 8\cos[\frac{\pi n}{4} + \frac{\pi N}{4}]$$

For periodicity $\frac{\pi n}{4}$ should be equal to integral multiple of 2π.

Let $\frac{\pi N}{4} = M \times 2\pi$; where M and N are integers $\xrightarrow{yields} N = 8M$

Here N is an integer for M = 1, 2, 3, ...

Let M = 1, \ N = 8

So $x[n]$ will be periodic with fundamental period 8 and fundamental frequency

$$\omega_0 = \frac{2\pi}{N} = \frac{2\pi}{8} = \frac{\pi}{4}.$$

Now go for the Fourier series expansion,

The Fourier coefficient a_k is given by,

$a_k = \frac{1}{N}\sum_{n=0}^{N-1} x[n]e^{\frac{-j2\pi kn}{N}}$; for $k = 0, 1, 2, ..N-1$

Here, N=8 and $x[n] = 8cos\frac{\pi n}{4}$

$a_k = \frac{1}{8}\sum_{n=0}^{7} 8cos\frac{\pi n}{4}e^{\frac{-j2\pi kn}{8}}$; for $k = 0, 1, 2, 3, 4, 5, 6, 7$

$$= \frac{8}{8}\sum_{n=0}^{7} cos\frac{\pi n}{4}e^{\frac{-j\pi kn}{4}} = \sum_{n=0}^{7} cos\frac{\pi n}{4}\left(cos\frac{\pi kn}{4} - jsin\frac{\pi kn}{4}\right)$$

$$= cos0(cos0 - jsin0) + cos\frac{\pi}{4}\left(cos\frac{\pi k}{4} - jsin\frac{\pi k}{4}\right) + cos\frac{\pi}{2}\left(cos\frac{\pi k}{2} - jsin\frac{\pi k}{2}\right)$$
$$+ cos\frac{3\pi}{4}\left(cos\frac{3\pi k}{4} - jsin\frac{3\pi k}{4}\right) + cos\pi(cos\pi k - jsin\pi k)$$
$$+ cos\frac{5\pi}{4}\left(cos\frac{5\pi k}{4} - jsin\frac{5\pi k}{4}\right) + cos\frac{3\pi}{2}\left(cos\frac{3\pi k}{2} - jsin\frac{3\pi k}{2}\right)$$
$$+ cos\frac{7\pi}{4}\left(cos\frac{7\pi k}{4} - jsin\frac{7\pi k}{4}\right)$$

As, $cos0 = 1, cos\pi = -1, cos\frac{\pi}{4} = sin\frac{\pi}{4} = sin\frac{3\pi}{4} = \frac{\sqrt{2}}{2}, cos\frac{3\pi}{4} = -\frac{\sqrt{2}}{2}, cos\frac{\pi}{2} = 0, sin\frac{\pi}{2} = 1, sin\pi = 0, cos\frac{5\pi}{4} = sin\frac{5\pi}{4} = -\frac{\sqrt{2}}{2}, cos\frac{3\pi}{2} = 0, sin\frac{3\pi}{2} = -1, cos\frac{7\pi}{4} = \frac{\sqrt{2}}{2}, sin\frac{7\pi}{4} = -\frac{\sqrt{2}}{2}$

$$a_k = 1 + \frac{\sqrt{2}}{2}\left(\frac{\sqrt{2}}{2}k - j\frac{\sqrt{2}}{2}k\right) - \frac{\sqrt{2}}{2}\left(-\frac{\sqrt{2}}{2}k - j\frac{\sqrt{2}}{2}k\right) + k - \frac{\sqrt{2}}{2}\left(-\frac{\sqrt{2}}{2}k + j\frac{\sqrt{2}}{2}k\right)$$
$$+ \frac{\sqrt{2}}{2}\left(\frac{\sqrt{2}}{2}k + j\,\frac{\sqrt{2}}{2}k\right)$$

$$a_k = 1 + \frac{2}{4}k + \frac{2}{4}k + k + \frac{2}{4}k + \frac{2}{4}k$$

When k=0, $a_k = a_0 = 1$

When k=1, $a_k = a_1 = 1 + \frac{2}{4} + \frac{2}{4} + 1 + \frac{2}{4} + \frac{2}{4} = 4$

When k=2, $a_k = a_2 = 1 + 1 + 1 + 2 + 1 + 1 = 7$

When k=3, $a_k = a_3 = 1 + \frac{6}{4} + \frac{6}{4} + 3 + \frac{6}{4} + \frac{6}{4} = 10$

When k=4, $a_k = a_4 = 1 + 2 + 2 + 4 + 2 + 2 = 13$

When k=5, $a_k = a_5 = 1 + \frac{5}{2} + \frac{5}{2} + 5 + \frac{5}{2} + \frac{5}{2} = 16$

When k=6, $a_k = a_6 = 1 + 3 + 3 + 6 + 3 + 3 = 19$

When k=7, $a_k = a_7 = 1 + \frac{7}{2} + \frac{7}{2} + 7 + \frac{7}{2} + \frac{7}{2} = 22$

The Fourier series representation of $x[n]$ is,

$$x[n] = \sum_{k=0}^{N-1} a_k e^{\frac{j2\pi kn}{N}} = \sum_{k=0}^{7} a_k e^{\frac{j2\pi kn}{8}} = \sum_{k=0}^{7} a_k e^{\frac{j\pi kn}{4}}$$

$$= a_0 + a_1 e^{\frac{j\pi n}{4}} + a_2 e^{\frac{j\pi n}{2}} + a_3 e^{\frac{j3\pi n}{4}} + a_4 e^{j\pi n} + a_5 e^{\frac{j5\pi n}{4}} + a_6 e^{\frac{j3\pi n}{2}} + a_7 e^{\frac{j7\pi n}{4}}$$

$$x[n] = 1 + 4e^{\frac{j\pi n}{4}} + 7e^{\frac{j\pi n}{2}} + 10e^{\frac{j3\pi n}{4}} + 13e^{j\pi n} + 16e^{\frac{j5\pi n}{4}} + 19e^{\frac{j3\pi n}{2}} + 22e^{\frac{j7\pi n}{4}}$$

3.11 Discrete Time Fourier Transform (DTFT) Representation

3.11.1 Definition of DTFT

The Fourier transform (FT) of discrete-time signals is called Discrete Time Fourier Transform (DTFT).

Let, $x[n]$=Finite energy discrete time signal

$X[e^{j\omega}]$=Discrete time Fourier transform of signal $x[n]$

$$X[e^{j\omega}] = F\{x[n]\} = \sum_{n=-\infty}^{+\infty} x[n]e^{-j\omega n} \quad (3.64)$$

The discrete time Fourier transform exists only for the absolutely summable signals. That means the Fourier transform exists for the signal $x[n]$ if,

$$\sum_{n=-\infty}^{+\infty} |x[n]| < \infty$$

3.11.2 Definition of Inverse DTFT

Let, $x[n]$=Finite energy discrete time signal

$X[e^{j\omega}]$=Discrete time Fourier transform of signal $x[n]$

The inverse Fourier transform (IFT) of discrete-time signal is written as,

$$x[n] = F^{-1}\{X[e^{j\omega}]\} = \frac{1}{2\pi}\int_{-\pi}^{\pi} X[e^{j\omega}]e^{j\omega n}d\omega \quad (3.65)$$

As $X[e^{j\omega}]$ is periodic with period 2π, the limits of integral can be either from "$-\pi$ to $+\pi$ ", or from "0 to 2 π ", or any interval of 2π.

3.12 Properties of DTFT

3.12.1 Linearity

If $x_1[n] \overrightarrow{FT} X_1[e^{j\omega}]$,

$x_2[n] \overrightarrow{FT} X_2[e^{j\omega}]$

Then,

$$F\{a_1x_1[n] + a_2x_1[n]\} = a_1 X_1[e^{j\omega}] + a_2 X_2[e^{j\omega}] \quad (3.66)$$

Proof: By definition of FT,

$$X[e^{j\omega}] = F\{x[n]\} = \sum_{n=-\infty}^{+\infty} x[n]e^{-j\omega n}$$

$$\therefore\ X_1[e^{j\omega}] = \sum_{n=-\infty}^{+\infty} x_1[n]\, e^{-j\omega n}$$

$$\therefore\ X_2[e^{j\omega}] = \sum_{n=-\infty}^{+\infty} x_2[n]\, e^{-j\omega n}$$

Consider linear combination, $a_1x_1[n] + a_2x_1[n]$

$\therefore\ F\{a_1x_1[n] + a_2x_1[n]\} = \sum_{n=-\infty}^{+\infty}(a_1x_1[n] + a_2x_1[n])e^{-j\omega n}$

$= \sum_{n=-\infty}^{+\infty}[a_1x_1[n]e^{-j\omega n} + a_2x_1[n]e^{-j\omega n}]$

$= a_1\sum_{n=-\infty}^{+\infty} x_1[n]e^{-j\omega n} + a_2\sum_{n=-\infty}^{+\infty} x_1[n]e^{-j\omega n}$

$= a_1\, X_1[e^{j\omega}] + a_2\, X_2[e^{j\omega}]$

3.12.2 Time Shifting:

If $x[n] \xrightarrow{FT} X[e^{j\omega}]$,

Then,

$F\{x[n-n_0]\} = X[e^{j\omega}]\, e^{-j\omega n_0}$ (3.67)

Proof: By definition of FT,

$$X[e^{j\omega}] = F\{x[n]\} = \sum_{n=-\infty}^{+\infty} x[n]e^{-j\omega n}$$

$\therefore F\{x[n-n_0]\} = \sum_{n=-\infty}^{+\infty} x[n-n_0]e^{-j\omega n}$

Let $n - n_0 = m,\quad \therefore n = m + n_0$

$$\therefore F\{x[n-n_0]\} = \sum_{m=-\infty}^{+\infty} x[m]e^{-j\omega(m+n_0)}$$

$$= \sum_{m=-\infty}^{+\infty} x[m]e^{-j\omega m}e^{-j\omega n_0}$$

$$= e^{-j\omega n_0}\sum_{m=-\infty}^{+\infty} x[m]e^{-j\omega m}$$

Replace m by n

$$= X[e^{j\omega}]\, e^{-j\omega n_0}$$

3.12.3 Periodicity

If $x[n] \overrightarrow{FT} X[e^{j\omega}]$, then $X[e^{j\omega}]$ is periodic with period 2π

$$\therefore X\left[e^{j\omega}\right] = X\left[e^{j(\omega+2\pi k}\right] \qquad (3.68)$$

Where k is an integer.

3.12.4 Time Reversal:

If $x[n] \overrightarrow{FT} X[e^{j\omega}]$, then,

$$F\{x[-n]\} = X[e^{-j\omega}] \qquad (3.69)$$

If a signal is folded about the origin in discrete time, its magnitude spectrum does not change and the phase spectrum changes in sign i.e., phase reversal happens.

Proof:

By definition of FT,

$$X\left[e^{j\omega}\right] = F\{x[n]\} = \sum_{n=-\infty}^{+\infty} x[n]e^{-j\omega n}$$

$$\therefore F\{x[-n]\} = \sum_{n=-\infty}^{+\infty} x[-n]e^{-j\omega n}$$

Let $-n = m$, $\quad \therefore when\, n \to -\infty,\ m \to +\infty\ and\ when\, n \to +\infty,\ m \to -\infty$

$$\therefore F\{x[-n]\} = \sum_{m=-\infty}^{+\infty} x[m]e^{j\omega m}$$

$$F\{x[-n]\} = \sum_{m=-\infty}^{+\infty} x[m]e^{(-j\omega)-m}$$

$$F\{x[-n]\} = X[e^{-j\omega}]$$

3.12.5 Conjugation:

If $x[n] \overrightarrow{FT} X[e^{j\omega}]$, then

$$F\{x^*[n]\} = X^*[e^{-j\omega}] \qquad (3.70)$$

Proof: By definition of FT,

$$X\left[e^{j\omega}\right] = F\{x[n]\} = \sum_{n=-\infty}^{+\infty} x[n]e^{-j\omega n}$$

$$F\{x^*[n]\} = \sum_{n=-\infty}^{+\infty} x^*[n]e^{-j\omega n}$$

$$= \left[\sum_{n=-\infty}^{+\infty} x[n]e^{(-j\omega)-n}\right]^*$$

$$= \left[X\left[e^{-j\omega}\right]\right]^*$$

$$= X^*[e^{-j\omega}]$$

3.12.6 *Frequency Shifting:*

If $x[n] \overrightarrow{FT} X[e^{j\omega}]$, then

$$F\left\{e^{j\omega_0 n}x[n]\right\} = X[e^{j(\omega-\omega_0)}] \tag{3.71}$$

Proof: By definition of FT,

$$X\left[e^{j\omega}\right] = F\{x[n]\} = \sum_{n=-\infty}^{+\infty} x[n]e^{-j\omega n}$$

$$F\left\{e^{j\omega_0 n}x[n]\right\} = \sum_{n=-\infty}^{+\infty} e^{j\omega_0 n}x[n]e^{-j\omega n}$$

$$= \sum_{n=-\infty}^{+\infty} x[n]e^{-j(\omega-\omega_0)n}$$

$$= X[e^{j(\omega-\omega_0)}]$$

3.12.7 *Differentiation in Frequency*

If $x[n] \overrightarrow{FT} X[e^{j\omega}]$, then

$$F\{n\, x[n]\} = j\frac{d}{d\omega}X[e^{j\omega}] \tag{3.72}$$

Proof: By definition of FT,

$$X\left[e^{j\omega}\right] = F\{x[n]\} = \sum_{n=-\infty}^{+\infty} x[n]e^{-j\omega n}$$

$$F\{nx[n]\} = \sum_{n=-\infty}^{+\infty} nx[n]e^{-j\omega n}$$

$$F\{nx[n]\} = \sum_{n=-\infty}^{+\infty} nx[n]j(-j)e^{-j\omega n}$$

$$= j\sum_{n=-\infty}^{+\infty} x[n](-jn)e^{-j\omega n}$$

As, $(-jn)e^{-j\omega n} = \frac{d}{d\omega}e^{-j\omega n}$

$$= j\sum_{n=-\infty}^{+\infty} x[n]\frac{d}{d\omega}e^{-j\omega n}$$

$$= j\frac{d}{d\omega}\sum_{n=-\infty}^{+\infty} x[n]e^{-j\omega n}$$

$$= j\frac{d}{d\omega}X[e^{j\omega}]$$

3.12.8 Convolution

If $x_1[n] \overrightarrow{FT} X_1[e^{j\omega}]$

$x_2[n] \overrightarrow{FT} X_2[e^{j\omega}]$ then,

$$F\{x_1[n] * x_2[n]\} = X_1[e^{j\omega}]X_2[e^{j\omega}] \tag{3.73}$$

Proof: By definition of FT,

$$X\left[e^{j\omega}\right] = F\{x[n]\} = \sum_{n=-\infty}^{+\infty} x[n]e^{-j\omega n}$$

$$\therefore\ X_1\left[e^{j\omega}\right] = \sum_{n=-\infty}^{+\infty} x_1[n]\, e^{-j\omega n}$$

$$\therefore\ X_2\left[e^{j\omega}\right] = \sum_{n=-\infty}^{+\infty} x_2[n]\, e^{-j\omega n}$$

$$\therefore F\{x_1[n] * x_2[n]\} = \sum_{n=-\infty}^{+\infty} (x_1[n] * x_2[n])\, e^{-j\omega n}$$

Using convolution formula,

$$F\{x_1[n] * x_2[n]\} = \sum_{n=-\infty}^{+\infty} \left[\sum_{k=-\infty}^{+\infty} (x_1[k] * x_2[n-k]) \right] e^{-j\omega n}$$

$$= \sum_{n=-\infty}^{+\infty} \sum_{k=-\infty}^{+\infty} (x_1[k] * x_2[n-k])\, e^{-j\omega n} e^{-j\omega k} e^{j\omega k}$$

$$= \sum_{k=-\infty}^{+\infty} x_1[k]\, e^{-j\omega k} \sum_{n=-\infty}^{+\infty} x_2[n-k]\, e^{-j\omega(n-k)}$$

Let, n-k=m

$$= \sum_{k=-\infty}^{+\infty} x_1[k]\, e^{-j\omega k} \sum_{m=-\infty}^{+\infty} x_2[m]\, e^{-j\omega m}$$

Replace k *and* m *to* n,

$$\therefore F\{x_1[n] * x_2[n]\} = X_1[e^{j\omega}] X_2[e^{j\omega}]$$

3.12.9 Parseval's Theorem:

If $x_1[n] \overrightarrow{FT} X_1[e^{j\omega}]$

$x_2[n] \overrightarrow{FT} X_2[e^{j\omega}]$ then, Parseval's relation says that,

$$\sum_{n=-\infty}^{+\infty} (x_1[n] * x_2[n]) = \frac{1}{2\pi j} \int_{-\pi}^{\pi} \left| X[e^{j\omega}] \right|^2 d\omega \qquad (3.74)$$

Proof: By definition of FT,

$$X\left[e^{j\omega}\right] = F\{x[n]\} = \sum_{n=-\infty}^{+\infty} x[n] e^{-j\omega n}$$

Using inverse FT

$$x[n] = \frac{1}{2\pi j} \int_{-\pi}^{\pi} X[e^{j\omega}]\, e^{j\omega n} d\omega$$

Using R.H.S of Eq. (3.74),

$$\frac{1}{2\pi j}\int_{-\pi}^{\pi}\left|X[e^{j\omega}]\right|^2 d\omega = \frac{1}{2\pi j}\int_{-\pi}^{\pi} X_1[e^{j\omega}]X_2{}^*[e^{j\omega}]d\omega$$

$$= \frac{1}{2\pi j}\int_{-\pi}^{\pi}\left[\sum_{n=-\infty}^{+\infty} x_1[n]e^{-j\omega n}\right]X_2{}^*[e^{j\omega}]d\omega$$

$$= \sum_{n=-\infty}^{+\infty} x_1[n]\left[\frac{1}{2\pi j}\int_{-\pi}^{\pi} X^*[e^{j\omega}]e^{-j\omega n}d\omega\right]$$

$$=\sum_{n=-\infty}^{+\infty}(x_1[n] * x_2[n])$$

3.13 Discrete Fourier Transform (DFT) Representation

The above discrete time Fourier transform (DTFT) concept provides analysis for a discrete time signal in frequency domain where it is a continuous function of ω and so it cannot be processed by digital system. Hence, we have to represent this ω into a discrete function of ω, so that frequency analysis of discrete time signals can be presented using digital system.

Basically, the DFT of a discrete time signal is obtained by sampling the DTFT of the signal at uniform frequency intervals. These samples must be sufficient to avoid aliasing effect. DFT is represented as a sequence of complex numbers represented as $X(k)$ for k = 0, 1, 2, 3, …. The magnitude and phase of each sample of $X(k)$ can also be computed.

The plot of *magnitude* versus k is called ***magnitude spectrum*** and the plot of *phase* versus k is called ***phase spectrum (frequency spectrum).***

3.13.1 Definition of DFT

Let $X[e^{j\omega}]$ be DTFT of the discrete time signal $x[n]$. The discrete Fourier transform (DFT) $x[n]$is calculated by sampling one period of the DTFT $X[e^{j\omega}]$ at a finite number of frequency points.

Let one period consists of N equally spaced points, $0 \leq \omega \leq 2\pi$.

Each frequency point is represented by ratio,

$$\omega_k = \frac{2\pi k}{N}; \quad \text{for } k = 0, 1, 2 \ldots N-1$$

Hence, the sampling of DTFT at frequency points is written as,

$$X[k] = X[e^{j\omega}]\Big|_{\omega_k=\frac{2\pi k}{N}}; \quad \text{for } k = 0, 1, 2 \ldots N-1 \tag{3.75}$$

DFT is also called as N point DFT, where the number of samples N for a finite duration sequence x[n] of length L should be such that, N ≥ L, in order to avoid aliasing.

Let, $x[n]$ = Discrete time signal having length as L

$X[k]$= DFT of $x[n]$

Hence, n-point DFT of $x[n]$ is defined as,

$X[k] = \sum_{n=0}^{N-1} x[n] e^{-\frac{j2\pi kn}{N}}$; for $k = 0, 1, 2 \ldots N-1$ (3.76)

3.13.2 Definition of Inverse DFT

Let, $x[n]$ = Discrete time signal having length as L

$X[k]$= N-point DFT of $x[n]$

Hence, inverse DFT of $X[k]$ is defined as,

$x[n] = \frac{1}{N} \sum_{k=0}^{N-1} X[k] e^{\frac{j2\pi kn}{N}}$; for $n = 0, 1, 2 \ldots N-1$ (3.77)

The relation between DTF and inverse DFT is expressed as,

$$x[n] \quad \overleftrightarrow{DFT, IDFT} \quad X[k]$$

3.14 Properties of DFT

3.14.1 Linearity

If $x_1[n] \overrightarrow{DFT} X_1[k]$,

$x_2[n] \overrightarrow{DFT} X_2[k]$

Then,

$DFt\{a_1 x_1[n] + a_2 x_1[n]\} = a_1 X_1[k] + a_2 X_2[k]$ (3.78)

Proof: By definition of FT,

$$X[k] = DFT\{x[n]\} = \sum_{n=0}^{N-1} x[n] e^{\frac{-j2\pi kn}{N}}$$

$$\therefore X_1[k] = \sum_{n=0}^{N-1} x_1[n]\, e^{\frac{-j2\pi kn}{N}}$$

$$\therefore X_2[k] = \sum_{n=0}^{N-1} x_2[n]\, e^{\frac{-j2\pi kn}{N}}$$

Consider linear combination, $a_1 x_1[n] + a_2 x_1[n]$

$\therefore DFT\{a_1 x_1[n] + a_2 x_1[n]\} = \sum_{n=0}^{N-1} (a_1 x_1[n] + a_2 x_1[n]) e^{\frac{-j2\pi kn}{N}}$

$= \sum_{n=0}^{N-1} [a_1 x_1[n] e^{\frac{-j2\pi kn}{N}} + a_2 x_1[n] e^{\frac{-j2\pi kn}{N}}]$

$$= a_1 \sum_{n=0}^{N-1} x_1[n] e^{\frac{-j2\pi kn}{N}} + a_2 \sum_{n=0}^{N-1} x_1[n] e^{\frac{-j2\pi kn}{N}}$$

$$= a_1 X_1[k] + a_2 X_2[k]$$

3.14.2 Circular Time Shifting:

If $x[n] \xrightarrow{DFT} X[k]$,

Then,

$$DFT\{x[(n-m)_N]\} = X[k]\, e^{\frac{-j2\pi km}{N}} \quad (3.79)$$

Proof: By definition of DFT,

$$X[k] = DFT\{x[n]\} = \sum_{n=0}^{N-1} x[n] e^{\frac{-j2\pi km}{N}}$$

$$\therefore DFT\{x[(n-m)_N]\} = \sum_{n=0}^{N-1} x[(n-m)_N] e^{\frac{-j2\pi kn}{N}}$$

Let $n - m = p, \quad \therefore n = p + m$

$$\therefore DFT\{x[n-n_0]\} = \sum_{n=0}^{N-1} x[(n-m)_N] e^{\frac{-j2\pi k(p+m)}{N}}$$

$$= \sum_{p=0}^{N-1} x[(p)_N] e^{\frac{-j2\pi k(p+m)}{N}}$$

$$= e^{\frac{-j2\pi km}{N}} \sum_{p=0}^{N-1} x[p] e^{\frac{-j2\pi kp}{N}}$$

Replace p by n

$$= X[k]\, e^{\frac{-j2\pi km}{N}}$$

3.14.3 Periodicity

If $x[n] \xrightarrow{DFT} X[k]$, i. e., If a sequence $x[n]$ is periodic with periodicity of N samples then N-point DFT, X(k) is also periodic with periodicity of N samples.

Hence, if $x[n]$ and $X[k]$ are N point DFT pair then,

$$X[n + N] = x[n] \text{ ; for all } n \quad (3.80)$$

$$X[k + N] = X[k] \text{ ; for all } k \quad (3.81)$$

Proof: By definition of DFT,

$$X[k] = DFT\{x[n]\} = \sum_{n=0}^{N-1} x[n]e^{\frac{-j2\pi km}{N}}$$

$$\therefore X[k+N] = \sum_{n=0}^{N-1} x[n]e^{\frac{-j2\pi n(k+N)}{N}}$$

$$= \sum_{n=0}^{N-1} x[n]e^{\frac{-j2\pi nk}{N}}e^{\frac{-j2\pi nN}{N}}$$

$$= \sum_{n=0}^{N-1} x[n]e^{\frac{-j2\pi nk}{N}}e^{-j2\pi n}$$

$$= \sum_{n=0}^{N-1} x[n]e^{\frac{-j2\pi nk}{N}}$$

$$\therefore X[k+N] = X[k]$$

3.14.4 Time Reversal:

If $x[n] \overrightarrow{DFT} X[k]$, then,

$$DFT\{x[N-n]\} = X[N-k] \tag{3.82}$$

If a signal is folded about the origin in discrete time, its magnitude spectrum does not changes and the phase spectrum changes in sign i.e., phase reversal happens.

Proof:

By definition of DFT,

$$X[k] = F\{x[N-n]\} = \sum_{n=0}^{N-1} x[N-n]e^{\frac{-j2\pi kn}{N}}$$

Let, $N - n = m, \therefore n = N - m$

$$= \sum_{m=0}^{N-1} x[m]e^{\frac{-j2\pi k(N-m)}{N}}$$

$$= \sum_{m=0}^{N-1} x[m]e^{\frac{-j2\pi m(N-k)}{N}}$$

$$= X[N-k]$$

3.14.5 Conjugation:

If $x[n] \overrightarrow{DFT} X[k]$, then

$$DFT\{x^*[n]\} = X^*[N-k] \tag{3.83}$$

Proof: By definition of DFT,

$$DFT\{x^*[n]\} = \sum_{n=0}^{N-1} x^*[n]e^{\frac{-j2\pi kn}{N}}$$

$$= \left[\sum_{n=0}^{N-1} x[n]e^{\frac{j2\pi kn}{N}}\right]^*$$

$$= \left[\sum_{n=0}^{N-1} x[n]e^{\frac{j2\pi kn}{N}} e^{-j2\pi}\right]^* \quad \text{As, } e^{-j2\pi} = 1$$

$$= \left[\sum_{n=0}^{N-1} x[n]e^{\frac{-j2\pi k(N-n)}{N}}\right]^*$$

$$= X^*[N-k]$$

3.14.6 Circular Frequency Shifting:

If $x[n] \overrightarrow{DFT} X[k]$, then

$$DFT\left\{e^{\frac{j2\pi mn}{N}} x[n]\right\} = X[(k-m)_N] \tag{3.84}$$

Proof: By definition of FT,

$$X[k] = F\left\{e^{\frac{j2\pi mn}{N}} x[n]\right\} = \sum_{n=0}^{N-1} e^{\frac{j2\pi mn}{N}} x[n]e^{\frac{-j2\pi kn}{N}}$$

$$= \sum_{n=0}^{N-1} x[n]e^{\frac{-j2\pi(k-m)n}{N}}$$

$$= X[(k-m)_N]$$

3.14.7 Multiplication

If $x_1[n] \overrightarrow{DFT} X_1[k]$,

$x_2[n] \overrightarrow{DFT} X_2[k]$

Then,

$$DFT\{x_1[n]x_1[n]\} = \frac{1}{N}\,[X_1[k] \circledast X_2[k]] \qquad (3.85)$$

Proof: By definition of FT,

$$X[k] = DFT\{x[n]\} = \sum_{n=0}^{N-1} x[n]e^{\frac{-j2\pi kn}{N}}$$

$$DFT\{x_1[n]x_1[n]\} = \sum_{n=0}^{N-1} x_1[n]x_2[n]e^{\frac{-j2\pi kn}{N}}$$

$$= \sum_{n=0}^{N-1}\left[\frac{1}{N}\sum_{m=0}^{N-1} X_1[m]e^{\frac{j2\pi mn}{N}}\right]x_2[n]e^{\frac{-j2\pi kn}{N}}$$

$$= \frac{1}{N}\sum_{m=0}^{N-1} X_1[m]\left[\sum_{n=0}^{N-1} x_2[n]e^{\frac{-j2\pi kn}{N}}e^{\frac{j2\pi mn}{N}}\right]$$

$$= \frac{1}{N}\sum_{m=0}^{N-1} X_1[m]\left[\sum_{n=0}^{N-1} x_2[n]e^{\frac{-j2\pi(-(m-k))n}{N}}\right]$$

$$= \frac{1}{N}\sum_{m=0}^{N-1} X_1[m]X_2[(m-k)]_N$$

$$= \frac{1}{N}\,[X_1[k] \circledast X_2[k]]$$

3.14.8 Convolution

If $x_1[n]\overrightarrow{DFT}\ X_1[k]$,

$x_2[n]\overrightarrow{DFT}\ X_2[k]$

Then,

$$DFT\{x_1[n] \circledast x_1[n]\} = X_1[k]\,X_2[k] \qquad (3.86)$$

Proof: By definition of FT,

$$X[k] = DFT\{x[n]\} = \sum_{n=0}^{N-1} x[n]e^{\frac{-j2\pi kn}{N}}$$

$$\therefore X_1[k] = \sum_{n=0}^{N-1} x_1[n] e^{\frac{-j2\pi kn}{N}}$$

$$\therefore X_2[k] = \sum_{n=0}^{N-1} x_2[n] e^{\frac{-j2\pi kn}{N}}$$

Considering the product of $X_1[k]$ and $X_2[k]$ and taking inverse DFT of the product the convolution property ccan be proved.

Hence,

$$X_1[k]\, X_2[k] = DFT\{x_1[n] \circledast x_1[n]\}$$

3.14.9 Parseval's Theorem:

If $x_1[n] \overrightarrow{DFT}\ X_1[k]$,

$x_2[n] \overrightarrow{DFT}\ X_2[k]$

then, Parseval's relation says that,

$$\sum_{n=0}^{N-1} x_1[n]\ x^*{}_2[n] = \frac{1}{N} \sum_{k=0}^{N-1} X_1[k]\ X^*{}_2[k] \tag{3.87}$$

Unit Summary

Fourier series and Fourier transform are fundamental tools in signal processing, mathematics, physics, and engineering. They are used to analyze and represent periodic and non-periodic functions in terms of sinusoidal or complex exponential functions. Fourier series decomposes a periodic function into a sum of sinusoidal functions (sine and cosine). It's applicable to functions with periodicity, allowing representation in terms of a discrete set of harmonics. The series comprises a constant term (DC component) and an infinite sum of harmonic terms, each with its own amplitude and phase. Fourier transform extends the concept of Fourier series to non-periodic functions or signals. It transforms a function from the time or spatial domain into the frequency domain. It decomposes a function into its constituent frequencies, represented by a continuous spectrum. Fourier series and Fourier transform are indispensable tools in various fields for analyzing, synthesizing, and processing signals and functions. Understanding these concepts facilitates advanced analysis and manipulation of signals in diverse applications.

Exercises

1. Find the Fourier series coefficients for the signals shown in figure.

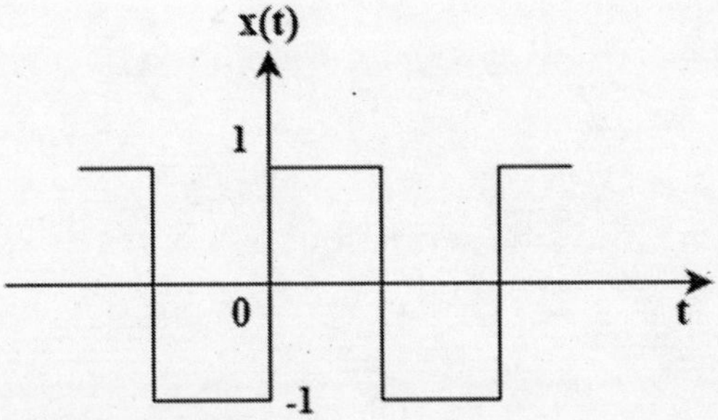

2. Find the inverse CTFT of the following:

a. $X(j\Omega) = \frac{4+j\Omega}{13-\Omega^2-4j\Omega}$

b. $X(j\Omega) = \frac{e^{-j\Omega}}{1+j\Omega}$

c. $X(j\Omega) = \frac{2+j\Omega}{6-\Omega^2+7j\Omega}$

3. Find the output $y(t)$ of an LTI system for an input $x(t) = e^{-2t}u(t) + e^{-5t}u(-t)$ and impulse response $h(t) = e^{-t}u(t)$ by using CTFT.

4. Given the FT of $x(t)$ as,

$$X(j\Omega) = \frac{2 + j\Omega}{(j\Omega)^2 + 6j\Omega + 31}$$

Find the transform for the following signals by using properties of CTFT:

a. $x\left(\frac{t}{6}\right) + x(6t)$

b. $x(-3t + 1)$

c. $\frac{d}{dt}x(t)$

d. $tx(t)$

5. Find the convolution of following signals using CTFT:

$x(t) = te^{-4t}u(t), \quad h(t) = te^{-2t}u(t)$

6. If the function $y = x$ in the range 0 to π is expanded as a sine series, show that it is equal to

$$2\left(\frac{\sin x}{1} - \frac{\sin 2x}{2} + \frac{\sin 3x}{3} + \cdots \dots \dots\right)$$

7. Expand $\frac{\pi x}{8}$ $(\pi - x)$ in a sine series valid when

$$0 \le x \le \pi$$

8. Find a sine series for

$$f(x) = x; \quad 0 < x < \frac{\pi}{2}$$

$= 0; \ \frac{\pi}{2} < x < \pi$

9. Show that in the range $(0, \pi)$, the sine series for $\pi x - x^2$ is $\frac{8}{\pi}\left(\sin x + \frac{1}{3^3}\sin 3x + \frac{1}{5^3}\sin 5x + \cdots\right)$

10. Find a Fourier cosine series corresponding to the function $f(x) = x$, defined in the interval $(0,\pi)$.

11. Find the Fourier sine series and the Fourier cosine series corresponding to the function ,

$$f(x) = \pi - x \text{ when } 0 < x < \pi$$

Defined in the interval 0 to π.

12. A function $f(t)$ can be expressed as a sum of an odd part and even part:
$f(t) = f_e(t) + f_0(t)$

Show that Re $[F(\omega)]$ is the transform of $f_e(t)$
$j\text{Im}[F(\omega)]$ is the transform of $f_0(t)$

13. Find the N-point Discrete Fourier Transform (DFT) of

$h(n) = \frac{1}{3}$, for $n = 0,1,2,$ and zero otherwise.

14. Find the DFT of $x(n)$ if

$$x(n) = 1, \text{for } n = 2 \text{ to } 6$$
$$x(n) = 0, \text{for } n = 0,1,7,8,9$$

Assume $x(n)$ is periodic beyond this interval $0 - 9$

15. Find the response of the following system to the input:

$$x(n) = 2 + 2\cos\left(\frac{n\pi}{4}\right) + \cos\left(\frac{2\pi n}{3} + \frac{\pi}{2}\right)$$

System: $H(\omega) = e^{-j\omega}\cos(\frac{\omega}{2})$

16. Show that the Hilbert Transform of $\exp(j\omega t)$ is $(-\text{sgn } f)\exp(j\omega t)$

17. Without using a calculator or computer find the dot products of (a) w1 and w-1, (b) w1 and w-2 (c) w11 and w37, where

$$w_k = \begin{bmatrix} w_4^0 \\ w_4^k \\ w_4^{2k} \\ w_4^{3k} \end{bmatrix} \text{ and } w_{N_F = e^{j2\pi/N_F}}$$

to show that they are orthogonal.

18. Find the DTFS harmonic function of a signal x[n]with period 4 for which x[0]= 3, x[1]=1, x[2] = -5, and x[3]=0 using the matrix multiplication $X = \frac{W^H x}{N_F}$

19. One period of a periodic function with period 4 is described by $x[n] = \delta[n] - \delta[n-2], 0 \leq n < 4$. Using the summation formula for the DTFS harmonic function and not using the tables or properties, find the harmonic function X[k].

20. Find the DTFS harmonic function of

$$x[n] = \sum_{m=-\infty}^{n} \delta_3[m] - \delta_3[m-1]$$

with $N_F = N_0 = 3$.

21. A periodic signal x[n] is exactly described for all discrete time by its DTFS

$$X[k] = (\delta_8[k-1] + \delta_8[k+1] + j2\delta_8[k+2] - j2\delta_8[k-2])e^{-j\pi k/4}$$

Using one fundamental period as the representation time.

a) Write a correct analytical expression for x[n] in which $\sqrt{1}$ (j) does not appear

b) What is the value of x[n] at $n = -10$?

22. Based on a representation time $N_F = 4$, the DTFS harmonic function X[k] of a signal x[n] has the following values.

$$X[-1] = 2 - j2, \quad X[0] = 4, \quad X[1] = 2 + j2, \quad X[2] = 3$$

a) What is the Value of X[3]?

b) What is the Value of X[22]?

c) What is the average value of x[n]?

Multiple-Choice Questions

1. A CT periodic signal x(t) is represented in Fourier series representation as

a. $x(t) = \sum_{k=-\infty}^{\infty} a_k e^{jk\Omega_0 t}$

b. $x(t) = \sum_{n=-\infty}^{\infty} a_{-n} e^{-jn\Omega_0 t}$

c. $x(t) = \sum_{n=-\infty}^{\infty} a_n e^{-jn\Omega_0 t}$

d. $x(t) = \sum_{k=-\infty}^{\infty} a_{-k} e^{j\Omega_0 t} / k$

2. If the function f(x) is even, then which of the following is zero?

a. a_n

b. b_n

c. a_0

d. nothing is zero

3. The spectrum of a continuous periodic rectangular signal is a

a. Discrete periodic sinc function

b. Continuous periodic sinc function

c. Discrete aperiodic sinc function

d. Continuous aperiodic sinc function

4. If the function f(x) is odd, then which of the only coefficient is present?

a. a_n

b. b_n

c. a_0

d. Everything is present

5. Find a_n if the function $f(x) = x - x^3$.

a. finite value

b. infinite value

c. zero

d. can't be found

6. The Fourier series coefficients of a continuous periodic signal x(t) are a_k. Fourier series coefficients of $x(-t)$ are

a. a_{-k}

b. $-a_k$

c. a_k

d. $\frac{1}{a_k}$

7. If the Fourier series coefficients of a signal x(t) are a_k, then

a. $a_k = a_{-k}^*$

b. $a_k = a_k^*$

c. $-a_k = a_k^*$

d. $a_k = -a_k^*$

8. x(t) is a continuous periodic signal with period T, fundamental frequency Ω_0 and Fourier series coefficients a_k. The Fourier series coefficients of x(2t) are

a. a_{2k}

b. a_k

c. $2a_k$

d. $\frac{1}{2}a_k$

9. The CTFT of a signum function is

a. $2j\Omega$

b. $\delta(\Omega)$

c. $\frac{2}{j\Omega}$

d. $\frac{1}{j\Omega}$

10. If the Fourier transform of $x(t)$ is $X(j\Omega)$, then Fourier transform of $x(-t)$ is

a. $X(-j\Omega)$

b. $-X(j\Omega)$

c. $-X(-j\Omega)$

d. $X(j\Omega)$

KNOW MORE

To delve deeper into the realm of Fourier series and Fourier transform is to embark on a journey of profound mathematical elegance and practical utility. One can uncover the secrets of convergence theorems, unravel the mysteries of orthogonality in function spaces, and master the art of manipulating signals in both time and frequency domains. Advanced analytical techniques open doors to solving complex differential equations, paving the way for applications in fields as diverse as physics, engineering, and finance. Moreover, the realm of Fourier transform beckons with promises of understanding the very essence of signals, be they audio waves, images, or quantum phenomena. From fast algorithms powering digital signal processors to cutting-edge applications in medical imaging and quantum computing, Fourier analysis continues to shape our modern world. As we journey forward, the exploration of Fourier series and transform promises not only a deeper understanding of mathematics and science but also an endless stream of possibilities for innovation and discovery.

REFERENCES AND SUGGESTED READINGS

1. Signals and Systems by Simon Haykin
2. Signals and Systems - Course (nptel.ac.in)

Dynamic QR Code for Further Reading

4 Laplace Transform

UNIT SPECIFICS

Through this unit we have discussed the following aspects:

- *What is Laplace transform, why it was developed?*
- *Review of the Laplace Transform for continuous-time signals and systems*
- *Poles and zeros of system functions and signals*
- *Laplace domain analysis of the signals*
- *The solution to differential equations, and system behavior.*

RATIONALE

The unit on "Laplace Transform" provides students to understand the behavior of Continuous and Discrete-time signals and systems in s-domain or Laplace domain. The Laplace transform is one of the most important tools used for solving ODEs and specifically, PDEs as it converts partial differentials to regular differentials.

Laplace transform can convert complex differential equations that describe the dynamic behavior of a system into simpler algebraic equations that describe the frequency response of a system

PRE-REQUISITES

1. *Strong understanding of mathematics, including algebra, calculus, and complex numbers.*
2. *Familiarity with basic concepts in signals and systems, such as time-domain and periodic, non-periodic signals.*
3. *Proficiency in solving ordinary differential equations and understanding linear algebra concepts.*

UNIT OUTCOMES

List of outcomes of this unit is as follows:

U4-O1: Understand the need for bilateral and unilateral Laplace transform for continuous-time signals and systems.

U4-O2: Understand the relationship between continuous-time Fourier transform and Laplace transform.

U4-O3: Learn the properties of Laplace transform.

U3-O4: Learn the applications of Laplace transform in the analysis of CT LTI systems.

U3-O5: Learn to solve the differential equations using Laplace transform.

Unit-4 Outcomes	***EXPECTED MAPPING WITH COURSE OUTCOMES*** *(1- Weak Correlation; 2- Medium correlation; 3- Strong Correlation)*					
	CO-1	***CO-2***	***CO-3***	***CO-4***	***CO-5***	***CO-6***
U4-O1	3	-	-	-	-	-
U4-O2	-	-	3	-	-	-
U4-O3	2	-	-	-	-	-
U4-O4	-	3	-	-	-	-
U4-O5		3				

4.1 Introduction

In the 3rd chapter we have discussed the Fourier series and Fourier transform along with their magnitude and frequency spectrum. In this chapter, the Laplace transform is discussed which is used to transform a time signal to complex frequency domain and this complex frequency domain is called as Laplace domain or s-domain. Laplace transformation was proposed by Laplace in the year 1780; hence this transformation is called as Laplace transform. In time domain the equations to represent a system are written in terms of differential equations whereas in s-domain, the differential equations are transformed to algebraic equations for easier analysis. In this chapter a brief discussion about Laplace transform, its properties and applications for analysis of signals and systems are presented.

4.2 Definition of Complex Frequency

The complex frequency is represented as,

$$s = \sigma + j\Omega$$

where, σ = Neper frequency in neper per second

Ω = Radian (or Real) frequency in radian per second

Let, $x(t) = Ae^{st} = Ae^{(\sigma+j\Omega)t}$ (4.1)

Let us analyze the signal of Eq. (3.1) for various choice of σ and Ω.

When, $\sigma = 0$,

$x(t) = Ae^{st} = Ae^{(j\Omega)t}$

$= A(\cos\Omega t + j\sin\Omega t) = A\cos\Omega t + jA\sin\Omega t$ (4.2)

The real part of Eq. (3.2) represents a cosine signal and the imaginary part represents a sinusoidal signal.

Real part= $A\cos\Omega t$

Imaginary part= $A\sin\Omega t$

When, $\Omega = 0$,

$x(t) = Ae^{st} = Ae^{\sigma t}$ (4.3)

In Eq. (3.3), if σ is positive, signal will be an exponentially increasing.

In Eq. (3.3), if σ is negative, signal will be an exponentially decreasing.

4.2.1 Complex Frequency Plane (s-Plane)

The complex frequency is defined as,

Complex frequency, s = σ + jΩ

where, σ = Real part of s

Ω= Imaginary part of s

Real part σ and imaginary part Ω can take values from -∞ to +∞. They are represented on a two dimensional complex plane along with horizontal axis and vertical axis as shown in fig 4.1 is called ***complex frequency plane*** or ***s-plane.***

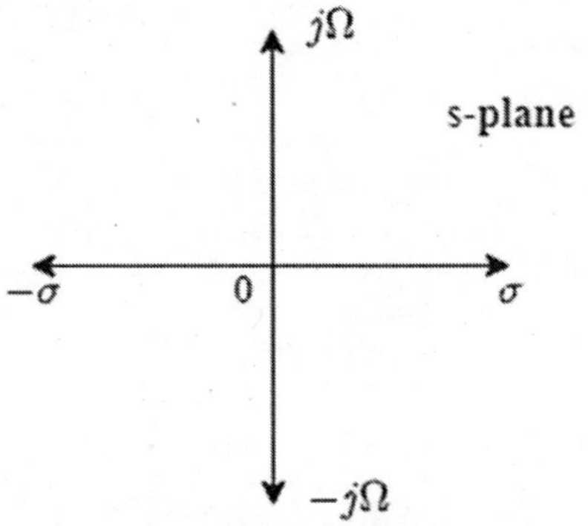

Fig 4.1 s-plane

4.2.2 Definition of Laplace Transform (LT)

A time domain signal $x(t)$ can be transformed into s-domain by multiplying the signal by e^{-st} and integrate from -∞ to +∞. The transformed signal is represented by $X(s)$ and the transformation is denoted by the letter $\mathcal{L}$.

Laplace transform is represented as,

$X(s) = \mathcal{L}\{x(t)\}$

Let $x(t)$ be a continuous time signal defined for all values of t. Let $X(s)$ be Laplace transform of $x(t)$ then the Laplace transform of $x(t)$ is defined as,

$$\mathcal{L}\{x(t)\} = X(s) = \int_{-\infty}^{+\infty} x(t)e^{-st}dt \qquad (4.4)$$

For causal input signal,

$$\mathcal{L}\{x(t)\}=X(s) = \int_0^{\infty} x(t)e^{-st}dt \qquad (4.5)$$

4.2.3 Definition of Inverse Laplace Transform (ILT)

The s-domain signal $X(s)$ can be represented to time domain signal $x(t)$ by using inverse Laplace transform (ILT).

Laplace transform is represented as,

$$\mathcal{L}^{-1}= x(t) = \frac{1}{2\pi j}\int_{s=\sigma-j\Omega}^{s=\sigma+j\Omega} X(s)e^{st}ds \qquad (4.6)$$

Input signal $x(t)$ and transformed signal $X(s)$ are called Laplace transform pair and are expressed as,

$$x(t) \Leftrightarrow X(s)$$

4.3 Region of Convergence (RoC)

The Laplace transform of a signal is given by, $\int_{-\infty}^{+\infty} x(t)e^{-st}dt$. The values of s for which the given LT equation converges is called ***Region of Convergence (RoC)***. The RoC is expressed for three types of cases given below:

Case I: Right Sided Signal

Let $x(t) = e^{-bt}u(t)$, where $b > 0$

$= e^{-bt}$ where $t \geq 0$

Take Laplace transform on both sides,

Using definition of LT,

$$x(s) = \int_{-\infty}^{\infty} x(t)\, e^{-st}\, dt$$

$$= \int_{-\infty}^{\infty} e^{-bt}\, u(t)\, e^{-st}\, dt$$

$$= \int_{0}^{\infty} e^{-bt}\, e^{-st}dt = \int_{0}^{\infty} e^{-(b+s)t}\, dt$$

$$= \left[\frac{e^{-(b+s)\,t}}{-(b+s)}\right]_0^{\infty}$$

$$= \frac{1}{-(b+s)} \left[e^{-(b+s)t}\right]_0^\infty$$

$$= \frac{1}{-(s+b)} \left[e^{-\infty} - e^0\right]$$

$$= \frac{1}{-(s+b)} [0-1] = \frac{1}{s+b}$$

X(s) Converges for $\sigma = -b$ where $s = \sigma + j\Omega$

Therefore, for causal signal ROC is the right side of pole at $\sigma = -b$ as shown in following fig 4.2.

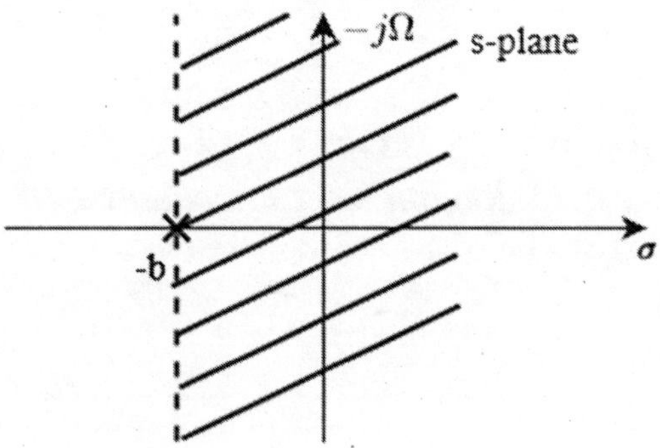

Fig 4.2 RoC for right sided signal

Case II: Left sided signal

Let $x(t) = e^{-bt}\, u(t)$, where $b > 0$, for $t \leq 0$

Take Laplace, transform on both sides,

Using definition of LT,

$$x(s) = \int_{-\infty}^{\infty} x(t)e^{-st}dt$$

$$= \int_{-\infty}^{\infty} e^{-bt}\, u(t)e^{-st}\, dt$$

$$\int_{-\infty}^{0} e^{-bt}\, e^{-st}\, dt = \int_{-\infty}^{0} e^{-(s+b)t}dt$$

$$= \left[\frac{e^{-(s+b)t}}{-(s+b)}\right]_{-\infty}^{0}$$

$$= \frac{1}{-(s+b)}\left[e^{-(s+b)\times 0} - e^{(s+b)\times\infty}\right]$$

Let $s = \sigma + j\Omega$,

$$\therefore X(S) = -\frac{1}{(s+b)}\left[e^{-0} - e^{(\sigma+j\Omega+b)\infty}\right]$$

$$= -\frac{1}{s+b} + \frac{e^{(\sigma+b)\infty}\, e^{j\Omega\times\infty}}{s+b}$$

Let $p = \sigma + b$

If $\sigma + b > 0$, $\sigma > -b$, $i.e., e^{\infty} = \infty$

If $\sigma + b < 0$, $\sigma < -b$ $i.e., e^{-\infty} = 0$

Hence, $x(s)$ converges when $\sigma < -b$

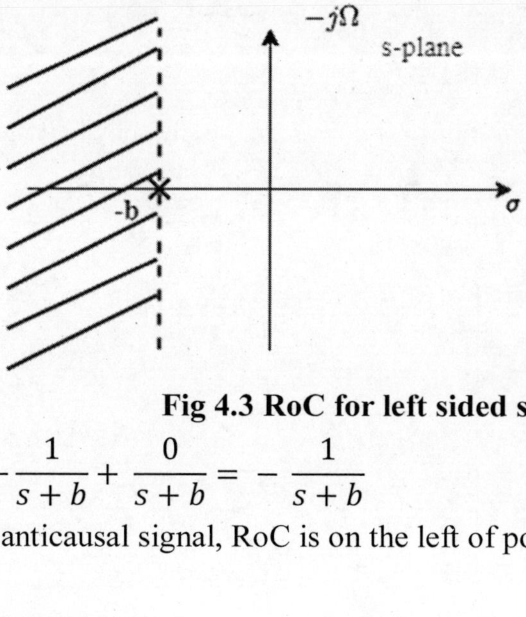

Fig 4.3 RoC for left sided signal

$$\therefore X(s) = -\frac{1}{s+b} + \frac{0}{s+b} = -\frac{1}{s+b}$$

Therefore, for an anticausal signal, RoC is on the left of pole $\sigma = -b$ shown in figure.

Case III: Two sided signal

Let $x(t) = e^{-at}u(t) + e^{-bt}u(-t)$ where $a, b, > 0$ and $a > b$.

Using definition of Laplace Transform,

$$X(s) = \int_{-\infty}^{\infty} x(t)e^{-st}\, dt$$

$$= \int_{-\infty}^{\infty} [e^{-at}\, u\,(t) + e^{-bt} u(-t)] e^{-st} dt$$

$$= \int_{0}^{\infty} e^{-at}\, e^{-st} dt + \int_{-\infty}^{0} e^{-bt}\, e^{-st} dt$$

$$= \int_{0}^{\infty} e^{-(s+a)t}\, dt + \int_{-\infty}^{0} e^{-(s+b)t}\, dt$$

$$= \left[\frac{e^{-(s+a)t}}{-(s+a)}\right]_0^{\infty} + \left[\frac{e^{-(s+b)t}}{-(s+b)}\right]_{-\infty}^{0}$$

Here also,

When, $s + a > 0,\ s > -a \rightarrow e^{-\infty} = 0$

$s + a < 0,\ s < -a \rightarrow e^{\infty} = \infty$

$s + b > 0,\ s > -b \rightarrow e^{\infty} = \infty$

$s + b < 0,\ s < -b \rightarrow e^{-\infty} = 0$

$$\therefore X(s) = \frac{1}{s+a} - \frac{1}{s+b}$$

Therefore, for two sided signal, ROC includes all points on s-plane lies between poles –a to –b as shown in figure.

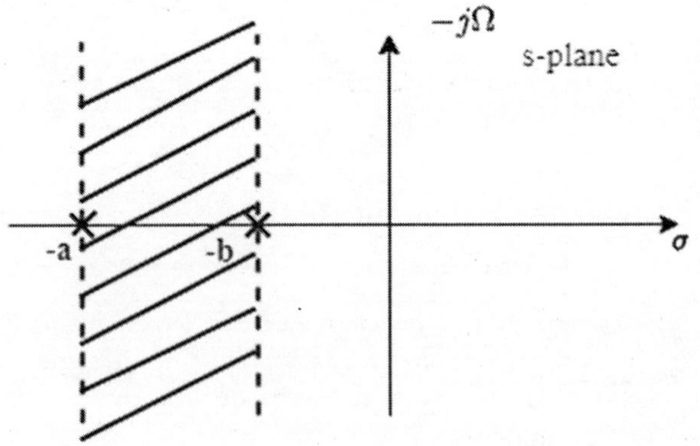

Fig 4.4 RoC for two sided signal

Example 4.1

Determine the Laplace transform of the following continuous time signals & find their ROC

1) $x\,(t) = A\,u\,(t)$

2) $x(t) = t\,u(t)$

3) $x(t) = e^{-8t}\,u(t)$

4) $x(t) = e^{-8t}\,u(-t)$

5) $x(t) = e^{-8|t|}$

Solution:

1.Given, $x(t) = A\,u(t)$

Using definition of LT,

$$X(s) = \int_{-\infty}^{\infty} x(t)e^{-st}\,dt$$

$$\int_{-\infty}^{\infty} A\,u(t)e^{-st}\,dt$$

$$x(s) = \int_{0}^{\infty} A\,e^{-st}\,dt = A\int_{0}^{\infty} e^{-st}\,dt$$

$$= A\left[\frac{e^{-st}}{-s}\right]_0^{\infty} = \frac{A}{-s}\,[e^{-st}]_0^{\infty}$$

$$\therefore X(s) = \frac{A}{s}\,[e^{-\infty} - e^{0}] = -\frac{A}{s}\,[0-1]$$

$\therefore X(s) = \frac{A}{s}$ where for $s > 0$ the X(s) converges.

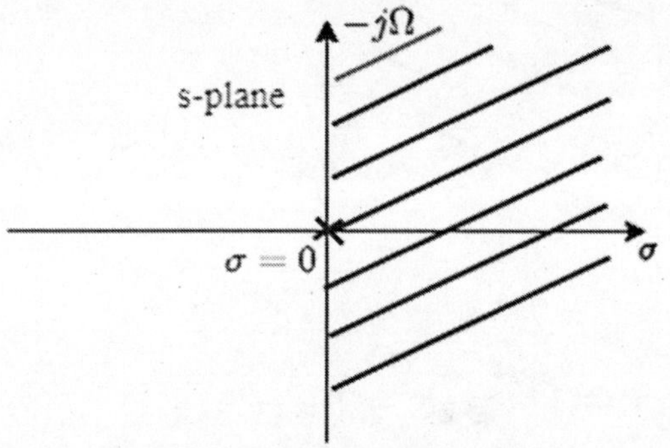

Fig 4.5 ROC of $x(t) = A\,u(t)$

∴ ROC is the Right half of S-plane

2. Given, $x(t) = t\,u\,(t)$

Using definition of LT,

$$X(s) = \int_{-\infty}^{\infty} x(t)\, e^{-st}\, dt$$

$$= \int_{-\infty}^{\infty} t\,u(t)\, e^{-st}\, dt$$

$$= \int_{0}^{\infty} t\, e^{-st}\, dt$$

Using $\int uv = u \int v - \int[du \int v]$ rule,

$$X(s) = t \int e^{-st}\, dt - \int \left[\frac{d}{dt}(t) \int e^{-st}\, dt\right]$$

$$= \left[t\frac{e^{-st}}{-s}\right]_0^{\infty} - \int_0^{\infty} 1\, \frac{e^{-st}}{-s}\, dt$$

$$= \left[t\frac{e^{-st}}{-s}\right]_0^{\infty} - \left[\frac{e^{-st}}{s^2}\right]_0^{\infty}$$

$$= [e^{-\infty} - 0] - \frac{1}{s^2}\,[e^{-\infty} - e^0]$$

$$= \frac{1}{s^2}$$

When, $s > 0$, $X(s)$ converges and ROC lies to the right of line passing through $\sigma = 0$.

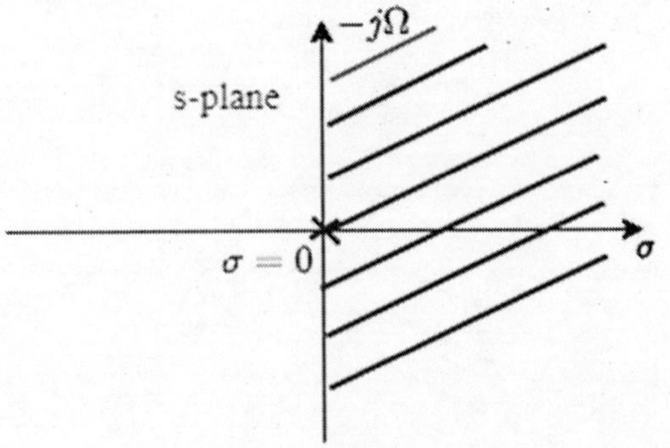

Fig 4.6 ROC of $x(t) = t\,u\,(t)$

3. Given , x (t) = e^{-8t} u (t)

Using definition of LT,

$$x(s) = \int_{-\infty}^{\infty} x(t)e^{-st}\, dt$$

$$= \int_{-\infty}^{\infty} e^{-8t}\, u(t)\, e^{-st}\, dt$$

$$= \int_{0}^{\infty} e^{-8t}\, e^{-st}\, dt$$

$$= \int_0^{\infty} e^{-(s+8)t}\, dt = \left[\frac{e^{-(s+8)t}}{-(s+8)}\right]_0^{\infty}$$

$$= -\frac{1}{s+8}\left[e^{-\infty} - e^{0}\right] = \frac{1}{s+8}$$

For, $S + 8 > 0$, X (s) converges for $S > -8$ and ROC lies to the right of line passing through $\sigma = -8$

4. Given, x(t) = e^{-8t} u (−t)

Using definition of LT,

$$X(s) = \int_{-\infty}^{\infty} x(t)e^{-st}\, dt$$

$$= \int_{-\infty}^{\infty} e^{-8t}\, u(-t)\, e^{-st}\, dt$$

$$= \int_{-\infty}^{0} e^{-8t}\, e^{-st}\, dt = \int_{-\infty}^{0} e^{-(s+8)t}\, dt$$

$$= \left[\frac{e^{-(s+8)t}}{-(s+8)}\right]_{-\infty}^{0} = -\frac{1}{s+8}\left[e^{-(s+8)t}\right]_{-\infty}^{0}$$

Here, for S < - ∞, X (s) converges

$$\therefore x(s) = -\frac{1}{s+8}$$

ROC contains all points in s – place on the left side of line passing through $\sigma = -8$

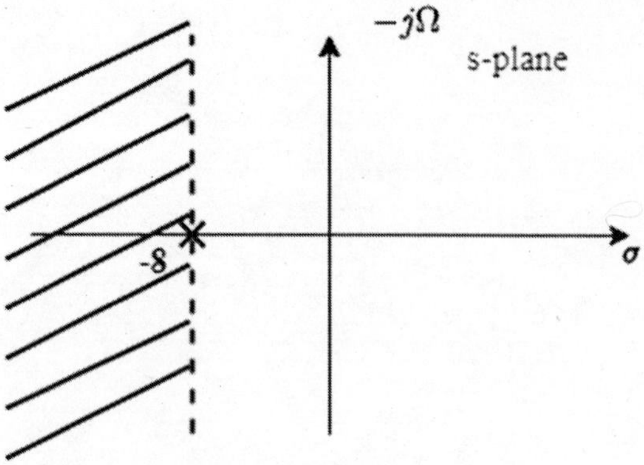

Fig 4.7 ROC of $\mathbf{x(t) = e^{-8t}\, u\,(-t)}$

5. Given $\mathbf{x(t) = e^{-3\,|t|}}$

Using definition of LT,

$$x(s) = \int_{-\infty}^{\infty} x(t)\, e^{st}\, dt$$

$$= \int_{-\infty}^{\infty} e^{-3\,|t|}\; e^{-st}\, dt$$

$$\int_{-\infty}^{0} e^{4t}\; e^{-st}\, dt + \int_{0}^{\infty} e^{-4t}\; e^{-st}\, dt$$

$$\int_{-\infty}^{0} e^{-(s-4)t}\; dt + \int_{0}^{\infty} e^{-(s+4)t}\; dt$$

$$= \left[\frac{e^{-(s-4)t}}{-(s-4)}\right]_{-\infty}^{0} + - \left[\frac{e^{-(s+4)t}}{-(s+4)}\right]_{0}^{\infty}$$

$$= -\frac{1}{s-4}\,[e^{0} - e^{\infty}] - \frac{1}{s+4}\,[e^{-\infty} - e^{0}]$$

$$X(s) = -\frac{1}{s-4} + \frac{1}{s+4} = -\frac{8}{s^2 - 16}$$

ROC lies between the points $\sigma = -4$ to $\sigma = 4$

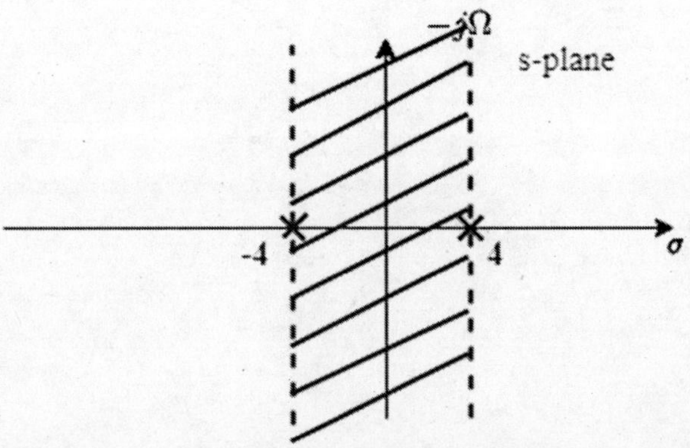

Fig 4.8 ROC of $\mathbf{x(t) = e^{-3\,|t|}}$

Example 4.2: Determine the Laplace Transform of the following signals.

1. $x(t) = \sin \Omega_0 t\, u(t)$
2. $x(t) = \cos \Omega_0 t\, u(t)$
3. $x(t) = e^{-at} \sin \Omega_0 t\, u(t)$
4. $x(t) = e^{-at} \cos \Omega_0 t\, u(t)$

Solution:

1. Given $\boldsymbol{x(t) = \sin \Omega_0 t\, u(t) = \sin \Omega_0 t\,; \quad t \geq 0}$

Using definition of Laplace Transform,

$$X(s) = \int_{-\infty}^{\infty} x(t)e^{-st}\, dt$$

$$= \int_{-\infty}^{\infty} \sin \Omega_0 t\, u(t)e^{-st}\, dt$$

$$= \int_{0}^{\infty} \sin \Omega_0 t\, e^{-st}\, dt$$

Using formula, $\sin\emptyset = \frac{e^{j\emptyset} - e^{-j\emptyset}}{2j}$

$$X(s) = \int_{0}^{\infty} \left[\frac{e^{j\Omega_0 t} - e^{-j\Omega_0 t}}{2j}\right] e^{-st}\, dt$$

$$= \frac{1}{2j}\int_0^{\infty}\left[e^{j\,\Omega_0\,t} - e^{-j\,\Omega_0\,t}\right]e^{-st}dt$$

$$= \frac{1}{2j}\int_0^{\infty}\left[e^{-st}e^{j\,\Omega_0\,t} - e^{-st}e^{-j\,\Omega_0\,t}\right]dt$$

$$= \frac{1}{2j}\int_0^{\infty}\left[e^{-(s-j\,\Omega_0)t} - e^{-(s+j\,\Omega_0)t}\right]dt$$

$$= \frac{1}{2j}\left[\frac{e^{-(s-j\,\Omega_0)t}}{-(s-j\,\Omega_0)} - \frac{e^{-(s+j\,\Omega_0)t}}{-(s+j\,\Omega_0)}\right]_0^{\infty}$$

$$= \frac{1}{2j}\left[\frac{e^{-\infty}}{-(s-j\,\Omega_0)} - \frac{e^{-\infty}}{-(s+j\,\Omega_0)} - \frac{e^0}{-(s-j\,\Omega_0)} + \frac{e^0}{-(s+j\,\Omega_0)}\right]$$

$$= \frac{1}{2j}\left[0 - 0 + \frac{1}{s-j\,\Omega_0} - \frac{1}{s+j\,\Omega_0}\right]$$

$$= \frac{1}{2j}\left[\frac{s+j\,\Omega_0 - s+j\,\Omega_0}{(s-j\,\Omega_0)(s+j\,\Omega_0)}\right]$$

$$= \frac{1}{2j}\left[\frac{2j\,\Omega_0}{s^2 + {\Omega_0}^2}\right]$$

$$= \frac{\Omega_0}{s^2 + {\Omega_0}^2}$$

as, $j^2 = -1$

$$\therefore \mathcal{L}\{\sin\,\Omega_0 t u(t)\} = \frac{\Omega_0}{s^2 + {\Omega_0}^2}$$

2. Given that $x(t) = cos\;\Omega_0\;t\;u(t) = cos\;\Omega_0\;t\;;\qquad t \geq 0$

Using definition of Laplace Transform,

$$X(s) = \int_{-\infty}^{\infty} x(t)e^{-st}\,dt$$

$= \int_{-\infty}^{\infty} \cos \Omega_0\, t\, u(t) e^{-st}\, dt$

$= \int_{0}^{\infty} \cos \Omega_0\, t\, e^{-st}\, dt$

Using formula, $\cos\emptyset = \frac{e^{j\emptyset} + e^{-j\emptyset}}{2}$

$X(s) = \int_{0}^{\infty} \left[\frac{e^{j\Omega_0 t} + e^{-j\Omega_0 t}}{2}\right] e^{-st}\, dt$

$= \frac{1}{2}\int_{0}^{\infty} \left[e^{-st} e^{j\Omega_0 t} + e^{-st} e^{-j\Omega_0 t}\right] dt$

$= \frac{1}{2}\int_{0}^{\infty} \left[e^{-(s-j\Omega_0)t} + e^{-(s+j\Omega_0)t}\right] dt$

$= \frac{1}{2}\left[\frac{e^{-(s-j\Omega_0)t}}{-(s-j\Omega_0)} + \frac{e^{-(s+j\Omega_0)t}}{-(s+j\Omega_0)}\right]_0^{\infty}$

$= \frac{1}{2}\left[0 + 0 + \frac{1}{s-j\Omega_0} + \frac{1}{s+j\Omega_0}\right]$

$= \frac{1}{2}\left[\frac{s+j\Omega_0 + s-j\Omega_0}{(s-j\Omega_0)(s+j\Omega_0)}\right]$

$= \frac{1}{2}\left[\frac{2s}{s^2 + \Omega_0^{\,2}}\right]$

$= \frac{s}{s^2 + \Omega_0^{\,2}}$

3. Given that $x(t) = e^{-at} \sin \Omega_0\, t\, u(t)$

$= e^{-at} \sin \Omega_0\, t; \quad t \geq 0$

Using definition of Laplace Transform,

$X(s) = \int_{-\infty}^{\infty} x(t) e^{-st}\, dt$

$= \int_{0}^{\infty} e^{-st} \sin \Omega_0\, t\, e^{-st}\, dt$

$$= \frac{1}{2j}\int_{0}^{\infty}\left[e^{-(s+a-j\Omega_0)t - e^{-(s+a-j\Omega_0)t}}\right]dt$$

$$= \frac{1}{2j}\left[\frac{e^{-(s+a-j\Omega_0)t}}{-(s+a-j\Omega_0} - \frac{e^{-(s+a-j\Omega_0)t}}{-(s+a+j\Omega_0}\right]_0^{\infty}$$

$$= \frac{\Omega_0}{(s+a)^2 + \Omega^2{}_0}$$

$$\therefore L\{e^{-at}\sin\Omega_0\, t\, u(t)\} = \frac{\Omega_0}{(s+a)^2 + \Omega^2{}_0}$$

Given that $x(t) = e^{-at}\cos\Omega_0\, t\, u\,(t)$

$= e^{-at}\cos\Omega_0 t; \quad t \geq 0$

Using definitiion of laplace Trasnform.

$$x(s) = \int_{-\infty}^{\infty} x(t)\, e^{-st}\, dt$$

$$= \int_{0}^{\infty} e^{-at}\cos\Omega_0 t\; e^{-st}dt$$

$$= \frac{1}{2}\int_{0}^{\infty}\left[e^{-(s+a-j\Omega_0)t + e^{-(s+a+j\Omega_0)t}}\right]dt$$

$$= \frac{1}{2}\left[\frac{e^{-(s+a-j\Omega_0)t}}{-(s+a-j\Omega_0} - \frac{e^{-(s+a+j\Omega_0)t}}{-(s+a+j\Omega_0}\right]_0^{\infty}$$

$$= \frac{1}{2}\left[0 + 0 + \frac{1}{s+a-j\Omega_0} + \frac{1}{s+a+j\Omega_0}\right]$$

$$= \frac{s+a}{(s+a)^2 + \Omega^2{}_0}$$

$$\therefore \mathcal{L}\{e^{-at}\cos\Omega_0\, t\, u(t)\} = \frac{s+a}{(s+a)^2 + \Omega^2{}_0}$$

Table 4.1 Some Standard Pairs of Laplace Transform with ROC

$\boldsymbol{x(t)}$	$\boldsymbol{x(s)}$	$\boldsymbol{ROC}$
$\delta(t)$	1	$Entire\ S - Plane$
$u(t)$	$\frac{1}{s}$	$\sigma > 0$
$tu(t)$	$\frac{1}{s^2}$	$\sigma > 0$
$\frac{t^{n-1}}{(n-1)!}u(t)$	$\frac{1}{s^n}$	$\sigma > 0$
$e^{-at}u(t)$	$\frac{1}{s+a}$	$\sigma > -a$
$-e^{-at}u(-t)$	$\frac{1}{s+a}$	$\sigma < -a$
$t^n u(t)$	$\frac{n!}{s^{n+1}}$	$\sigma > 0$
$te^{-at}\ u(t)$	$\frac{1}{(s+a)^2}$	$\sigma > -a$
$t^n e^{-at}\ u(t)$	$\frac{n!}{(s+a)^{n+1}}$	$\sigma > -a$
$sin\Omega_0 t\ u(t)$	$\frac{\Omega_0}{s^2+{\Omega_0}^2}$	$\sigma > 0$
$cos\Omega_0 t\ u(t)$	$\frac{s}{s^2+{\Omega_0}^2}$	$\sigma > 0$
$e^{-at}sin\Omega_0 t\ u(t)$	$\frac{\Omega_0}{(s+a)^2+{\Omega_0}^2}$	$\sigma > -a$
$e^{-at}cos\Omega_0 t\ u(t)$	$\frac{s+a}{(s+a)^2+{\Omega_0}^2}$	$\sigma > -a$

4.4 Properties of Laplace Transform

4.4.1 Scaling of amplitude

If amplitude is scaled in time domain by constant K then it's Laplace transform is multiplied by same constant

i.e. if $L\{x(t)\} = X(s)$

then,

$L\{Kx(t)\} = KX(s)$

Proof: Using definition of LT

$X(s) = \int_{-\infty}^{\infty} x(t)e^{-st}\, d$ (4.7)

$= \int_{-\infty}^{\infty} Kx(t)e^{-st}\, dt$

$= K\int_{-\infty}^{\infty} x(t)e^{-st}\, dt$

$= KX(s)$ Using Eq. (4.7)

4.4.2 Linearity

This property states that weighted sum of two or more signals is equal to similar weighted sum of individual's Laplace transform.

i.e. if $L\{x_1(t)\} = X_1(s)$

$L\{x_2(t)\} = X_2(s)$, then

$L\{ax_1(t) + bx_2(t)\} = aX_1(s) + bX_2(s)$

Proof: Using definition of LT

$X_1(s) = \int_{-\infty}^{\infty} x_1(t)e^{-st}dt$ (4.8)

$X_2(s) = \int_{-\infty}^{\infty} x_2(t)e^{-st}dt$ (4.9)

$L\{ax_1(t) + bx_2(t)\} = \int_{-\infty}^{\infty} [ax_1(t) + bx_2(t)]e^{-st}dt$

$= a\int_{-\infty}^{\infty} x_1(t)e^{-st}dt + b\int_{-\infty}^{\infty} x_2(t)e^{-st}dt$

$= aX_1(s) + bX_2(s)$

4.4.3 Time differentiation

If derivative is taken in time domain then it's Laplace transform is $SX(s) - x(0)$

i.e. if $L\{x(t)\} = X(s)$, then

$L\left\{\frac{d}{dt}x(t)\right\} = SX(s) - x(0)$, Where $x(0)$ is value of $x(t)$ at $t = 0$

Proof: Using definition of LT

$$X(s) = \int_{-\infty}^{\infty} x(t)e^{-st}dt \qquad (4.10)$$

$$\therefore L\left\{\frac{d}{dt}x(t)\right\} = \int_{-\infty}^{\infty} \frac{d}{dt}x(t)e^{-st}dt$$

$$= \int_{0}^{\infty} e^{-st}\frac{dx(t)}{dt}dt \qquad \text{... for causal } x(t)$$

Using $\int uv = u\int v - \int[du\int v]$

$$L\left\{\frac{d}{dt}x(t)\right\} = [e^{-st}x(t)]_0^{\infty} - \int_0^{\infty} -se^{-st}x(t)dt$$

$$= e^{-\infty}x(\infty) - e^{0}x(0) + s\int_0^{\infty} x(t)e^{-st}dt$$

$$= S\int_0^{\infty} x(t)e^{-st}dt - x(0)$$

$$= SX(s) - x(0) \qquad \text{Using Eq. (4.10)}$$

4.4.4 Integration in time domain

If $L\{x(t)\} = X(s)$, then

$$L\{\int x(t)dt\} = \frac{X(S)}{S} + \frac{[\int x(t)dt]|_{t=0}}{S}$$

Proof: Using definition of LT

$$X(S) = \int_0^{\infty} x(t)e^{-st}dt \qquad \text{...for causal signal}$$

$$L\{\int x(t)dt\} = \int_0^{\infty}[Sx(t)dt]\,e^{-st}dt$$

Using, $\int uv = u\int v - \int[du\int v]$

$$L\{\int x(t)dt\} = \left[[\int x(t)dt]\frac{e^{-st}}{-s}\right]_0^{\infty} - \int_0^{\infty} x(t)\frac{e^{-st}}{-s}dt$$

$$= \frac{1}{s}[\int x(t)dt]|_{t=0} + \frac{1}{s}\int_0^{\infty} x(t)e^{-st}dt$$

$$= \frac{X(S)}{S} + \frac{[\int x(t)dt]|_{t=0}}{S}$$

4.4.5 Shifting in frequency domain

If $L\{x(t)\} = X(s)$, then

$L\{e^{\pm at}x(t)\} = X(S \mp a)$

Proof : Using definition of LT,

$X(S) = \int_{-\infty}^{\infty} x(t)e^{-st}\,dt$

$L\{e^{\pm at}x(t)\} = \int_{-\infty}^{\infty} e^{\pm at}\,x(t)e^{-st}dt$

$= \int_{-\infty}^{\infty} x(t)e^{-(S\mp a)t}dt$

$= X(S \mp a)$

4.4.6 Shifting in time domain

If $L\{x + (t)\} = X(s)$, then

$$L\{x(t \pm a)\} = e^{\pm as}x(s)$$

Proof: Using definition of LT,

$$X(s) = \int_{-\infty}^{\infty} x(t)e^{-st}\,dt \qquad (4.11)$$

$$L\{x(t \pm a)\} = \int_{-\infty}^{\infty} x(t \pm a)e^{-st}dt$$

let $t \mp a = \tau$

$$\therefore t = \tau \mp a, dt = d\tau$$

$$\therefore L\{x(t \pm a)\} = \int_{-\infty}^{\infty} x(\tau)e^{-s(\tau\mp a)}\,d\tau$$

$$= \int_{-\infty}^{\infty} x(t)e^{-s\tau}\,e^{\pm as}d\tau$$

$$= e^{\pm\,as} \int_{-\infty}^{\infty} x(\tau)e^{-s\tau}\,d\tau$$

$= e^{\pm as}\,X(s)$ Using Eq (4.11)

4.4.7 Differentiation in frequency

If $L\{x(t)\} = X(s)$, then,

$$L\{tx(t)\} = -\frac{d}{ds}X(s)$$

Proof: Using definition of LT,

$$X(s) = \frac{d}{ds}\left[\int_{-\infty}^{\infty} x(t)e^{-st}dt\right]$$

$$= \int_{-\infty}^{\infty} x(t)\left(\frac{d}{ds}e^{-st}\right)dt$$

$$= \int_{-\infty}^{\infty} x(t)(-t\,e^{-st})\,dt$$

$$= \int_{-\infty}^{\infty} [-t\,x(t)]e^{-st}\,dt$$

$$= L\{-t\,x(t)\}$$

$$= -L\{t\,x(t)\}$$

$$\therefore L\{t\,x(t)\} = -\frac{d}{ds}X(s)$$

4.4.8 Time Scaling

If $L\{x(t)\} = X(s)$, then

$$L\{x(at)\} = \frac{1}{|a|}X\left(\frac{s}{a}\right)$$

Proof: Using definition of LT,

$$X(s) = \int_{-\infty}^{\infty} x(t)\,e^{-st}\,dt$$

$$\therefore L\{x(at)\} = \int_{-\infty}^{\infty} x(at)\,e^{-st}\,dt$$

$$\text{let } at = \tau$$

$$t = \frac{\tau}{a},\ dt = \frac{d\tau}{a}$$

$$X(s) = \int_{-\infty}^{\infty} x(\tau)e^{-\left(\frac{s}{a}\right)\tau}\frac{d\tau}{a}$$

$$= \frac{1}{a}\int_{-\infty}^{\infty} x(\tau)e^{-\left(\frac{s}{a}\right)\tau}d\tau$$

$$L\{x(at)\} = \frac{1}{a}X\left(\frac{s}{a}\right) \qquad (4.12)$$

Above equation is true when a is positive for negative a,

$$L\{x(at)\} = -\frac{1}{a}X\left(\frac{s}{a}\right) \qquad (4.13)$$

$\therefore$ Combining Eq. (4.12)& Eq. (4.13)

$$L\{x(at)\} = \frac{1}{|a|}X\left(\frac{s}{a}\right)$$

4.4.9 Initial Value theorem

If $L\{x(t)\} = X(s)$, then

Initial Value of signal x (t) at t=0 is,

$$x(0) = \lim_{t\to 0} x(t) = \lim_{s\to\infty} sX(s)$$

4.4.10 Final Value theorem

If $L\{x(t)\} = X(s)$. then

Final value of signal $x(t)$ at $t = \infty$ is,

$$x(\infty) = \lim_{t\to\infty} x(t) = \lim_{s\to 0} sX(s)$$

4.4.11 Convolution Property

The convolution theorem of LT says that the convolution of two signals in time domain is equivalent to multiplication of their Laplace transforms in S domain.

i.e. If $L\{x, (t)\} = X_1(s)$

$L\{x_2(t)\} = X_2(s)$ then,

$$L\{x_1(t) * x_2(t)\} = X_1(s)X_2(s)$$

4.5 Poles and Zeros of System Functions and Signals

The Laplace transform is represented in terms of rational, i.e. it is a ratio of polynomials in the complex variable *s*.

$$X(s) = \frac{N(s)}{D(s)}$$

Where *N* and *D* are the numerator and denominator polynomials respectively.

In fact, *X*(*s*) will be rational whenever *x*(*t*) is a linear combination of real or complex exponentials. **Rational transforms** also arise when we consider **LTI systems specified in terms of linear, constant coefficient differential equations**.

We can mark the roots of *N* and *D* in the *s*-plane along with the ROC

4.5.1 Poles and Zeros:

The roots of *N*(*s*) are known as the zeros. For these values of *s*, *X*(*s*) is zero.

The roots of *D*(*s*) are known as the poles. For these values of *s*, *X*(*s*) is infinite, the Region of Convergence for the Laplace transform cannot contain any poles, because the corresponding integral is infinite

The set of poles and zeros completely characterise *X*(*s*) to within a scale factor (+ ROC for Laplace transform)

$$X(s) \propto \frac{\prod_i (s - z_i)}{\prod_j (s - p_j)}$$

The graphical representation of *X*(*s*) through its poles and zeros in the s-plane is referred to as the **pole-zero** plot of *X*(*s*).

Example 4.3: Poles and Zeros

Consider the signal below signal and arrange in pole zero form showing the ROC.

$$x(t) = \delta(t) - \frac{4}{3}e^{-t}u(t) + \frac{1}{3}e^{2t}u(t)$$

Solution: By linearity we can evaluate the second and third terms

The Laplace transform of the impulse function is:

$$L\{\delta(t)\} = \int_{-\infty}^{\infty} \delta(t)e^{-st}\,dt = 1$$

which is valid for any s. Therefore,

$$X(s) = 1 - \frac{4}{3}\frac{1}{s+1} + \frac{1}{3}\frac{1}{s-2}$$

$$= \frac{(s-1)^2}{(s+1)(s-2)}, \qquad \text{Re}\{s\} > 2$$

That means ROC lies on the RHS of right most pole which is 2.

4.6 ROC Properties for Laplace Transform:

Depending upon the location of poles and the criteria of convergence the following properties are given.

Property-1: The ROC of X(s) consists of strips parallel to the jW - axis in the s-plane.

Property-2: If x(t) is of finite duration and is absolutely integrable, then the ROC is the entire s- plane.

Property-3: If x(t) is right sided, and if the line passing through Re(s) = s0 is in ROC, then all values of s for which Re(s) > s0 will also be in ROC.

Property-4: If x(t) is left sided, and if the line passing through Re(s) = s0 is in ROC, then all values of s for which Re(s) < s0 will also be in ROC.

Property-5: If x(t) is two sided, and if the line passing through Re(s) = s0 is in ROC, then the ROC will consists of a strip in the s-plane that includes the line passing through Re(s) = s0 .

Property-6: If X(s) is rational, (where X(s) is Laplace transform of x(t)), then its ROC is bounded by poles or extends to infinity.

Property-7: If X(s) is rational, (where X(s) is Laplace transform of x(t)), then ROC does not include any poles of X(s).

Property-8: If X(s) is rational, (where X(s) is Laplace transform of x(t)), and if x(t) is right sided, then ROC is the region in s-plane to the right of the rightmost pole.

Property-9: If X(s) is rational, (where X(s) is Laplace transform of x(t)), and if x(t) is left sided, then ROC is the region in s-plane to the left of the leftmost pole.

4.7 Inverse Laplace Transform by Partial Fraction Expansion Method

Let Laplace transform of x(t) be X(s). The s-domain signal X(s) will be a ratio of two polynomials in s (i.e., rational function of s). The roots of the denominator polynomial are called poles. The roots of numerator polynomials are called zeros. In signals and systems, three different types of s-domain signals are encountered. They are, with separate poles, with multiple poles, with complex conjugate poles.

The inverse Laplace transform (ILT) by partial fraction expansion method of all the three cases are explained with an example.

Type 1: When s-Domain Signal X(s) has Distinct Poles

Let $X(S) = \frac{\text{A}}{\text{s(s+p1)(s+p2)}}$

Using partial fraction expansion, above equation can be written as,

$$X(S) = \frac{\text{A1}}{\text{s}} + \frac{\text{A2}}{(\text{s} + \text{p1})} + \frac{\text{A3}}{(\text{s} + \text{p2})}$$

The residues $\text{A1}, \text{A2}, \text{A3}$ will be found for s=0, s=-p1, s=-p2.

Type 2: When s-Domain Signal X(s) has Multiple Poles

Let $X(S) = \frac{\text{A}}{\text{s(s+p1)(s+p2)}^2}$

Using partial fraction expansion, above equation can be written as,

$$X(S) = \frac{\text{A1}}{\text{s}} + \frac{\text{A2}}{(\text{s} + \text{p1})} + \frac{\text{A3}}{(\text{s} + \text{p2})} + \frac{\text{A4}}{(\text{s} + \text{p2})^2}$$

The residues A1, A2, A4, will be found for s=0, s=-p1, s=-p2.

For residue A3,

$$A3 = \frac{d}{ds}[X(s)(s+p2)^2]\Big|_{s=-p2}$$

Type 3: When s-Domain Signal X(s) has Complex Conjugate Poles

Let $X(S) = \frac{A}{(s+p1)(s^2+bs+c)}$

Using partial fraction expansion, above equation can be written as,

$$X(S) = \frac{A1}{(s+p1)} + \frac{A2s + A3}{(s^2+bs+c)}$$

The residues A2 and A3 are solved by cross multiplying the above equation and then equating the

coefficients of like power of s.

Examples 4.4: On Inverse Laplace Transform

1. Find the ILT of given signal

$$X(s) = \frac{1}{(s+1)(s+2)} \qquad \mathrm{Re}\{s\} < -2$$

<u>Solution:</u> Like the inverse Fourier transform, expand as partial fractions

$$X(s) = \frac{1}{(s+1)(s+2)} = \frac{A}{(s+1)} + \frac{B}{(s+2)} = \frac{1}{(s+1)} - \frac{1}{(s+2)}$$

Pole-zero plots and ROC for combined & individual terms

$$-e^{-t}u(-t) \overset{L}{\leftrightarrow} \frac{1}{s+1}, \quad \mathrm{Re}\{s\} < -1$$

$$-e^{-2t}u(-t) \overset{L}{\leftrightarrow} \frac{1}{s+2}, \quad \mathrm{Re}\{s\} < -2$$

$$x(t) = (-e^{-t} + e^{-2t})u(-t) \overset{L}{\leftrightarrow} \frac{1}{(s+1)(s+2)}, \quad \mathrm{Re}\{s\} < -2$$

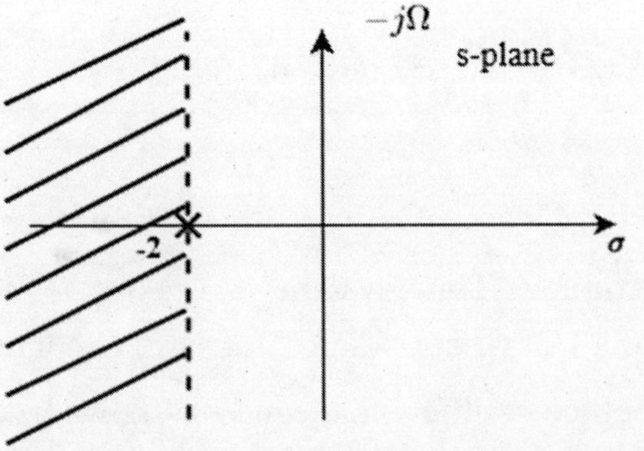

2. Find the ILT of $X(S) = \frac{4}{(s+2)(s+4)}$ if the ROC is

i. $-2 > Re\{s\} > -4$
ii. $Re\{s\} < -4$
iii. $Re\{s\} > -2$

Solution: Given $X(S) = \frac{4}{(s+2)(s+4)} = \frac{A1}{s+2} + \frac{A2}{s+4}$

Residue A1 is,

$$A1 = X(s)(s+2)|_{s=-2} = \frac{4}{(s+2)(s+4)} \times (s+2)\Big|_{s=-2} = 2$$

Residue A2 is,

$$A2 = X(s)(s+4)|_{s=-2} = \frac{4}{(s+2)(s+4)} \times (s+4)\Big|_{s=-4} = -2$$

$$X(S) = \frac{2}{s+2} - \frac{2}{s+4}$$

i. For $-2 > Re\{s\} > -4$

Given that ROC lies between lines passing through s = 2 to s = 4. Hence, x(t) will be two sided signal.

$$\boldsymbol{x(t) = -2e^{-2t}u(-t) - 2e^{-4t}u(t)}$$

ii. $Re\{s\} < -4$

Given that ROC is left of the line passing through s = 4. Hence x(t) will be anticausal signal

$$\boldsymbol{x(t) = -2e^{-2t}u(-t) + 2e^{-4t}u(-t)}$$

iii. $Re\{s\} > -2$

Given that ROC is right of the line passing through s = – 2. Hence x(t) will be causal signal.

$$\boldsymbol{x(t) = 2e^{-2t}u(t) - 2e^{-4t}u(t)}$$

4.8 Laplace domain analysis

4.8.1 Transfer Function of LTI Continuous Time System

In general, the input-output relation of a LTI (Linear Time Invariant) continuous time system is represented by the constant coefficient differential equation shown below,

$$\frac{d^n}{dt^n}y(t) + p_1\frac{d^{n-1}}{dt^{n-1}}y(t) + p_2\frac{d^{n-2}}{dt^{n-2}}y(t) + \cdots + p_{n-1}\frac{d}{dt}y(t) + p_n y(t) = z_0\frac{d^m}{dt^m}x(t) +$$

$$z_1\frac{d^{m-1}}{dt^{m-1}}x(t) + z_2\frac{d^{m-2}}{dt^{m-2}}y(t) + \cdots + z_{m-1}\frac{d}{dt}x(t) + z_m x(t) \qquad (4.14)$$

Where n is order of system and $m \leq n$

On taking LT of above equation and taking zero initial conditions,

$$\frac{Y(s)}{X(s)} = \frac{z_0 s^m + z_1 s^{m-1} + z_2 s^{m-2} + \cdots + z_{m-1}s + z_m}{p_0 s^n + p_1 s^{n-1} + p_2 s^{n-2} + \cdots + p_{n-1}s + p_n} \qquad (4.15)$$

The transfer function of a continuous time system is defined as the ratio of Laplace transform of output and Laplace transform of input. Hence the equation (4.15) is the transfer function of an LTI continuous time system.

4.8.2 Impulse Response and Transfer Function

Let, $x(t)$=input to LTI system

$y(t)$=output for input $x(t)$

$h(t)$=Impulse response

Now, the response y(t) of the continuous time system is given by convolution of input and impulse response. Recall the formula of convolution,

$$y(t) = x(t) * h(t) = \int_{-\infty}^{+\infty} x(\tau)h(t-\tau)d\tau \qquad (4.16)$$

Taking LT,

$$Y(s) = X(s)H(s) \qquad (4.17)$$

$$H(s) = \frac{Y(s)}{X(s)} = K\frac{(s - z_1)(s - z_2)(s - z_3) \dots \dots (s - z_m)}{(s - p_1)(s - p_2)(s - p_3) \dots \dots (s - p_n)}$$

The transfer function of LTI continuous time system is also given by Laplace transform of the impulse response.

4.9 Solving Differential Equations by Using Laplace Transform

Given a differential equation of LTI system as shown by Eq. (4.17), the system function can be written as,

$$H(s) = \frac{Y(s)}{X(s)} \qquad (4.18)$$

Which is obtained by taking the Laplace transform of the differential equation. The inverse Laplace transform of system function $H(s)$ can be obtained to get the impulse response of the system $h(t)$. For the stable system, i.e., if ROC includes the $j\Omega$ axis, then by substituting $s = j\Omega$, the frequency response of the system $H(j\Omega)$ can be obtained.

Unit Summary

The Laplace transform, a powerful mathematical tool, transcends mere computation to offer profound insights into the behavior of dynamic systems across various disciplines. Beginning with its historical roots and fundamental properties, the journey into Laplace transform theory elucidates its superiority over conventional methods in solving differential equations, thanks to its ability to convert complex time-domain problems into simpler algebraic ones. Techniques such as partial fraction decomposition and theorems for initial and final values amplify its practicality in diverse applications, from control systems analysis and electrical circuit design to signal processing and probability theory. Advanced topics unveil its versatility in handling generalized functions and partial differential equations, while its integration into modern engineering workflows underscores its indispensable role in modeling and analysis. As we reflect on its enduring impact, it becomes evident that the Laplace transform not only revolutionizes problem-solving but also fosters a deeper understanding of dynamic systems, paving the way for innovation and discovery across scientific and engineering frontiers.

Exercise

1. Using final value theorem, find the final value of the signal x(t) given

a. $X(s) = \frac{20}{s(s+4)}$

b. $X(s) = \frac{s}{s+4}$

c. $X(s) = \frac{s+12}{s^2+3s+2}$

d. $X(s) = \frac{s+3}{s^2+2s-3}$

e. $X(s) = \frac{s+9}{s^2+11s+30}$

2. Find the inverse Laplace transform of the following:

a. $X_1(s) = \frac{-4}{(s+2)(S-1)}$; ROC: $-2 < Re\{s\} < 1$

b. $X_2(s) = \frac{15s+72}{s^2-3s-28}$; $-7 < Re\{s\} < 4$

c. $X_3(s) = \frac{50}{s^2-225}$; ROC: $-15 < Re\{s\} < 15$

3. Using convolution property, find the following:

a. $y_1(t) = e^{-4t}u(t) * u(t)$

b. $y_2(t) = u(t) * u(t-5)$

c. $y_3(t) = \delta(t) * e^{-t}u(t)$

d. $y_4(t) = e^{-8t}u(t) * e^{-8t}u(t)$

e. $y_5(t) = e^{-4t}u(t) * e^{4t}u(-t)$

4. Sketch the pole-zero plot and ROC (if exists) for the following signals:

a. $x_1(t) = e^{-3t}u(t)$

b. $x_2(t) = e^{3t}u(-t)$

c. $x_3(t) = te^{-t}u(t)$

d. $x_4(t) = 3e^{-|t|}$

e. $x_5(t) = \frac{4}{3}e^{(4/3)t}u(-t)$

5. Using Laplace transform, solve the following differential equations:

a. $\frac{d}{dt}y(t) + 5y(t) = 5; y(0^-) = 1$

b. $\frac{d^2}{dt^2}y(t) + 7\frac{d}{dt}y(t) + 12y(t) = 3$

c. $\frac{d^2}{dt^2}x(t) + 3\frac{d}{dt}x(t) + 2x(t) = 4; x(0^-) = 1 = x'(0^-)$

d. $\frac{d^3}{dt^3}y(t) + 11\frac{d^2}{dt^2}y(t) + 30y(t) = e^{-t}u(t); y(0^-) = y'(0^-) = y''(0^-) = 0$

e. $\frac{d^2}{dt^2}y(t) + 4\frac{d}{dt}y(t) + 4y(t) = 1;\ y(0^-) = 1, y'(0^-) = -1,\ y''(0^-) = 0$

6. Find the Laplace transform of the signal

$$x(t) = -e^{-at}u(-t)$$

7. Find the Laplace transform of the signal

$$x(t) = e^{-2|t|}$$

8. Find the Laplace transform of the signal and its corresponding ROC.

$$x(t) = e^{-4t}[u(t) - u(t-4)]$$

9. Find the Laplace transform of $x(t) = e^{-2t}u(t) + e^{-4t}u(t)$

10. Find the Laplace transform of the signal $x(t) = e^{3t}u(t) + e^{9t}u(-t)$

11. Find the Laplace transform of $x(t) = \delta(t) - \frac{1}{5}e^{-3t}u(t) + \frac{1}{6}e^{-4t}u(t)$

12. Find the Laplace transform of $x(t) = e^{-at}u(t) + e^{bt}u(-t-1)$

13. Find the Laplace transform of $x(t) = u(t)$

14. Find the Laplace transform of $x(t) = tu(t)$

15. Find the Laplace transform of $x(t) = e^{j\Omega t}u(t)$.

16. Find the Laplace transform of $x_1 t = u(2t)$ by using the time-scaling property

17. Find the Laplace transform of $y(t) = x_1(t) * x_2(t)$, where $x_1(t) = e^{-t}u(t), x_2(t) = \delta(t)$.

18. Find the Laplace transform of $y(t) = -te^{-t}u(t)$. Using the differentiation in time domain property.

19. Find the Laplace transform of the output of an LTI system $y(t) = 3tx(t)$ by using the differentiation in s-domain property. Given

$$X(s) = \frac{s+2}{s^2 + 4s + 4}$$

20. Find the initial value and final value of $x(t)$ with Laplace transform

$$X(s) = \frac{2}{s(s^2 + 3s + 5)}$$

21. Find the inverse Laplace transform of

$$X(s) = \frac{2}{s^2+3s+2}, \text{ Re}\{s\} > -1$$

22. Find the inverse Laplace transform of

$$X(s) = \frac{2s+1}{s+3}$$

For (a) ROC: Re$\{s\} > -3$.

23. Find the inverse Laplace transform of

$$X(s) = \frac{1}{(s+5)(s-3)}$$

For the following ROCs:

$(a) - 5 < Re\{s\} < 3$
(b) $Re\{s\} > 3$

(c) $Re\{s\} < -5$

24. Find the inverse Laplace transform of

$$X(s) = \frac{s(s+3)}{(s+3)^2},$$

ROC: $Re\{s\} > -3$

25. Find the inverse Laplace transform of

(a) $X(s) = \frac{1}{(s+2)^2}$; ROC: $Re\{s\} > -2$

(b) $X(s) = \frac{s}{s^2+4}$; ROC: $Re\{s\} > -2$

(c) $X(s) = \frac{2}{(s+1)^2+4}$; ROC: $Re\{s\} > -1$

Multiple-Choice Questions

1. For a causal signal x(t), the ROC of X(s) is

a) Right-half of s-plane
b) Left-half of s-plane
c) Entire s-plane
d) jΩ-axis

2. The Laplace transform of $x(t) = 2\delta(t)$ is

a) 2
b) b) $2/s$
c) c) 2s
d) d) s

3. The Laplace transform of $x(t) = e^{-4t}u(t)$ is

a) $\frac{1}{s-4}$

b) $\frac{1}{s+4}$

c) $\frac{1}{(s+4)^2}$

d) $\frac{1}{(s-4)^2}$

4. ROC of X(s) of $e^{4t}u(-t)$ is

a) $Re\{s\} > 4$

b) $Re\{s\} < -4$

c) $Re\{s\} < 4$

d) $Re\{s\} > -4$

5. If $X(s) = \frac{s-10}{s^2-5s}$ then $x(0^-)$ is

a) 0

b) ∞

c) 1

d) 2

6. Given $(t) \overset{LT}{\leftrightarrow} X(s)$, then $-4\frac{d}{dt}x(t) \overset{LT}{\leftrightarrow}$ is

a) $4sX(s)$

b) $-4sX(s)$

c) $\frac{4}{s}X(s)$

d) $-\frac{4}{s}X(s)$

7. The Laplace transform of $\delta(t) * u(t)$ is

a) $\frac{1}{s}$

b) s

c) $\frac{1}{s+1}$

d) $\frac{1}{s-1}$

8. The Laplace transform of $x(2t)$ is

a) $\frac{1}{2}X\left(\frac{s}{2}\right)$

b) $2X(2s)$

c) $\frac{1}{2}X(2s)$

d) $2\frac{X}{s/2}$

9. The inverse Laplace transform of $X(s) = \frac{10s}{(s+1)(s+3)}$ is

a) $5(3e^{3t} - e^{t})u(t)$
b) $5(3e^{-3t} - e^{-t})u(t)$
c) $5(3e^{-3t} - e^{t})u(t)$
d) $5(3e^{-3t} - e^{t})u(-t)$

10. The Laplace transform of $x(t) = e^{t}u(t)$ is

a) $\frac{1}{s-1}$; Re{s} > 1
b) $\frac{1}{s+1}$; Re{s} > 1
c) $\frac{1}{s-1}$; Re{s} < 1
d) $\frac{1}{s+1}$; Re{s} < 1

11. The Laplace transform of $\delta(4t)$ is

a) 1/4s
b) 1/4
c) s/4
d) 4s

12. The output of an LTI system $\frac{d}{dt}y(t) + y(T) = x(t)$ initially at rest, for given $x(t) = \delta(t)$ is

a) $e^{-t}u(t)$
b) $u(t)$
c) $\delta(t)$
d) $\delta(t-1)$

13. If $x(t)$ is a left-sided signal, then its ROC is

a) entire s-plane
b) left-half of s-plane
c) right-half of s-plane
d) entire jΩ- axis

14. A causal LTI system has a transfer fraction $H(s)$, whose ROC will be

a) Right-sided in the s-plane

b) Left-sided in the s-plane
c) Entire s-plane
d) $s = j\Omega$- axis

15. The ROC of a stable LTI system will
a) include the $j\Omega$- axis
b) be $Re\{s\} > 1$
c) be $Re\{s\} + 1$
d) be $Re\{s\} > 0$

KNOW MORE

The Laplace transform is a mathematical technique that is used to simplify solving differential equations, particularly those with initial conditions. It transforms functions of time into functions of complex frequency. This transformation makes it easier to solve linear differential equations by turning them into algebraic equations. Understanding the Laplace transform's definition and its properties is crucial. This includes linearity, time-shifting, scaling, and differentiation properties. Additionally, understanding the region of convergence is important for ensuring convergence of the transformed function. Knowing how to convert a Laplace-transformed function back into the time domain is essential. Techniques such as partial fraction decomposition, contour integration, and the use of tables of Laplace transforms are commonly employed. Laplace transform is extensively used in solving ordinary and partial differential equations, including those arising in engineering, physics, and other fields. It simplifies solving differential equations with initial conditions, boundary conditions, and forcing functions. Laplace transform finds applications in signal processing for analyzing and manipulating continuous-time signals. It aids in filtering, modulation, demodulation, and system identification tasks, contributing to various fields such as telecommunications, audio processing, and medical imaging. We have to stay updated on recent advancements and ongoing research in Laplace transform theory, applications, and computational methods. Investigating emerging trends, challenges, and potential interdisciplinary collaborations in areas such as data science, machine learning, and quantum computing along with Laplace transform is needed.

REFERENCES AND SUGGESTED READINGS

1. Signals and Systems by Simon Haykin
2. Signals and Systems by Ganesh Rao
3. Signals and Systems - Course (nptel.ac.in)

Dynamic QR Code for Further Reading

5 Z - Transform

UNIT SPECIFICS

Through this unit we have discussed the following aspects:

- *What is z- Transform, why it was developed?*
- *z-Transform and ROC of finite and infinite duration sequences*
- *Relation between Discrete Time Fourier Transform (DTFT) and z-Transform*
- *Properties of z-Transform.*
- *Inverse z-Transform and methods of analysis*

RATIONALE

The unit on "z-Transform" provides students to understand the relationship between DTFT and z-Transform. The students will understand the conversion of a discrete-time signal, which is a sequence of real or complex numbers, into a complex valued frequency-domain (the z-domain or z-plane) representation.

The unit focuses on z-Transform and ROC of finite and infinite duration sequences along with the properties. The students can analyse the behaviour of the linear time-invariant (LTI) system using the Z transform.

PRE-REQUISITES

1. *Strong understanding of mathematics, including algebra, calculus, and complex numbers.*

2. *Familiarity with basic concepts in signals and systems, such as periodic, non-periodic signals, unilateral and bilateral sequences.*

3. *Proficiency in solving ordinary differential equations and understanding linear algebra concepts.*

UNIT OUTCOMES

List of outcomes of this unit is as follows:

U5-O1: Be able to understand the need for bilateral and unilateral z-transforms to analyze discrete-time (DT) signals and systems.

U5-O2: Be able to understand the relationship between DT Fourier Transform (DTFT) and z-transform.

U5-O3: Be able to learn the properties of z-transform.

U5-O4: Be able to learn the applications of bilateral and unilateral z-transform.

Unit-5 Outcomes	***EXPECTED MAPPING WITH COURSE OUTCOMES*** *(1- Weak Correlation; 2- Medium correlation; 3- Strong Correlation)*					
	CO-1	***CO-2***	***CO-3***	***CO-4***	***CO-5***	***CO-6***
U5-O1	-	-	-	2	3	-
U5-O2	-	-	-	2	3	-
U5-O3	-	-	-	-	3	-
U5-O4	-	-	-	-	3	-

5.1 Introduction

The Z-transform is a mathematical technique used in signal processing and control theory to analyze and process discrete-time signals and systems. It is the discrete-time counterpart of the Laplace transform, which is used for continuous-time signals and systems.

The Z-transform is beneficial for several reasons:

Frequency Analysis: It allows for the analysis of signals and systems in the frequency domain. By taking the Z-transform of a discrete signal or system, you can analyze its frequency components and behavior.

System Representation: The Z-transform can be used to represent and analyze discrete-time linear time-invariant (LTI) systems, which are essential in fields like control theory and digital signal processing.

Transfer Functions: It helps in finding the transfer function of a system, which relates the input and output in the Z-domain. This is useful for designing and analyzing control systems and filters.

Stability Analysis: The Z-transform can be used to analyze the stability of discrete-time systems. It's crucial in control theory to ensure that a system doesn't become unstable over time.

Differential Equations: It can be used to solve linear difference equations, which often arise in discrete-time systems modeling.

The Z-transform is a powerful tool for the analysis and design of discrete-time systems and is widely used in various engineering and scientific fields. It helps in simplifying the analysis of complex systems and understanding their behavior in both the time and frequency domains.

5.2 Need of Z-transform

There are some signals which are not absolutely summable and there Fourier transform does not exist. Instead of taking transform of x[n], we can do a little change in the signal so that the signal becomes absolutely summable and then apply the transform. Let us multiply the signal x[n] with r^{-n}. r^{-n} is a slow decaying exponential signal. This transform is named as Z-transform.

$$Z.T.\{x(n)\} = X(z) = \sum_{-\infty}^{\infty}\{x[n]r^{-n}\}\,e^{-jwn}$$

$$=\sum_{-\infty}^{\infty} x[n]\{r^{-n}e^{-jwn}\}$$

$$=\sum_{-\infty}^{\infty} x[n]\{re^{jw}\}^{-n}$$

Substituting into z = r e^{jw} the above equation, the difficulty is resolved by generalizing the DTFT of the signal x(n) can be expressed as sum of complex exponential, z^n.

$$X(z) = \sum_{-\infty}^{\infty} x[n]z^{-n} \qquad (5.1)$$

The Z-transform reduces to DTFT for the value of r = 1.

Inverse Z-transform is given by,

$$x[n] = \frac{1}{2\pi j}\oint_C X(z)z^{n-1}dz$$

It is denoted as,

$$x(n) \overset{Z.T}{\leftrightarrow} X(z)$$

$$\Rightarrow \text{Z.T.}\{x(n)\} = X(z)$$

$$\Rightarrow \text{I.Z.T.}\{X(z)\} = x[n]$$

5.3 Types of Z-transforms

There are mainly two types of Z-transforms: the unilateral Z-transform and the bilateral Z-transform. Both are mathematical techniques used in the analysis and design of discrete-time systems, but they differ in their definitions and applications.

5.3.1 Unilateral Z-Transform:

Definition: The unilateral Z-transform is defined for signals that are causal, meaning they start at a finite time and continue indefinitely.

Formula: The unilateral Z-transform of a discrete-time signal x[n] is given by:

$$X(z) = \sum_{0}^{\infty} x[n]z^{-n} \qquad (5.2)$$

Application: It is commonly used when dealing with signals that are causal and have a starting point in time.

5.3.2 Bilateral Z-Transform:

Definition: The bilateral Z-transform is defined for signals that may be non-causal, extending over both past and future time indices.

Formula: The bilateral Z-transform of a discrete-time signal x[n] is given by:

$$X(z) = \sum_{-\infty}^{\infty} x[n]z^{-n} \qquad (5.3)$$

Application: It is more general and can be applied to a wider range of signals, including non-causal ones. However, it may not converge for all signals, and caution is needed in its application.

In practical applications, the unilateral Z-transform is often more commonly used, especially in the context of causal systems and signals. The choice between unilateral and bilateral Z-transform depends on the nature of the problem and the characteristics of the signals involved.

5.4 The Z-plane

The Z-plane is a graphical representation used in the analysis and design of discrete-time systems, particularly in the context of Z-transforms as shown in the figure below. The Z-plane is a complex plane where the Z-transform is visualized and analyzed. In the Z-plane, complex numbers are represented as points, and each point corresponds to a specific frequency response or characteristic of a discrete-time system.

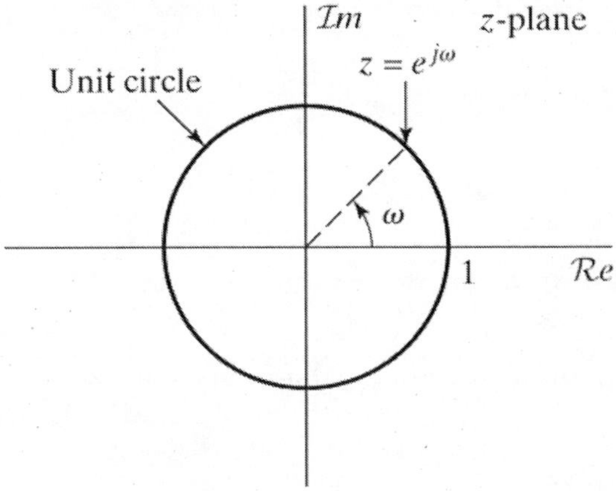

Fig 5.1: Z-plane

The Z-transform is a mathematical transformation that converts a discrete-time signal, represented by a sequence x[n], into a complex function of a complex variable z. The Z-plane provides a way to understand and interpret the properties of this complex function.

The point at the origin (z = 0) represents the DC (zero-frequency) component of the signal. The unit circle in the Z-plane corresponds to the unit circle in the complex plane, where the magnitude of z is equal to 1. Points on the unit circle are associated with frequencies equal to the sampling frequency. The unit circle is particularly important for analyzing frequency response characteristics.

Poles and zeros of the Z-transform are represented as points in the Z-plane. Zeros are locations where the Z-transform is zero, and poles are locations where the Z-transform becomes infinite. The distribution of poles and zeros in the Z-plane provides insights into the stability and frequency response of a discrete-time system.

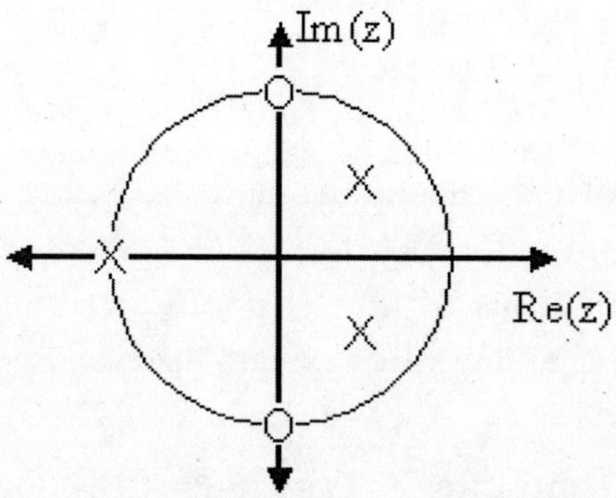

Fig 5.2: Poles and zeros in the Z-plane

5.4.1 Poles:

Poles are the values of Z for which the transfer function becomes infinite (the denominator of the transfer function becomes zero). The poles are denoted with the cross sign in the above figure. They represent the natural frequencies of the system and provide information about the system's stability and response to input signals.

The locations of the poles in the Z-plane determine how the system responds to different frequencies. Poles closer to the origin ($Z = 0$) correspond to faster decaying modes, while poles farther from the origin may represent dominant resonant frequencies.

The system is considered stable if all poles are inside the unit circle in the Z-plane. If any poles are outside the unit circle, the system is unstable.

5.4.2 Zeros:

Zeros are the values of Z for which the transfer function becomes zero (the numerator of the transfer function becomes zero). The zeros are denoted with a small circle sign in the above figure. They represent the frequencies at which the system's response is zero, indicating points in the Z-plane where the system does not respond to certain input frequencies.

Zeros can affect the system's frequency response, leading to resonant peaks or notches in the frequency domain. The location of zeros in the Z-plane indicates the frequencies at which the system has no response.

In summary, poles and zeros in the Z-transform provide valuable information about the frequency response and stability of a discrete-time system. By analyzing the distribution of poles and zeros in the Z-plane, one can understand how a system responds to different frequencies and make design decisions to achieve desired system performance.

The Z-plane is also associated with the concept of the Region of Convergence (ROC), which is the set of values of z for which the Z-transform converges. The ROC is often specified to ensure the convergence of the Z-transform. We will discuss about this later in this chapter. The location of poles in the Z-plane is crucial for stability analysis. For a discrete-time system to be stable, all poles must lie inside the unit circle.

The Z-plane is a valuable tool for visualizing and analyzing the properties of discrete-time systems in the context of Z-transforms. It provides insights into the frequency response, stability, and convergence properties of these systems, making it an essential concept in the field of digital signal processing and control system analysis.

5.5 Region of Convergence (ROC) for Z-Transform

We have already seen that the Z-Transform of x[n] is the Fourier Transform of x[n] r^{-n}, that is,

$$x(z) = \sum_{-\infty}^{\infty} \{x[n]r^{-n}\}e^{-jwn} \qquad (5.4)$$

Hence, is guaranteed to converge if x[n] r^{-n} is absolutely summable. So, if x[n] r^{-n} is absolutely assumable then $|X(z)| < \infty$.

For a given Z-transform X(z), the Region of Convergence (ROC) is the set of values of the complex variable z for which the Z-transform converges. The ROC is crucial because it determines the set of values for which the Z-transform is well-defined.

Let us see few signals and their Z-Transform.

Example 5.1 Determine the Z.T. and ROC of the following finite duration signals:

(a) $x[n] = \{1,2,3,-1,0,1\}, -2 \le n \le 3$
(b) $x[n] = \{0,0,1,2,1\},\ 0 \le n \le 4$
(c) $x[n] = \{1,2,3,-1,0,\}, -4 \le n \le 0$

Solution:

(a) $x[n] = \{1,2,\mathbf{3},-1,0,1\}, -2 \le n \le 3$

By definition,

$$X(z) = \sum_{-\infty}^{\infty} x[n]z^{-n}$$

The given signal is of finite duration $-2 < n < 3$.

$$= \sum_{-2}^{3} x[n]z^{-n}$$

$$= x(-2)z^{2} + x(-1)z^{1} + x(0)z^{0} + x(1)z^{-1} + x(2)z^{-2} + x(3)z^{-3}$$

Substituting values of x[n] we get,

$$X(z) = 1z^{2} + 2z + 3 - z^{-1} + z^{-3}$$

ROC for X(z) is entire z-plane except z = 0 and z = ∞.

(b) $x[n] = \{\mathbf{0}, 0, 1, 2, 1\}, 0 \le n \le 4$

By definition,

$$X(z) = \sum_{-\infty}^{\infty} x[n]z^{-n}$$

The given signal is of finite duration 0 ≤ n ≤ 4.

Change the limits of summation,

$$X(z) = \sum_{0}^{4} x[n]z^{-n}$$

$$= x(0) + x(1)z^{-1} + x(2)z^{-2} + x(3)z^{-3} + x(4)z^{-4}$$

$$X(z) = 0 + 0z^{-1} + 1z^{-2} + 2z^{-3} + 1z^{-4}$$

$$= z^{-2} + 2z^{-3} + z^{-4}$$

$$\therefore ROC\ of\ X(z) is\ entire\ z - plane\ except\ z = 0.$$

(c) $x[n] = \{1, 2, 3, -1, \mathbf{0}\}, -4 \le n \le 0.$

By definition,

$$X(z) = \sum_{-\infty}^{\infty} x[n]z^{-n}$$

The signal x[n] has non-zero values of n = –4, –3, –2, – 1, 0. i.e. –4 ≤ n ≤ 0.

$$X(z) = \sum_{-4}^{0} x[n]z^{-n}$$

$$= x(-4)z^{-(-4)} + x(-3)z^{-(-3)} + x(-2)z^{-(-2)} +$$

$$x(-1)z^{-(-1)} + x(0)z^{0}$$

$$= 1z^{4} + 2z^{3} + 3z^{3} + (-1)z + 0$$

$$= 1z^{4} + 2z^{3} + 3z^{2} + (-1)z + 0$$

$$X(z) = z + 3z^2 + 2z^3 + z^4$$

The ROC for X(z) is entire z-plane except z = ∞.

Example 5.2

Consider the Signal x[n] = a^nu(n). Find Z-Transform of x[n] Where |a| < 1.

Given : x[n] = a^n u(n), |a| < 1

Solution: The signal x[n] is right sided i.e. causal and infinite duration.

Z.T. of x[n] can be found by using equation below,

$$X(z) = \sum_{-\infty}^{\infty} x[n]z^{-n}$$

$$= \sum_{-\infty}^{\infty} a^n\, u(n)z^{-n}$$

We know,

$$u(n) = \begin{cases} 1, & n \geq 0 \\ 0, & o.w. \end{cases}$$

$$X(z) = \sum_{0}^{\infty} a^n .1.z^{-n}$$

$$= \sum_{0}^{\infty} (a.z^{-1})^n$$

We know,

$$\sum_{0}^{\infty} a^n\ .u(n) = \frac{1}{1-a}, \qquad |a| < 1$$

Applying this to X(z) we get,

$$X(z) = \sum_{0}^{\infty} (az^{-1})^n = \frac{1}{1 - az^{-1}} = \frac{z}{z-a}$$

$|z - a| > 0, |z| > |a|$ It will be the ROC.

The zeros can be obtained by equating numerator to zero and poles by equation denominator to zero.

z – a=0 ⇒ z = a

One pole is located at z = a.

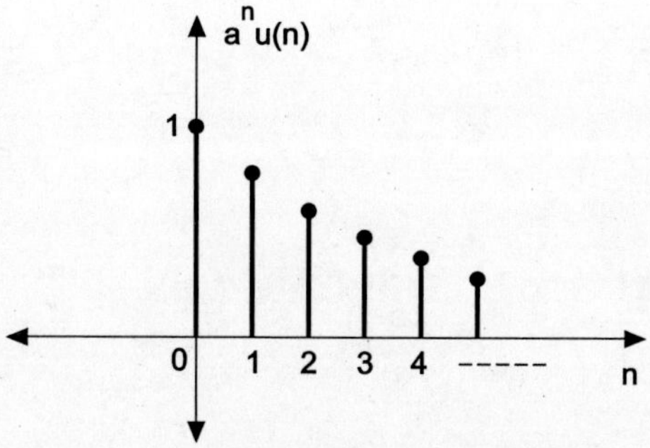

Fig. 5.3 $x(n) = a^n u(n)$

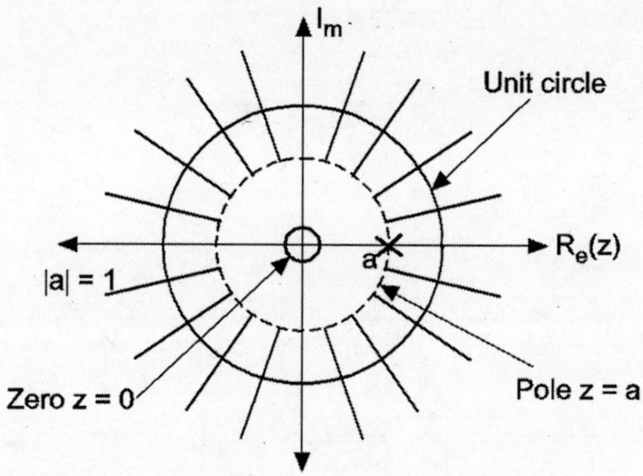

Fig. 5.4 Pole-zero plot and ROC $|z| > |a|$

Observe here that the signal x[n] is causal, therefore the ROC of X(z) is outside the circle having radius $|a|$.

<u>Example 5.3</u>: Determine the Z.T. of the another signal given below

$$x[n] = -a^n u[-n-1], |a| < 1$$

<u>Solution:</u> It is an infinite duration left sided, anticausal signal.

The Z.T. of the x[n] can be evaluated as,

$$X(z) = \sum_{-\infty}^{\infty} x[n] z^{-n}$$

Substituting value of x[n] in X(z) we get,

$$X(z) = \sum_{-\infty}^{\infty} -a^n\, u(-n-1) z^{-n}$$

Here, u(–n – 1) is 1 only when n ∈ [– ∞, – 1].

$$\therefore X(z) = -\sum_{n=-\infty}^{\infty} a^n (u(n-1) z^{-n}$$

$$= -\sum_{n=-\infty}^{-1} a^n .1. z^n$$

$$= -\sum_{-\infty}^{-1} (az^{-1})^n$$

Replacing n by –n we get,

$$= -\sum_{1}^{\infty} (a^{-1}z)^n$$

As the lower limit starts from 1, we cannot directly find the answer. We will do some adjustments so that it will start from 0.

$$= -\left[\sum_{0}^{\infty} (a^{-1}z)^n - 1\right]$$

$$= 1 - \sum_{n=0}^{\infty} \left(\frac{Z}{a}\right)^n$$

$$= 1 - \frac{1}{1 - a^{-1}z} = \frac{z}{z-a}$$

This series converges,

$$|a^{-1}z| < 1$$

$$\Rightarrow |z| < \lceil a \rceil$$

$$\therefore X(z) = \frac{z}{z-a}\ ; ROC\ |z| < |a|$$

$x[n] = -a^n\, u\,(-n-1)$ is a non-causal infinite duration signal.

The ROC is inside the circle of radius |a| as shown below.

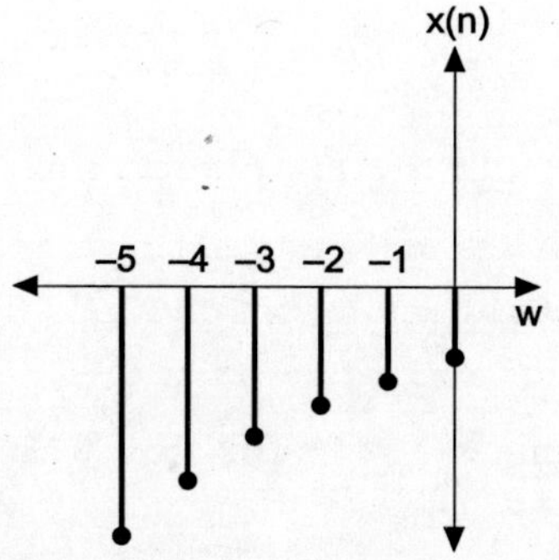

Fig. 5.5 x[n]=– a^n u(– n – 1)

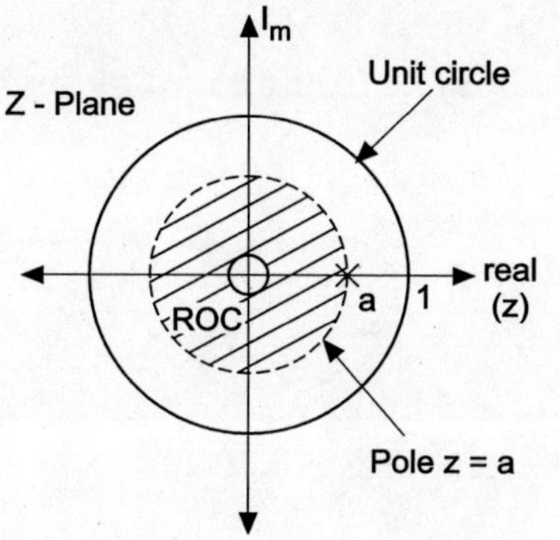

Fig. 5.6 Pole-zero plot and ROC |z| < |a|·

It is an interesting thing to observe that the signals: $x[n] = a^n u\,(n), |a|\; 1\; and\; x\;[n] = -a^n u(\,-n-1)$are having same value of $X(z) = \frac{z}{z-a}$ Here the ROC is playing an important role of differentiating the two signals. For causal signal the ROC of X(z) is outside the circle having radial |a| and anti-causal signal the ROC of X(z) is inside the circle having radial |a|. These two examples explain the importance of specifying ROC.

5.6 Properties of ROC

The ROC determines the validity and convergence of the Z-transform expression. If a specific Z value is within the ROC, the Z-transform is well-defined and finite for that value. Outside the ROC, the Z-transform might not exist or could be infinite, leading to undefined results. In this section, let us go through the properties of ROC.

1. The ROC of X(z) consists of a ring in the z-plane centered about the origin.
2. If X(z) is rational, then The ROC must not contain any pole because at pole location the Z.T. becomes infinity.

3. If x[n] is of finite duration, then the ROC is the entire z-plane, except possibility z = 0 and/or z = ∞.
4. If x[n] is right sided and of infinite duration sequence, then ROC is the region of the z-plane outside the outermost pole.
5. If x[n] is a left sided and of infinite duration sequence, then ROC is the region of the z-plane inside the innermost pole.
6. If x[n] is two sided and if the circle |z| = r_0 is the ROC, then the ROC will consist of a ring in the z-plane that includes the circle |z| = r_0.
7. If the z-transform X(z) of x[n], is rational, then its ROC is bounded by poles or extends to infinity.
8. If the Z.T. of X(z) of x[n] is rational and if x[n] is right sided, then ROC is the region in the z-plane outside the outermost pole. i.e. outside the circle of radius equal to the largest magnitude of the pole of X(z).

   If signal x[n] is causal then ROC includes z = ∞.
9. If the Z.T. X(z) of x[n] is rational and if x[n] is left sided, then ROC is the region in the z-plane inside the innermost nonzero pole.

i.e. Inside the circle of radius equal to the smallest magnitude including z = 0 in particular, if x[n] is anti-causal then the ROC also includes z = 0.

5.7 Properties of the Z-transform

The Z-transform is a mathematical tool used in the analysis and processing of discrete-time signals and systems. It has several important properties that make it a valuable tool in various engineering and scientific fields. Here are some of the key properties of the Z-transform:

5.7.1 Linearity:

The Z-transform is a linear operation, which means it satisfies the superposition principle. If you have a linear combination of signals, you can compute the Z-transform of each signal separately and then sum them to find the Z-transform of the combined signal.

Linearity property states that,

$$x_1(n) \overset{Z.T}{\leftrightarrow} X_1(z) \; with\; ROC : \; R_1$$

$$x_2(n) \overset{Z.T}{\leftrightarrow} X_2(z) \; with\; ROC : \; R_2$$

Then, $y(n) = a\,x_1(n) + b\,x_2\,(n) \overset{Z.T}{\leftrightarrow} Y(z) = a\,X_1(z) + b\,X_2(z)$ with ROC $R_1 \cap R_2$ (5.5)

Proof : The Z.T. of Y[n] is given by,

$$Y(z) = \sum_{n=-\infty}^{\infty} y(n).\ z^{-n}$$

$$= \sum_{-\infty}^{\infty} \{ax_1\,(n) + b\,x_2\,(n)\}z^{-n}$$

$$= a\sum_{-\infty}^{\infty} x_1(n).z^{-n} + b\sum_{-\infty}^{\infty} x_2\,(n)z^{-n}$$

$$X_1(z) \qquad\qquad X_2(z)$$

$$Y(z) = a\,X_1(z) + b\,X_2(z)\ with\ ROC\ R_1 \cap R_2$$

Hence proved.

The linearity property can be generalized for any number of arbitrary signals.

It implies that the Z.T. of a linear combination of signals is the same as linear combination of their Z.T.

5.7.2 Time Shifting:

If you delay (advance) a discrete signal in the time domain, the Z-transform of the shifted signal is related to the original Z-transform by multiplying it by a power of Z.

If $x[n] \overset{Z.T}{\leftrightarrow} X(z)\ with\ ROC\ :R$

then, $y(n) = x\,(n - n_0) \overset{Z.T}{\leftrightarrow} Y(z) = z^{-n_0}\,X_{(z)}$ $\qquad ROC\ : R \cap \{0 < |z| < \infty\}$ (5.6)

Proof : Let, y[n] = x[n – n₀]

By the definition of the Z.T. we have,

$$Y[z] = \sum_{-\infty}^{\infty} y[n]\,z^{-n}$$

$$= \sum_{-\infty}^{\infty} x(n - n_0)z^{-n}$$

Let, $n - n_0 = m\,, \quad n_0 + m = n$

$Y[z] = \sum_{-\infty}^{\infty} x[m]z^{-(m+n_0)}$ (5.7)

$=\sum_{-\infty}^{\infty} x[m]z^{-m}\,z^{-n_0}$ (5.8)

$= z^{-n_0}\sum_{m=-\infty}^{\infty} x(m)z^{-m}$ (5.9)

$$Y(z) = z^{-n_0}\,X_{(z)} \qquad ROC\ : R \cap \{0 < |z| < \infty\}$$

Hence proved.

5.7.3 Time Reversal:

The Z-transform of a time-reversed signal is related to the complex conjugate of the Z-transform of the original signal.

Time reversal property states that,

if $x[n] \overset{Z.T}{\leftrightarrow} X(z)$ with ROC : R and $y(n) = x\,(-n)$

then, $Y\,(z) = X\,(z^{-1}) with\ ROC\ \frac{1}{R}$ (5.10)

Proof : We have, $y(n) = x\,(-n)$

By the definition of Z.T.

$$Y(z) = \sum_{-\infty}^{\infty} y(n) z^{-n}$$

$= \sum_{-\infty}^{\infty} x(-n) z^{-n}$ (5.11)

Substituting $-n = m$

$$Y(z) = \sum_{-m=-\infty}^{\infty} x[m] z^{m}$$

$= \sum_{m-\infty}^{\infty} x[m][z^{-1}]^{-m}$ (5.12)

$$Y(z) = X\,(z^{-1})$$

then, $Y(z) = X\,(z^{-1}) with\ ROC\ \frac{1}{R}$.

which is same as R.H.S. Hence proved.

5.7.4 Scaling in z-domain:

If you multiply a discrete signal by a constant in the time domain, the Z-transform of the scaled signal is obtained by multiplying the original Z-transform by the same constant.

Let, $x[n] \overset{Z.}{\leftrightarrow} X\,(z) with\ ROC\ R.$

' x[n] (z) with ROC R.

then, $y[n] = a^n . x[n] \overset{Z.T}{\leftrightarrow} y\,(z) = X\left(\frac{z}{a}\right) with\ ROC :\ |a|\,R.$ (5.13)

Proof : Let $Z.T. of\ y\,[n] = a^n . x[n] z[n] is,$

Z.T. of $y[n] = a^n . x[n]$ is,

$$Y[z] = \sum_{-\infty}^{\infty} y(n) z^{-n} = \sum_{-\infty}^{\infty} a^n . x[n] z^{-n}$$

$$= \sum_{-\infty}^{\infty} x[n].\left(\frac{z}{a}\right)^{-n}$$

$$Y(z) = X\left(\frac{z}{a}\right) with\ ROC:\ |a|\ R.$$

then, $Y(z) = X\left(\frac{z}{a}\right)$ $with\ ROC:\ |a|R.$

$||a|$ R is scaled version of R.

If X(z) has a pole or zero at z = b then $X\left(\frac{z}{a}\right)$ has a pole or zero at z = a · b.

If b is +ve number, the scaling can be interpreted as shrinking or expanding of the z-plane.

5.7.5 Time scaling:

$$Let, x_m[n] = \begin{cases} x\left(\frac{n}{m}\right) & \text{if n is multiple of m;} \\ 0 & \text{if n is not multiple of m ;} \end{cases}$$

$x_m[n]$ is obtained from x[n] by inserting (m – 1) zeros between successive sample values of x(m).

if, $x_m(n) = \longleftrightarrow$X (z)

then, y(n) = $X_m(n) \overset{Z}{\longleftrightarrow} X(z^m)$ = Y(z) with ROC : $R^{1/m}$. (5.14)

Proof : We know that,

$$X(z) = \sum_{-\infty}^{\infty} x[n]z^{-n}$$

$$X(z^m) = \sum_{-\infty}^{\infty} x[n](z^m)^{-n}$$

$$= \sum_{-\infty}^{\infty} x[n]z^{-mn}$$

k = mn then n=k/m,

$$X(z^m) = \textstyle\sum_{-\infty}^{\infty} x\left[\frac{k}{m}\right] z^{-k} \qquad (5.15)$$

Replacing k by n,

$$X(z^m) = \sum_{-\infty}^{\infty} x\left[\frac{n}{m}\right] z^{-n}$$

$Y(z) = X(z^m)$ with ROC : $R^{1/m}$.

5.7.6 Convolution:

Convolution in the time domain corresponds to multiplication in the Z-domain. This property is particularly useful for analyzing the behavior of linear time-invariant systems. Convolution property states that,

$$x_1(n) \overset{z}{\leftrightarrow} X_1(z) with\ ROC\ R_1$$

$$x_2(n) \overset{z}{\leftrightarrow} X_1(n) with\ ROC\ 2$$

then, $y(n) = x_1(n) * x_2(n) \overset{z}{\leftrightarrow} Y(z) = X_1(z).X_2(z) \quad ROC : R_1 \cap R_2$ (5.16)

Proof : By definition of Z.T.

We have,

$$y(z) = \sum_{-\infty}^{\infty} y(n) z^{-n}$$

$$\sum_{-\infty}^{\infty} [x_1(n) * x_2(n)]\ z^{-n}$$

But, we know,

$$y(x) = x_1(n) * x_2(n)$$

$$= \textstyle\sum_{-\infty}^{\infty} x_1(m) x_2(n-m) \quad (5.17)$$

Substituting y (n) in y (z) as,

$$y(z) = \textstyle\sum_{-\infty}^{\infty} \sum_{-\infty}^{\infty} x_1(m).x_2(n-m) z^{-n} \quad (5.18)$$

$$= \textstyle\sum_{-\infty}^{\infty} x_1(m) \sum_{-\infty}^{\infty} x_2(n-m) z^{-n} \quad (5.19)$$

Using time shifting property,

$$= \textstyle\sum_{-\infty}^{\infty} x_1(m).z^{-m} X_2(z) \quad (5.20)$$

Putting $\sum_{-\infty}^{\infty} x_1(m).z^{-m} = X_1(z)$ into the above equation,

$$Y(z) = X_1(z).X_2(z) \quad ROC : R_1 \cap R_2$$

Hence proved.

5.7.7 Differentiation in z-domain:

Taking the Z-transform of a signal's derivative in the time domain is related to the Z-transform of the original signal through multiplication by Z (i.e., differentiation in the time domain corresponds to multiplication by Z in the Z-domain).

$If\ x[n] \overset{ZT}{\leftrightarrow} X(z) with\ ROC\ R.$

Then, $y(n) = n.x[n] \overset{ZT}{\leftrightarrow} Y(z) = -z\frac{d}{dz} X(z) with\ ROC\ R.$ (5.21)

Proof : We know,

$$X(z) = \sum_{-\infty}^{\infty} x[n]z^{-n}$$

Differentiate X(z) w.r.t. z we get,

$\frac{d}{dz}X(z) = \sum_{-\infty}^{\infty} x[n].\frac{d}{dz}(z^{-n})$ (5.22)

$\frac{d}{dz} X(z) = \sum_{-\infty}^{\infty} x[n].(-n).z^{-n-1}$ (5.23)

$\frac{d}{dz} X(z) = -z^{-1}\sum_{-\infty}^{\infty} n.x[n].z^{-n}$ (5.24)

$-z.\frac{d}{dz} X(z) = \sum_{-\infty}^{\infty} n.x[n]z^{-n}$ (5.25)

It is the $Z.T.\{n.x[n]\}$

Hence, $n.x[n] \overset{ZT}{\leftrightarrow} -z\frac{d}{dz} X(z)$

5.7.8 Conjugation:

Convolution property states that

It states that, if $x[n] \overset{ZT}{\leftrightarrow} X(z)\ with\ ROC\ R$

then, $y(n) = x^*(n) \overset{ZT}{\leftrightarrow} y(z) = X^*(z^*)\ with\ ROC\ R.$ (5.26)

Proof: The $Z.T. of\ x[n] is\ given\ by,$

$X(z) = \sum_{-\infty}^{\infty} x[n]z^{-n}$

Taking conjugate of the above equation we get,

$X^*(z) = (\sum_{-\infty}^{\infty} x[n]z^{-n})^*$ (5.27)

$X^*(z) = \sum_{-\infty}^{\infty} x^*(n).z^{n} = \sum_{-\infty}^{\infty} x^*(n)(z^*)^{-n}$ (5.28)

Putting z = z* we get,

$$X^*(z^*) = \sum_{-\infty}^{\infty} x^*(n).z^{-n}$$

Hence, $x^*(n) \overset{ZT}{\leftrightarrow} X^*(z^*)$

5.7.9 Initial Value Theorem:

The initial value of a signal can be found from its Z-transform. This property is useful for analyzing the behavior of signals as they start at time zero.

It states that, if x[n] is causal signal i.e. x[n] = 0, n < 0.

then, $x(0) = \lim_{z\to\infty} X(z)$ (5.29)

5.7.10 Final Value Theorem:

The final value of a signal can also be determined from its Z-transform. This property is useful for understanding the long-term behavior of signals as time approaches infinity.

It states that, $x(\infty) = \lim_{z\to 1}(1 - z^{-1})X(z)$ (5.30)

where, $x(\infty)$ is the final value of causal signal.

This expression is possible only when the poles of $(1 - z^{-1})\,X(z)$ are inside the unit circle.

Proof : We have, $x[n] - x(n-1) \overset{z}{\leftrightarrow} (1 - z^{-1})X(z)$

L.H.S.$y(n) = x[n] - x\,(n-1)$

Taking the Z.T. of above,

$$y(z) = \sum_{-\infty}^{\infty} \{x[n] - x(n-1)\}z^{-n}$$

$$= \overset{Lt}{N \to \infty} \sum_{n=0}^{N} \{x[n] - x(n-1)\}z^{-n}$$

$$\lim_{n\to 1}(1 - z^{-1})X(z) = \lim_{n\to\infty}\{x[n] - x(n-1)\}z^{-n} = x(\infty)$$

$$x(\infty) = \lim_{n\to 1}(1 - z^{1}).X(z)$$

Hence proved.

5.7.11 Accumulation:

$$Let, y[n] = \sum_{k=-\infty}^{n} x[k]$$

Then

$Y(z) = \frac{X(z)}{(1-z^{-1})}$ (5.31)

Proof :

$$y(n) - y(n-1) = \sum_{-\infty}^{n} x[k] - \sum_{\infty=k}^{n-1} x[k]$$

$y(n) - y(n-1) = x[n]$

Taking Z.T. on both sides, we get

$$Y(z) - z^{-1}Y(z) = X(z)$$
$$Y(z)(1 - z^{-1}) = X(z)$$

$$Y(z) = \frac{X(z)}{(1 - z^{-1})}$$

This is the Z.T. of accumulator. It adds poles at z = 1 and ROC 1 < |z| < R.

These properties make the Z-transform a powerful tool for analyzing and solving problems in discrete-time signal processing, control theory, and other related fields. They simplify the analysis of discrete-time systems and help in understanding their behavior in the Z-domain.

Example 5.4

Determine the Z.T. of the following signals $\boldsymbol{x[n] = a^n . u[n] - b^n u[-n-1]}$.

for $\boldsymbol{|a| < |b|, we\ have\ |z| > a, |z| < b}$.

Solution: $Given : x[n] = a^n u[n] - b^n\ u[n-1]$

The given signal is two sided; the Z.T. is given by,

$$X(z) = \sum_{-\infty}^{\infty} x[n] z^{-n}$$

$= \sum_{-\infty}^{\infty} (a^n\ u(n) - b^n\ u(-n-1))\ z^{-n}$

$$= \sum_{-\infty}^{\infty} a^n\, u(n) z^{-n} - \sum_{-\infty}^{\infty} b^n\, u(-n-1) z^{-n}$$

$$= \sum_{-\infty}^{\infty} (az^{-1})^n + \sum_{1}^{\infty} -(b^{-1}z)^n$$

$$= \frac{1}{1-az^{-1}} + \frac{1}{1-\frac{z}{b}} - 1$$

$$X(z) = \frac{z}{z-a} + \frac{z}{z-b}$$

There are two different causes for ROC.

For $|a| < |b|, we\ have, |z| > a, |z| < b$

These two ROC's overlap as shown and X(z) exists and given by,

$$X(z) = \frac{z}{z-a} + \frac{z}{z-b} \quad ROC|a| < |z| < |b|$$

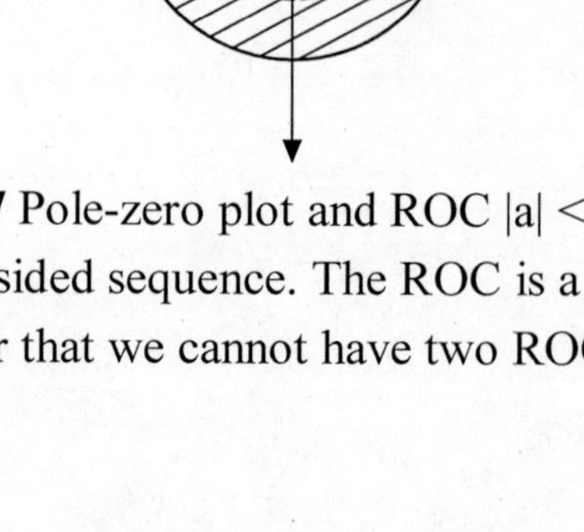

Fig. 5.7 Pole-zero plot and ROC |a| < |z| < |b|

For an infinite duration two sided sequence. The ROC is a ring in the z-plane. From this example, it is clear that we cannot have two ROC's.

Example 5.5

Determine the Z.T. of the signal,

$$x[n] = \left(\frac{1}{3}\right)^n u\,(n) + \left(\frac{1}{4}\right)^n u(n).$$

Solution: We know that Z.T. of,

$$a^n u\,(n) \overset{Z.T.}{\longleftrightarrow} \frac{z}{z-a}, \qquad ROC\ |z| > |a|.$$

Hence,

$$\left(\frac{1}{3}\right)^n u(n) \overset{Z.T}{\longleftrightarrow} \frac{z}{z-\frac{1}{3}}, \qquad |z| > \frac{1}{3}$$

$$\left(\frac{1}{4}\right)^n u(n) \overset{z.T}{\longleftrightarrow} \frac{z}{z-\frac{1}{4}} : |z| > \frac{1}{4}$$

Therefore, z-transform of x[n] is given by,

$$X(z) = \frac{z}{z-\frac{1}{3}} + \frac{z}{z-\frac{1}{4}}$$

$$= \frac{4z}{4z-1} + \frac{3z}{3z-1} = \frac{3z}{3z-1} + \frac{4z}{4z-1}$$

The first series converges for $|z| > \frac{1}{3}$. Second series converges for $|z| > \frac{1}{4}$. The common values of z for which both the series converges is $|z| > \frac{1}{3}$. This is shown in the figure below.

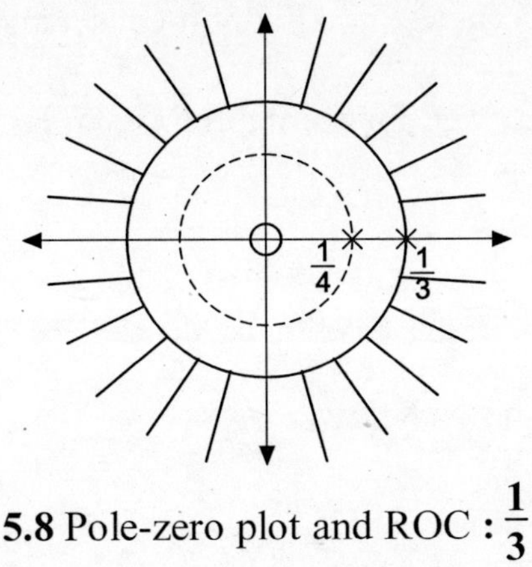

Fig. 5.8 Pole-zero plot and ROC : $\frac{1}{3} < |z|$

Example 5.6

Determine the Z.T. of x[n],

$$\boldsymbol{x[n] = \left(\frac{1}{4}\right)^2 u(-n-1) + \left(\frac{1}{3}\right)^n u(-n-1)}$$

$$x[n] = \left(\frac{1}{4}\right)^n u(-n-n) + \left(\frac{1}{3}\right)^n u(-n-1)$$

Solution: The Z.T. of x[n] is given by,

$$X(z) = \sum_{-\infty}^{\infty} [\left(\frac{1}{4}\right)^n u(-n-1) + \left(\frac{1}{3}\right)^n u(-n-1)] z^{-n}$$

$$= \sum_{-\infty}^{-1} \left(\frac{1}{4} z^{-1}\right)^n + \sum_{-\infty}^{-1} \left(\frac{1}{3} z^{-1}\right)^n$$

$$= \sum_{1}^{\infty} (4z)^n + \sum_{1}^{\infty} (3z)^n$$

$$X(z) = \frac{4z}{1-4z} + \frac{3z}{1-3z}$$

First series converges for $|z| < \frac{1}{4}$ because signal is non-causal and second series converges for $|z| < \frac{1}{3}$. Therefore, x(z) will be converge for common ROC of R_1 and R_2.

i.e. $|z| < \frac{1}{4}$

The ROC of X(z) is inside the circle of radius $|z| < \frac{1}{4}$

∴ Pole zero plot and ROC is shown below.

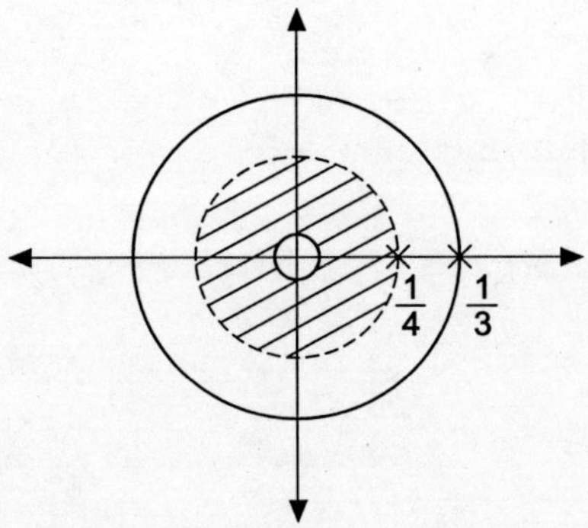

Fig. 5.9: Pole-zero plot and ROC $|z| < \frac{1}{4}$

5.8 Relationship between DTFT and z-transform:

The relationship between CTFT and L.T. we have seen.

DTFT and Z.T.exhibits similar relation as CTFT and L.T.

Let, $z = r \cdot e^{j\omega}$

Here, r is the magnitude and $\angle z = \omega$ is the phase.

We know, $z = re^{j\omega}$

$$X(z) = \sum_{-\infty}^{\infty} x[n].z^{-n}$$

$= \sum_{-\infty}^{\infty} x[n]re^{j\omega^{-n}}$ (5.32)

$= \sum_{-\infty}^{\infty} \{r^{-n}.x[n]\}e^{-j\omega n}$ (5.33)

and we have, DTFT given by

$\sum_{-\infty}^{\infty} x[n]e^{-j\omega n}$ (5.34)

On comparing (1) and (2), it is clear that DTFT of $r^{-n} \cdot x[n]$ is Z.T.

$$r^{-n}x[n] \overset{F.T.}{\longleftrightarrow} X(re^{jw})$$

When r = 1.

$$We\ get, (1)^n\ x[n] = x[n] \overset{F.T.}{\longleftrightarrow} X(e^{jw})$$

Hence, $|z| = |r| = 1$, DTFT is Z.T. obtained on the unit circle.

$$X(z)|_{z=e^{jw}} = X\left(e^{j\omega}\right) = F.T.\{x[n]\}$$

5.9 Inverse Z- transform

We know that Z.T. of x[n] which is defined as

$$X(z) = \sum_{-\infty}^{\infty} x[n]z^{-n}$$

$$z = r.e^{j\omega}$$

$X(re^{j\omega}) = F.T.\{x[n]r^{-n}\}$ (5.35)

Applying I.Z.T.to above equation we get,

$$x[n]r^{-n} = I.F.T\{X(re^{j\omega})\}$$

$$x[n] = r^n I.F.T.\{X(re^{j\omega})\}$$

Using I.F.T. expression, we have

$x[n] = r^n \frac{1}{2\pi} \int X(re^{jw})(e^{j\omega n})dw$ (5.36)

$$\frac{1}{2\pi}\int X(re^{jw})(r.e^{j\omega})^n \, d\omega$$

If we put,

$$z = re^{j\omega}$$

$$dz = jr.e^{jw}d\omega \Rightarrow d\omega = dz/(jr.e^{j\omega})$$

Substituting in above equation is obtained.

$x[n] = 1/(2\pi j) \oint X(re^{j\omega}).(r.e^{j\omega})^n.1/(jr.e^{j\omega})dz$ (5.37)

The symbol $\oint$ represents contour integration.

$$x[n] = 1/2(\pi j) \oint X(z).(z)^n \ (z)^{-1} \, dz$$

$$x[n] = 1/(2\pi j) \oint X(z).z^{n-1} \, dz$$

This is the expression for I.Z.T. indicates the integration around a counter clockwise closed circular contour centered at the origin with radius r.

This is a formal definition of I.Z.T. This is a direct method of computing I.Z.T. I.Z.T. There are other methods to find a time domain sequence when its z-transform is known. These are,

a) Power series expansion or Long division method

b) Partial fraction method

5.9.1. Power series expansion method

The power series expansion method for the inverse Z-transform is a useful technique for finding the time-domain sequence when an explicit inverse Z-transform expression is not readily available. The power series expansion method can be employed to find the inverse Z-transform by representing X(z) as a power series and then finding the inverse Z-transform of each term in the series.

The power series expansion is typically expressed as:

$$X(z) = \sum_{-\infty}^{\infty} c_n \, . \, z^{-n}$$

where c_n = x[n] are the coefficients in the power series. When X(z) is rational, the expansion can be performed by long division. Thus, it is also called as long division method.

We will learn this method through solved examples.

<u>Example 5.7</u>

Using long division method find the I.Z.T. of

$$\boldsymbol{X(z) = \frac{1 + z^{-1}}{1 + \left(\frac{1}{3}\right) z^{1}}} \text{ assuming ROC to be } |\boldsymbol{z}| > \frac{\boldsymbol{1}}{\boldsymbol{3}}.$$

<u>Solution:</u>

The ROC is outside the circle of radius z = 1/3. So, its corresponding time domain signal is causal.

Causal signals have negative power series expansion of z.

$$1 + \frac{2}{3} z{-1} - \frac{2}{9} z{-2} + \frac{2}{27} z{-3} \ldots$$

$$1 + \left(\frac{1}{3}\right) z{-} \;\Big)\; 1 + z{-1}$$

$$1 + \frac{1}{3} z{-1}$$

$$\frac{2}{3}z^{-1}$$

$$-\quad \frac{2}{3}z^{-1} + \frac{2}{9}z^{-2}$$

$$-\frac{2}{9}z^{-2}$$

$$-\frac{2}{9}z^{-2} + \frac{2}{27}z^{-3}$$

$$\frac{2}{27}z^{-3}$$

$$X(z) = 1 + \frac{2}{3}z^{-1} - \frac{2}{9}z^{-2} + \frac{2}{27}z^{-3}$$

Taking I.Z.T.

$$x[n] = \left\{1, \frac{2}{3}, -\frac{2}{9}, \frac{2}{27}, \ldots\ldots\right\}$$

Example 5.8

Using long division method find the I.Z.T. of $X(z) = \dfrac{z}{z-a}$; ROC $|z| < |a|$

Solution:

The ROC is inside the circle of radius z = a. So, its corresponding time domain signal is anti-causal.

Anti-causal signals have positive power series expansion of z.

So, the I.Z.T. of $\dfrac{z}{z-a}$ can be evaluated by using following method (the terms are written in opposite sequence so as to get positive power series expansion of z) as,

$$-\frac{1}{a}z - \left(\frac{1}{a}\right)^2 z^2 - \left(\frac{1}{a}\right)^3 z^3$$

$$-a + z \,)\; z$$

$$z - \frac{1}{a}z^2 \; z\,)\; z$$

$$\frac{1}{a}z^2$$

$$\frac{1}{a}z2 - \left(\frac{1}{a}\right)^2 z3$$

$$\left(\frac{1}{a}\right)^2 z3$$

$$\left(\frac{1}{a}\right)^2 z3 - \left(\frac{1}{a}\right)^3 z4$$

$$\left(\frac{1}{a}\right)^3 z4$$

$$\left(\frac{1}{a}\right)^3 z4 - \left(\frac{1}{a}\right)^4 z5$$

We know that quotient is the power series of X(z).

Therefore,

$$X(z) = -\left(\frac{1}{a}\right)z - \left(\frac{1}{a}\right)^2 z^2 - \left(\frac{1}{a}\right)^2 z^3 \ldots$$

$$= -\left[\left(\frac{1}{a}\right)z + \left(\frac{1}{a}\right)^2 z^2 + \left(\frac{1}{a}\right)^3 z^3 \ldots\ldots\right]$$

So, x[n] is given by,

$$x[n] = -\left[\left(\frac{1}{a}\right)z + \left(\frac{1}{a}\right)^2 z2 + \left(\frac{1}{a}\right)^3 z3 \ldots\right]$$

={…… a–3, a–2, a–1, 0}

$$= \{\ldots\ldots\ldots a^{-3}, a^{-2}, a^{-1}, 0\}$$

We can write, $x[n]\ as$

$$x[n] = --a^n u(-n-1)$$

∴ We can write relation X(z) and x[n] as,

$$-a^n u(-n-1) \overset{z}{\leftrightarrow} \frac{z}{(z-a)}; ROC\ |z| < |a|$$

5.9.2 Partial fraction method

The inverse Z.T. can be evaluated by partial fraction method. If the Z.T.is represented as a rational function given by,

$$X(z) = \frac{N(z)}{D(z)} = \frac{a_o + a_1 z^{-1} + a_2 z^{-2} + \cdots \ldots a_m z^{-M}}{b_o + b_1 z^{-1} + b_2 z^{-2} + \cdots \ldots b_N z^{-N}} \qquad (5.38)$$

With its corresponding ROC, then partial expansion can be used to find the inverse Z.T.

1. If the denominator D(z) can be factorized and if it has distinct real roots as given by,

$$\frac{X(z)}{z} = \frac{C_0}{z} + \frac{C_1}{z} \qquad (5.39)$$

$$= \frac{A_1}{z - z}$$

$$X(z) = \frac{N(z)}{D(z)} = \frac{k.(z - z_1)(z - z_2).....((z - z_m)}{(z - p_1)((z - p_2)......((z - p_n)} \qquad (5.40)$$

Case I) P1, P2, P3, …, Pn are different poles.

$$\frac{X(z)}{z} = \frac{C_0}{z} + \frac{C_1}{z - P_1} + \frac{C_2}{z - P_2} + \cdots \ldots \frac{C_n}{z - P_n}$$

$$= \frac{C_0}{z} + \sum_{k=1}^{n} \frac{C_k}{z - P_k} \qquad (5.41)$$

The C0, C1, C2 … Cn can be evaluated by following equations,

$$C_0 = X(z)_z = 0$$

$$C_k = (z - P_k)X(z)_{z = p_k}$$

$$X(z) = C_0 + \frac{zC_1}{(z - P_1)} + \frac{zC_2}{(z - P_2)} + \cdots \ldots \frac{C_n z}{(z - p_n)} \qquad (5.42)$$

We can compute I.Z.T. of $\frac{z}{z - p_1}, \frac{z}{z - p_2} \ldots . \frac{z}{z - p_n}$

Case II) If X(z) has poles with multiplicity with greater than one or if X(z) has more than one poles at same location.

Let Pi is pole location with multiplicity r then X(z)/z will have term of the following form

$$\frac{X(z)}{z} = \frac{\lambda_1}{z-P_i} + \frac{\lambda_2}{(z-p_i)^2} + \cdots \frac{\lambda_r}{(z-p_i)^r} \qquad (5.43)$$

$$\lambda_{r-k} = \frac{1}{k!}\frac{d^k}{dz^k}\left[\left[(z-P_i)^r\frac{X(z)}{z}\right]\right]_{z=p_i} \qquad (5.44)$$

From the above equation we can find the coefficients of poles which are located at same location.

Example 5.9

Determine the inverse Z.T. of the following X(z) by the partial fraction method.

$$X(z) = \frac{z+2}{2z^2 - 7z + 3}$$

With ROC $(a)|z| > 3, (b)|z| < \frac{1}{2}, (c)\frac{1}{2} > |z| < 3.$

Solution: Let,

$$\frac{X(z)}{z} = \frac{(z+2)}{z(2z^2 - 7z + 3)}$$

$$\frac{X(z)}{z} = \frac{z+2}{2z\left(z-\frac{1}{2}\right)(z-3)}$$

$$\frac{X(z)}{.z} = \frac{C_0}{z} + \frac{C_1}{\left(z-\frac{1}{2}\right)} + \frac{C_2}{(z-3)}$$

$$C_0 = X(z)|_{z=0} = \frac{0+2}{2+\frac{1}{2}*3} = \frac{2}{3}$$

$$C_1 = \left(z-\frac{1}{2}\right)\left[\frac{(z+2)}{2z\left(z-\frac{1}{2}\right)(z-3)}\right]$$

$$= \frac{(z+2)}{2z(z-3)}\bigg|_{z=\frac{1}{2}}$$

$$= \frac{\frac{1}{2}+2}{2 * \frac{1}{2\left(\frac{1}{2} * 3\right)}} = \frac{\frac{5}{2}}{-\frac{5}{2}} = -1$$

$$C_2 = (z-3)\frac{(z+2)}{2z\left(z-\frac{1}{2}\right)(z-3)}\Bigg|_{z=3}$$

$$= \frac{3+2}{2 * 3\left(z-\frac{1}{2}\right)} + \frac{5}{6 * \frac{5}{2}} = \frac{1}{3}$$

$\therefore$ Substituting values of C_0, C_1 and C_2 we get,

$$X(z) = \frac{2}{3} - \frac{z}{\left(z-\frac{1}{2}\right)} + \frac{1}{3}\frac{z}{(z-3)}$$

(a) ROC : $|z| > 3$

X(z) has 2 poles at $z = \frac{1}{2}$, $z = 3$.

$\therefore$ The I.Z.T. of X(z) is given by,

$$\frac{2}{3} \overset{I.Z.T.}{\longleftrightarrow} \frac{2}{3}\delta[n]$$

$$\frac{z}{\left(z-\frac{1}{2}\right)} \overset{I.Z.T.}{\longleftrightarrow} \left(\frac{1}{2}\right)^n u(n)$$

$$\frac{z}{(z-3)} \overset{I.Z.T.}{\longleftrightarrow} (3)^n u(n)$$

$$x[n] = \frac{2}{3}\delta[n] - \left(\frac{1}{2}\right)^n u(n) + (3)^n u(n)$$

(b) ROC $|z| < \frac{1}{2}$

The ROC is inside the circle of radius $z = \frac{1}{2}$.

$$x[n] = \frac{2}{3}\delta[n] + \left(\frac{1}{2}\right)^n u(-n-1) - \frac{1}{3}(3)^n u(-n-1)$$

(c) ROC : $\frac{1}{2} > |z| < 3$

$$(c) ROC : \frac{1}{2} k|z| < 3$$

∴ The ROC is ring between the poles at $z = \frac{1}{2} and\ z = 3.$

The corresponding time domain signal of $\frac{z}{(z-3)}$ is anti-causal and of $\frac{z}{z-\frac{1}{2}}$ is causal.

$$x[n] = \frac{2}{3}\delta[n] + \left(\frac{1}{2}\right)^n u(n) - \frac{1}{3}(3)^n u(-n-1)$$

5.10 Z – Domain Causality and stability analysis

A causal linear time invariant system is one whose unit sample response h(n) satisfies the condition,

$$h[n] = 0\ for\ n < 0 \qquad (5.45)$$

We have also seen that the ROC of the Z-transform of a causal sequence is the exterior of a circle outside the outermost pole.

When we talk about stability we want to refer to the so called BIBO (bounded-input, bounded-output) stability. As the name already implies, a BIBO stable system should respond with a bounded output to a bounded input.

The output y[n] is commonly known as the convolution of x[n] and the impulse response, h[n]. So, with a bounded input, output will be bounded if and only if the impulse response is finite. For the impulse response to be finite, we need to ensure that h[n] is absolutely summable. This would ensure that the system will be stable. Hence, the bottom line is that we need an absolutely summable impulse response, i.e.

$$\sum_{-\infty}^{\infty} |h[n]| < \infty \qquad (5.46)$$

By definition, $H(z) = \sum_{-\infty}^{\infty} h(n)\, z^{-n}$, it follows

$$|H(z)| = \sum_{-\infty}^{\infty} |h(n)\, z^{-n}| = \sum_{-\infty}^{\infty} |h(n)||\, z^{-n}| \qquad (5.47)$$

For |z| = 1 i.e. on the unit circle, it will become,

$$H(z) = \sum_{-\infty}^{\infty} |h[n]| \qquad (5.48)$$

In turn this condition implies that H(z) must contain the unit circle within its ROC.

Example 5.10

A linear time-invariant system is characterized by the system function

$$H(z) = \frac{3 - 4z^{-1}}{1 - 3.5z^{-1} + 1.5z^{-2}}$$

Specify the ROC of H(z) and determine h(n) for the following conditions:

(a) The system is stable.

(b) The system is causal.

(c) The system is anticausal.

Solution:

$$H(z) = \frac{3 - 4z^{-1}}{1 - 3.5z^{-1} + 1.5z^{-2}}$$

By applying partial fractions,

$$H(z) = \frac{1}{1 - 0.5z^{-1}} + \frac{2}{1 - 3z^{-1}}$$

The system has poles at z= 0.5 and z= 3.

(a) Since the system is stable, its ROC must include the unit circle and hence it is $0.5 < |z| < 3$. Consequently, h(n) is non-causal and is given as,

$$h(n) = (0.5)^n u(n) - 2(3)^n u(-n-1)$$

(b) Since the system is causal, it ROC is $|z| > 3$. Hence,

$$h(n) = (0.5)^n u(n) + 2(3)^n un)$$

and the system is unstable in this case.

(c) If the system is anti-causal, it ROC is $|z| < 0.5$. Hence,

$$h(n) = -(0.5)^n u(n-1) - 2(3)^n u(-n-1)$$

and the system is unstable in this case.

Unit Summary

The Z-transform, a powerful mathematical tool in discrete-time signal processing, offers a comprehensive framework for analyzing discrete signals and systems. Understanding its definition and properties, including linearity, time-shifting, scaling, and convolution properties, forms the foundation of its application. The inverse Z-transform facilitates the conversion of transformed signals back into the time domain, employing techniques such as partial fraction decomposition and contour integration. In practical terms, the Z-transform finds extensive use in digital filter design, system analysis, and control theory, allowing engineers to analyze and design discrete-time systems with precision. Its applications extend to fields such as telecommunications, audio processing, and image processing, where it enables efficient manipulation of discrete signals. Advanced topics, including the relationship between Z-transform and Laplace transform, as well as multirate signal processing, deepen the understanding of its theoretical underpinnings and broaden its scope of application. As technology continues to evolve, the Z-transform remains a vital tool for digital signal processing, offering insights into the behavior of discrete systems and paving the way for innovative solutions in a digital world.

Exercise

1) Determine the Z-transform of the following signals, also mention the ROC.

a) $x(n) = \{1, 2, 3, 3, 2, 1\}\ for\ 0 \leq n \leq 5$

b) $x(n) = \{-1, 0, 1, 0, -1, 0, +1\}\ for - 2 \leq n \leq 4$

c) $x(n) = \{3, 2, 1, 1, 2, 3\}\ for - 5 \leq n \leq 0$

2) Determine the z-transform of the following signals, also plot the ROC.

a) $x(n) = a^n \sin(w_0 n) . u(n)$

b) $x(n) = (0.3)^n [u(n) - u(n-2)]$

3) Determine the causal signal $x(n)$ if Z-transform is given by

$$x(z) = \frac{2 - 1.5z^{-1}}{1 - 1.5z^{-1} + 0.5z^{-2}}$$

4) Determine the Z-transform of the signal $x(n) = -a^n u(-n-1)$ and plot the ROC.

5) Evaluate the inverse z-transform of

a) $X(z) = \frac{1}{1-0.5z^{-1}}$ $\quad |z|<0.5$

b) $X(z) = \frac{2}{(z-0.2)(z+0.4)}$

6) For the given sequences $x_1(n) = 5\delta(n) - 2\delta(n-2)$ and $x_2(n) = 3\delta(n-3)$, find $x_3(n) = x_1(n) * x_2(n)$ using the convolution property of z-transform.

7) A linear time invariant system is characterized by the system function $H(z) = \frac{3-4z^{-1}}{1-3.5z^{-1}+1.5z^{-2}}$ Specify the ROC of H(z) and determine h(n) for the following convolutions

a) The system is stable

b) The system is causal

c) The system is anticausal.

Multiple choice questions

1. The Z – transform of $a^{-n}u(-n-1)$ is,

a) $\frac{-z}{z-1/a}$

b) $\frac{z}{z-1/a}$

c) $\frac{z}{z-a}$

d) $\frac{-z}{z-a}$

2. The ROC of the sequence $x(n) = u(-n)$ is,

a) |z|>1

b) b) |z|<1

c) c) no ROC

d) d) -1<|z|<1

3. The inverse Z – $transform\ of\ \frac{3}{z-4}, |z| > 4\ is,$

a) $3(4)^n u(n-1)$
b) $3(4)^{n-1} u(n)$
c) $3(4)^{n-1} u(n+1)$
d) $3(4)^{n-1} u(n-1)$

4. ROC of x(n) contains

a) Poles
b) zeros
c) no poles
d) no zeros

5. The Z – $transform\ of\ x(n) = [u(n) - u(n-3))], for\ ROC\ |z| > 1\ is,$

a) $X(z) = \frac{z-z^{-3}}{z-1}$

b) $X(z) = \frac{z^{-2}}{(z-1)^2}$

c) $X(z) = \frac{z-4z^{-2}+3z^{-3}}{(z-1)^2}$

d) none of the above

6. If all the poles of the system function H(z) have magnitude smaller than 1, then the system will be,

a) Stable
b) unstable
c) BIBO stable
d) a and c

7. $If\ x(n) = \{0.5, -0.25, 1\}, then\ Z - transform\ of\ the\ signal\ is,$

a) $\frac{z^2}{0.5z^2-0.25z+1}$
b) $\frac{z^2}{z^2-0.5z+0.25}$
c) $\frac{0.5z^2-0.25z+1}{z^2}$
d) $\frac{2z^2+4z+1}{z^2}$

8. $The\ ROC\ of\ the\ signal\ x(n) = a^n for -5 < n < 5\ is,$

a) Entire z-plane
b) entire z-plane except z=0 and z=∞
c) Entire z-plane except z=0
d) entire z-plane except z=∞

9. $If\ Z - transform\ of\ x(n)\ is\ X(z) then\ Z - transform\ of\ x(-n) is,$

a) $-X(z)$
b) $X(-z)$
c) $-X(z^1)$
d) $X(z^{-1})$

10. $The\ inverse\ Z - transform\ of\ X(z) can\ be\ defined\ as,$

a) $x(n) = \frac{1}{2\pi}\oint X(z)z^{n-1}\,dz$
b) $x(n) = \frac{1}{2j}\oint X(z)z^{n-1}dz$
c) $x(n) = \frac{1}{2\pi j}\oint X(z)z^{n-1}dz$
d) $x(n) = \frac{1}{2\pi j}\oint X(z)z^{-n}\,dz$

11. *The Z – transform is a,*

a) finite series

b) infinite power series

c) geometric series

d) both a and c

12. *The Z – transform of correlation of the sequence* $x(n)$ *and* $y(n)$ *is,*

a) $X^*(z)Y^*(z^{-1})$ b) $X(z)Y(z^{-1})$ c) $X(z) * Y(z)$ d) $X(z^{-1})Y(z^{-1})$

13. For a stable LTI discrete time system poles should lie______ and unit circle should be______

a) Outside unit circle, included in ROC

b) inside unit circle, outside of ROC

c) inside unit circle, included in ROC

d) outside unit circle, outside of ROC

14. *An LTI system with impulse response,* $h(n) = (-a)^n\, u(n)$ *and* $-a < -1$ *will be,*

a) stable system

b) unstable system

c) anticausal system

d) neither stable nor causal

15. *If* $X(z)$ *has a single pole on the unit circle, on negative real axis then,* $x(n)$ *is,*

a) signed constant sequence

b) signed decaying sequence

c) signed growing sequence

d) constant sequence

16. *If* $x(n)$ *has Z – Transform* $X(z)$ *with ROC* $\rightarrow R_1$ *then ROC of* $a^n x(n) \overset{Z}{\leftrightarrow} X\left(\frac{z}{a}\right)$ *is,*

a) $\frac{R_1}{a}$ b) aR_1 c) R_1 d) $\frac{1}{R_1}$

17. *The Z – transform of a ramp function* $x(n) = n\, u(n)$ *is,*

a) $X(z) = \frac{z}{(z-1)^2}$; *ROC is* $|z| > 1$ b) $X(z) = \frac{-z}{(z-1)^2}$; *ROC is* $|z| > 1$

c) $X(z) = \frac{z}{(z-1)^2}$; $ROC\ is\ |z| < 1$

d) $X(z) = \frac{-z}{(z-1)^2}$; $ROC\ is\ |z| < 1$

Answers to the multiple choice questions:

1. a	2. b	3. d	4. c	5. d	6. a	7. c	8. b	9. d
10. c	11. b	12. b	13. c	14. a	15. a	16. a	17. a	

KNOW MORE

Z-transform reveals a rich tapestry of mathematical intricacies and practical applications. Beyond its fundamental properties lie advanced techniques and insights that amplify its utility in discrete signal analysis and system design. Understanding the intricacies of Z-transform inversion methods, such as residue calculus and contour integration, empowers engineers and researchers to unravel complex system behaviors with precision and accuracy. The Z-transform's role extends far beyond mere signal processing; it serves as a cornerstone in areas ranging from digital control theory to communication systems design, enabling the development of robust algorithms and efficient data processing techniques. Exploring the connections between the Z-transform and other mathematical tools, such as Fourier analysis and Laplace transform, unveils deeper insights into the interplay between time and frequency domains in discrete systems. Moreover, ongoing research in areas such as multirate signal processing and adaptive filtering continues to push the boundaries of Z-transform theory, paving the way for innovative applications in emerging technologies. As we delve deeper into the intricacies of the Z-transform, we unlock a world of possibilities, where mathematical abstraction converges with real-world engineering challenges, driving forward progress and innovation in the digital age.

REFERENCES AND SUGGESTED READINGS

1. Signals and Systems by Simon Haykin
2. Signals and Systems by Ganesh Rao
3. Signals and Systems - Course (nptel.ac.in)

Dynamic QR Code for Further Reading

6 Sampling & Reconstruction

UNIT SPECIFICS

Through this unit we have discussed following aspects:

- *The necessity of sampling theorem*
- *Sampling theorem for Continuous Time & Discrete time signal*
- *Understanding of discrete time processing of continuous time signals*
- *Frequency domain spectra of the sampled signals*
- *Interpolation methods for reconstruction of sampled signals*
- *Zero-order & first order hold interpolation methods*
- *Effects of under sampling and oversampling on the signals*
- *Using spectra to understand aliasing and its effects*
- *Understanding continuous and discrete time systems*

RATIONALE

The unit "Sampling and Reconstruction" is not only important to understand signals but also will be helpful in Communications. We can call on simple intuition to motivate and describe the processes of sampling and reconstruction from samples, because in communication systems that are closely related to sampling or rely fundamentally on using a sampled version of the signal to be transmitted.

This unit focuses on sampling of continuous and discrete time signals. The effects of under sampling and oversampling are discussed in detail with various examples. Frequency domain analysis i.e. Fourier transform of signals is extensively used for the better understanding of the topic. The effects of 'aliasing' are explained in lucid manner. Various methods to avoid aliasing are also discussed in this topic. Both continuous time and discrete time signals are considered for discussions. For reconstruction of the sampled signal, various interpolation methods are discussed with detailed mathematical analysis and distinct examples. Different filtering techniques are studied for proper reconstruction of the signal.

The discrete and continuous time systems are also discussed to give overview of the working of how systems work.

PRE-REQUISITES

1. *Strong understanding of mathematics, including algebra, calculus, and complex numbers.*
2. *Familiarity with basic concepts in signals and systems, such as time-domain and frequency-domain representations, Fourier analysis, and convolution.*
3. *Proficiency in solving ordinary differential equations and understanding linear algebra concepts.*
4. *Basic knowledge of electronics and circuit analysis for understanding continuous-time LTI systems.*
5. *Knowledge of digital signal processing concepts for understanding discrete-time LTI systems.*

UNIT OUTCOMES

List of outcomes of this unit is as follows:

U6-O1: Understand need of sampling theorem

U6-O2: Apply sampling theorem to continuous and discrete time signals

U6-O3: Study the effects of under sampling and oversampling

U6-O4: Perform Zero-order and first order hold interpolation

U6-O5: Study aliasing and its effects

U6-O6: Understand aliasing and its effects through Fourier analysis

U6-O7: Study relationship between continuous time & discrete time systems

Unit-6 Outcomes	***EXPECTED MAPPING WITH COURSE OUTCOMES*** *(1- Weak Correlation; 2- Medium correlation; 3- Strong Correlation)*					
	CO-1	***CO-2***	***CO-3***	***CO-4***	***CO-5***	***CO-6***
U6-O1	-	-	-	-	-	*3*
U6-O2	*2*	-	-	*2*	-	*3*
U6-O3	-	-	-	-	-	*3*
U6-O4	-	-	-	-	-	*3*
U6-O5	-	-	-	-	-	*3*
U6-O6	-	-	*3*	-	-	*3*
U6-O7	-	*2*	-	*2*	-	*2*

6.1 Introduction

A continuous time signal can entirely be represented by its samples which are equally spaced in time. The sampling theorem is associated with these samples. This theorem is widely used in applications where digital data is preferred over analog. Sampling theorem is one of the most important theorems in signals & systems as it acts bridge between continuous time signals and discrete time signals.

Nowadays, technically advanced digital systems are developed to effectively process continuous time signals. Hence, there is need to convert these continuous time signals into discrete time signals. Sampling process provides some insight, to deal with the problem of conversion mentioned above. Sampling is the process which involves conversion of continuous time signal to discrete time signal. The sampling is performed by taking samples of continuous time signal at definite intervals of time. This sampled (discrete time) signal is easily processed by discrete time systems. The original continuous time signal is reconstructed from this discrete time signal.

In the following discussion, we introduce and develop concept of sampling and process of reconstructing CT signals from its samples. In the following discussion, we will analyze the conditions under which sampling rate is sufficient to be able to exactly reconstruct the original continuous time signal. And we will also observe when sampling rate is low what will happen to original continuous time signal while trying to reconstruct from its samples. Finally, we examine the sampling of discrete time signals & related concepts of decimation & interpolation.

6.2 Sampling Theorem

First, we need to clearly see some examples of continuous time signals which can be uniquely specified by a sequence of equally spaced samples. For example, figure 6.1 illustrate three different continuous time signals, all of which have identical values at integer multiples of T (T is sampling time/sampling period/sampling interval) that is,

$$x_1(kT) = x_2(kT) = x_3(kT)$$

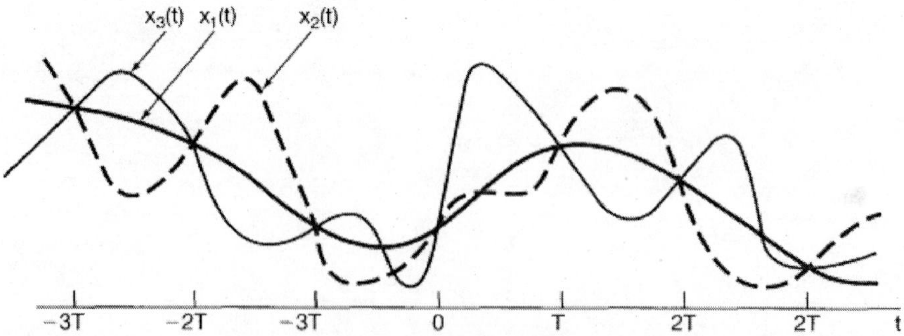

Fig 6.1: Three continuous time signals

6.2.1 Impulse train sampling

To sample a continuous time signal at regular intervals we need a convenient way to develop sampling theorem. One useful way is to use periodic impulse train multiplied by continuous time signal $x(t)$ which is the signal we wish to sample. This mechanism is known as impulse-train sampling and is shown in figure 6.2. The periodic impulse train $p(t)$ is referred to as sampling function, the period T as sampling period and the fundamental frequency of $p(t)$, $\omega_s = \frac{2\pi}{T}$ as the sampling frequency. In time domain, we can write,

$$x_p(t) = x(t)p(t) \tag{6.1}$$

Where,

$$p(t) = \sum_{n=-\infty}^{+\infty} \delta(t - nT) \tag{6.2}$$

Now, by using sampling property of unit impulse function, we know that multiplying x(t) by a unit impulse sample the value of signal at the point at which the impulse is located i.e. $x(t)\delta(t - t_0) = x(t_0)\delta(t - t_0)$. Applying this to Eq. (6.1) we see the result which is illustrated in figure 6.2, that $x_p(t)$ is an impulse train with amplitudes of impulses equal to the samples of x(t) at intervals spaced at time interval T; that is,

$$x_p(t) = \sum_{n=-\infty}^{+\infty} x(nT)\delta(t - nT) \tag{6.3}$$

From multiplication property, we know that

$$X_p(j\omega) = \frac{1}{2\pi}\int_{-\infty}^{+\infty} X(j\theta)P\big(j(\omega - \theta)\big)d\theta \tag{6.4}$$

Using earlier properties,

$$P(j\omega) = \frac{2\pi}{T}\sum_{k=-\infty}^{+\infty} \delta(\omega - k\omega_s) \tag{6.5}$$

Since, convolution with the impulse function simply shifts a signal, it follows that,

$$X_p(j\omega) = \frac{1}{T}\sum_{k=-\infty}^{+\infty} X(j(\omega - k\omega_s)) \tag{6.6}$$

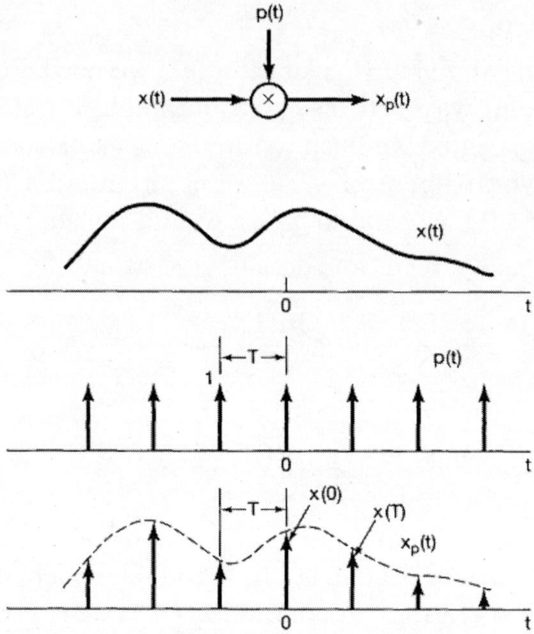

Fig 6.2: Impulse-train sampling

So, $X_p(j\omega)$ is periodic function of ω consisting of superposition of shifted replicas of $X(j\omega)$, scaled by $1/T$ as illustrated in figure 6.3. In figure 6.3(c), $\omega_m < (\omega_s - \omega_M)$, or equivalently, $\omega_s > 2\omega_M$ and hence there is no overlap between shifted replicas of $X(j\omega)$, whereas in figure 6.3(d), with $\omega_s > 2\omega_M$, x(t) can be recovered exactly from $x_p(t)$ by means of a low pass filter with gain T and cut off frequency greater than ω_M and less than $\omega_s - \omega_M$ and is indicated in figure 6.4.

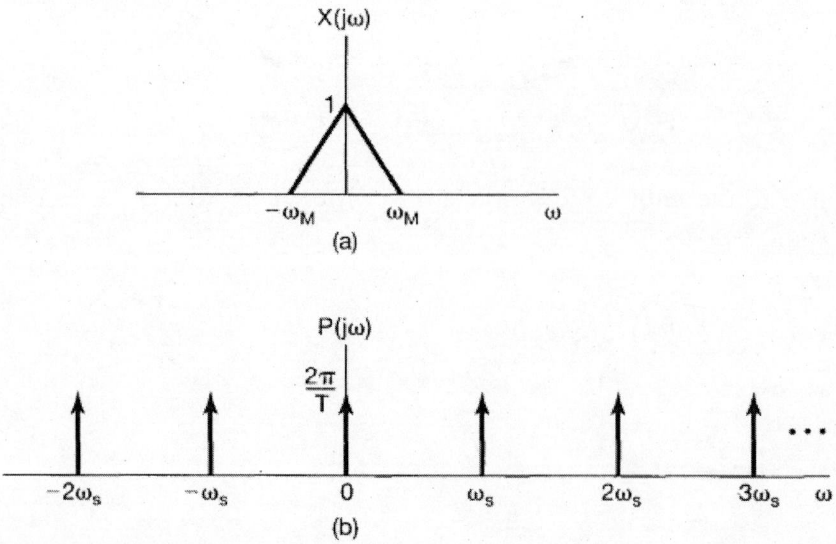

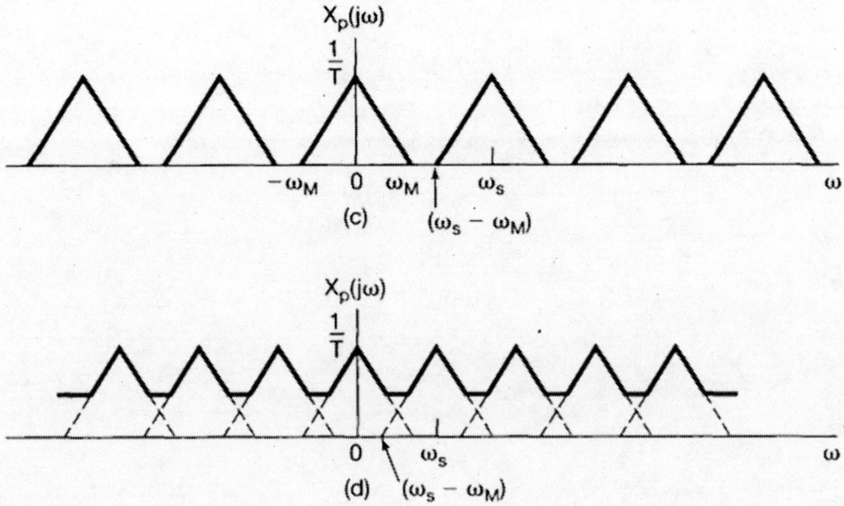

Fig. 6.3: Frequency domain representation due to sampling in time domain: (a) Spectrum of original signal; (b) Spectrum of sampling function; (c) Spectrum of sampled signal with $\omega_s > 2\omega_M$; (d) Spectrum of sampled signal $\omega_s < 2\omega_M$

Sampling Theorem:

Let x(t) be a band limited signal with $X(j\omega) = 0 \; for \; |\omega| > \omega_M$. Then x(t) is uniquely determined by its samples x(nT), $n = 0, \pm 1, \pm 2, \ldots \ldots$, if

$$\omega_s > 2\omega_M$$

Where,

$$\omega_s = \frac{2\pi}{T}$$

Given these samples, we can reconstruct x(t) by generating a periodic impulse train in which successive impulses have amplitudes that are successive sample values. This impulse train is then processed through an ideal lowpass filter with gain T and cutoff frequency greater than ω_M and less than $\omega_s - \omega_M$. The resulting output will be exactly equal to x(t).

We have seen sampling theorem, where impulse train sampling method was discussed. However, in practice the frequency of the original continuous time signal which comes under sampling theorem must be excess than the sampling frequency is referred to as 'Nyquist Rate'. In real life applications a non-ideal lowpass filter is used instead of ideal lowpass filter as shown in figure 6.4. The non-ideal filter has filter characterictics as $|H(j\omega)|$ where $|H(j\omega)| \cong 1 \; for \; \omega < \omega_M$ and $|H(j\omega)| \cong 0 \; for \; \omega_s - \omega_M$. For understanding basic principles of sampling theorem for convenience we will regularly use ideal filters throughout this chapter.

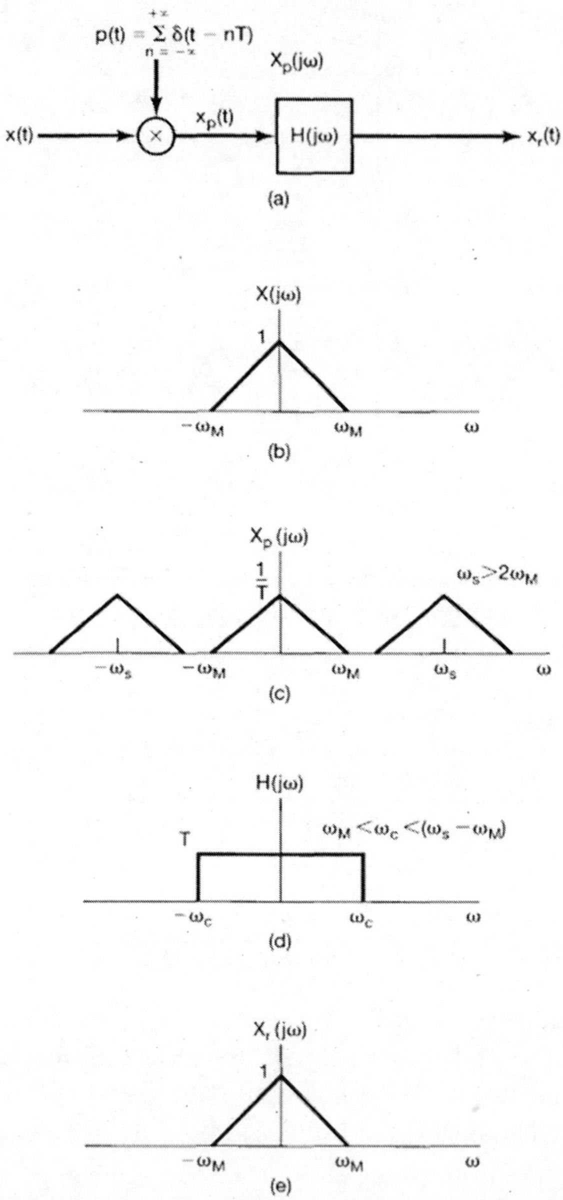

Fig 6.4: Recovery of original signal by using ideal lowpass filter

(a) System for sampling & reconstruction (b) Representative spectrum for x(t) (c) Corresponding spectrum for $x_p(t)$ (d) Ideal lowpass filter to recover $X(j\omega)$ from $X_p(j\omega)$ (e) Spectrum of $x_r(t)$

6.2.2 Sampling with Zero-Order Hold

In sampling theorem a band limited signal is uniquely represented by its samples using the impulse-train sampling. However, in practice, large narrow amplitude pulses are difficult generate and transmit. So, it is often more convenient to generate sampled signal in a form referred to as 'Zero-Order hold. Such system samples the given continuous time signal at given instant and holds that value until the next instant at which sample is taken as shown in figure 6.5.

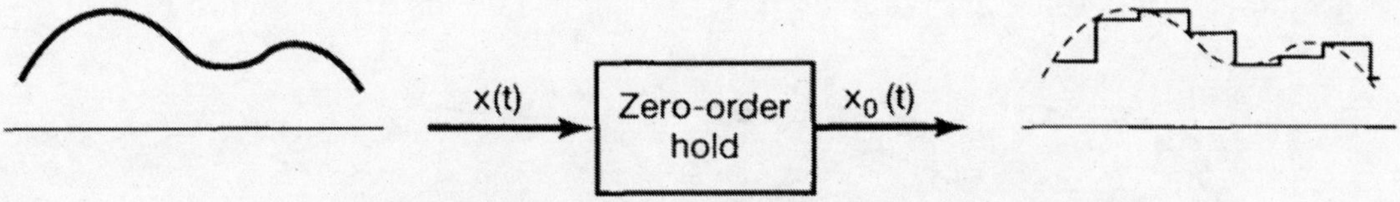

Fig 6.5: Sampling using Zero-Order Hold

Now, the output $x_0(t)$ of zero order hold can be generated by impulse train sampling followed by LTI system. The impulse response is shown in figure 6.6 as shown below,

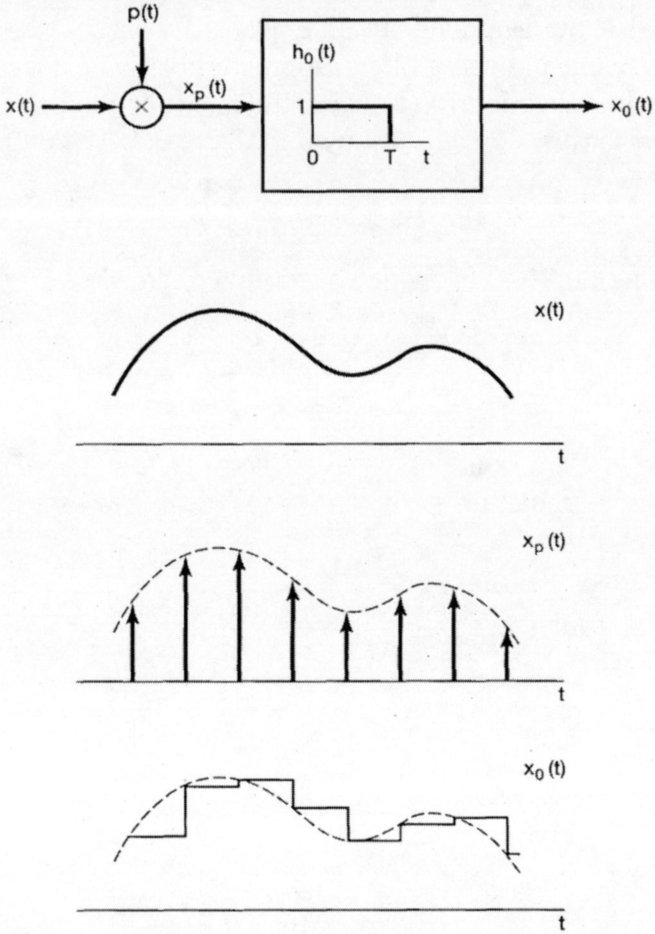

Fig 6.6: Zero order hold as impulse- train sampling followed by an LTI system with ractangular response

6.3 Reconstruction of a signal from its samples using interpolation

Interpolation, to fit a continuous signal to a set of sample values, is a widely used for reconstructing a function from its samples. One simple interpolation procedure is the zero-order hold discussed in Section 6.1.2. Another useful form of interpolation is *linear interpolation,* whereby adjacent sample points are connected by a straight line, as illustrated in Figure 6.7

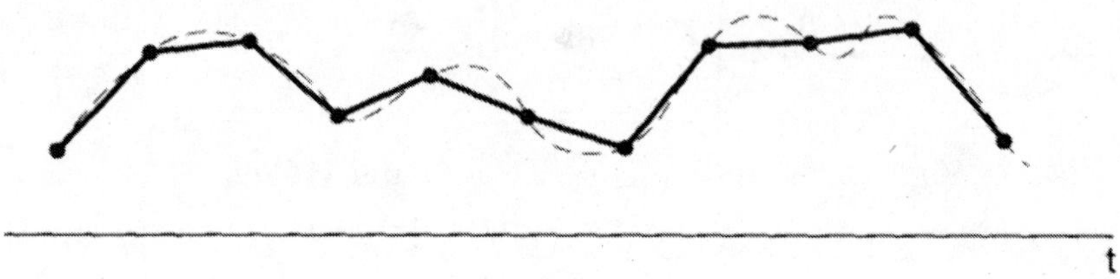

Fig 6.7: Interpolation between samples, solid curve represents interpolation

For a band-limited signal if the sampling instants are sufficiently close then signal can be reconstructed exactly. By using a lowpass filter, exact interpolation can be carried out between sample points. For the reconstruction of $x(t)$ using the interpolation process we will consider the effect of lowpass filter in time domain as shown in figure 6.4. The output of reconstruction is written as,

$$x_r(t) = x_p(t) * h(t)$$

Substituting for $x_p(t)$ using Eq. (6.3) in above equation, we can write

$$x_r(t) = \sum_{n=-\infty}^{+\infty} x(nT)h(t - nT) \tag{6.7}$$

Eq. (6.7) describes how to fit a continuous curve between the sample points $x(nT)$ and consequently represent an interpolation formula. For the ideal lowpass filter $H(j\omega)$ in Figure 6.4, the impulse response $h(t)$ is,

$$h(t) = \frac{\omega_c T \sin(\omega_c t)}{\pi \omega_c t} \tag{6.8}$$

we will get,

$$x_r(t) = \sum_{n=-\infty}^{+\infty} x(nT)h(t - nT) \tag{6.9}$$

$$x_r(t) = \sum_{n=-\infty}^{+\infty} x(nT)\frac{\omega_c T}{\pi}\frac{sin(\omega_c(t - nT))}{\omega_c(t - nT)} \tag{6.10}$$

The reconstruction according to Eq. (6.10) with $\omega_c = \omega_s/2$ is illustrated in Figure 6.8 Figure 6.8(a) represents the original band-limited signal $x(t)$, and Figure 6.8(b) represents $x_p(t)$, the impulse train of samples. In figure 6.8(c), the superposition of the individual terms in Eq. (6.10) is illustrated.

Interpolation using the impulse response of an ideal lowpass filter as in Eq. (6.10) is commonly referred to as *band-limited interpolation,* since it implements exact reconstruction if $x(t)$ is band limited and the sampling frequency satisfies the conditions of the sampling theorem. As we have indicated, in many cases it is preferable to use a less accurate, but simpler, filter or, equivalently, a simpler interpolating function than the function in Eq. (6.8). For example, the zero-order hold can be viewed as a form of interpolation between sample values in which the interpolating function $h(t)$ is the impulse response $h_0(t)$ depicted in figure 6.6. In that sense, with $x_0(t)$ in the figure corresponding to the approximation to $x(t)$, the system $h_0(t)$ represents an approximation to the ideal lowpass filter required for the exact interpolation. Figure 6.9 shows the magnitude of the transfer function of the zero-order-hold interpolating filter, superimposed on the desired transfer function of the exact interpolating filter.

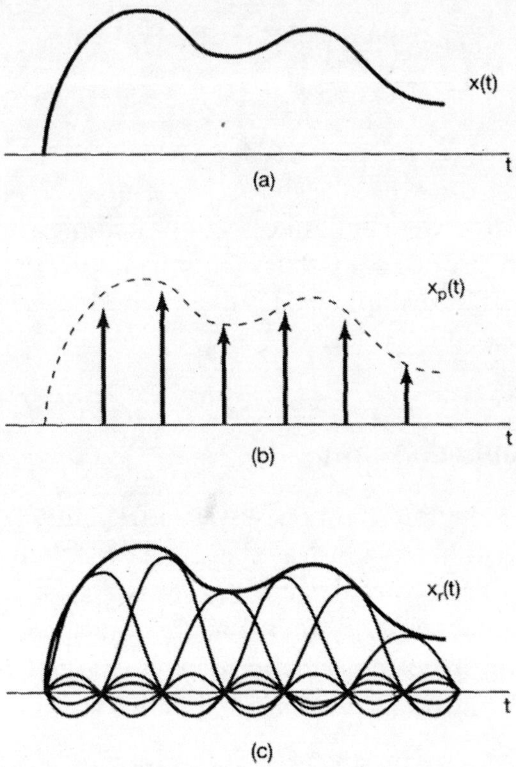

Fig 6.8: Band-limited interpolation using Sinc function: (a) Band-limited signal x(t) (b) Impulse train sampling of x(t) (c) Ideal band-limited interpolation in which impulse train is replaced by superposition of Sinc functions.

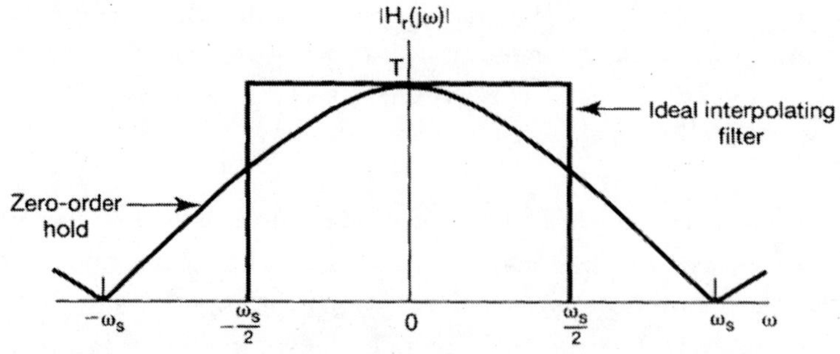

Fig 6.9: Transfer function for zero-order hold

If the interpolation provided by zero-order hold is insufficient then we can opt for interpolation strategies which are of higher order holds. We know from figure 6.5 that the zero-order hold produces an output signal that is not continuous in time. On the other hand, the linear interpolation, as shown in figure 6.7 gives us reconstructions which are continuous. The linear interpolations are sometimes also known as first-order hold and can also be viewed as in figure 6.6. The associated transfer function is also shown in figure and is given by

$$H(j\omega) = \frac{1}{T}\left(\frac{\sin\left(\frac{\omega T}{2}\right)}{\frac{\omega}{2}}\right)^2 \tag{6.11}$$

The transfer function of the first-order hold is shown superimposed on the transfer function for the ideal interpolating filter. Now, we can define second- and higher order holds that produce reconstructions with a higher degree of smoothness. For example, the output of a second-order hold provides an interpolation of the sample values that is continuous and has a continuous first derivative and discontinuous second derivative.

6.3.1 The effect of under sampling: Aliasing

Till now we assumed that the sampling frequency was sufficiently high that the conditions of the sampling theorem were satisfied. As illustrated in figure 6.3, with $\omega_s > 2\omega_M$ the spectrum of the sampled signal consists of scaled replications of the spectrum of $x(t)$, and this forms the basis for the sampling theorem. When $\omega_s < 2\omega_M$, $X(j\omega)$ the spectrum of $x(t)$, is no longer replicated in $X_p(j\omega)$ and thus it is not possible to recover original continuous time signal by lowpass filtering. This effect is known as *aliasing,* and in this section, we explore its effect and consequences.

Clearly, if the system of figure 6.4 is applied to a signal with $\omega_s < 2\omega_M$ the reconstructed signal $x_r(t)$ will no longer be equal to *x(t)*. However, as explored in earlier section, the original signal, and the signal $x_r(t)$ that is reconstructed using band- limited interpolation will always be equal at the sampling instants; that is, for any choice ω_s,

$$x_r(nT) = x(nT), \qquad n = 0, \pm 1, \pm 2 \dots \dots \tag{6.12}$$

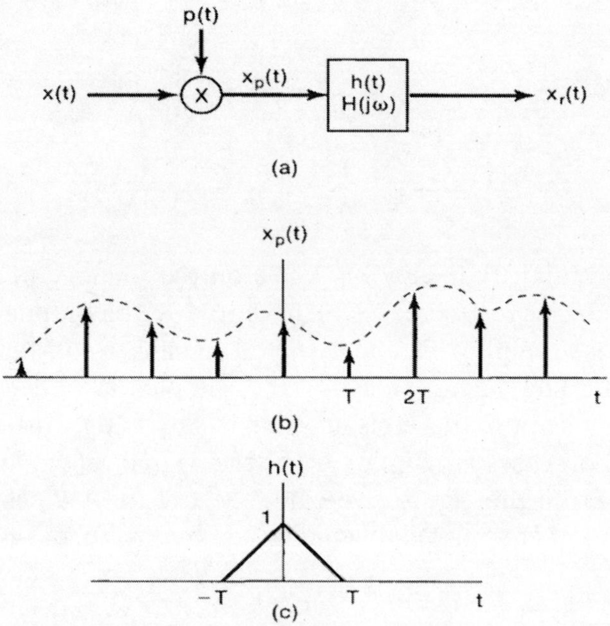

Fig 6.10: Linear Interpolation (First-order hold) as impulse-train sampling followed with convolution a triangular impulse response: (a) system for sampling & reconstruction; (b) Impulse train of samples; (c) Impulse response representing a first-order hold; (d) First-order hold applied to sampled signal; (e) Comparison of transfer function of ideal interpolating filter & first order hold.

We will try to understand the relationship between $x(t)$ and $x_r(t)$ when $\omega_s < 2\omega_M$ for the simple case of sinusoidal case thus let,

$$x(t) = \cos(\omega_0 t) \tag{6.13}$$

with Fourier transform $X(j\omega)$ as indicated in Figure 6.11(a). In this figure, we have graphically distinguished the impulse at w_0 from that at $-w_0$ for convenience. Let us consider $X_p(j\omega)$, the spectrum of the sampled signal, and focus on the effect of a change in the frequency ω_0 with the sampling frequency ω_s fixed. In figure 6.11(b)-(e), we illustrate $X_p(j\omega)$ for several values of ω_0. Also indicated by a dashed line is the passband of the lowpass filter of figure 6.4 with $\omega_c = \omega_s/2$. Note that no aliasing occurs in (b) and (c), since $\omega_0 < \omega_s/2$, whereas aliasing does occur in (d) and (e). For each of the four cases, the lowpass filtered output $x_r(t)$ is given as follows:

$$(a)\quad \omega_0 = \frac{\omega_s}{6}; \qquad x_r(t) = \cos\omega_0 t = x(t)$$

$$(b)\quad \omega_0 = \frac{2\omega_s}{6}; \qquad x_r(t) = \cos\omega_0 t = x(t)$$

$$(c)\quad \omega_0 = \frac{4\omega_s}{6}; \qquad x_r(t) = \cos(\omega_s - \omega_0)t \neq x(t)$$

$$(d)\quad \omega_0 = \frac{5\omega_s}{6}; \qquad x_r(t) = \cos(\omega_s - \omega_0)t \neq x(t)$$

When aliasing occurs, the original frequency ω_0 takes on the identity of a lower frequency, $\omega_s - \omega_0$. For $\omega_s/2 < \omega_0 < \omega_s$, as ω_0 increases relative to ω_s , the output frequency $\omega_s - \omega_0$ decreases. When $\omega_s = \omega_0$, for example, the reconstructed signal is a constant. This is consistent with the fact that, when sampling once per cycle, the samples are all equal and would be identical to those obtained by sampling a constant signal ($\omega_0 = 0$). In figure 6.12, we have depicted, for each of the four cases in Figure 6.11, the signal $x(t)$, its samples, and the reconstructed signal $x_r(t)$. From the figure, we can see how the lowpass filter interpolates between samples. Consider another sinusoidal signal given by Eq. (6.14) as,

$$x(t) = \cos(\omega_0 t + \varphi) \tag{6.14}$$

In this case, the Fourier transform of $x(t)$ is essentially the same as Figure 6.11(a), except that the impulse indicated with a solid line now has amplitude $\pi e^{j\varphi}$, while the impulse indicated with a dashed line has amplitude with the opposite phase, namely, $\pi e^{-j\varphi}$ If we now consider the same set of choices for ω_0 as in Figure 6.11, the resulting spectra for the sampled versions of $\cos(\omega_0 t + \varphi)$ are exactly as in the figure, with all solid impulses having amplitude $\pi e^{j\varphi}$ and all dashed ones having amplitude $\pi e^{-j\varphi}$ Again, in cases (b) and (c) the condition of the sampling theorem is met, so that $x_r(t) = \cos(\omega_0 t + \varphi) = x(t)$, while in (d) and (e) we again have aliasing. but we now see that there has been a reversal in the solid and dashed impulses appearing in the passband of the lowpass filter. As a result, we find that in these cases, $x_r(t) = \cos[(\omega_s - \omega_0)t + \varphi)]$, where we have a change in the sign of the phase φ i.e., a *phase reversal.*

It is important to note that the sampling theorem explicitly requires that the sampling frequency be *greater than* twice the highest frequency in the signal, rather than greater than or equal to twice the highest frequency. The next example illustrates that sampling a sinusoidal signal at exactly twice its frequency (i.e., exactly two samples per cycle) is not sufficient.

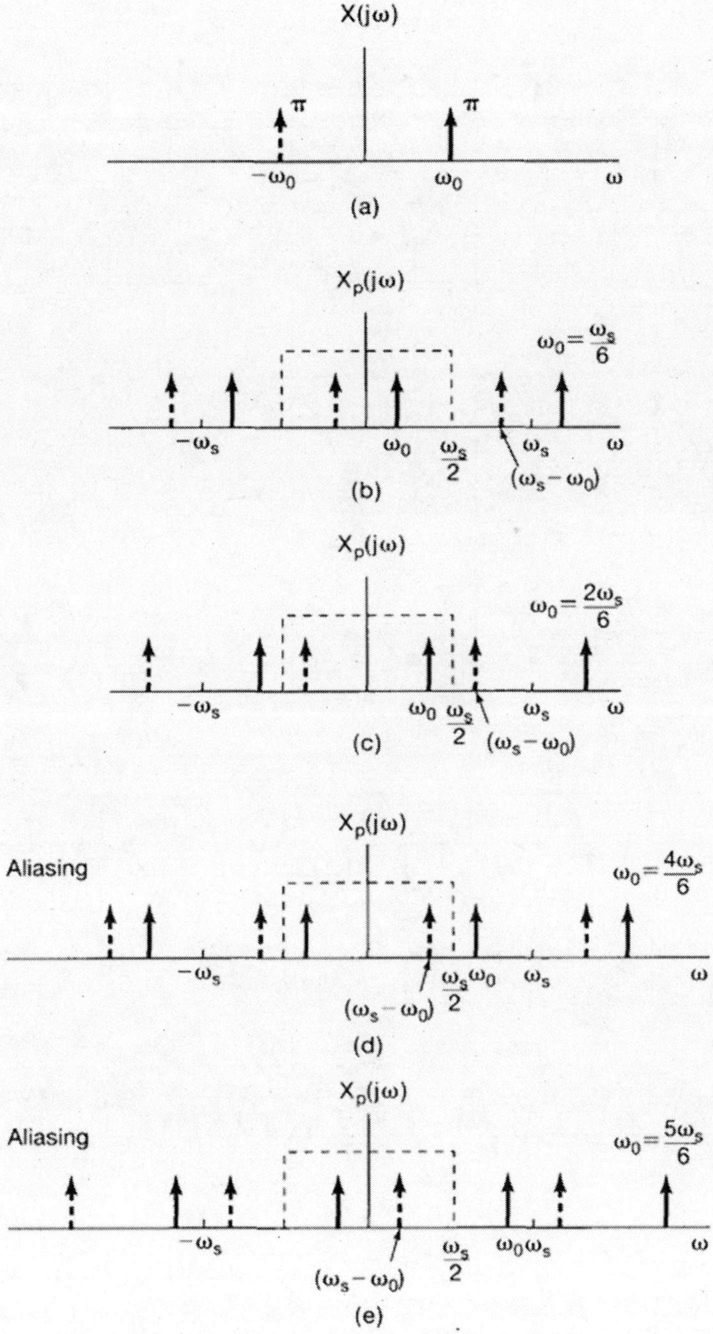

Fig 6.11: Effect of oversampling & under sampling: (a) Spectrum of original sinusoidal signal; (b) (c) Spectrum of sampled signal with $\omega_s > 2\omega_0$; (d) (e) Spectrum of sampled signal with $\omega_s < 2\omega_0$;

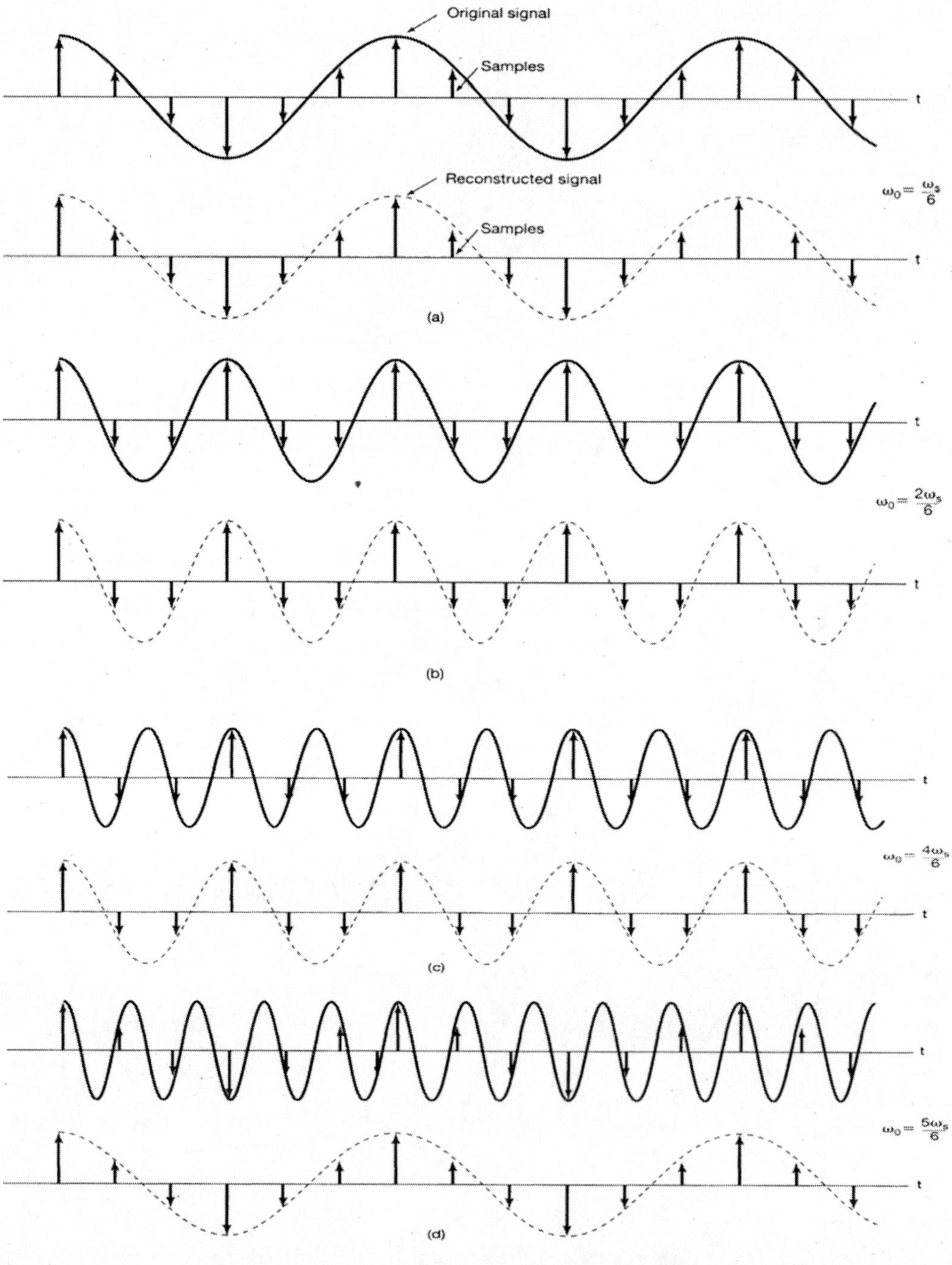

Fig 6.12: Effect of aliasing on sinusoidal signal. For each of the four values of ω_0, the original sinusoidal signal (solid curve), its samples, and reconstructed signal (dashed curve) are illustrated: (a) $\omega_0 = \frac{5\omega_s}{6}$, in (a) and (b) no aliasing occurs, whereas in (c) & (d) there is aliasing

Example 6.1

Consider a sinusoidal signal

$$x(t) = \cos\left(\frac{\omega_s}{2}t + \varphi\right),$$

And suppose that the above signal is sampled using impulse sampling at exactly the twice the frequency of the sinusoid that is with sampling frequency ω_s. Now if this impulse sampled signal is applied as input to an ideal low pass filter with cut-off frequency $\omega_s/2$ the resulting output is

$$x_r(t) = (\cos\varphi)\cos\left(\frac{\omega_s}{2}t\right)$$

It is observed that the perfect reconstruction of $x(t)$ is only possible when $\varphi = 0$ or when φ is integer multiple of 2π. Otherwise $x_r(t) \neq x(t)$. So, the perfect reconstruction of original continuous time signal becomes conditional, which is not desirable.

Now, let us consider the case in which $\varphi = -\pi/2$ so that,

$$x(t) = \sin\left(\frac{\omega_s}{2}t\right)$$

The signal corresponding to above signal is sketched in figure 6.12. The values of the signal at integer multiples of the sampling period $2\pi/\omega_s$ are zero. So, sampling at this rate will produce a signal which is zero. Now these zero inputs will be given to the ideal low pass filter, the resulting output $x_r(t)$ will also be zero.

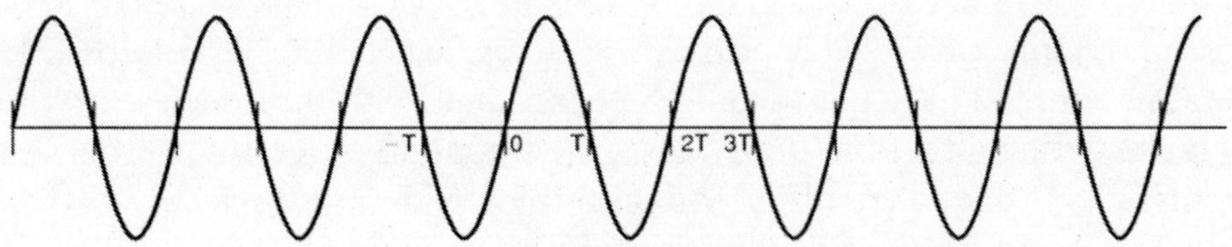

Fig 6.13: Sinusoidal signal for example 6.1

Due to under sampling, stroboscopic effect is observed where higher frequencies are reflected into lower frequencies, is the principle on which the it is based. Consider, for example, the situation depicted in Figure 6.13, in which we have a disc rotating at a constant rate with a single radial line marked on the disc.

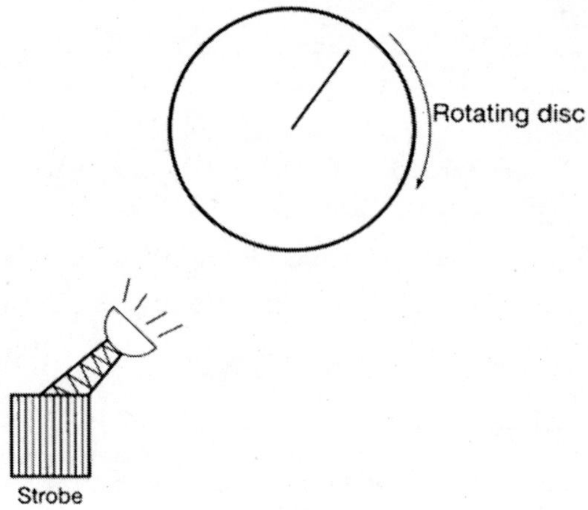

Fig 6.14 Strobe effect

The flashing strobe can be considered to act as a sampling system, since it illuminates the disc for extremely brief time intervals at a periodic rate. It is observed that when the rotational speed of the disc is less than the strobe frequency then the speed of the rotation of the disc is perceived correctly. Now, when the strobe frequency is less than twice the rotational frequency of the disc, then rotation appears to be at lower frequency than the actual. Sometimes because of phase reversal disc will appear to be rotating in the wrong direction. Now, if we track the position of line on the disc at successive samples then when $\omega_0 < \omega_s < 2\omega_0$ such that sampling rate per revolution is increased so that so that we sample somewhat more frequently than once per revolution, samples of the disc will show the fixed line in positions that are successively displaced in a counterclockwise direction, opposite to the clockwise rotation of the disc itself. At one flash per revolution, corresponding to $\omega_s = \omega_0$, the radial line appears stationary (i.e., the rotational frequency of the disc and its harmonics have been aliased to zero frequency). A similar effect is commonly observed in western movies, where the wheels of a stagecoach appear to be rotating more slowly than would be consistent with the coach's forward motion, and sometimes in the wrong direction. In this case, the sampling process corresponds to the fact that moving pictures are a sequence of individual frames with a rate (usually between 18 and 24 frames per second) corresponding to the sampling frequency.

The preceding discussion suggests interpreting the stroboscopic effect as an example of a useful application of aliasing due to under sampling. Another practical application of aliasing arises in a measuring instrument referred to as a *sampling oscilloscope.* This instrument is intended for observing very high-frequency waveforms and exploits the principles of sampling to alias these frequencies into ones that are more easily displayed.

6.4 Discrete Time Processing of Continuous Time Signals

In many applications, there is a significant advantage offered in processing a continuous time signal by first converting it to a discrete-time signal and, after discrete-time processing, converting back to a continuous-time signal. The discrete-time signal processing can be implemented by a special purpose computer, with various DSP processors, or with any of the variety of devices that are specifically designed for discrete-time signal processing.

In broad terms, this approach to continuous-time signal processing can be viewed as the cascade of three operations, as indicated in Figure 7.13, where $x_c(t)$ and $y_c(t)$ are continuous-time signals and $x_d(n)$ and $y_d(n)$ are the discrete-time signals corresponding $x_c(t)$ to $y_c(t)$ and. The overall system is, of course, a continuous-time system in the sense that its input and output are both continuous-time signals. The theoretical basis for converting a continuous-time signal to a discrete-time signal and reconstructing a continuous-time signal from its discrete-time representation lies in the sampling theorem. By satisfying simple conditions of sampling theorem and through the process of periodic sampling with the sampling frequency consistent with the conditions of the sampling theorem, the continuous-time signal $x_c(t)$ is exactly represented by a sequence of instantaneous sample values $x_c(nT)$; that is, the discrete-time sequence $x_d(n)$ is related to $x_c(t)$ by

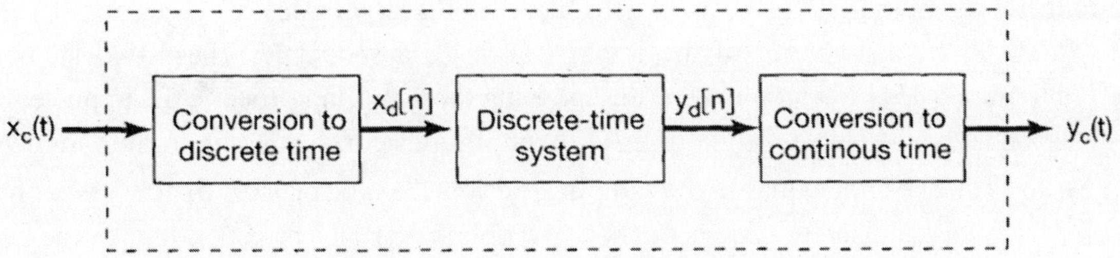

Fig 6.15: Discrete-time processing of Continuous Time signals

$$x_d(n) = x_c(nT) \tag{6.15}$$

The continuous time signal is applied to the first block of the figure 6.13 and $x_c(t)$ is converted to the discrete time signal $x_d(n)$. It will be abbreviated as C/D conversion. The third block in figure 6.13 converts the discrete time signal $y_d(n)$ to continuous signal. This conversion is known is abbreviated as D/C. The D/C operation uses the interpolation technique between sample values provided to it as input. The continuous time signal produced is expressed as

$$y_d(n) = y_c(nT)$$

This notation is made explicit in Figure 6.14. In systems such as digital computers and digital systems for which the discrete-time signal is represented in digital form, the device commonly used to implement the *C/D* conversion is referred to as an *analog-to-digital* (A- to-D) converter, and the device used to implement the *D/C* conversion is referred to as a *digital-to-analog* (D-to-A) converter.

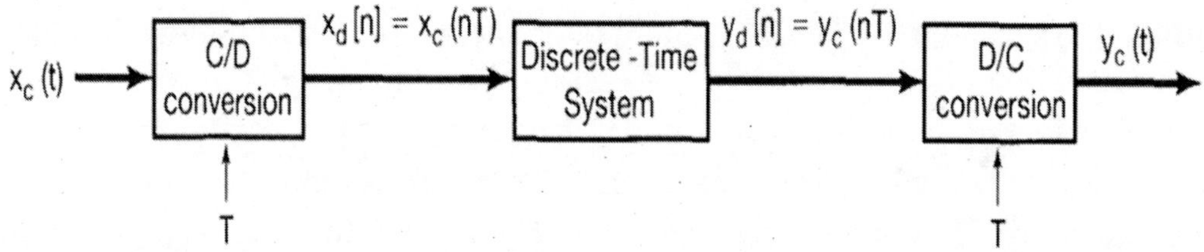

Fig 6.16: Notation for A/D conversion and D/A conversion

To understand further the relationship between the continuous-time signal $x_c(t)$ and its discrete-time representation $x_d(n)$, it is helpful to represent *C/D* as a process of periodic sampling followed by a mapping of the impulse train to a sequence. These two steps are illustrated in Figure 6.15. First step is to represent using the sampling process, the impulse train $x_p(t)$ corresponds to a sequence of impulses with amplitudes corresponding to the samples of $x_c(t)$ and with a time spacing equal to the sampling period *T*. In the process of conversion from the impulse train to the discrete-time sequence, we obtain $x_d(n)$, corresponding to the same sequence of samples of $x_c(t)$, but with unity spacing in terms of the new in- dependent variable *n*. Thus, in effect, the conversion from the impulse train sequence of samples to the discrete-time sequence of samples can be thought of as a normalization in time. This normalization is evident in Figures 6.15 (b) and (c).

It is also instructive to examine the processing stages in Figure 6.13 in the frequency domain. Since we will be dealing with Fourier transforms in both continuous and discrete time, in this section only we distinguish the continuous-time and discrete-time frequency variables by using ω in continuous time and Ω in discrete time. For example, the continuous-time Fourier transforms of $x_c(t)$ and $y_c(t)$ are $X_c(j\omega)$ and $Y_c(j\omega)$, respectively, while the discrete-time Fourier transforms of $x_d(n)$ and $y_d(n)$ are $X_d(j\Omega)$ and $Y_d(j\Omega)$, respectively.

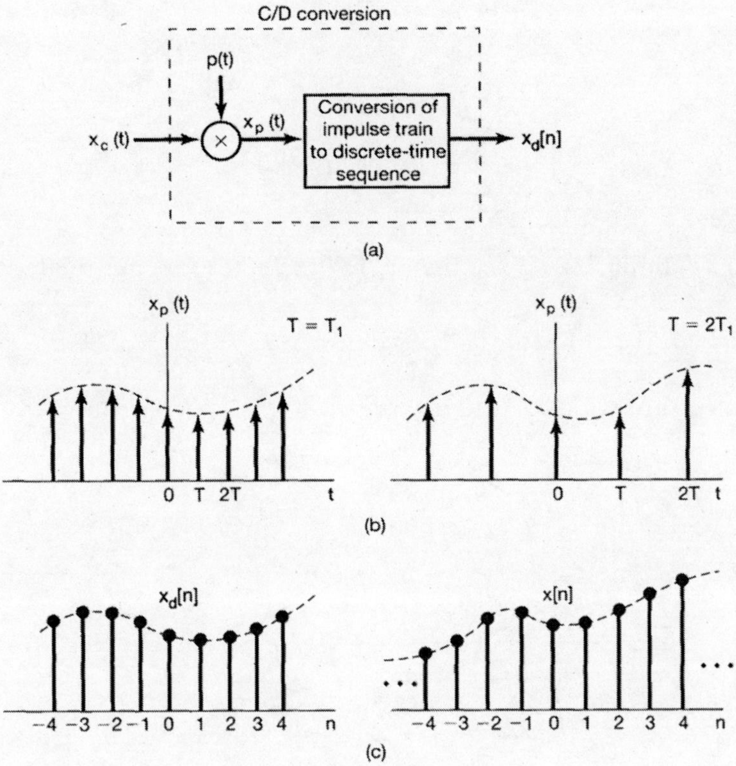

Fig 6.17: Sampling then followed by conversion to Discrete-time sequence: (a) Overall System; (b) $x_p(t)$ for two sampling rates. Dashed envelop represents $x_c(t)$; (c) The output sequence for two different sampling rates.

Let us, apply Fourier Transform to $x_p(t)$ to get $X_p(j\omega)$, then we will get,

$$x_p(t) = \sum_{n=-\infty}^{\infty} x_c(nT)\delta(t - nT) \tag{6.16}$$

Now, we know the transform of $\delta(t - nT)$ is $e^{-j\omega nT}$ it follows that

$$X_p(j\omega) = \sum_{n=-\infty}^{\infty} x_c(nT)e^{-j\omega nT} \tag{6.17}$$

On similar lines the discrete-time Fourier Transform of $x_d(n)$ will be

$$X_d(j\Omega) = \sum_{n=-\infty}^{\infty} x_d(n)e^{-j\Omega n} \tag{6.18}$$

Using the equation 6.15

$$X_d\left(e^{-j\Omega}\right) = \sum_{n=-\infty}^{+\infty} x_c(nT)e^{-j\Omega n} \tag{6.19}$$

Comparing equation 6.17 and 6.19 we see that $X_d\left(e^{j\Omega}\right)$ & $X_p(j\omega)$ are related as

$$X_d\left(e^{j\Omega}\right) = X_p(j\Omega/T) \tag{6.20}$$

With the help of equation 6.6, we can further write

$$x_p(j\omega) = \frac{1}{T}\sum_{k=-\infty}^{+\infty} X_c(j(\omega - k\omega_s)) \tag{6.22}$$

Similarly,

$$x_d\left(e^{j\Omega}\right) = \frac{1}{T}\sum_{k=-\infty}^{+\infty} X_c(j(\Omega - 2\pi k)/T) \tag{6.23}$$

The relationship among $X_c(j\omega), X_p(j\omega)$ and $X_d(e^{j\Omega})$ is illustrated in figure 6.16 for two different sampling rates. Here, $X_d(e^{j\Omega})$ is a frequency scaled version of $X_p(j\omega)$ and in particular is periodic in Ω with period 2π. This is the characteristic of any discrete-time Fourier transform. The spectrum of $x_d(n)$ is related to that of $x_c(t)$ through periodic replication, represented by eq. (6.22), followed by linear frequency scaling, represented by eq. (6.20). The periodic replication is a consequence of the first step in the conversion process in Figure 6.15, namely, the impulse-train sampling. The linear frequency scaling in eq. (6.20) can be thought of informally because of the normalization in time introduced by converting from the impulse train $x_p(t)$ to the discrete-time sequence $x_d(n)$.

In the overall system of Figure 6.13, after processing with a discrete-time system, the resulting sequence is converted back to a continuous-time signal. This process is the reverse of the steps in Figure 6.15. Specifically, from the sequence $y_d(n)$, a continuous time impulse train $y_p(t)$ can be generated. Recovery of the continuous-time signal $y_c(t)$ from this impulse train is then accomplished by means of lowpass filtering, as illustrated in Figure 6.17.

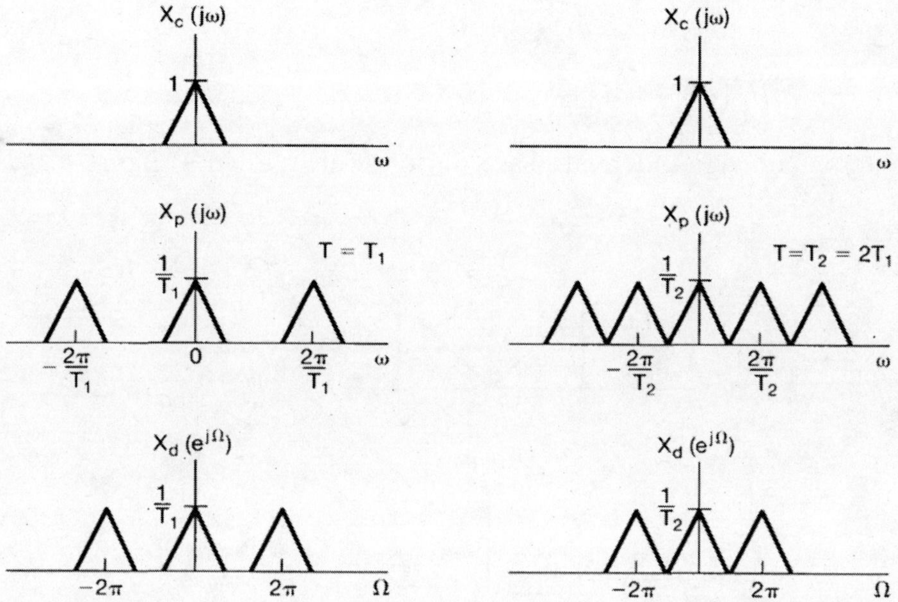

Fig 6.18: The relationship among $X_c(j\omega), X_p(j\omega)$ and $X_d(e^{j\Omega})$ with different sampling rates

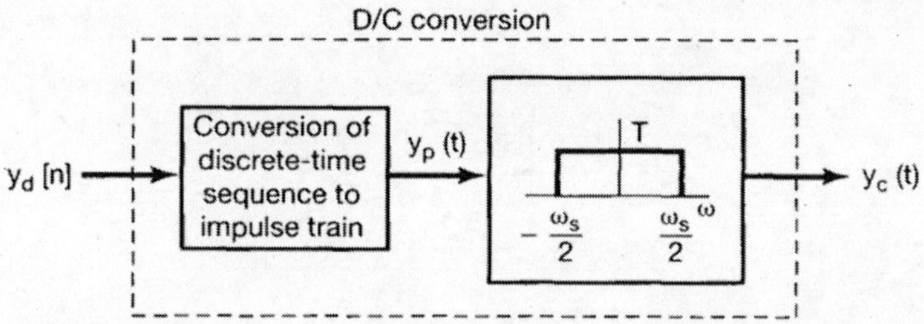

Fig. 6.19: Conversion of discrete time sequence to a continuous time signal

6.4.1 Digital differentiator

Consider the discrete-time implementation of a continuous-time band-limited differentiating filter. As discussed in earlier section, the frequency response of a continuous-time differentiating filter is,

$$H_c(j\omega) = j\omega \tag{6.24}$$

And band-limited differentiator with cutoff frequency ω_c is

$$H_c(j\omega) = \begin{cases} j\omega, & |\omega| < \omega_c \\ 0, & |\omega| > \omega_c \end{cases} \tag{6.25}$$

With sampling frequency $\omega_s = 2\omega_c$, we see that corresponding discrete-time transfer function is,

$$H_d(e^{j\Omega}) = j\left(\frac{\Omega}{T}\right), \quad |\Omega| < \pi \tag{6.26}$$

For the above filters, the magnitude and phase response are shown in figure 6.19 and figure 6.20

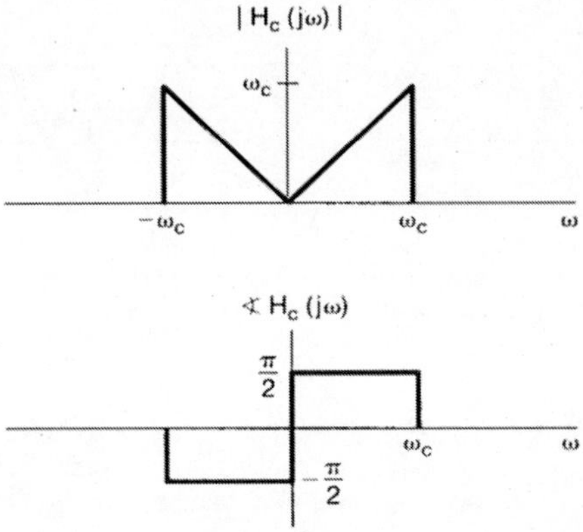

Fig 6.20: Frequency Response of ideal band-limited differentiator

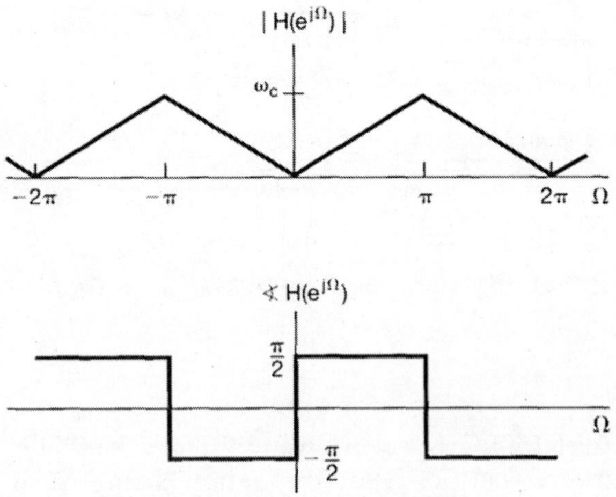

Fig 6.21: Frequency Response of discrete-time filter used to implement a continuous time band-limited differentiator

Example 6.2

By considering the output of the digital differentiator for a continuous time sine input, we may conveniently determine the impulse response $h_d(n)$ of the discrete-time filter in the implementation of the digital differentiator.

$$x_c(t) = \frac{\sin(\pi t/T)}{\pi t} \tag{6.27}$$

Where T is sampling period, then

$$X_c(j\omega) = f(x) = \begin{cases} 1, & |\omega| < \pi/T \\ 0, & Otherwise \end{cases}$$

which is sufficiently band limited to ensure that sampling $x_c(t)$ at frequency $\omega_s = 2\pi/T$ does not give rise to any aliasing. It follows that the output of the digital differentiator is,

$$y_c(t) = \frac{d}{dt}x_c(t) = \frac{\cos(\pi t/T)}{Tt} - \frac{\sin\left(\frac{\pi t}{T}\right)}{\pi t^2} \tag{6.28}$$

The $x_c(t)$ is given by equation (6.27) the corresponding signal $x_d(n)$ is

$$x_d(n) = x_c(nT) = \frac{1}{T}\delta(n) \tag{6.29}$$

Which can be verified from l'Hospital's rule,

$$y_d(n) = y_c(nT) = \begin{cases} \frac{-1^n}{nT^2}, & n \neq 0 \\ 0, & n = 0 \end{cases} \tag{6.30}$$

So when input to the filter is given by equation 6.26 is the scaled unit impulse in equation (6.29) The resulting output is given by eq. 6.30. So, impulse response of this filter is given by,

$$h_d(n) = \begin{cases} \frac{-1^n}{nT^2}, & n \neq 0 \\ 0, & n = 0 \end{cases} \tag{6.30}$$

6.5 Sampling of discrete time signals

Thus far in this chapter, we have considered the sampling of continuous-time signals, and in addition to developing the analysis necessary to understand continuous-time sampling, we have introduced several of its applications. As we will see in this section, a very similar set of properties and results with several important applications can be developed for sampling of discrete-time signals.

6.5.1 Impulse train sampling

In analogy with continuous-time sampling as carried out using the system of Figure 6.14, sampling of a discrete-time signal can be represented as shown in Figure 6.20. Here, the new sequence $x_p(n)$ resulting from the sampling process is equal to the original sequence $x(n)$ at integer multiples of the sampling period *N* and is zero at the intermediate samples; that is,

$$x_p(n) = \begin{cases} x(n), & if\ n = an\ integer\ multiple\ of\ N \\ x, & Otherwise \end{cases} \tag{6.31}$$

Using the multiplication property developed early in this section, discrete time sampling in frequency domain can be written as,

$$x_p(n) = x(n)p(n) = \sum_{k=-\infty}^{+\infty} x(kN)\delta(n - kN) \tag{6.32}$$

We have, in frequency domain,

$$x_p(e^{j\omega}) = \frac{1}{2\pi}\int P(e^{j\theta})X(e^{j(\omega-\theta)})d\theta \tag{6.33}$$

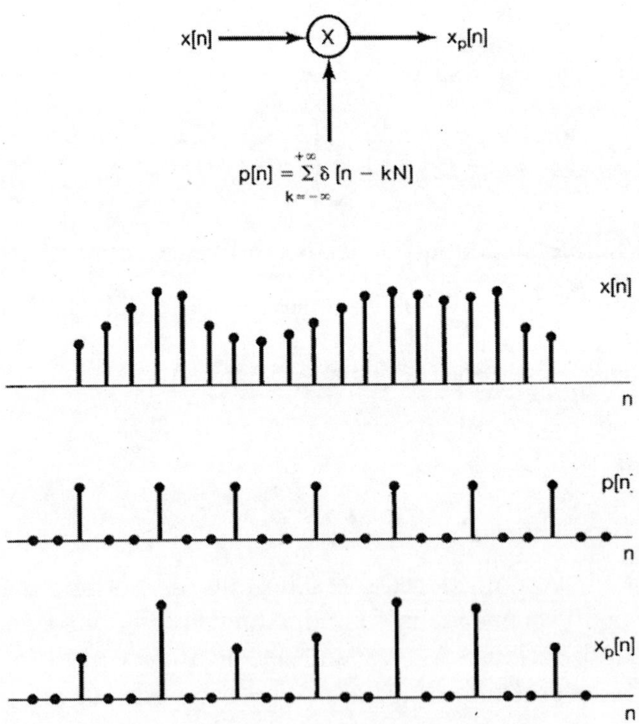

Fig 6.22: Discrete time sampling

Fourier Transform of sampling space $p(n)$ is,

$$P(e^{j\omega}) = \frac{2\pi}{N}\sum_{k=-\infty}^{+\infty} \delta(\omega - k\omega_s) \tag{6.34}$$

Equation (6.42) is the counterpart for discrete-time sampling of eq. (6.6) for continuous-time sampling and is illustrated in figure 6.21. In Figure 6.21(c), with $\omega_s - \omega_M > \omega_M$, or equivalently, $\omega_s > \omega_M$ there is no aliasing (i.e., the nonzero portions of the replicas of $X(e^{j\omega})$ do not overlap), whereas with $\omega_s < \omega_M$, as in figure 6.21(d), frequency domain aliasing results. In the absence of aliasing, $X(e^{j\omega})$ is faithfully reproduced around $\omega = 0$ and integer multiples of 2π. Consequently, $x(n)$ can be recovered from $x_p(n)$ by means of a lowpass filter with gain N cutoff frequency greater than ω_m and less than $\omega_s - \omega_M$, where we have specified cutoff frequency of the low pass filter as $\omega_s/2$. If overall system from figure 6.22 (a) is applied to a sequence for which $\omega_s < \omega_M$, so that there are aliasing results $x_r(n)$ will no longer will equal to $x(n)$. But with continuous time sampling, the two sequences will be equal at multiple time of sampling period. Now, we have,

$$x_r(kN) = x(kN), \qquad k = 0, \pm1, \pm2 \dots \dots \dots, \tag{6.35}$$

independently of whether aliasing occurs

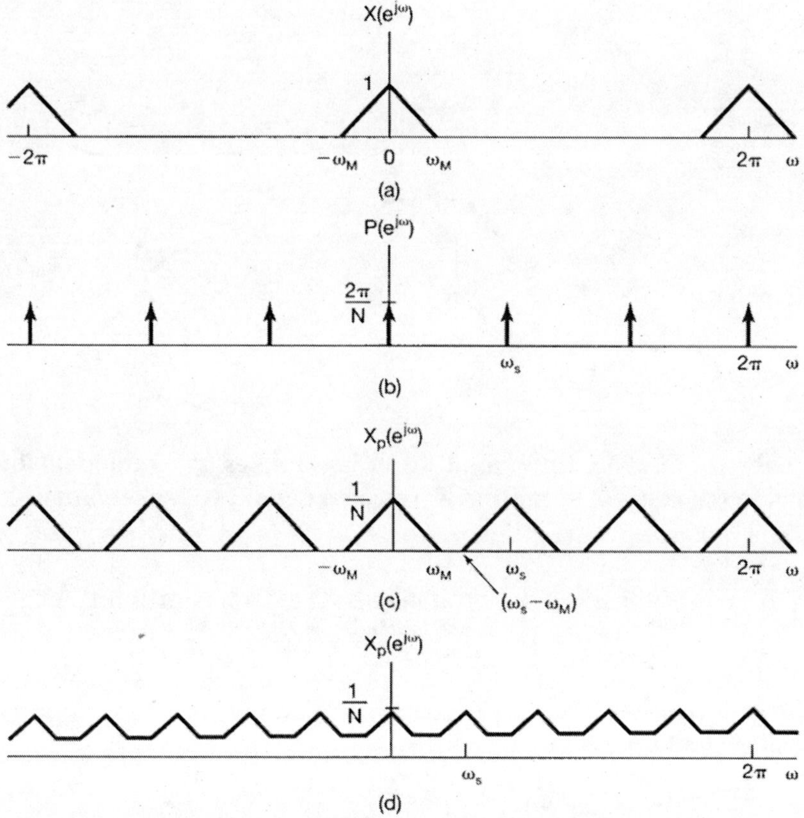

Fig 6.23: Impulse-train sampling of discrete-time signal in frequency domain: (a) Original signal spectrum; (b) Spectrum of sampling sequence; (c) Spectrum of sampled signal with $\omega_s > \omega_M$; (d) Spectrum of sampled signal with $\omega_s < \omega_M$. No aliasing occurs.

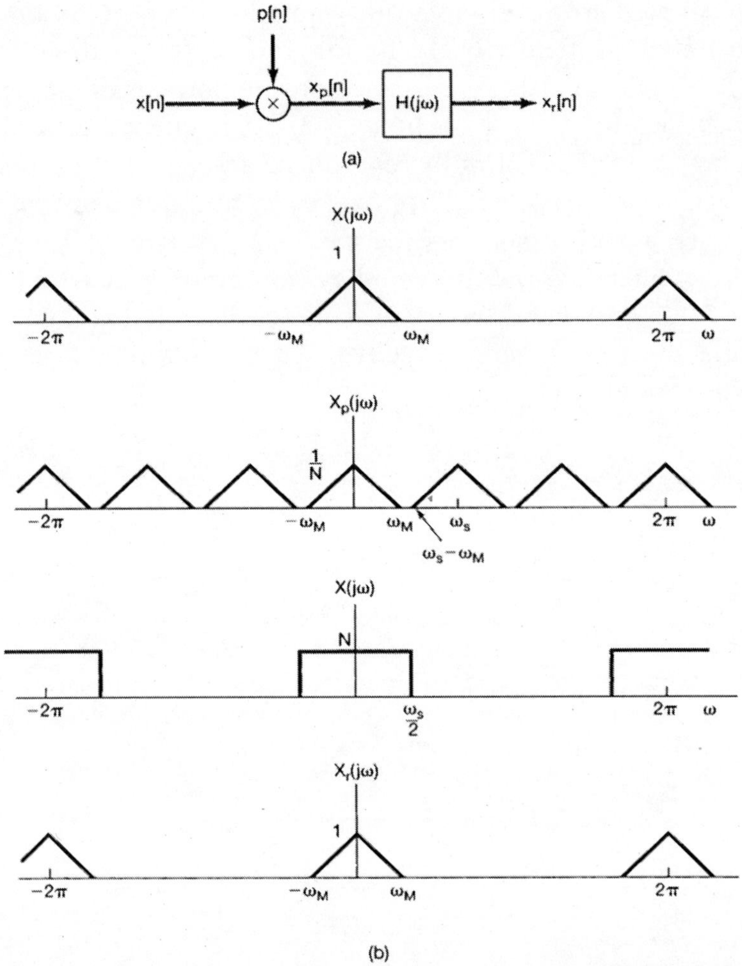

Fig 6.24: Exact recovery of discrete time signal from its samples using an ideal low pass filter: (a) Block diagram for sampling & reconstruction; (b) spectrum of $x(n)$;

Example 6.3

Consider a sequence of $x(n)$ whose Fourier transform $X(e^{j\omega})$ has property that

$$X(e^{j\omega}) = 0 \qquad for \quad 2\pi/9 \leq |\omega| \leq \pi$$

To determine the lowest rate at which $x(n)$ may be sampled without the possibility of aliasing, we must find the largest N such that

$$\frac{2\pi}{N} \geq 2\left(\frac{2\pi}{9}\right) \Rightarrow N \leq \frac{9}{2}$$

We conclude that $N_{max} = 4$ and corresponding sampling frequency is $\frac{2\pi}{4} = \frac{\pi}{2}$

The reconstruction of $x(n)$ using a lowpass filter applied to $x_p(n)$ can be interpreted in the time domain as an interpolation formula like eq. (6.10). With $h(n)$ denoting the impulse response of the lowpass filter, we have

$$h(n) = \frac{N\omega_c}{\pi} \frac{\sin(\omega_c n)}{\omega_c n} \tag{6.36}$$

The reconstructed sequence is then

$$x_r(n) = x_p(n) * h(n) \tag{6.37}$$

Or equivalently,

$$x_r(n) = \sum_{n=-\infty}^{+\infty} x(kN)h_r(n - kN) \tag{6.38}$$

Where $h_r(n)$ is impulse response of interpolating filter

6.5.2 Discrete time decimation and interpolation

There are a variety of important applications of the principles of discrete-time sampling, such as in filter design and implementation or in communication applications. In many of these applications it is inefficient to represent, transmit, or store the sampled sequence $x_p(n)$ directly in the form depicted in Figure 6.20, since, in between the sampling instants, $x_p(n)$ is known to be zero. Thus, the sampled sequence is typically replaced by a new sequence $x_b(n)$, which is simply every Nth value of $x_p(n)$; that is,

$$x_b(n) = x_p(nN) \tag{6.39}$$

Similarly,

$$x_b(n) = x(nN) \tag{6.40}$$

since $x_p(n)$ and $x(n)$ are equal at integer multiples of N. The operation of extracting every N^{th} sample is commonly referred to as *decimation.* The relationship between $x(n), x_p(n)$, $x_b(n)$ is illustrated in figure 6.23.

To determine the effect of decimation in the frequency domain, we wish to determine the relationship between $X_b(e^{j\omega})$ the Fourier transform of $X_b(n)$ and $X(e^{j\omega})$. To this end, we note that,

$$X_b\left(e^{j\omega}\right) = \sum_{k=-\infty}^{+\infty} x_b[k]e^{-j\omega k} \tag{6.41}$$

Using the Eq. (6.39)

$$X_b(e^{j\omega}) = \sum_{k=-\infty}^{+\infty} x_p[kN]e^{-j\omega k} \tag{6.42}$$

If we let $n = kN$, or equivalently $k = n/N$, we can write

$$X_b(e^{j\omega}) = \sum_{\substack{n=integer \\ multiple \\ of\ N}} x_p[n]e^{-j\omega n/N} \tag{6.43}$$

And since $x_p[n] = 0$ when n is not integer multiple of N, we can also write,

$$X_b(e^{j\omega}) = \sum_{k=-\infty}^{+\infty} x_p[n]e^{-j\omega n/N} \tag{6.44}$$

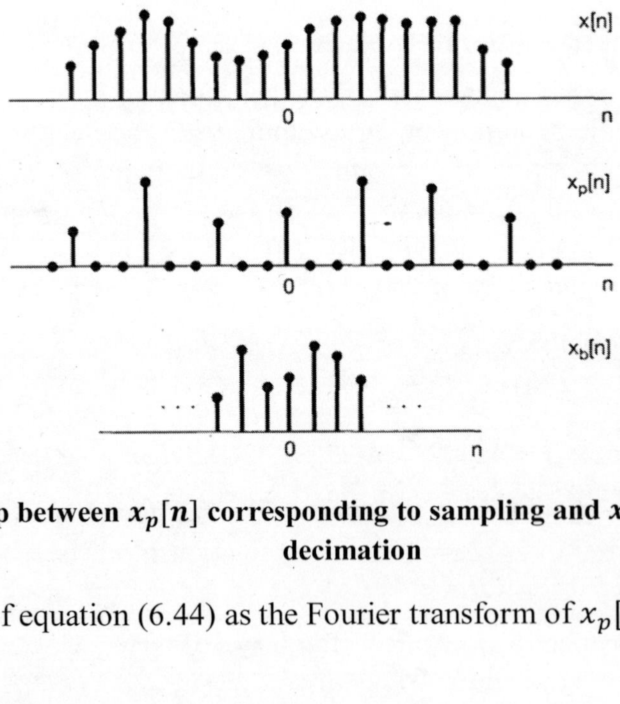

Fig 6.25: Relationship between $x_p[n]$ corresponding to sampling and $x_b[n]$ corresponding to decimation

Also, right hand side of equation (6.44) as the Fourier transform of $x_p[n]$; so,

$$\sum_{k=-\infty}^{+\infty} x_p[n]e^{-j\omega n/N} = X_p(e^{j\omega/N}) \tag{6.45}$$

Thus, from equation (6.44) & (6.45) we can conclude that

$$X_b(e^{j\omega}) = X_p(e^{j\omega/N}) \tag{6.46}$$

This relationship is illustrated in Figure 6.24, and from it, we observe that the spectra for the sampled sequence and the decimated sequence differ only in a frequency scaling or normalization. If the original spectrum $X(e^{j\omega})$ is appropriately band limited, so that there is no aliasing present in $X_p(e^{j\omega})$, then, as shown in the figure, the effect of decimation is to spread the spectrum of the original sequence over a larger portion of the frequency band.

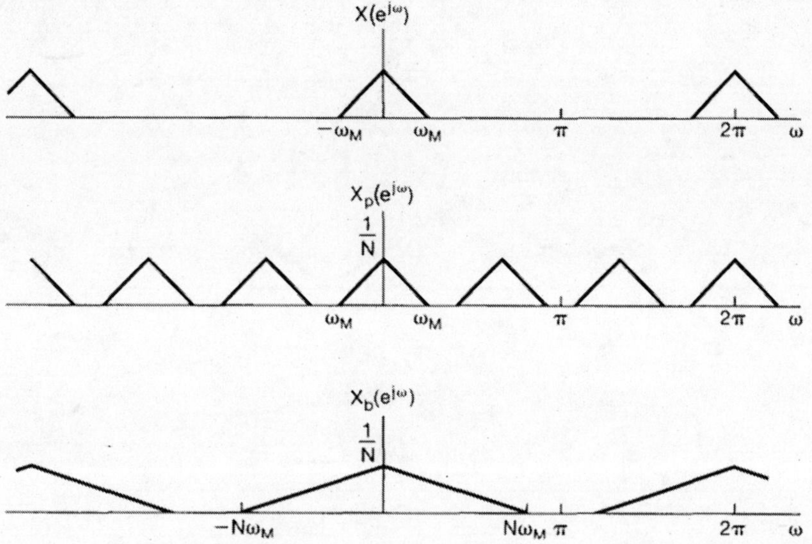

Fig 6.26: Frequency domain illustration of the relationship between sampling & decimation

If the original sequence $x(n)$ is obtained by sampling a continuous-time signal, the process of decimation can be viewed as reducing the sampling rate on the signal by a factor of N. To avoid aliasing, $X(e^{j\omega})$ cannot occupy the full frequency band. In other words, if the signal can be decimated without introducing aliasing, then the original continuous- time signal was oversampled, and thus, the sampling rate can be reduced without aliasing. With the interpretation of the sequence $x(n)$ as samples of a continuous-time signal, the process of decimation is often referred to as downsampling.

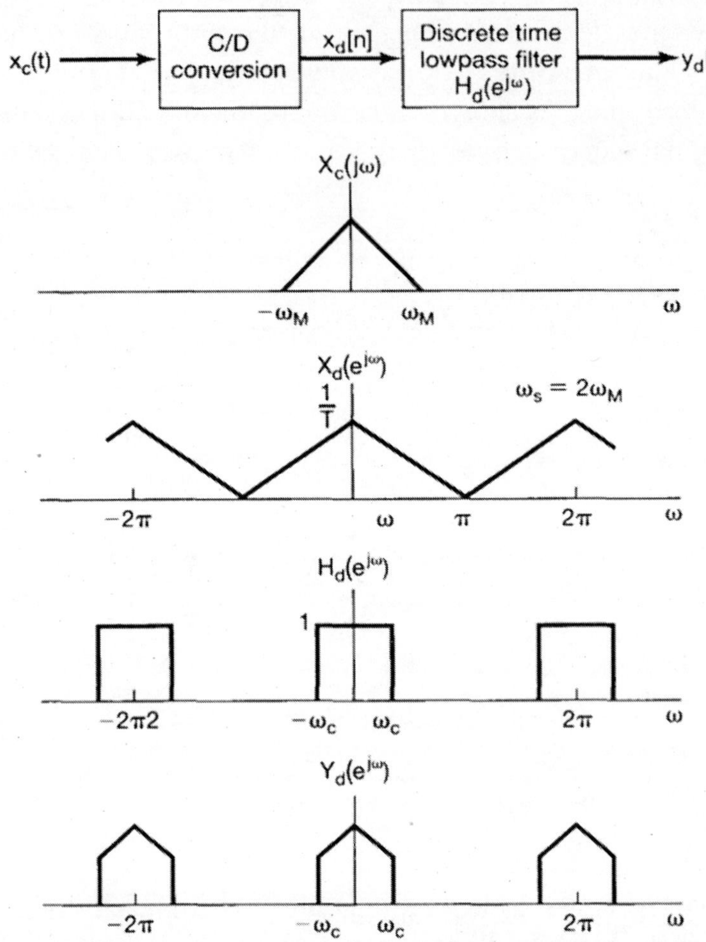

Fig 6.27: Continuous time signal that was originally sampled at Nyquist rate. After discrete time filtering, the resulting sequence can be further downsampled. Here $X_c(j\omega)$ is the continuous time Fourier Transform of $x_c(t), X_d(e^{j\omega})$ and $Y_d(e^{j\omega})$ are the discrete time Fourier transforms of $x_d(n)$ & $y_d(n)$ respectively. And $H_d(e^{j\omega})$ is the frequency response of the discrete time low pass filter depicted in the block diagram.

In some applications in which a sequence is obtained by sampling a continuous- time signal, the original sampling rate may be as low as possible without introducing aliasing, but after additional processing and filtering, the bandwidth of the sequence may be reduced. An example of such a situation is shown in Figure 6.25. Since the output of the discrete-time filter is band limited, downsampling or decimation can be applied.

Just as in some applications it is useful to downsample, there are situations in which it is useful to convert a sequence to a *higher* equivalent sampling rate, a process referred to as *upsampling* or *interpolation.* Upsampling is basically the reverse of decimation or downsampling. As illustrated in Figures 6.23 and 6.24, in decimation we first sample and then retain only the sequence values at the sampling instants. To upsample, we reverse the process. For example, referring to Figure 6.23, we consider upsampling the sequence $x_b[n]$ to obtain $x[n]$. From $x_b[n]$, we form the sequence $x_p[n]$ by inserting *N* - 1 points with zero amplitude between each of the values in $x_b[n]$. The interpolated sequence $x[n]$ is then obtained from $x_p[n]$ by lowpass filtering. The overall procedure is summarized in Figure 6.26.

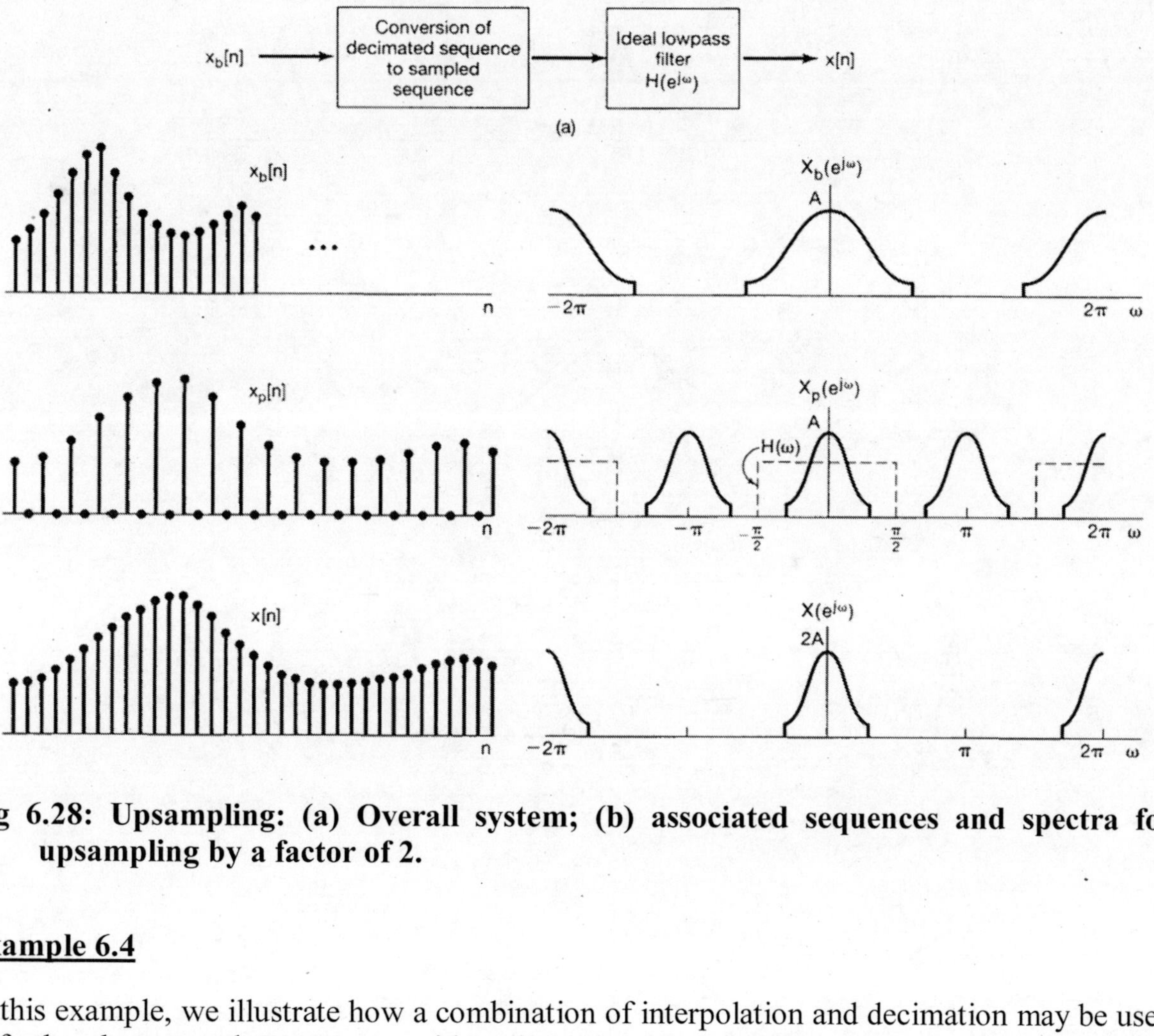

Fig 6.28: Upsampling: (a) Overall system; (b) associated sequences and spectra for upsampling by a factor of 2.

Example 6.4

In this example, we illustrate how a combination of interpolation and decimation may be used to further downsample a sequence without incurring aliasing. It should be noted that maximum possible downsampling is achieved once the non-zero portion of one period of the discrete-time spectrum has expanded to fill the entire band from $-\pi\ to + \pi$.

Consider the sequence $x[n]$ whose Fourier transform $X(e^{j\omega})$ is illustrated in Figure 6.27(a). The lowest rate at which impulse-train sampling may be used on this sequence without incurring aliasing is $2\pi/4$. This corresponds to,

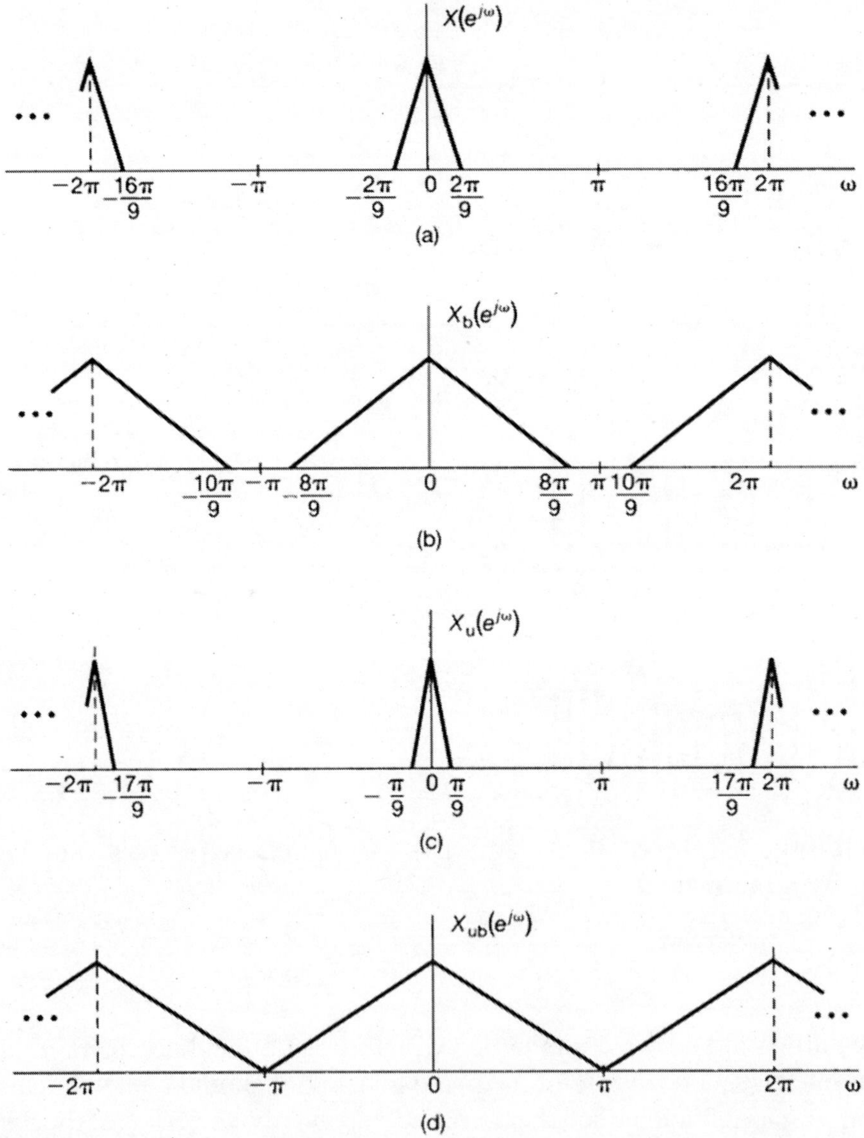

Fig 6.29: Spectra associated with example 6.4: (a) Spectrum of $x[n]$; (b) Spectrum after downsampling by 4; (c) Spectrum after upsampling of $x(n)$ by factor of 2; (d) Spectrum after upsampling $x[n]$ by 2 then downsampling by 9

sampling every 4th value of $x(n)$. If the result of such sampling is decimated by a factor of 4, we obtain a sequence $x_b[n]$ whose spectrum is shown in Figure 6.27(b). Clearly, there is still no aliasing of the original spectrum. However, this spectrum is zero for $8\pi/9 \leq |\omega| \leq \pi$, which suggests there is room for further downsampling.

Specifically, examining Figure 6.27(a) we see that if we could scale frequency by a factor of 9/2, the resulting spectrum would have nonzero values over the entire frequency interval from $-\pi\ to + \pi$. However, since 9/2 is not an integer, we cannot achieve this purely by downsampling. Rather we must first upsample $x[n]$ by a factor of 2 and then downsample by a factor of 9. In particular, the spectrum of the signal $x_u[n]$ obtained when $x[n]$ is upsampled by a factor of 2, is displayed in Figure 6.27(c). When $x_u[n]$ is then downsampled by a factor of 9, the spectrum of the resulting sequence $x_{ub}[n]$ is as shown in Figure 6.27(d). This combined result effectively corresponds to downsampling $x[n]$ by a no integer amount, 9/2. Assuming that $x[n]$ represents unaliased samples of a continuous-time signal $x_c(t)$, our interpolated and decimated sequence represents the maximum possible (aliasing-free) downsampling of $x_c(t)$.

Unit Summary

In this chapter we have developed the concept of sampling, whereby a continuous-time or discrete-time signal is represented by a sequence of equally spaced samples. The conditions under which the signal is exactly recoverable from the samples is embodied in the sampling theorem. For exact reconstruction, this theorem requires that the signal to be sampled be band limited and that the sampling frequency be greater than twice the highest frequency in the signal to be sampled. Under these conditions, exact reconstruction of the original signal is carried out by means of ideal lowpass filtering. The time-domain interpretation of this ideal reconstruction procedure is often referred to as ideal band- limited interpolation. In practical implementations, the lowpass filter is approximated and the interpolation in the time domain is no longer exact. In some instances, simple interpolation procedures such as a zero-order hold or linear interpolation (a first-order hold) suffice.

If a signal is undersampled (i.e., if the sampling frequency is less than that required by the sampling theorem), then the signal reconstructed by ideal band-limited interpolation will be related to the original signal through a form of distortion referred to as aliasing. In many instances, it is important to choose the sampling rate to avoid aliasing. However, there are a variety of important examples, such as the stroboscope, in which aliasing is exploited.

Sampling has several important applications. One particularly significant set of applications relates to using sampling to process continuous-time signals with discrete- time systems, by means of minicomputers, microprocessors, or any of a variety of devices specifically oriented toward discrete-time signal processing.

The basic theory of sampling is similar for both continuous-time and discrete- time signals. In the discrete-time case there is the closely related concept of decimation, whereby the decimated sequence is obtained by extracting values of the original sequence at equally spaced intervals. The difference between sampling and decimation lies in the fact that, for the sampled sequence, values of zero lie in between the sample values, whereas in the decimated sequence these zero values are discarded, thereby compressing the sequence in time. The inverse of decimation is interpolation.

Solved examples on DTFS

Example 6.1:

Shown in figure below is a system in which sampling signal is an impulse train with alternating sign

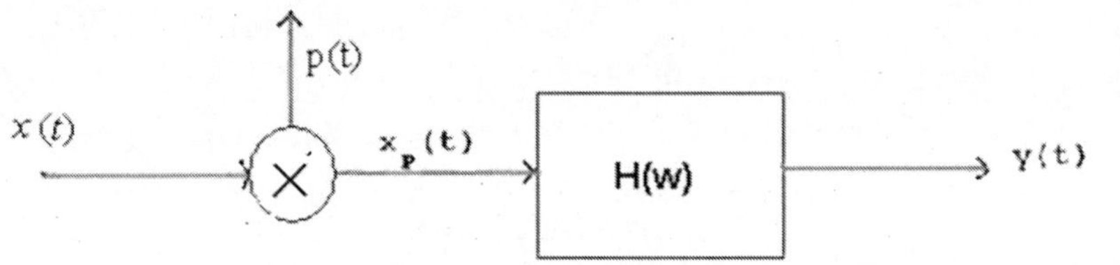

The sampling signal $p(t)$, the Fourier transform of signal $x(t)$ and frequency response of filter are shown below

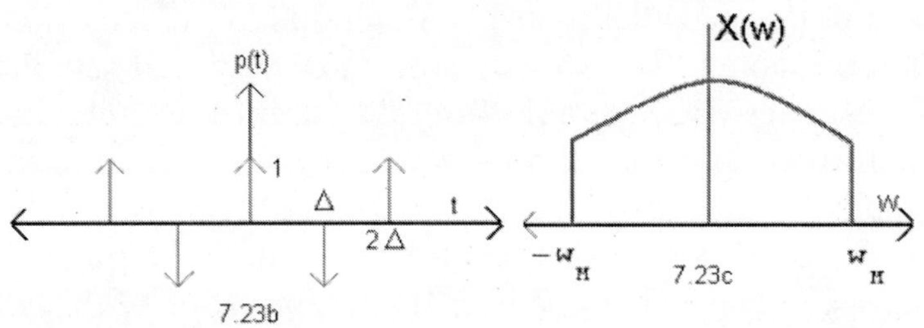

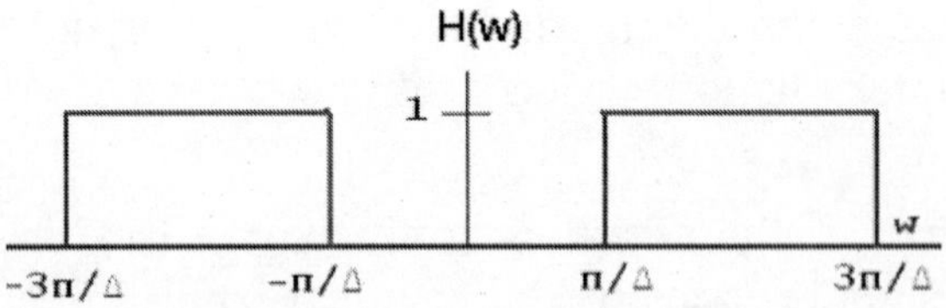

(a) For $\Delta < \frac{\pi}{\omega m}$, Sketch the Fourier Transform of $x_p(t)$ and $y(t)$

(b) For $\Delta < \frac{\pi}{\omega m}$, Determine a system that will recover $x(t)$ from $x_p(t)$ and another that will recover $x(t)$ from $y(t)$

(c) What is the maximum value of Δ in relation to ω_m for which $x(t)$ can be recovered from either $x_p(t)$ or $y(t)$

Solution:

We know that $x_p(t) = x(t)p(t)$, by dual of convolution theorem, we have,

$X_p(\omega) = X(\omega)P(\omega)$,

So we first find Fourier transform of $p(t)$ as follows

The Fourier transform of periodic function is an impulse train at intervals of $\omega = \frac{2\pi}{2\Delta} = \frac{\pi}{\Delta}$

Strength of impulse at $\frac{k\pi}{\Delta}$ being

$$C_k = \frac{\pi}{\Delta}\int p(t)\, e^{j\frac{2\pi k}{2\Delta}t} dt$$

$$C_k = \frac{\pi}{\Delta}\left(1 - e^{j\frac{2\pi k}{2\Delta}\Delta}\right) = \frac{\pi}{\Delta}\left(1 - e^{jk\pi}\right)$$

$$C_k = \frac{\pi}{\Delta}\left(1 - (-1)^k\right)$$

Thus, we can sketch $P(\omega)$

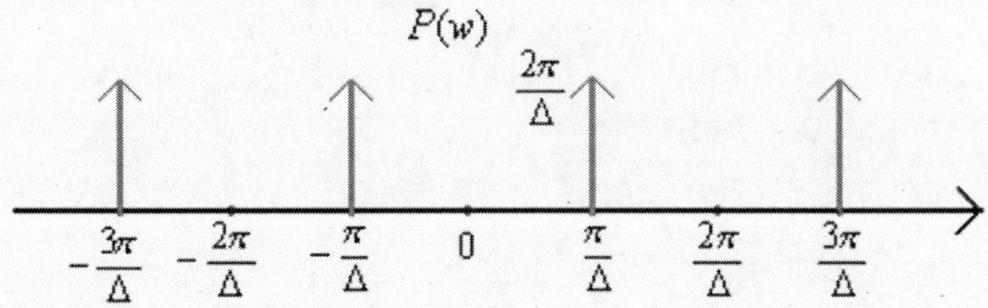

Thus, we can also sketch $X_p(\omega)$ and hence $Y(\omega)$:

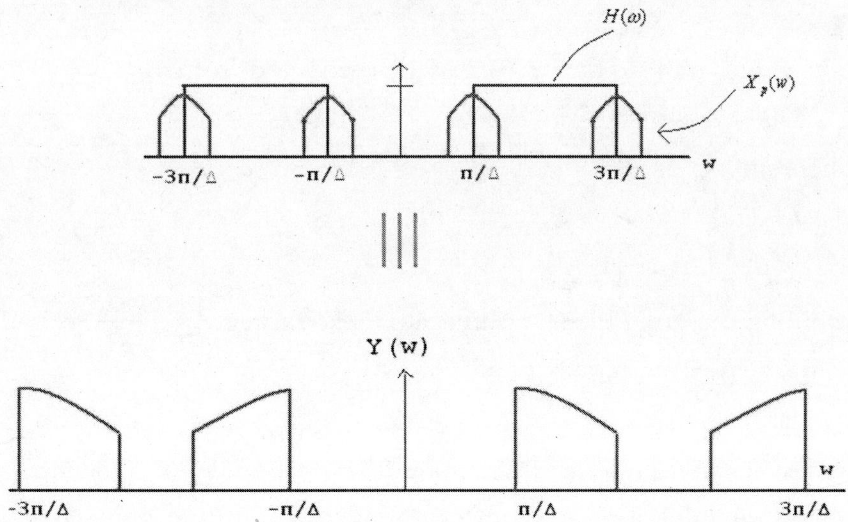

(b) Recover $x(t)$ from $x_p(t)$

Modulate $x_p(t)$ with $\cos(\frac{\pi}{\Delta}t)$

$\cos(\frac{\pi}{\Delta}t)$ has spectrum with impulses of equal strength at $\frac{\pi}{\Delta}$ & $-\frac{\pi}{\Delta}$. Thus, new signal will have copies of the original spectrum (modulated by constant of course) at all even multiples of $\frac{\pi}{\Delta}$

Now, an appropriate low pass filter can extract the original spectrum

To recover $x(t)$ from $y(t)$

Here too, notice from the figures that modulation with $\cos(\frac{\pi}{\Delta}t)$ will do the job. Here too the modulated signal will have copies of the original spectrum at all even multiples of $\frac{\pi}{\Delta}$

(c) So long as adjacent copies of the original spectrum do not overlap in $X_p(\omega)$, theoretically one can reconstruct the original signal. Therefore, the condition is,

$$2\omega_m < \frac{2\pi}{\Delta} \Rightarrow \Delta < \frac{\pi}{\omega_m}$$

Example 6.2:

The signal $y(t)$ is obtained by convolving signals $x_1(t)$ and $x_2(t)$ where:

$|X_1(\omega)| = 0 \qquad for\ |\omega| > 1000\pi$ &

$|X_2(\omega)| = 0 \qquad for\ |\omega| > 2000\pi$

Impulse train sampling is performed on $y(t)$ to get

$$y_p(t) = \sum_{-\infty}^{+\infty} y(nT)\delta(t - nT)$$

Specify the range of values of T so that $y(t)$ may be recovered from $y_p(t)$

Solution:

By Convolution theorem

$$Y(\omega) = X_1(\omega)X_2(\omega)$$

$$Y(\omega) = 0 \qquad for\ |\omega| > 1000\pi$$

Thus, from the sampling theorem, the sampling rate must exceed $2 * \frac{1000\pi}{2\pi} = 1000$

So, T must be less than 10^{-3} i.e. 1mSec

Example 6.3:

In the figure below, we have a sampler, followed by an ideal low pass filter, for reconstruction of $x(t)$ from its samples $x_p(t)$. From sampling theorem, we know that if $\omega_s = \frac{2\pi}{T}$ is greater than twice the highest frequency present in $x(t)$ $\omega_c = \frac{\omega_s}{2}$, then reconstructed signal will exactly equal $x(t)$. If this condition on bandwidth of $x(t)$ is violated, then $x_r(t)$ will not equal $x(t)$. We seek to show in this problem that if $\omega_c = \frac{\omega_s}{2}$ then for any choice of T,

$x_r(t)$ & $x(t)$ will be always equal at the sampling instants; that is, $x_r(kT) = x(kT),\ k = 0, \pm1, \pm2, \dots\dots$

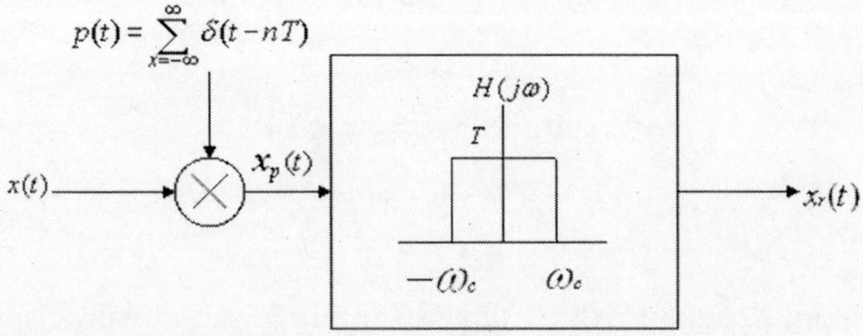

To obtain this result, consider the following equation which expresses $x_r(t)$ in terms of samples $x(t)$:

$$x_r(t) = \sum_{n=-\infty}^{\infty} x(nT)T\frac{\omega_c}{\pi}\frac{\sin[\omega_c(t-nT)]}{\omega_c(t-nT)}$$

With $\omega_c = \frac{\omega_s}{2}$ this becomes,

$$x_r(t) = \sum_{n=-\infty}^{\infty} x(nT)\frac{\sin\left[\frac{\pi}{T}(t-nT)\right]}{\frac{\pi}{T}(t-nT)}$$

By considering value of μ for which $\frac{[\sin\mu]}{\mu} = 0$, show that without any restrictions on $x(t), x_r(kT) = x(kT)$ for any integer value of k.

Solution:

To show that $x_r(t)$ and $x(t)$ are equal at the sampling instants, consider

$$\lim_{t\to kT} x_r(t) = \lim_{t\to kT}\sum_{n=-\infty}^{\infty} x(nT)\frac{\sin\left[\frac{\pi}{T}(t-nT)\right]}{\frac{\pi}{T}(t-nT)}$$

$$= \sum_{n=-\infty}^{+\infty}\left\{\lim_{t\to kT} x(nT)\frac{\sin\left[\frac{\pi}{T}(t-nT)\right]}{\frac{\pi}{T}(t-nT)}\right\}$$

$$= \sum_{n=-\infty, n\neq k}^{\infty}\left\{x(nT)\frac{\sin\left[\frac{\pi}{T}(kT-nT)\right]}{\frac{\pi}{T}(kT-nT)}\right\} + \lim_{t\to kT}\left\{x(kT)\frac{\sin\left[\frac{\pi}{T}(t-kT)\right]}{\frac{\pi}{T}(t-kT)}\right\}$$

$$= \sum_{n=-\infty, n\neq k}^{\infty}\left\{x(nT)\frac{\sin[\pi(k-n)]}{\pi(k-n)}\right\} + x(kT)\lim_{t\to kT}\left\{\frac{\sin\left[\frac{\pi}{T}(t-kT)\right]}{\frac{\pi}{T}(t-kT)}\right\}$$

$$= 0 + x(kT) \times 1 \because (k-n) \in Z \Leftrightarrow \sin[\pi(k-n)] = 0 \ \& \ \lim_{x \to 0} \frac{\sin x}{x} = 1$$

Thus,

$$\lim_{x \to kT} x_r(t) = x(kT)$$

Assuming continuity of $x_r(t)$ at $t = kT$, $x_r(kT) = x(kT), \forall k \in z$

Example 6.4:

This problem deals with one procedure of bandpass sampling & reconstruction. This procedure, used when $x(t)$ is real, consists of multiplying $x(t)$ by a complex exponential and then sampling the product. The sampling system is shown below figure a with $x(t)$ real with $X(j\omega)$ non-zero only for $\omega_1 < |\omega| < \omega_2$, the frequency chosen to be $\omega_0 = \frac{1}{2}(\omega_2 + \omega_1)$ and low pass filter $H_1(j\omega)$ has cutoff frequency $\left(\frac{1}{2}\right)(\omega_2 + \omega_1)$

(a) For $X(j\omega)$ shown in figure b, Sketch $X_p(j\omega)$

(b) Determine maximum sampling period T such that $x(t)$ is recoverable from $x_p(t)$

(c) Determine a system to recover $x(t)$ from $x_p(t)$

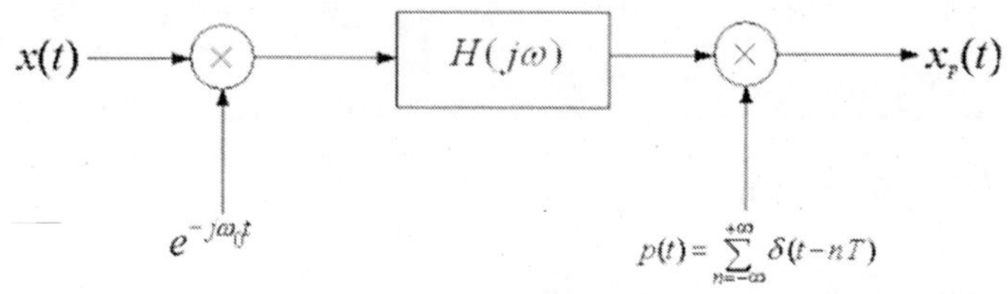

Fig. (a)

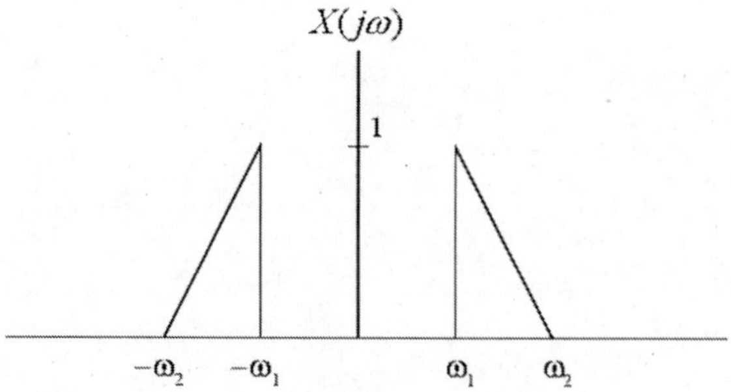

Fig. (b)

Solution:

(a) Multiplication by the complex exponential $e^{-j\omega t}$ in time domain is equivalent to shifting left the Fourier transform by an amount ω in frequency domain. Therefore, resultant transform looks as shown below

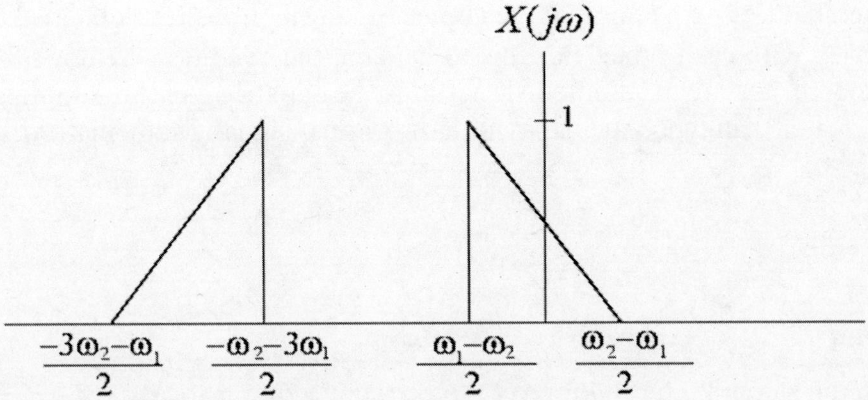

After passing through filter, the Fourier transform becomes,

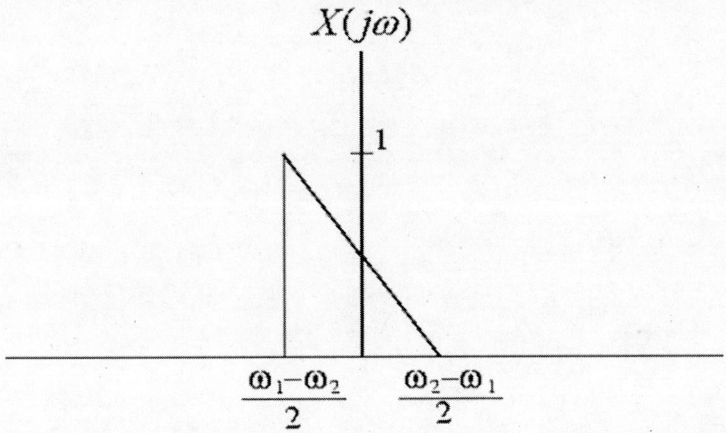

Now sampling the signal amounts to making copies of the Fourier transform, the center of each separated from the other by the sampling frequency in the frequency domain. Thus, $X_p(j\omega)$ has the following form

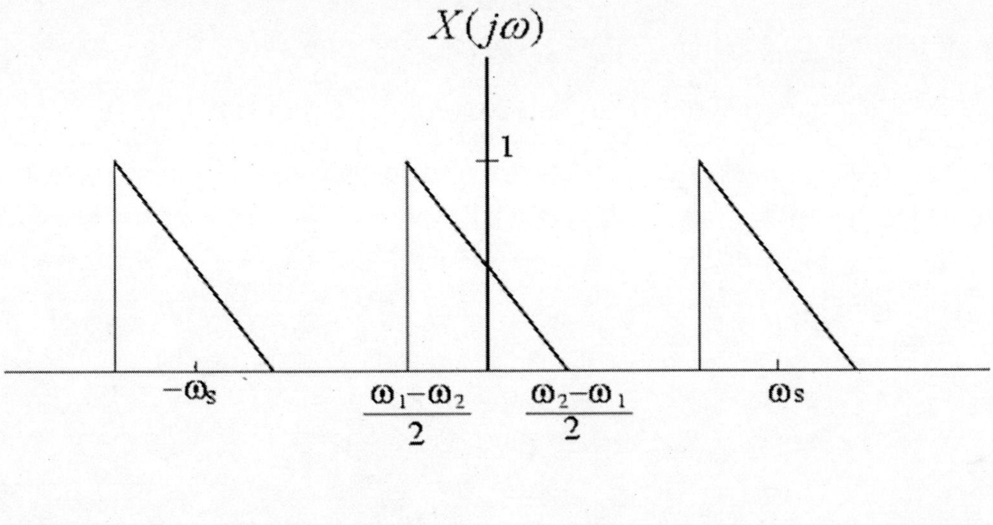

(b) $x(t)$ is recoverable from $x_p(t)$ only if the copies of Fourier transform obtained by sampling do not overlap with each other. For this to happen, the condition set down by Shannon-Nyquist theorem for a band-limited signal must be satisfied i.e. the sampling frequency should be greater than twice the bandwidth of original signal. Mathematically,

$$\omega_s > 2\omega_m$$

$$\frac{2\pi}{T} > 2\left(\frac{\omega_2-\omega_1}{2}\right)$$

$$T < \frac{2\pi}{\omega_2 - \omega_1}$$

Hence the maximum sampling period for $x(t)$ to be recoverable from $x_p(t)$ is $\frac{2\pi}{\omega_2-\omega_1}$

(c) The system to recover $x(t)$ from $x_p(t)$ is outlined below:

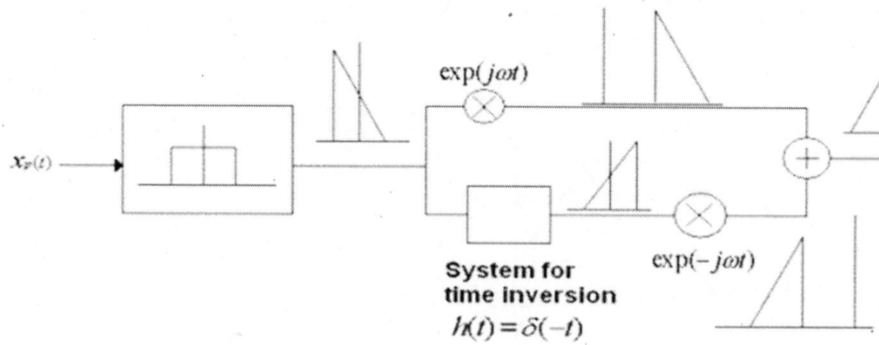

Example 6.5:

Shown in the figures is a system in which the sampling signal is an impulse train with alternating sign. The Fourier transform of the input signal is as indicated in figures below.

(i) For $\Delta < \frac{\pi}{2\omega_m}$, Sketch the Fourier Transform of $x_p(t)$ and $y(t)$

(ii) For $\Delta < \frac{\pi}{2\omega_m}$, determine a system that will recover $x(t)$ from $x_p(t)$

(iii) For $\Delta < \frac{\pi}{2\omega_m}$, determine a system that will recover $x(t)$ from $y(t)$

(iv) What is the maximum value of Δ in relation to ω_m for which $x(t)$ can be recovered from either $x_p(t)$ or $y(t)$?

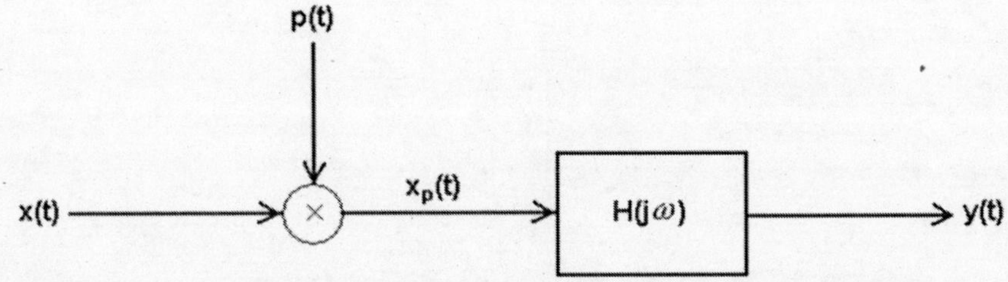

Fig (a)

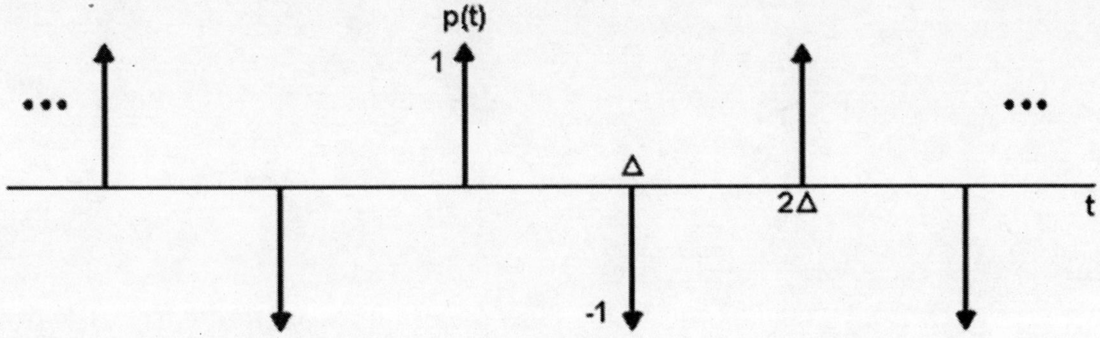

Fig (b)

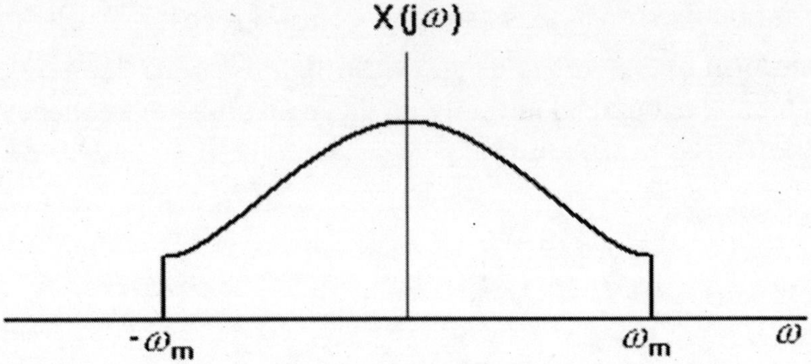

Fig (c)

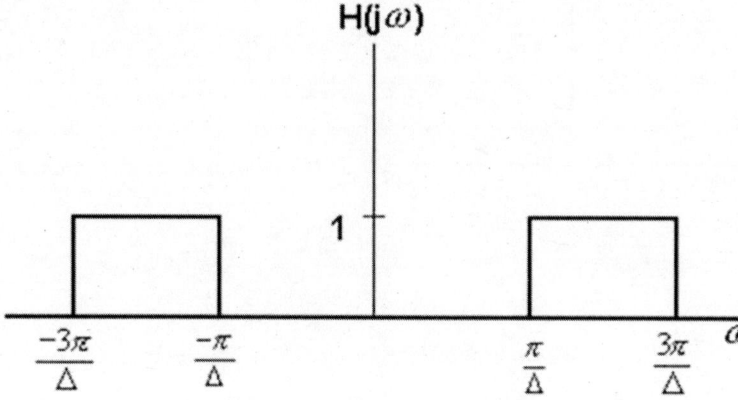

Fig (d)

Solution:

(a) As $x_p(t) = x(t)p(t)$, by dual of convolution theorem we have $X_p(j\omega) = X(j\omega)P(j\omega)$ so we first find Fourier transform of $p(t)$ as follows

The Fourier transform of a periodic function is an impulse train at intervals of $\omega = \frac{2\pi}{2\Delta} = \frac{\pi}{\Delta}$

Each impulse being of magnitude:

$$P(j\omega)_k = 2\pi/2\Delta \int p(t)e^{-jk\omega_0 t}\, dt$$

$$= \pi/\Delta(1 - \cos(\pi k))$$

Here, we see that the impulses on ω axis vanish at even values of k

Hence, Fourier transform of $X_p(j\omega)$ is as shown in figure (a). In the frequency domain, the output signal Y can be found by multiplying the input with the frequency response. Hence $Y(j\omega)$ is as shown below in figure (b)

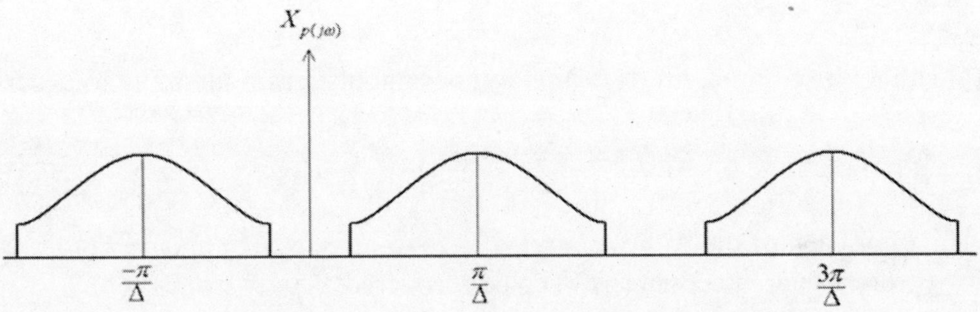

Figure (a)

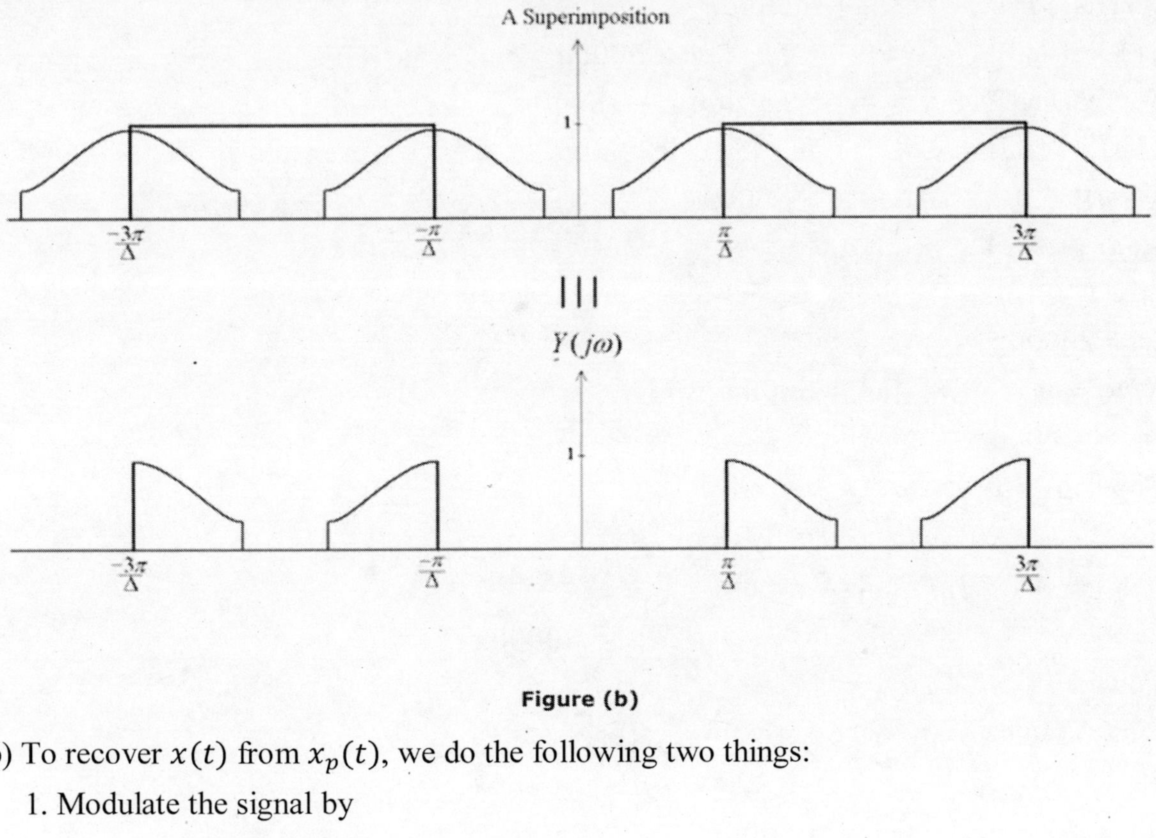

Figure (b)

(b) To recover $x(t)$ from $x_p(t)$, we do the following two things:

1. Modulate the signal by

$$\cos((2\pi/\Delta)t)$$

2. Apply a low pass filter of bandwidth $\pi/2\Delta$

(c) To recover $x(t)$ from $y(t)$ we do following two things

1. Modulate signal by $2\cos((2\pi/\Delta)t)$
2. Apply a low pass filter of bandwidth $\pi/2\Delta$

(d) Maximum value for recoverability is π/ω_m as can be seen from graphs

Example 6.6:

A signal $x(t)$ with Fourier transform $X(j\omega)$ undergoes impulse train sampling to generate

$$x_p(t) = \sum_{n=-\infty}^{+\infty} x(nT)\delta(t - nT)$$

Where $T = 10^{-4}$ For each of the following set of constraints on $x(t)$ and/or $X(j\omega)$, does the sampling theorem guarantee that $x(t)$ can be recovered exactly from $x_p(t)$?

(a) $X(j\omega) = 0 \quad for \ \ |\omega| > 5000\pi$

(b) $X(j\omega) = 0 \quad for \ \ |\omega| > 15000\pi$

(c) $\Re\{X(j\omega)\} = 0 \quad for\ |\omega| > 5000\pi$

(d) $x(t)$ real and $X(j\omega) = 0 \quad for\ |\omega| > 5000\pi$

(e) $x(t)$ real and $X(j\omega) = 0 \quad for\ |\omega| < -15000\pi$

(f) $X(j\omega) * X(j\omega) = 0 \quad for \ \ |\omega| > 15000\pi$

(g) $|X(j\omega)| = 0 \quad for \ \ \omega > 5000\pi$

Solution:

We have $T = 10^{-4}$

So, $\omega_s = 20000\pi$

(a) $X(j\omega) = 0 \quad for \ \ |\omega| > 5000\pi$

$2\omega_m = 10000\pi$

Here, obviously $\omega_s < 2\omega_m$

Hence $x(t)$ can be recovered exactly from $x_f(t)$

(b) $X(j\omega) = 0 \quad for \ \ |\omega| > 15000\pi$

$$2\omega_m = 30000\pi$$

Here, obviously $\omega_s < 2\omega_m$

Hence $x(t)$ can be recovered exactly from $x_f(t)$

(c) $\Re\{X(j\omega)\} = 0 \quad for\ |\omega| > 5000\pi$

Real part of $X(j\omega) = 0$, but we cannot say anything particular about imaginary part of the $X(j\omega)$, thus, not necessary that $X(j\omega) = 0$ for this range

Hence $x(t)$ cannot be recovered exactly from $x_f(t)$

(d) $x(t)$ real and $X(j\omega) = 0 \quad for\ |\omega| > 5000\pi$

As $x(t)$ is real we have $X(j\omega) = \overline{X(-j\omega)}$

Taking mod on both sides

$$X(j\omega) = \overline{X(-j\omega)} = 0 \quad for\ \omega > 5000\pi$$

$$\Rightarrow \overline{|X(-j\omega)|} = |X(-j\omega)| = 0 \qquad for\ \ \omega > 5000\pi$$

$$\Rightarrow X(-j\omega) = 0 \quad for\ \omega > 5000\pi$$

$$\Rightarrow X(j\omega) = 0 \quad for\ \omega < -5000\pi$$

So, we get

$$X(j\omega) = 0 \quad for \quad |\omega| > 5000\pi$$

Here, obviously $\omega_s > 2\omega_m$

Hence $x(t)$ can be recovered exactly from $x_f(t)$

(e) $x(t)$ real and $X(j\omega) = 0 \qquad for\ |\omega| < -15000\pi$

Proceeding as above we get

$$X(j\omega) = 0 \quad for \quad |\omega| > 15000\pi$$

Here, obviously $\omega_s < 2\omega_m$

Hence $x(t)$ can not be recovered exactly from $x_f(t)$

(f) $X(j\omega) * X(j\omega) = 0 \qquad for \quad |\omega| > 15000\pi$

When we convolve two functions with domain $\omega_1\ to\ \omega_2$ and $\omega_3\ to\ \omega_4$ then domain of their convolution function varies from $\omega_1 + \omega_3$ to $\omega_2 + \omega_4$

Here, $\omega_1 = \omega_3$ & $\omega_2 = \omega_4$

$$2\omega_1 = 15000$$

$$\Rightarrow \omega_1 = 7500$$

Therefore,

$$X(j\omega) = 0 \quad for \quad |\omega| > 7500\pi$$

Here, obviously $\omega_s > 2\omega_m$

Hence $x(t)$ can be recovered exactly from $x_f(t)$

(g) $|X(j\omega)| = 0 \qquad for\ \ \omega > 5000\pi$

We can not say anything about $X(j\omega)\ \ for \quad \omega < -5000\pi$,

Hence $x(t)$ can not be recovered exactly from $x_f(t)$

Example 6.7:

Figure I shows overall system for filtering a continuous time signal using a discrete time filter. If $X_c(j\omega)$ and $H(e^{j\omega})$ are as shown in figure II with $\frac{1}{T} = 20KHz$ sketch $X_p(j\omega), X(e^{j\omega})$, $Y(e^{j\omega})$, $Y_p(j\omega)$ & $Y_c(j\omega)$

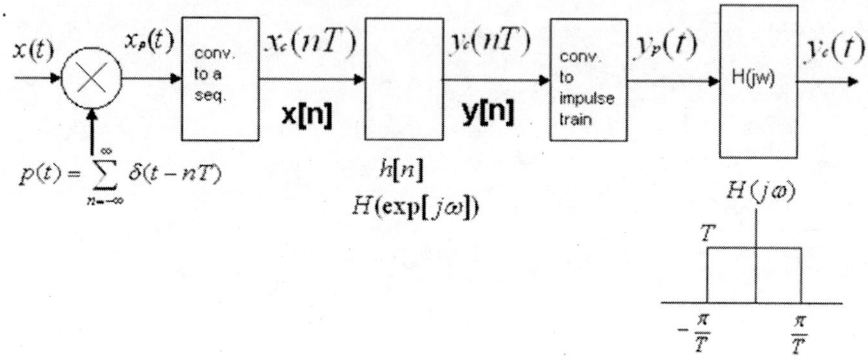

Figure (I)

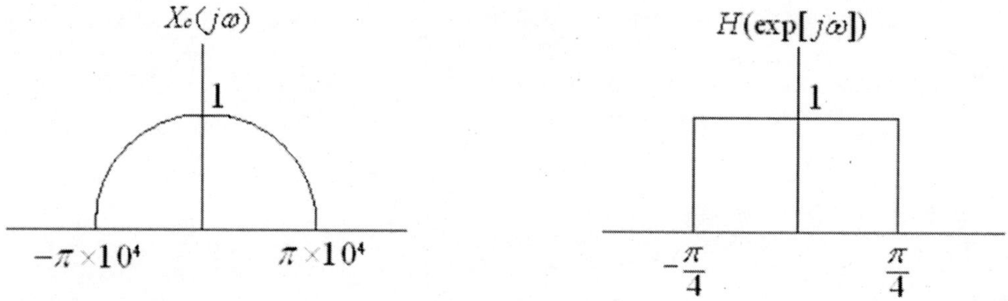

Figure (II)

Solution:

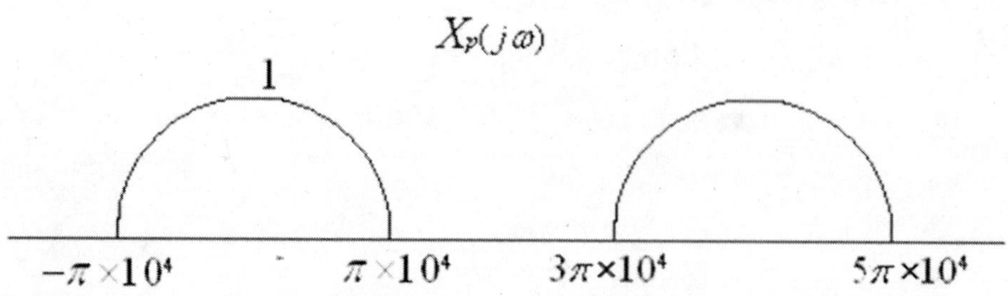

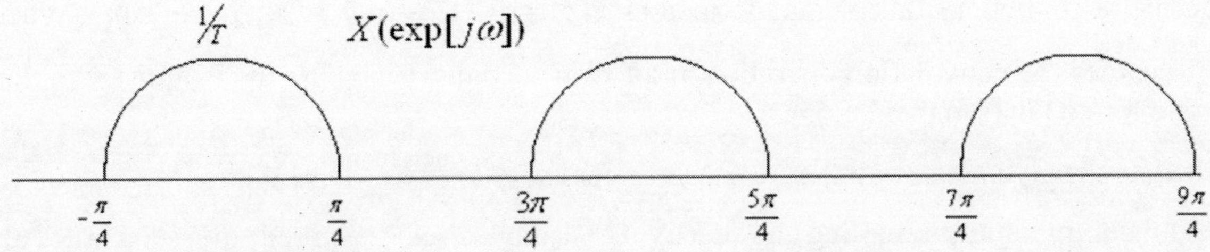

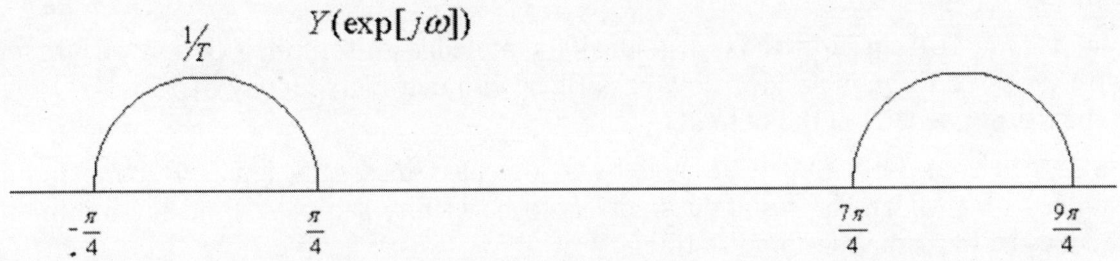

EXERCISES

1) The signal $x(t) = \sin(14000\pi t)$, where t is in seconds, is sampled at a rate of 9000 samples per second. The sampled signal is the input to an ideal lowpass filter with frequency response $H(f)$ as following:

$$H(f) = \begin{cases} 1, & |f| \leq 12KHz \\ 0, & |f| > 12KHz \end{cases}$$

What is number of sinusoids in the output and their frequency in KHz?

2) Consider a continuous time signal defined as $x(t) = \frac{Sin\ (\pi t/2)}{(\frac{\pi t}{2})} * \sum_{n=-\infty}^{+\infty} \delta(t - 10n)$. Where * denotes the convolution operation and t is in seconds. Calculate the Nyquist sampling rate for x(t) in (samples/sec).

3) Calculate the Nyquist sampling rate for the signal $s(t) = \frac{\sin(500\pi t)}{\pi t} \times \frac{\sin(700\pi t)}{\pi t}$

4) Calculate minimum sampling frequency (in samples/sec) required to reconstruct the following signal from its samples without distortion

$$x(t) = 5\left(\frac{\sin 2\pi 1000t}{\pi t}\right)^3 + 7\left(\frac{\sin 2\pi 1000t}{\pi t}\right)^2$$

5) A signal $m(t)$ with bandwidth 500Hz is first multiplied by a signal g(t) where

$$g(t) = \sum_{k=-\infty}^{+\infty} (-10)^k \delta(t - 0.5x10^{-4}k)$$

The resulting signal is then passed through an ideal low pass filter with bandwidth 1KHz. Write the output of the low pass filter.

6) A 1KHz signal is ideally sampled at 1500 samples/sec and the sampled signal is passed through an ideal low pass filter with cut off frequency of 800 Hz. Calculate frequency of the output signal

7) A signal $x(t) = 100\cos(24\pi \times 10^3)$ is ideally sampled with sampling period of $50\mu sec$ and then passed through an ideal low pass filter with cutoff frequency of 15 KHz. What will be the frequencies at the output?

8) A 4 GHz carrier is DSB-SC modulated by a low pass message signal with maximum frequency of 2 MHz. The resultant signal is to be ideally sampled. Find the minimum frequency of the sampling impulse train.

9) Find the Nyquist sampling interval for the signal $Sinc\ (700t) + sinc(500t)$

10) A low pass signal $m(t)$ band-limited to B Hz is sampled by a periodic rectangular pulse train $p_\tau(t)$ of period $T_s = 1/3B$ sec. Assuming natural sampling and that the pulse amplitude and pulse width are A volts $1/30B$ sec., respectively, obtain an expression for the frequency spectrum of the sampled signal $m_s(t)$.

11) A real valued signal $x(t)$ is known to be uniquely determined by its samples, when the sampling frequency is $\omega_s = 10000\pi$. For what values of ω is $X(j\omega)$ guaranteed to be zero.

12) A continuous time signal $x(t)$ at the output of of ideal low pass filter with cutoff frequency $\omega_c = 1000\pi$. If impulse train sampling is performed on $x(t)$, Which of the following sampling periods would guarantee that $x(t)$ can be recovered from its sampled version using an appropriate low pass filter

(a) $T = 0.5 \times 10^{-3}$

(b) $T = 2 \times 10^{-3}$

(c) $T = 10^{-4}$

13) For the following figure shows a system consisting of a continuous time LTI system followed by a sampler, conversion to a sequence, an LTI discrete time system. The continuous time LTI system is causal and satisfies the linear, constant coefficient differential equation,

$$\frac{dy_c(t)}{dt} + y_c(t) = x_c(t)$$

The input $x_c(t)$ is unit impulse $\delta(t)$

(a) Determine $y_c(t)$

(b) Determine frequency response $H(e^{j\omega})$ and impulse response $h[n]$ such that $w[n] = \delta[n]$

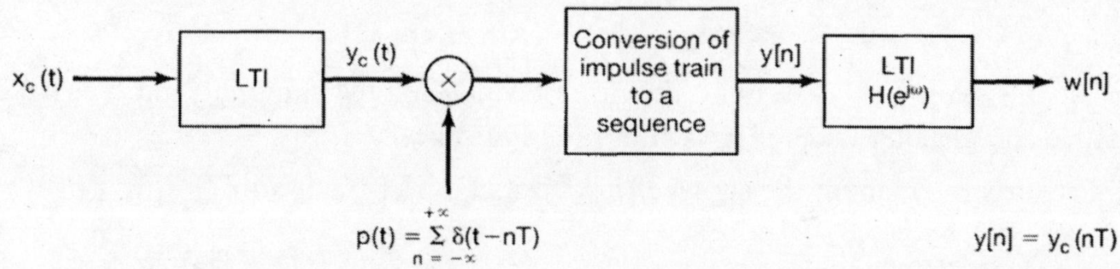

14) A signal $x_p(t)$ is obtained through impulse train sampling of a sinusoidal signal $x(t)$ whose frequency is equal to half the sampling frequency ω_s

$$x(t) = \cos\left(\frac{\omega_s}{2}t + \phi\right)$$

And

$$x_p(t) = \sum_{n=-\infty}^{+\infty} x(nT)\delta(t - nT)$$

Where $T = 2\pi/\omega_s$

(a) Find $g(t)$ such that

$$x(t) = \cos\phi \cos\left(\frac{\omega_s}{2}t\right) + g(t)$$

(b) Show that

$$g(nT) = 0 \qquad for\; n = 0, \pm 1, \pm 2, \dots \dots$$

15) Suppose $x[n] = \cos\left(\frac{\pi}{4}n + \phi_0\right)$ with $0 \le \phi_0 \le 2\pi$ and $g[n] = x[n]\sum_{k=-\infty}^{+\infty}\delta[n - 4k]$, what additional constraints must be imposed on ϕ_0 to ensure that

$$g[n] * \left(\frac{\sin \frac{\pi}{4} n}{\frac{\pi}{4}} \right) = x[n]$$

16) With reference to the filtering approach, assume that sampling period used is T and input $x_c(t)$ is band limited so that $X_c(j\omega) = 0$ for $|\omega| \geq \pi/T$. If the overall system has the property $y_c(t) = x_c(t - 2T)$ determine the impulse response $h[n]$ of the discrete time filter.

17) Repeat the previous problem except this time assume that

$y_c(t) = \frac{d}{dt} x_c\left(t - \frac{T}{2}\right)$.

18) Impulse train sampling of $x(n)$ is used to obtain

$$g[n] = \sum_{k=-\infty}^{+\infty} x[n]\delta[n - kN]$$

If $X(e^{j\omega}) = 0$ for $3\pi/7 \leq |\omega| \leq \pi$, determine the largest value for the sampling interval N which ensures that no aliasing takes place while sampling $x[n]$.

19) The following facts are given about the signal $x[n]$ and its Fourier transform:

1. $x[n]$ is real

2. $X(e^{j\omega}) \neq 0 \quad for \quad 0 < \omega < \pi$

3. $x[n] \sum_{k=-\infty}^{\infty} \delta[n - 2k] = \delta[n]$

Determine $x[n]$.

20) Consider a signal $x(t) = \left(\frac{\sin 50\pi t}{\pi t}\right)^2$,

Which we wish to sample with a sampling frequency of $\omega_s = 150\pi$ to obtain a signal $g(t)$ with Fourier transform $G(j\omega)$. Determine the maximum value of ω_0 for which it is guaranteed that

$$G(j\omega) = 75X(j\omega) \ for \ |\omega| \leq \omega_0$$

Where $X(j\omega)$ is Fourier transform of $x(t)$.

Multiple-Choice Questions

1. Sampling can be done by:

a) Impulse train sampling

b) Natural sampling

c) Flat-top sampling

d) All of above

Ans: d)

2. Sampled data technique is appropriate as:

   a) For long distance data transmission
   b) Pulses are transferred by little loss of accuracy
   c) More than one channel of information is sequentially sampled and transmitted.
   d) All of the mentioned

   Ans: d)

3. Signal sampling reduces the power demand made on the signal.

a) True

b) False

   Ans: a)

4. The signal is reconstructed back with the help of

   a) Zero order hold circuits
   b) Extrapolations
   c) Signal is reconstructed with zero order holds and extrapolations
   d) Signal is not reconstructed

   Ans: c)

5. Aliasing is caused when:

   a) Sampling frequency must be equal to the message signal
   b) Sampling frequency must be greater to the message signal
   c) Sampling frequency must be less to the message signal
   d) Sampling frequency must be greater than or equal to the message signal

   Ans: c)

6. The first step required to convert Analog signal to digital is:

   a) Sampling
   b) Holding
   c) Reconstruction
   d) Quantization

   Ans: a)

7. ________________ is a sampling pattern which is repeated periodically

   a) Single order sampling
   b) Multi order sampling
   c) Zero order sampling
   d) Unordered sampling

   Ans: b)

8. Choose minimum sampling rate required to avoid aliasing when continuous time signal $x(t) = 5\cos 400\pi t$ is sampled:

a) 200 Hz

b) 500 Hz

c) 400 Hz

d) 450Hz

Ans: c)

9. Find Nyquist rate and Nyquist interval of sinc[t]

a) 1 Hz, 1 sec

b) 2 Hz, 2 sec

c) ½ Hz, 2 sec

d) 2 Hz, ½ sec

Ans: a)

10. Determine the Nyquist rate of signal $x(t) = 1 + \cos 2000\pi t + \sin 4000\pi t$

a) 2000 Hz

b) 4000 Hz

c) 500 Hz

d) 3000 Hz

Ans: b)

11. Which of the following requires interpolation filtering?

a) UP-Sampler

b) D to A Converter

c) Both (a) & (b)

d) None of these

Ans: c)

12. Which process requires Low Pass Filter.

a) UP-sampling

b) Down-sampling

c) Up-sampling & Down-sampling

d) None of the above mentioned

Ans: c)

13. Which device is needed for the reconstruction of signal?

a) Low pass filter

b) Equalizer

c) Low pass filter & Equalizer

d) None of the above mentioned

Ans: c)

14. Decreasing the data rate is called as

a) Aliasing

b) Down-sampling

c) Up-sampling

d) None of the above mentioned

Ans: b)

15. Instantaneous sampling

a) Has a train of impulses

b) Has the pulse width approaching zero value

c) Has negligible power content

d) All of the above

Ans: d)

16. The spectrum of sampled signal may be obtained without overlapping only if

a) $f_s \geq 2f_m$

b) $f_s < 2f_m$

c) $f_s > f_m$

d) $f_s < f_m$

Ans: a)

17. Decimation is a process in which the sampling rate is __________

a) Enhanced

b) Stable

c) Reduced

d) Unpredictable

Ans: c)

18. To change the sampling rate for better efficiency in two or multiple stages, the decimation & interpolation factors must be ______________ unity.

a) Greater than

b) Less than

c) Equal to

d) None of the above

Ans: a)

19. How is the sampling rate conversion achieved by factor I/D

a) By increase in sampling rate with (I)

b) By filtering the sequence to remove unwanted images of spectra of original signal.

c) By decimation of filtered signal with factor D

d) All of the above

Ans: d)

20. The first step required to convert Analog signal to digital is:

a) Aliasing

b) Holding

c) Quantization

d) Sampling

Ans: d)

KNOW MORE

Our treatment of sampling is concerned primarily with the sampling theorem and its implications. However, to place this subject in perspective we begin by discuss the general concepts of representing a continuous-time signal in terms of its samples and the reconstruction of signals using interpolation. After using frequency-domain methods to derive the sampling theorem, we consider both the frequency and time domains to provide intuition concerning the phenomenon of aliasing resulting from under sampling. One of the very important uses of sampling is in the discrete-time processing of continuous time signals. Which is discussed thoroughly. Following this, we turn to the sampling of discrete-time signals. The basic result underlying discrete-time sampling is developed in a manner that parallels that used in continuous time, and the applications of this result to problems of decimation and interpolation are described. Again, a variety of other applications, in both continuous and discrete time, are addressed in the problems.

Both the sampling and reconstruction are critical in maintaining the integrity and fidelity of signals as they transition between the continuous and discrete domains. Careful consideration of the sampling rate, anti-aliasing, and reconstruction techniques is essential to avoid signal degradation and ensure accurate representation. These concepts are foundational in various fields, including telecommunications, audio processing, image processing, and more.

REFERENCES AND SUGGESTED READINGS

1. Signals and Systems by Simon Haykin
2. Signals and Systems by Ganesh Rao
3. Signals and Systems - Course (nptel.ac.in)

Dynamic QR Code for Further Reading

CO AND PO ATTAINMENT TABLE

Course outcomes (COs) for this course can be mapped with the programme outcomes (POs) after the completion of the course and a correlation can be made for the attainment of POs to analyze the gap. After proper analysis of the gap in the attainment of POs necessary measures can be taken to overcome the gaps.

Table for CO and PO attainment

Course Outcomes	Expected Mapping with Programme Outcomes (1- Weak Correlation; 2- Medium correlation; 3- Strong Correlation)											
	PO-1	PO-2	PO-3	PO-4	PO-5	PO-6	PO-7	PO-8	PO-9	PO-10	PO-11	PO-12
CO-1												
CO-2												
CO-3												
CO-4												
CO-5												
CO-6												

INDEX

Aliasing, 238
Convolution, 61, 204
Cascade systems, 64
Complex frequency, 153, 154
Conversion, 246, 247
Continuous time signal, 6
Continuous-Time Unit Impulse, 8
CT Unit Impulse Function Properties, 9
CT Unit Step Function, 10
CT Signum Function, 13
CT Ramp Function, 14
CT Exponential signal, 15
Complex Exponential Signal, 16
Complex Exponential Sequence, 17
CT Sinusoid Signal, 19
Discrete signal, 25
Differential equation, 67, 68
Exponential signal, 16, 17, 18
Energy signal, 27
ECG Signal, 5
Fourier series, 89, 90, 94
Fourier transform, 111, 112, 120
Final value theorem, 172
Gibbs phenomenon, 106, 107
Impulse signal, 8, 9, 10
Inverse Laplace transform, 155, 175
Initial value theorem, 206
Inverse Z transform, 212
LTI system, 57, 58
Laplace transform, 153, 154
Left sided signal, 156
Magnitude, 112
Periodic Signal, 23, 24
Parseval's Theorem, 118, 137
Poles, 173
Power series, 213
Partial fraction, 216
Ramp signal, 14, 15
Region of convergence, 155, 194
Right sided signal, 155
Reconstruction, 236
Real Exponential Signal, 16
Real Exponential Sequence,17
Step signal, 11, 12
Signum signal, 14
Sinusoid signal, 18, 19
System, 37, 38, 39, 42
State space representation, 69, 70
Sampling theorem, 230, 233
Strobe effect, 244
Waveform symmetry, 96, 97
Z transform, 190, 191
Z-plane, 192
Zeros, 193